Worlds in Motion

The International Union for the Scientific Study of Population Problems was set up in 1928, with Dr Raymond Pearl as President. At that time the Union's main purpose was to promote international scientific co-operation to study the various aspects of population problems, through national committees and through its members themselves. In 1947 the International Union for the Scientific Study of Population (IUSSP) was reconstituted into its present form.

It expanded its activities to:

- stimulate research on population
- develop interest in demographic matters among governments, national and international organizations, scientific bodies, and the general public
- foster relations between people involved in population studies
- disseminate scientific knowledge on population.

The principal ways through which the IUSSP currently achieves its aims are:

- organization of worldwide or regional conferences
- operations of Scientific Committees under the auspices of the Council
- organization of training courses
- publication of conference proceedings and committee reports.

Demography can be defined by its field of study and its analytical methods. Accordingly, it can be regarded as the scientific study of human populations primarily with respect to their size, their structure, and their development. For reasons which are related to the history of the discipline, the demographic method is essentially inductive: progress in knowledge results from the improvement of observation, the sophistication of measurement methods, and the search for regularities and stable factors leading to the formulation of explanatory models. In conclusion, the three objectives of demographic analysis are to describe, measure, and analyse.

International Studies in Demography is the outcome of an agreement concluded by the IUSSP and the Oxford University Press. The joint series reflects the broad range of the Union's activities; it is based on the seminars organized by the Union and important international meetings in the field of population and development. The Editorial Board of the series is comprised of:

John Cleland, UK   Henri Leridon, France
John Hobcraft, UK   Richard Smith, UK
Georges Tapinos, France

Worlds in Motion

Understanding International Migration at the End of the Millennium

Douglas S. Massey
Joaquín Arango
Graeme Hugo
Ali Kouaouci
Adela Pellegrino
J. Edward Taylor

CLARENDON PRESS · OXFORD

This book has been printed digitally and produced in a standard specification in order to ensure its continuing availability

OXFORD
UNIVERSITY PRESS

Great Clarendon Street, Oxford OX2 6DP

Oxford University Press is a department of the University of Oxford.
It furthers the University's objective of excellence in research, scholarship,
and education by publishing worldwide in

Oxford New York

Auckland   Cape Town Dar es Salaam   Hong Kong   Karachi
Kuala Lumpur Madrid Melbourne Mexico City   Nairobi
New Delhi Shanghai Taipei Toronto
With offices in
Argentina Austria Brazil Chile Czech Republic France Greece
Guatemala Hungary Italy Japan South Korea Poland Portugal
Singapore Switzerland Thailand Turkey Ukraine Vietnam

Oxford is a registered trade mark of Oxford University Press
in the UK and in certain other countries

Published in the United States
by Oxford University Press Inc., New York

© IUSSP 2008

ISBN 978-0-19-928276-0

*Dedicated
to the Memory of
Bruno Remiche*

Preface

The seeds of this book were sown in early 1991 when Massimo Livi-Bacci, then President of the International Union for the Scientific Study of Population, approached Douglas S. Massey with the idea of chairing a new scientific committee, whose charge would be to develop a fuller theoretical understanding of the forces producing contemporary international migration, not just in traditional receiving countries such as the USA, but throughout the world. In consultation with the Secretariat and Council of the IUSSP, they selected an international committee of population scientists to represent a diversity of disciplines and regions. The Committee on South-North Migration was formally appointed in November of 1991 and held its initial meeting in December of that year. The members of the committee are the co-authors of this book: Joaquín Arango, Graeme Hugo, Ali Kouaouci, Adela Pellegrino, J. Edward Taylor, and Douglas S. Massey, who served as chair.

Rather than focusing on data, measurement, or other methodological issues that are usually of greatest interest to demographers, the committee sought to develop a comprehensive theoretical understanding of the social and economic forces responsible for international migration between developing and developed nations in the late twentieth century. In order to accomplish this goal, committee members decided to examine in detail the processes responsible for initiating and sustaining international migration around the world. The committee deliberately chose not to address accompanying issues of migrant adaptation, integration, and assimilation, except as they encouraged or discouraged international movement. The committee thus focused on those forces that *produced* international migrants, leaving what happened to these people after they arrived in the receiving society to another committee and another time. The Committee on South-North Migration was more interested in the causes than the consequences of contemporary international migration.

In attempting to develop an integrated theoretical understanding of international migration at the end of the twentieth century, the committee self-consciously sought to be cross-disciplinary, cross-national, and eclectic, drawing upon the theoretical and substantive literatures of anthropology, demography, economics, geography, and sociology, and evaluating research conducted not only in historical countries of immigration such as the USA, Canada, Argentina, and Australia, but also in newer destination countries located in Europe, the Middle East, and Asia and the Pacific.

The committee's work proceeded in phases. It began with a systematic description and critical review of contemporary theories of international migration, and then moved on to undertake a substantive evaluation of how well these theories performed empirically in each of the world's principal migration systems: in North America, Western Europe, the Persian Gulf, the Western Pacific, and South America. In order to make the committee's work available to researchers in a timely way, and to generate critical comments and feedback from demographers around the world, the committee decided to present and publish its work as often as possible in public forums.

To this end, committee members published four articles and delivered one conference paper. Although these reports were presented roughly in the order they were produced, they always formed part of a broader plan for a volume that would be published to represent the end product of the committee's scientific work. That volume—the present book—was intended to describe the international migration systems that had emerged in different world regions by the decade of the 1980s; present and evaluate the leading contemporary theories proposed to explain the emergence and operation of these systems; evaluate the efficacy of the various theories as they applied to trends and patterns in North America, Western Europe, the Persian Gulf, Asia and the Pacific, and South America, and then to synthesize the results of these reviews to produce an integrated theoretical vision capable of providing a coherent guide for future research and policy formation. We also planned to devote special attention to the thorny issue of international migration and economic development.

The present volume represents the fruits of more than four years of collaborative work by members of the Committee on South-North Migration. Different committee members took primary responsibility for preparing initial drafts of different chapters and for putting the assembled material to the test of their respective disciplines (Massey: sociology; Arango: economics and sociology; Hugo: geography; Kouaouci: demography; Pellegrino: sociology; Taylor: economics). Drafts of each chapter were circulated to all committee members for critical comments and suggestions for addition or deletion. After changes were made, a final draft was recirculated to committee members for approval prior to publication or presentation. Final editorial and stylistic changes were made by the committee chair, who assumed responsibility for assembling the final volume. The book should be viewed as the collective product of all members of the Committee on South-North Migration and not the work of any one member.

Graeme Hugo wrote the initial draft of a paper on 'Contemporary International Migration Systems', which committee members originally planned to include in the volume as a separate chapter. This paper was presented at the Annual Meetings of the American Sociological Association in Washington, DC on 18–22 August, 1994. We later decided to break up this chapter and use the material describing each migratory system to introduce the empirical review of theoretical propositions in different world regions—the central chapters of the book. Hence, Hugo's paper provided initial drafts for the first sections of Chapters 3 through 7.

The first draft of Chapter 1, 'New Migrations, New Theories', was prepared by Joaquín Arango, who also assumed primary responsibility for preparing the initial version of Chapter 4, 'Coming to Terms with European Immigration'. The first drafts of Chapters 2 and 3, 'Contemporary Theories of International Migration' and 'Understanding the North American System', were written by Douglas S. Massey. In order to solicit comment and reaction from the field, the latter two chapters were published as separate articles in *Population and Development Review* (19: 431–66 and 20: 699–752, respectively). Ali Kouaouci prepared the preliminary version of Chapter 5, 'Labour Migration in the Gulf System'; Graeme Hugo undertook the writing of Chapter 6, 'Theory and Reality in Asia and the Pacific'; and Adela Pellegrino wrote the first draft of Chapter 7, 'International Migration in South America'.

Having considered the degree of empirical support for the theories proposed to account for the initiation and perpetuation of international migration in various systems around the world, Chapters 9 and 10 focus on the contentious and ideologically charged issue of international migration and economic development, a question that has occupied the attention of many researchers over the years. Drafts of these chapters were initially prepared by J. Edward Taylor. Chapter 9, 'International Migration and National Development', considers the relationship from the macroperspective of the nation State, and Chapter 10, 'International Migration and Community Development', examines it from the microperspective of the community. Given the intense interest in development that prevails in many quarters, we sought to bring these works to the early attention of researchers by publishing them in successive issues of *Population Index* (62: 181–212 and 62: 397–418).

Following the publication and presentation of papers, the committee received many helpful comments and suggestions, and these were incorporated into revisions of the text that occurred prior to their incorporation into the book as integrated chapters. A draft of the entire manuscript was circulated to all committee members and to two anonymous reviewers for Oxford University Press, and based on their criticisms, the book went through one final round of revisions and changes following the last meeting of the committee in May 1997.

The members of the IUSSP Committee on South-North Migration offer this book to their colleagues, peers, and associates as a comprehensive guide to the world's theoretical and empirical literature on international migration at century's end. We hope that it will stimulate more theoretically directed research; that it will reveal the common elements underlying geographically diverse migration systems; and that it will ultimately yield more enlightened and efficacious immigration policies throughout the world. Like Castles and Miller (1993), we believe that international migration will be the emblematic social, political, and economic issue of the twenty-first century, and that it merits the closest attention, the best research, and the most conscientious theorizing that social science has to offer. As committee members, we express our sincere thanks to the staff and officers of the IUSSP for their constant support, and particularly to Marc Lebrun, Jane Verall, and Renèe Latour, who served sequentially as staff liaisons to the committee. If this book makes a contribution to human understanding, it is due in no small way to their efforts. We owe a special debt of gratitude to Bruno Remiche, the late Secretary General of the IUSSP, whose untimely passing during this project deeply saddened committee members, and in whose memory they dedicate the present volume.

Contents

List of Figures

List of Tables

1 New Migrations, New Theories

Like many birds, but unlike most other animals, humans are a migratory species. Indeed, migration is as old as humanity itself. Of this fact there is no better proof than the spread of human beings to all corners of the earth from their initial ecological niche in sub-Saharan Africa (Davis 1974: 53). A careful examination of virtually any historical era reveals a consistent propensity towards geographic mobility among men and women, who are driven to wander by diverse motives, but nearly always with some idea of material improvement.

The modern history of international migration can be divided roughly into four periods. During the *mercantile period*, from 1500 to 1800, world immigration was dominated by flows out of Europe and stemmed from processes of colonization and economic growth under mercantilist capitalism. Over the course of 300 years, Europeans inhabited large portions of the Americas, Africa, Asia, and Oceania (Altman 1995; Heffernan 1995; Lucassen 1995; Tinker 1995). Although the exact number of colonizing emigrants is unknown, the outflow was sufficient to establish Europe's dominion over large parts of the world. During this period, emigrants generally fell into four classes: a relatively large number of agrarian settlers, a smaller number of administrators and artisans, an even smaller number of entrepreneurs who founded plantations to produce raw materials for Europe's growing mercantilist economies, and in a very few cases, convict migrants sent to penal colonies overseas.

Although the number of Europeans involved in plantation production was small, this sector had a profound impact on the size and composition of population in the Americas. Given a pre-industrial technology, plantations required large amounts of cheap labour, a demand met partially by indentured workers from East Asia (Gemery and Horn 1992; Hui 1995; Kritz 1992; Tinker 1977; Twaddle 1995; Vertovec 1995). The most important source of plantation labour, however, was the forced migration of African slaves (Palmer 1992). Over three centuries, nearly 10 million African slaves were imported into the Americas (Curtain 1969) and together with European colonists, they radically transformed the racial and ethnic composition of the New World.

The second, *industrial period* of emigration begins early in the nineteenth century and stemmed from the economic development of Europe and the spread of industrialism to former colonies in the New World (Hatton and Williamson 1994c). From 1800 to 1925, more than 48 million people left the industrializing countries of Europe in search of new lives in the Americas and Oceania. Of these emigrants, 85 per cent went to just five destinations:

Argentina, Australia, Canada, New Zealand, and the USA, with the latter receiving 60 per cent all by itself (Ferenczi 1929). Key sending nations were Britain, Italy, Norway, Portugal, Spain, and Sweden, each of which exported a large share of its potential population in the course of industrializing (Massey 1988).

The period of large-scale European emigration faltered with the outbreak of the First World War, which brought European emigration to an abrupt halt and ushered in a four-decade *period of limited migration* (Massey 1995). Although emigration revived somewhat during the early 1920s, by then several important receiving countries (most notably the USA) had passed restrictive immigration laws. The onset of the Great Depression stopped virtually all international movement in 1929, and except for a small amount of return migration, there was little movement during the 1930s. During the 1940s, international migration was checked by the Second World War. What mobility there was consisted largely of refugees and displaced persons and was not tied strongly to the rhythms of economic growth and development (Holmes 1995; Noiriel 1995; Sword 1995; Kay 1995), a pattern that persisted well into the subsequent decade.

The period of *post-industrial migration* emerged during the 1960s and constituted a sharp break with the past. Rather than being dominated by outflows from Europe to a handful of former colonies, immigration became a truly global phenomenon, as the number and variety of both sending and receiving countries steadily increased and the global supply of immigrants shifted from Europe to the developing countries of the Third World (Castles and Miller 1993). Whereas migration during the industrial era brought people from densely settled, rapidly industrializing areas to sparsely settled, rapidly industrializing regions, migration in the post-industrial era brought people from densely settled countries in the earliest stages of industrialization to densely settled post-industrial societies.

Before 1925, 85 per cent of all international migrants originated in Europe (Ferenczi 1929); but since 1960, Europeans have comprised an increasingly small fraction of world immigrant flows, and emigration from Africa, Asia, and Latin America has increased dramatically (Kritz *et al.* 1981; Stalker 1994). The variety of destination countries has also grown. In addition to traditional immigrant-receiving nations such as Canada, the USA, Australia, New Zealand, and Argentina, countries throughout Western Europe now attract significant numbers of immigrants—notably Germany, France, Belgium, Switzerland, Sweden, and the Netherlands (Abadan-Unat 1995; Anwar 1995; Hammar 1995; Hoffman-Nowotny 1995; Ogden 1995).

During the 1970s, even long-time nations of emigration such as Italy, Spain, and Portugal began receiving immigrants from the Mediterranean basin and Africa (Fakiolas 1995; Solé 1995); and after the rapid escalation of oil prices in 1973, several less developed but capital-rich nations in the Gulf region also began to sponsor massive labour migration at about the same time (Birks and

Sinclair 1980; Abella 1995). By the 1980s, international migration had spread into Asia, not just to Japan but also to newly industrialized countries such as Korea, Taiwan, Hong Kong, Singapore, Malaysia, and Thailand (Bun 1995; Fee 1995; Hugo 1995*a*; Loiskandl 1995).

A New Look at an Old Phenomenon

Human migration is rooted in specific historical conditions that define a particular social and economic context. Historically-specific explanations for international migration are frequently *ad hoc* and unsystematic rather than general. Nonetheless, ahistorical frameworks that offer universal explanations, immutable laws, and timeless regularities are not very helpful in trying to understand new patterns of international movement. The theoretical concepts now employed by social scientists to analyse and explain international migration were forged primarily during the industrial era and reflect its particular economic arrangements, social institutions, technology, demography, and politics.

These industrial-era theories gave rise to a conceptual framework that lasted for decades. Although fluid and creative when first derived, it grew rigid over time and now appears ill-suited to the dramatically different conditions of the late twentieth century. With the passage of time, reality changed but scientific thinking about international migration remained mired in the past. The classical approach has now entered a state of crisis, challenged by new ideas, concepts, and hypotheses. Although these new ways of thinking have not yet cohered into a single theory, they have reinvigorated conceptual development and spawned a new wave of empirical research grounded in the patterns and forms of international migration in the late twentieth century.

Sooner or later theories must change to reflect new social and economic realities. We are now well into a post-industrial, post-Cold War world and about to embark on a brand new century within which immigration will play a central role (Castles and Miller 1993). The time has come, therefore, to reassess theories of international migration and bring them into conformity with new empirical conditions. In the chapters that follow, we present and evaluate theories that have been put forth to explain the social, economic, and political forces that generate and perpetuate international migration around the world. Often discussed as 'the determinants of migration', we see the explication of these forces as one of two crucial tasks now confronting the field.

The other task is the theoretical elucidation of what might be called 'immigrant assimilation': the means, mechanisms, and policies by which immigrants adapt to and are incorporated within receiving societies. Although this issue is also of clear and unambiguous importance, we leave it aside for now and focus instead on the causes of international migration, not its consequences. Understanding the causes of global migration is of paramount importance, for whatever concepts and theories we derive will determine predictions about the magnitude, duration, and character of international migration in the next century, and, hence, the policies that will ultimately be adopted to meet this unique global challenge.

The New Face of International Migration

The emblematic international migrant of the late nineteenth and early twentieth centuries was a European crossing the ocean in search of a better life, exchanging an industrializing region intensive in labour for another industrializing region intensive in land (Hatton and Williamson 1994c). Traditional countries of immigration such as the USA, Canada, Australia, and Argentina had vast, sparsely inhabited territories as well as rapidly growing cities, whereas Europe's countryside was densely settled and the absorptive capacity of its crowded urban centres was often strained beyond practical limits (D. S. Thomas 1941; B. Thomas 1973; Lowell 1987).

Europe's passage through the initial and intermediate stages of economic development was accompanied by a demographic boom that, although small by contemporary Third World standards, was large enough to affect rates of emigration. Ebbs and flows in the volume of out-migration from Europe were closely tied to oscillating cohort sizes caused by earlier fluctuations in period fertility, which were themselves responses to prior economic cycles (D. S. Thomas 1941; Easterlin 1961; Germani 1966; B. Thomas 1973; Hatton and Williamson 1994a). The tonic of demographic growth continued well into the present century, and even witnessed a fleeting revival after the Second World War.

International migration into the countries of Western Europe began during the second half of the twentieth century (Rose 1969; Castles and Kosack 1973; Power 1979; Stalker 1994). During the third quarter of the century much of the movement was intracontinental. Workers left nations in southern Europe that were still relatively intensive in labour—Italy, Spain, Portugal, and Greece—for nations in the north and west that had become intensive in capital but scarce in labour—Germany, France, Belgium, the Netherlands, Sweden (Martin and Miller 1980; Schierup 1995). Although it was not clear at the time, by the late 1960s, southern Europe was itself on the verge of achieving the long-desired state of capital abundance and labour scarcity, and during the 1970s, Italy, Spain, and Portugal also began importing migrant workers, mainly from the Middle East and North Africa.

The European shift from exporting to importing labour was notable because it involved, for the first time, the widespread movement of migrants to countries that were not intensive in land. Another distinctive feature lay in the *way* European labour migrants were brought in. Faced with rapid economic growth, tight labour markets, and a demand for workers that was impossible to fill from domestic sources (see Kindleberger 1967), but lacking an indigenous tradition of immigration or an ideology that favoured permanent settlement, European governments sought to recruit 'temporary' migrants—*gastarbeiter* or 'guestworkers' in the language coined at the time—who would return to their countries of origin when the economic conditions that made their recruitment necessary disappeared (Martin 1991*a*).

When this moment finally arrived, however, the 'guests' failed to take the not-so-subtle hints of their 'hosts' and return home as anticipated. On the contrary, large numbers opted to settle permanently in Europe and began petitioning for the entry of their spouses, children, and other relatives. Although the number of immigrant *workers* stopped growing, foreign *populations* continued to swell (Martin and Miller 1980). In response, countries adopted more restrictive admissions policies after the mid-1970s, but by then the cow was out of the barn and European governments faced the prospect of integrating growing populations of immigrants and their descendants (Rose 1969; Castles and Kosack 1973). Without any popular referendum or explicit decision on the matter, Western Europe had become a multiracial, multi-ethnic society (Castles and Miller 1993).

It was only during the last quarter of the twentieth century, after the watershed event of the 1973 oil shock and the ensuing worldwide recession, that the outlines of the new post-industrial migratory order came into clear view, not just in Europe, but throughout the globe. The sudden infusion of petrodollars transformed the Persian Gulf into a capital-rich, labour-scarce region, and as in Europe, political leaders in the Gulf countries sought to recruit 'temporary' workers to fill the resulting demand for labour, this time from labour-rich, capital-poor States elsewhere in the Middle East and in Asia (Birks and Sinclair 1980). With even weaker traditions of immigration and pluralism than in Europe, the Gulf States placed harsher restrictions on migrant workers in an effort to keep them temporary (Dib 1988). Despite the restrictive nature of these policies, however, immigrants have become a permanent structural feature of economic and social life in the Gulf region.

By the 1980s, several 'Asian Tigers' had joined the ranks of wealthy, industrialized nations. In addition to Japan, which in some ways had become the world's dominant economic power, Taiwan, South Korea, Hong Kong, Singapore, Thailand, and Malaysia achieved stunning rates of economic growth during the 1970s; and by the 1980s, these nations also had become intensive in capital but poor in labour (Hugo 1995*a*). Like the countries of southern Europe during the 1970s, many switched from exporting to importing labour, while others continued simultaneously to import and export workers. Throughout Asia and the Pacific, efforts were made to keep the new labour migration temporary to avoid the problems and tensions of racial and ethnic diversity created by permanent settlement.

Finally, traditional immigrant-receiving nations also experienced a transformation in their migratory patterns after the mid-1960s. Not only did the number of immigrants rise sharply, but the sources shifted from Europe to Asia and Latin America (Massey 1981, 1995). As in other migration systems, international migrants going to Argentina, Australia, Canada, and the USA generally came from labour-rich but capital-poor countries. As these receiving countries imposed new restrictions on immigration to limit and regulate the expanding flows, undocumented migration began to grow, and over time it came to comprise a larger share of the total.

Although experiences may differ across the world's contemporary migration systems, several common denominators stand out. First, most immigrants today come from countries characterized by a limited supply of capital, low rates of job creation, and abundant reserves of labour. Indeed, the imbalance between labour supply and demand in the Third World today far exceeds that which prevailed in Europe during its period of industrialization. This imbalance stems not only from a relative scarcity of capital and investment, but from a disarticulation between demographic conditions and economic limits that in earlier periods had constrained them. Whereas public health measures were readily imported into poor developing countries to lower mortality, social and economic conditions within those countries did not change rapidly enough to stimulate a corresponding decline in fertility, yielding an unprecedented demographic boom. Variation from country to country in the timing and pace of fertility decline thus emerges as a significant factor explaining widening of intercountry differences in labour availability.

Second, today's immigrant-receiving societies are far more intensive in capital and much less intensive in land than destination countries of the past. In fact, nations such as Germany, Japan, Korea, Taiwan, Kuwait, and the USA are so intensive in capital and technology that they have been shedding workers in many sectors (particularly manufacturing) and full employment has become a serious social and political issue. Under present technological conditions, farms and factories today can produce the same output as earlier with a fraction of their earlier labour force (Rifkin 1995). While high rates of unemployment have been the most visible outcome of this process in Europe, low wages and a growing class of working poor have been its principal manifestation in the USA. Rather than comprising a basic input for core sectors of the economy, international migrants now fill marginal niches within a labour market that is highly segmented (Piore 1979).

The economic marginalization of immigrants is associated with another characteristic of the post-industrial period: immigrants are no longer perceived as wanted or even needed, despite the persistence of a demand for their services (see Espenshade and Calhoun 1993; Espenshade and Hemstead 1996; Espenshade 1997). Whereas officials in destination countries of the past saw immigration as necessary for industrialization and a vital part of nation building, today's political leaders view immigrants as a social and political problem to be managed. Receiving societies increasingly have implemented restrictive admissions policies designed to limit the number of immigrants, confine their activities to the labour market, discourage the entry of dependants, and deter or prevent ultimate settlement.

Some new destination countries such as Japan, Germany, and Kuwait have become *de facto* countries of immigration without ever considering themselves as such, and they continue to maintain *de jure* systems that deny this reality. Meanwhile, traditional immigrant-receiving societies such as the USA, Canada, Australia, and Argentina, have sought to change their *de facto* status as countries of immigration by adopting more restrictive *de jure* policies (Kubat 1979; Stalker 1994). Although governments in capital-rich countries may acknowledge a need for migrant workers, citizens express discomfort at the rising tide of immigration and the growing ethnic diversity that it brings, yielding a fundamental contradiction that politicians seek somehow to finesse.

The last distinctive characteristic of contemporary international migration is the sheer size of the disparities that exist between sending and receiving societies—in wealth, income, power, size, growth, and culture. Presently, there are five principal migratory systems clustered around well-defined regions: North America, Western Europe, Asia and the Pacific, the Gulf region, and the Southern Cone of South America. The specific countries feeding into these zones are diverse and depend on historical ties of colonization, trade, politics, and culture; but generally they are located in the south and are relatively poor.

Considering the great disparities in wealth, power, and population that prevail within these systems, the actual size of the migratory flows is really rather modest, only a fraction of what might potentially result if the systems were left to operate without state interference. It is not so much the *actual* size of flows that accounts for developed countries' current obsessive interest in immigration, but the *potential* size of the flows, as well as the conflicting interests that sending and receiving nations have in perpetuating them.

Thus, the panorama of international migration in the last quarter of the twentieth century is characterized by distinctive features that set it apart from the earlier industrial era: within sending nations there is a sharp imbalance between labour supply and demand; within receiving nations low birth rates and ageing populations produce a limited supply of workers while capital-intensive technologies yield a stratified demand producing plentiful opportunities for natives with skills and education, unemployment for those who lack schooling or special skills, and a segmented demand for immigrant workers. The continuing demand for immigrants, combined with high native unemployment and growing unease with ethnic diversity, yields a contradiction that governments seek to manage through restrictive polices that confine migrants to the labour market, limit the entry of dependants, discourage long-term settlement, and repatriate those who enter outside authorized channels. Compared to the earlier industrial era, contemporary patterns and processes of international migration are far more complex.

The Insufficiency of Traditional Approaches

The theoretical approach to immigration that has prevailed for the past fifty years does not adequately come to terms with the complexities of the current reality, and social scientists have consequently begun to question the two pillars upon which earlier models were built. At the micro-level, they question the conceptualization of migrants as rational actors responding to economic disparities between countries. At the macro-level, they question the 'push-pull' approach, which views migration as a means of establishing equilibrium between regions of labour supply and demand. With seeds of doubt planted about the primacy of economic motives, the conceptual edifice of neoclassical economics has begun to wobble as never before.

The Crisis of Rational Expectations

Standard economic models have a difficult time explaining a variety of commonplace observations in the post-industrial world: whereas one less developed country may have a high rate of emigration, its similarly developed neighbour may not; migrants do not always go to places where wages are highest; migration often ceases before wage disparities disappear; migration at times occurs in the absence of wage disparities. Other problems are the inability of models to account for moves that are not economic in nature and the assumption that migrants are homogeneous with respect to taste and risk so that, given a net real wage differential, movement becomes axiomatic.

The neoclassical economic perspective has led analysts to focus almost exclusively on economic disparities between areas of origin and destination, which are evaluated by rational actors seeking to maximize utility. At times researchers have seemingly found it sufficient simply to enumerate the economic and demographic disparities separating two regions, and then deduce an all but inevitable future flow of migrants between them (see Espenshade 1989; Chesnais 1991; Golini *et al.* 1991). Rarely do they stop and ask why such flows have not materialized before, given the long-standing nature of most economic differences.

Although migration is clearly related to differentials in wages and employment (little movement generally occurs in their absence), economic disparities alone are not enough to explain international movement. By themselves, they appear to be a necessary but not sufficient condition for labour migration to occur. Although there is still a substantial wage differential between Northern and Southern Europe, for example, little migration occurs between Spain, Portugal, and Italy, on the one hand, and Germany, Belgium, and Denmark, on the other. Wage differentials may have to be quite large for migration to occur, more than the 30 per cent 'cliff' mentioned by Lewis (1954) in his classic treatise.

International migration may require that economic conditions be perceived as insupportable—not simply inferior—in the country of origin. Above a certain level of economic well-being, the perceived costs—psychic as well as financial—may predominate over expected gains in explaining the propensity to move (Massey and García España 1987). If this is true, traditional explanations need to be modified to give more weight to non-pecuniary factors and also to expectations, necessarily subjective, about the future.

In traditional economic frameworks, migrants move because they expect to reap a net gain in income, and the larger the expected gain the more likely they are to move. Increases in wages within destination areas should therefore increase the volume of migration, and decreases should lower it. This vision bears little relationship to reality, however: without any increase in developed country wages, the number of candidates for international migration has steadily grown throughout the world. North–South wage differentials are presently such that they provide a virtually constant incentive to move. The volume of international migration would probably not change markedly were wages in core receiving areas suddenly to decline modestly. Indeed, over the past two decades, average wages have declined in real terms in the USA while immigration has steadily expanded.

Debates about whether real or nominal wages are most important in determining migration, or whether observed wages must be conditioned by employment rates to generate expected wages (Todaro 1969) may make sense for studies of internal migration; but they seem rather odd when applied to international migration. No matter how wages are measured, differentials between North and South are sufficient to yield large net returns to international movement from nearly all less developed countries, most of which are not major players in international migration today.

According to neoclassical economic theory, the departure of migrants raises wages in sending areas and lowers them in receiving areas. Migration should thus continue until wages are equalized, and then it should stop. Historical experience reveals, however, that transnational wage differentials rarely disappear, and when they do it is through a variety of mechanisms, among which migration is not necessarily the most important. If the world really worked as predicted by theory, far more people would move and international migration would continue to grow until it produced an equilibrium wage throughout the world.

Reality categorically refutes this hypothesis. Migration typically has not ended with the equalization of wages, but with the attainment of bearable conditions of life in areas of origin, after which people find migration not worth the effort. Despite the absence of legal barriers to movement and the persistence of a significant wage differential, sustained net migration between Puerto Rico and the USA mainland effectively ended in the early 1970s, as did migration between Spain and Germany. These observations thus suggest a need to revise standard economic theory, especially with respect to what it assumes about human motivations. Migrants may be motivated not simply by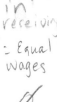

a desire for gain, but by an aversion to risk, a desire to be comfortable, or simply an interest in building better lives at home.

Rather than predicting a propensity to move for economic improvement, one might even posit the opposite: a propensity to stay at home that is overcome only during certain exceptional periods when unusual circumstances coincide to alter the socio-economic context for decision-making in ways that make migration appear to be a good and reasonable investment of time and resources. These 'unusual circumstances' seem to follow directly from economic development and its social and demographic consequences.

The influence of material development on the propensity to migrate is fundamental. Although economic growth in poor countries reduces the incentive to emigrate in the long run by raising living standards and closing economic gaps with potential destination countries, in the short run it increases pressures for emigration by fomenting a massive displacement of people from agriculture and from rural ways of life, a process that is inseparable from the process of development itself. As one of us has pointed out elsewhere, 'these displaced people constitute the source for the massive population movements that inevitably accompany development. Most become internal migrants . . . but some always migrate internationally' (Massey 1988: 384).

A corollary of the idea that emigration results from disparities between nations is that the volume of international migration is directly proportional to the size of the differential between them. But the number of exceptions to this rule is so large that its veracity must seriously be questioned. If it were true, there would be more countries in the 'sending' category than we now observe. Although the number of major sending countries continues to rise, there really aren't that many. A minority of nations account for the vast majority of the world's international migrants, and usually they are neither the poorest nor the least developed of nations.

Thus, economic disparities by themselves seem insufficient to explain international migration. At best they constitute a necessary but not a sufficient condition for emigration. Although they may be a precondition for international movement, wage and employment differentials are not necessarily the most important determinants of the propensity to leave home for a destination abroad.

It might be argued that migration costs represent more of a deterrent to international movement than is normally recognized by economic theory, with its traditional de-emphasis on transactions costs. This does not explain, however, differences in potential migrants' responses to income disparities across borders. Revolutions in global transportation and communication have dramatically lowered travel and information costs without triggering a proportional increase in international migration. Moreover, in some cases where these costs are low—as between Southern and Northern Europe and between Puerto Rico and the US mainland—net migration has virtually ceased despite ongoing wage differences. In these places, the absence of international movement can hardly be ascribed to the presence of unusually large information and transportation costs.

Until now we have focused primarily on economic disparities between countries, but the propensity for emigration that is built into the process of economic development is also aggravated by demographic forces *within* nations. Economic transformation is usually accompanied by demographic shifts that raise the rate of population growth and cause the number of potential job-seekers, consumers, and service users to swell. In practice, as well as in theory, conventional wisdom dictates that demographic factors may, under certain conditions, play a role in promoting international migration.

We do not concur, however, with the notion that demographic 'pressure' in sending regions translates directly into migration towards areas of lower 'pressure' overseas (e.g. Schaeffer 1993; Straubhaar 1993). This idea, corresponding to a certain 'hydraulic logic', can be categorically refuted: demographic disparities *per se* are irrelevant; people do not migrate because they perceive demographic differences. Countries with the highest rates of fertility, the fastest population growth, and the greatest density of settlement do not send the most emigrants worldwide.

Likewise, demographic conditions in countries of destination—above all low fertility and the ageing of the population—are much less important in their migratory effects than often assumed. There are many ways to balance labour supply and demand besides immigration: raising the retirement age, increasing the rate of female labour force participation, encouraging the internal movement of native workers, and raising worker productivity through capital investment. If there is a demand for foreign labour today, it appears to stem as much from the segmented structure of advanced industrial economies as from demographic conditions *per se* (Piore 1979).

Demographic conditions in countries of origin are indeed important, not because of their contrast with conditions in destination countries, as often assumed. Rather, they are important because of their influence within sending regions themselves. Demographic trends are relevant, not demographic disparities. High fertility and rapid population growth produce large birth cohorts that have migration-promoting effects within specific socio-economic contexts: they put pressure on social infrastructure such as schools, roads, hospitals, and clinics; they make the satisfaction of consumer desires more difficult; they make it harder to provide decent and affordable housing; they raise unemployment rates; and generally they channel state resources away from productive investment into current consumption, driving up public expenditures and contributing to state deficits and foreign debt. The latter outcomes may further exacerbate migratory pressure by leading public officials to adopt policies of structural adjustment that, in the short run, aggravate unemployment, consumer scarcity, and housing shortages to yield social tensions, impelling people to search for relief through international migration.

The integration of demographic factors into a broader theory of international migration is a goal that remains to be fully accomplished, despite the empirical connections established by Easterlin (1961), B. Thomas (1973), and more recently the historical analysis of Hatton and Williamson (1994*a*). One ambitious attempt to integrate demographic interrelations into a coherent, empirically informed framework was that of Zelinsky (1971), who proposed a theory of migration transition that offered general claims about human migration fashioned from demographic, geographic, and historic observations.

The extent to which Zelinksy's model continues to be valid is unclear, however, especially considering its strong emphasis on the crucial role of geography. One factor he considered central—physical distance—has certainly changed profoundly in character and importance over the past three decades. Proximity to a receiving area continues to be relevant, but it is not nearly as decisive as it once was. The importance of physical distance has diminished greatly as improvements in transportation and communication have allowed human beings to overcome the barriers of space and information in less time, with greater ease, and at lower cost than ever before.

Given current technologies, we must also question Zelinsky's view that migratory fields expand in concentric circles away from a point of labour supply, as well as his axiomatic acceptance of spatial diffusion as fundamental to the spread of migration. Although Zelinsky's effort to integrate demographic factors into a general theory of migration offers certain attractions, it now seems dated and in need of revision in light of post-industrial conditions that were not fully manifest at the time he was working.

Finally, most theoretical work to date has sought to explain potential rather than actual migratory flows. That is, it has focused on the patterns and processes of migration that would occur in the absence of legal or political obstacles to international movement. But reality continually demonstrates that between the potential act and its realization lies a considerable distance, typically mediated by national and transnational political structures. On what does the realization of migration potential depend, and to what extent? With this question we enter an area of obscurity, but one that is central to the research and theories that we review.

The Crisis of Push-Pull

Just as the traditional economic approach to migration has been questioned, so too has its inseparable companion, the 'push-pull' framework. For years analysts have relied upon the venerable concepts of 'push' and 'pull' to animate their models. Although useful heuristic devices, push-pull models do not constitute a theoretical framework so much as a means of classifying migration and ordering its determinants in space. Although never stated explicitly, the nature of the factors considered under the rubric of push-pull have always been exclusively economic.

The push-pull framework joined perfectly with standard microeconomics.

The paradigmatic application of the push-pull framework is the well-known analysis of Brinley Thomas (1973), who studied the great transatlantic migrations of the industrial era. He discovered that oscillations in the British economic cycle had countervailing ripples on American shores, creating successive waves of migration in which the forces of push and pull predominated at different times on different sides of the Atlantic: periods of push in Britain coincided with eras of pull in the USA, while periods of pull in Britain coincided with times of push in America.

The push-pull framework assumed that migration enabled a certain equilibrium to be achieved between forces of economic growth and contraction in different geographic locations. Investigators have discussed the consequences that follow from the predominance of one of the forces—push or pull—over the other (Singer 1971, 1975); and in the industrial period we find cases in which the forces of attraction predominate (D. S. Thomas 1941), cases where those of expulsion rule (Lowell 1987), and even changes in the sequence and predominance of forces over time (B. Thomas 1973).

In the post-industrial period, however, the forces of expulsion seem to have gained the upper hand, to the point of ending the equilibrium characteristic of the earlier industrial era. As already noted, North–South wage differentials now provide a constant incentive for migration irrespective of business cycles, and the growing importance of new forms of migration that did not exist in the industrial era—undocumented migration and the movement of asylees and refugees—attests to the growing importance of push over pull. Moreover, countries of destination have not just stopped labour recruitment; they actively try to keep immigrants out through legal obstacles and repressive border policies.

Restrictive admissions policies—virtually absent in the industrial era—are extraordinarily important, for they decisively condition the character and volume of international migration today. The imposition of qualitative and quantitative limits on entry creates different classes of migrants with differently selected traits who ultimately occupy different positions in the socioeconomic structure of the receiving society: legal immigrants, undocumented migrants, refugees, asylees, students, trainees, business executives, and 'temporary' workers. As countries of destination adjust their policies in response to changing conditions, migrants adjust their strategies and tailor their schemes to fit the prevailing rules and regulations.

As policies become more restrictive, the costs and risks of all kinds of migration rise, and so do the odds of failure (involuntary repatriation) with the consequent loss of resources invested in the move. The legal admissions policies of developed countries are now highly selective, and certain personal traits—education, skills, wealth, family connections—are essential in assuring success, or even putting a person in a position to be a realistic candidate for entry. For many aspiring migrants who cannot meet the legal requirements, a reasonable expectation of economic improvement is not enough to promote movement. Without documents, they need a very strong motivation or another source of comparative advantage (e.g. social connections to a person already in the receiving country) to overcome the obstacles and gain access to foreign employment.

The State and its policies are thus central to explaining contemporary migration for theoretical as well as practical reasons. Nothing invalidates traditional approaches to migration as effectively as border control policies. Indeed, 'it is precisely the control which states exercise over borders that defines international migration as a distinctive social process' (Zolberg 1989: 405). Border controls reduce the applicability of standard economic models by impeding the free circulation of labour as a factor of production, and, consequently, preventing the development of international migration to its fullest potential.

Although border controls and restrictive policies obviously reduce the flow of immigrants below what it would be in their absence, all borders remain 'porous' to some degree. Undocumented migrants enter and work by clandestine means, while others enter through legal exceptions made to restrictive policies for humanitarian reasons (family reunification, political asylum, flight from wars or natural disasters). In all cases, the size of the actual inflow exceeds that specified by policy or envisioned by officials and the public as ideal.

In some ways, this state of affairs is highly functional and even adaptive: labour demand is met by undocumented migrants, 'temporary' workers, and legal immigrants able to overcome the barriers, keeping employers happy; yet the government is not perceived as encouraging or promoting immigration, thus avoiding a political backlash (Andreas 1998). Whether the contemporary nature of immigration is functional or not, or whether it is even consciously sought, the key point is that international migration is no longer promoted by two equally important forces. Rather, push factors are now predominant and are paired with diminished, but constant pull factors, with governments acting as intermediaries to limit the size of the resulting flows through restrictive policies.

Thus, the dialectic is not so much between the forces of push and pull as between the push and 'intervening factors' described by Lee (1966). The most important forces operating to influence the volume and composition of international migration today are those that States deploy to regulate or impede the inflow: admission policies, *de jure* or *de facto*. Classical theorists mentioned these intermediate factors only in passing, if at all; and when they did, they usually confined their attention to the one factor that today matters least: distance. In the world of the late twentieth century, distances are small but the barriers erected by governments are large, and the latter have become the principal factor determining the size and character of contemporary international migrant flows.

New Theoretical Perspectives

It is thus clear that theory must move beyond the analysis of simple social, economic, demographic disparities between countries—beyond the mere cataloguing of push and pull factors—to account for contemporary trends and patterns of international migration. Perhaps the first victims of the new reality are the hoary 'laws of migration' proposed by Ravenstein (1885, 1889) more than a century ago and extended by Lee in 1966. Although useful in their day, their validity is now highly doubtful (Davis 1988), and they never constituted a theory so much as a collection of empirical regularities (Arango 1985).

Recognition of the complexity of international migration during the last quarter of the twentieth century reveals multiple insufficiencies in traditional theoretical approaches. Migrants clearly do not respond mechanically to wage and employment differentials, if they ever did; they are not homogeneous with respect to tastes and motivations; and the contexts within which they make their decisions are not the same.

Recognition of these problems has led to a renewed interest in the nature of migrant decision-making, a reconceptualization of the basic motivations that underlie geographic mobility, greater attention to the context within which the decisions are made, and more informed efforts to identify the specific social and economic dimensions that define this context. Thinking has moved away from reified, mechanical models towards more dynamic formulations that allow micro-level decisions to affect macro-level processes and vice versa. In these efforts, the field has moved away from a reliance on official statistics and aggregate data towards a more extensive use of household surveys, life histories, and in-depth community studies. Emphasis has shifted to the migrants themselves—to interactions with their environments, confrontations with restrictive state policies, comparisons with non-migrants, and contrasts between the first migrants and those that follow.

In this emphasis on migrants as active agents, macro-level factors have not been abandoned. The movement of the pendulum towards the study of migrant decision-making does not imply a neglect of the larger social and economic forces that constrain and condition individual decisions and actions. On the contrary, the thrust of much new theoretical work has been explicitly to study the interplay of socio-economic structure, household strategies, and individual decision-making. The need to combine macro- and micro-level approaches into coherent multilevel models is a clear desideratum.

In contrast to the classical theoretical explanations of the past, the new theoretical literature is well described by the Spanish philosopher José Ortega y Gasset: 'I am myself and my circumstances.' Contemporary theorists and researchers see migrants as much more 'I' than the reified, mechanical approaches of the past, but they have not forgotten the 'circumstances' either. In the new theory, neither the subject nor the context are sanitized to be consistent with a set of arbitrary assumptions, such as rational behaviour, homogeneous response to common incentives, perfect information, complete markets, little risk, irrelevance of non-pecuniary factors.

On the contrary, the interaction between subject and environment (geographic, social, economic, and political) has become the central focus of analysis to test these very assumptions. The interplay of individuals, motivations, and contexts defined at various levels of aggregation (household, community, national, and international) have become fundamental to building an accurate understanding of contemporary migration flows, and above all to answering the central question of why some people migrate while others do not—and concomitantly, why some countries send many migrants abroad while others, apparently equally situated, send few.

Widespread dissatisfaction with the push-pull framework and neoclassic economic explanations for migration have given rise to a series of new and exciting theoretical perspectives: the new economics of labour migration, segmented labour market theory, social capital theory, world systems theory, and the theory of cumulative causation. These theoretical approaches have opened new avenues of thought and investigation, but to date no successful attempt has been made to integrate them into a single theoretical vision.

In subsequent chapters, we apply ourselves to this goal, first by undertaking a complete and thorough examination of each theoretical model on its own terms, and then through a systematic empirical evaluation of the principal tenets of each theory against the research literature emanating from the world's principal migration systems: North America, Western Europe, the Gulf region, Asia and the Pacific, and the Southern Cone of South America. In doing so, we classify systems according to core countries of destination, reviewing the literature associated with flows into each set of core nations. Thus, whereas destination countries are considered as part of one and only one migration system, source countries may be discussed under several system rubrics. The Philippines, for example, simultaneously contributes immigrants to North America and the Persian Gulf, as well to nations throughout Asia and the Pacific. Research conducted in the Philippines is therefore reviewed under all three systems, depending on where migrants in each study go. By proceeding through the empirical research literature in an orderly fashion, system by system, we hope to develop a comprehensive theoretical basis for understanding international migration now, and in the century that is fast upon us.

2 Contemporary Theories of International Migration

At present, there is no single theory widely accepted by social scientists to account for the emergence and perpetuation of international migration throughout the world, only a fragmented set of theories that have developed largely in isolation from one another, sometimes but not always segmented by disciplinary boundaries. Current patterns and trends in international migration suggest, however, that a full understanding of contemporary migratory processes will not be achieved by relying on the tools of one discipline alone, or by focusing on a single level of analysis or one conceptual model. Rather, their complex, multifaceted nature requires a sophisticated theory that incorporates a variety of perspectives, levels, and assumptions.

In this chapter, we seek to explicate and integrate the leading contemporary theories of international migration. We begin by examining models that describe the initiation of international movement and then consider theories that account for why transnational population flows persist across space and time. Rather than favouring one theory over another a priori, we seek to understand each model on its own terms in order to illuminate key assumptions and hypotheses. Only after each theory has been considered separately do we compare and contrast the different conceptual frameworks to reveal areas of logical inconsistency and substantive disagreement. In undertaking this exercise, we seek to provide a sound basis for evaluating the models empirically, and to lay the groundwork for constructing a comprehensive theory of international migration for the twenty-first century.

The Initiation of International Migration

A variety of theoretical models have been proposed to explain why international migration begins, and although each ultimately seeks to explain the same thing, they employ radically different concepts, assumptions, and frames of reference. Neoclassical economics focuses on differentials in wages and employment conditions between countries, and on migration costs; it generally conceives of movement as an individual decision for income maximization. The new economics of migration, in contrast, considers conditions in a variety of markets, not just labour markets. It views migration as a household decision taken to minimize risk and to overcome constraints on family production or consumption attributable to failures in insurance, capital, or consumer credit markets. Segmented labour market theory and world systems theory generally ignore such micro-level decision processes, focusing instead on forces operating at higher levels of aggregation. The former links immigration to the structural requirements of modern industrial economies, and the latter sees immigration as a natural consequence of capitalist market penetration across national boundaries.

Given the fact that theories conceptualize causal processes at such different levels of analysis—individual, household, national, and international—they cannot be assumed, a priori, to be inherently incompatible. It is quite possible, for example, that individuals act to maximize income while families organize themselves to minimize risk, and that the context within which both decisions are made is shaped by structural forces operating at the national and international levels. Nonetheless, the various models reflect different research objectives, focuses, interests, and ways of decomposing an enormously complex subject into analytically manageable parts. A firm basis for judging their consistency requires that the inner logic, propositions, assumptions, and hypotheses of each theory be clearly specified and well understood.

S.D. of Labor   *Supply & Demand: ↑ Labor → ↓ Labor · ↓ wage → ↓ wage = Equilibrium*

Neoclassical Economics: Macro-Theory

Probably the oldest and best-known theory of international migration has its roots in models developed originally to explain internal labour migration in the process of economic development (Lewis 1954; Ranis and Fei 1961; Harris and Todaro 1970; Todaro 1976). According to this theory and its extensions, international migration, like its internal counterpart, is caused by geographic differences in the supply of and demand for labour (Todaro and Maruszko 1987). A country with a large endowment of labour relative to capital will have a low equilibrium market wage (and in the world of Lewis (1954), a labour surplus), while a nation with a limited endowment of labour relative to capital will be characterized by a high market wage, as depicted graphically by the familiar interaction of labour supply and demand curves. The resulting differential in wages causes workers from the low-wage or labour-surplus country to move to the high-wage or labour-scarce country. As a result of this movement, the supply of labour decreases and wages eventually rise in the capital-poor country, while the supply of labour increases and wages ultimately fall in the capital-rich country, leading, at equilibrium, to an international wage differential that reflects only the costs of international movement, pecuniary and psychic.

Mirroring the flow of workers from labour-abundant to labour-scarce countries is a flow of investment capital from capital-rich to capital-poor countries. The relative scarcity of capital in poor countries yields a rate of return that is high by international standards, thereby attracting investment. The movement of capital includes the migration of human capital, with highly skilled workers going from capital-rich to capital-poor countries in order to reap high returns on their skills in a human capital-scarce environment, leading to a parallel movement of managers, technicians, and other skilled workers. The international flow of labour, therefore, must be kept conceptually distinct from the associated international flow of human capital. Even in the most aggregated macro-level models, the heterogeneity of immigrants along skill lines must be clearly recognized.

The simple and compelling explanation for international migration offered by neoclassical macroeconomics has strongly shaped public thinking and has provided the intellectual basis for much immigration policy. The perspective contains several implicit propositions and assumptions:

1. The international migration of workers is caused by differences in wage rates between countries.
2. The elimination of wage differentials will end the movement of labour, and migration will not occur in the absence of such differentials.
3. International flows of human capital—that is, highly skilled workers— respond to differences in the rate of return to human capital, which may be different from the overall wage rate, yielding a distinct pattern of migration that may be the opposite that of unskilled workers.
4. International flows of workers are influenced primarily by labour market mechanisms; other kinds of markets do not have important effects on international migration.
5. The way for governments to control migration flows is to regulate or influence labour markets in sending and/or receiving countries.

Neoclassical Economics: Micro-Theory = Individual Choice & Net Returns

Corresponding to the macroeconomic model is a microeconomic model of individual choice (Todaro 1969, 1976, 1989; Borjas 1989). In this scheme, individual rational actors decide to migrate because a cost-benefit calculation leads them to expect a positive net return, usually monetary, from movement. International migration is conceptualized as a form of investment in human capital (Sjaastad 1962). People choose to move to where they can be most productive, given their skills; but before they can capture the higher wages associated with greater labour productivity, they must undertake certain investments, which include the material costs of travelling, the costs of maintenance while moving and looking for work, the effort involved in learning a new language and culture, the difficulty experienced in adapting to a new labour market, and the psychological costs of cutting old ties and forging new ones (Todaro and Maruszko 1987).

Potential migrants estimate the costs and benefits of moving to alternative international locations and migrate to where the expected discounted net returns are greatest over some time-horizon (Borjas 1989, 1990). Net returns in each future period are estimated by taking the observed earnings corresponding to the individual's skills in the destination country and multi-plying these by the probability of obtaining a job there (and for illegal migrants the likelihood of being able to avoid deportation) to obtain 'expected destina-tion earnings'. These expected earnings are then subtracted from those expected in the community of origin (observed earnings there multiplied by the probability of employment) and the difference is summed over a time-horizon from 0 to n, discounted by a factor that reflects the greater utility of money earned in the present than in the future. From this integrated differ-ence the estimated costs are subtracted to yield the expected net return to migration.

This decision-making process is summarized analytically by the following equation:

$$ER(0) = \int_0^n \left[P_1(t)P_2(t)Y_d(t) - P_3(t)Y_o(t) \right] e^{-rt} dt - C(0) \tag{1}$$

where $ER(0)$ is the expected net return to migration calculated just before departure at time 0; t is time; $P_1(t)$ is the probability of avoiding deportation from the area of destination (1.0 for legal migrants and <1.0 for undocu-mented migrants); $P_2(t)$ is the probability of employment at the destination; $Y_d(t)$ is earnings if employed at the place of destination; $P_3(t)$ is the probability of employment in the community of origin; $Y_o(t)$ is earnings if employed in the community of origin; r is the discount factor; and $C(0)$ is the sum total of the costs of movement (including a monetization of psychological costs).

If the quantity $ER(0)$ is positive for some potential destination, the rational actor migrates; if it is negative the actor stays; and if it is zero, the actor is indifferent between moving and staying. In theory, a potential migrant goes to wherever the expected net returns to migration are greatest, leading to several important conclusions that differ slightly from the earlier macroeconomic formulations:

1. International movement stems from international differentials in both earnings and employment rates, whose product determines expected earn-ings (the prior model, in contrast, downplayed employment rates, espe-cially at migrant destinations).
2. Individual human capital characteristics that increase the likely rate of remuneration or the probability of employment in the destination relative to the sending country (e.g. education, experience, training, language skills) will increase the likelihood of international movement, other things being equal.
3. Individual characteristics, social conditions, or technologies that lower migration costs increase the net returns to migration and, hence, raise the probability of international movement.
4. Because of 2 and 3, individuals within the same country can display very different proclivities to emigrate.

5. Aggregate migration flows between countries are simple sums of individual moves undertaken on the basis of individual cost-benefit calculations.

6. International movement does not occur in the absence of differences in earnings levels and/or employment rates between countries. Migration occurs until expected earnings (the product of earnings and employment rates) have been equalized internationally (net of the costs of movement), and movement does not stop until this product has been equalized.

7. The size of the differential in expected returns determines the size of the international flow of migrants between countries.

8. Migration decisions stem from disequilibria or discontinuities between labour markets; other markets do not directly influence the decision to migrate.

9. If conditions in receiving countries are psychologically attractive to prospective migrants, migration costs may be negative. In this case, a negative earnings differential may be necessary to halt migration between the countries.

10. Governments can control immigration primarily through policies that affect expected earnings in sending and/or receiving countries—for example, those that attempt to lower the likelihood of employment or raise the risk of underemployment in the destination area (through employer sanctions), those that seek to raise incomes at the origin (through long-term development programmes), or those that aim to increase the costs (both psychological and material) of migration.

The New Economics of Migration

In recent years, a 'new economics of labour migration' has arisen to challenge many of the assumptions and conclusions of neoclassical theory (Stark and Bloom 1985). A key insight of this new approach is that migration decisions are not made by isolated individual actors, but by larger units of related people—typically families or households, but sometimes communities, in which people act collectively not only to maximize expected income, but also to minimize risks and to loosen constraints associated with various kinds of market failures, apart from those in the labour market (Stark and Levhari 1982; Stark 1984a; Katz and Stark 1986; Taylor 1986, 1987; Lauby and Stark 1988; and articles by various authors reprinted in Stark 1991).

Unlike individuals, households are in a good position to control risks to their economic well-being by diversifying the allocation of resources at their disposal, such as family labour. Although individuals may use sequential short periods of seasonal migration as a means of spreading out their labour over time, this strategy is less feasible for international migrants who face large sunk costs of movement. Households, in contrast, can easily diversify income by allocating various family workers to different geographically discrete labour markets: some may undertake productive activities in the local economy; others may work elsewhere in the same country (for example, in a distant urban area); and still others may work in a foreign country.

As long as economic conditions in the non-local labour markets are negatively correlated or weakly associated with those in the home community, households will be in a position to control risks through diversification. In the event that economic conditions at home deteriorate and productive activities there fail to bring in sufficient income, the household can rely on migrant remittances for support. In most developed countries, risks to household income are minimized through private insurance and credit markets or governmental programmes, but in developing countries these institutional mechanisms for managing risk are imperfect, absent, or inaccessible to poor families, giving them incentives to diversify risks through foreign wage labour.

In developed countries, markets for capital and consumer credit are relatively complete and well-functioning, enabling families of modest means to finance new projects through borrowing, such as the adoption of new production technology, the construction of a home, or the purchase of an appliance. In most developing countries, in contrast, investment capital and consumer credit are unavailable or are procurable only at high cost. Thus, the absence of well-functioning capital and credit markets creates strong pressures for international movement as a strategy of capital accumulation. The manifold links between various market failures and international migration are illustrated by the following examples.

Crop insurance markets

Whenever farm households put time and money into sowing a crop, they are betting that the investment will pay off at a future date in the form of a product that can be sold for cash to purchase desired goods and services, or which can be consumed directly for subsistence. Between the time a crop is planted and harvested, however, human or natural events may reduce or eliminate the harvest, leaving the family with insufficient income or food for sustenance. Likewise, the introduction of new agricultural technology (such as high-yielding seeds or new methods of cultivation) may alter the objective and/or subjective risks confronting farm households. Using a new seed variety may increase a farmer's yield if the development expert is right; but if he or she is wrong, the household faces the prospect of having insufficient food or income, a risk to which farm families are naturally quite averse.

In developed countries, these sorts of objective and subjective risks are managed through formal insurance arrangements, whereby agricultural producers pay a fee to a company or a government agency to insure the crop against future loss. The insuring institution assumes the risk to the future crop, and should a drought or flood destroy the harvest or a new technology backfire, it pays the producer for the insured market value of the crop, thereby guaranteeing the economic well-being of the family. If crop insurance is not available, families have an incentive to self-insure by sending one or more workers abroad to remit earnings home, thereby guaranteeing family income even if the harvest fails.

Futures markets

Whenever a household sows a cash crop, it assumes that the crop, when harvested, can be sold for a price sufficient to sustain the family or improve its well-being. In making this bet, however, there is a risk that the price for the crop may drop below expected levels, once again leaving the family with insufficient income. In developed countries, price risk is managed through futures markets that allow farmers to sell all or part of their crop for future delivery at a guaranteed price. Investors assume the risk of loss should prices fall below the guaranteed price, and they reap the gain should prices rise above this level. Most developing countries lack futures markets, and when they exist, poor farm households generally have little access to them. Migration offers a mechanism by which farm families can self-insure against income risks arising from crop price fluctuations.

Unemployment insurance

Non-farm families, as well as many farm households, depend on wages earned by family workers. If local economic conditions deteriorate and employment levels fall, or if a family member is injured and cannot work, the household's livelihood may be threatened by a reduction or loss of income. In wealthy countries, governments maintain insurance programmes that protect workers and their families from this risk, but in poor countries such unemployment and disability programmes are absent or incomplete in their coverage, again giving families incentives to self-insure by sending workers abroad.

If employment conditions in foreign and local labour markets are negatively correlated or uncorrelated, then international migration provides a way of reducing the risk to family wages and guarantees a reliable stream of income, in the form of remittances, to support the family. Moreover, migration fulfils this insurance function whether or not remittances are actually observed. Migrants as insurers, like formal insurance contracts, only have to pay out if losses are realized. The existence of an implicit or explicit insurance contract among family members, however, can have an important effect on a household's economic behaviour, and the desire to acquire this insurance may be a primary motivation for families and households to participate in international migration.

Retirement insurance

The problem of how to support oneself after one's inevitable withdrawal from productive activities in old age is a universal human concern. Developed countries have evolved a mix of private pensions and government security programmes to reduce or eliminate the risk of penury in old age. Workers privately set aside a portion of their earnings during their productive years and invest them in financial instruments to generate a stock of capital capable of financing their retirement, essentially transferring some of their earnings from the present to the future. Most developed-country governments perform the same tasks publicly on behalf of their citizens, or they simply transfer current income from workers to retirees using powers of taxation and spending.

In most developing nations, however, public and private schemes for ensuring old-age support are rudimentary, incomplete in their coverage, or, very frequently, non-existent, creating serious problems for individuals and families seeking to provide for their retirement. By generating an additional stream of income that can be invested in productive assets at home or accumulated in savings accounts abroad, international migration offers a potential solution to this fundamental human problem. The extra earnings garnered through international migration yield a total household income stream sufficiently large to enable its diversification across time and, hence, the accumulation of assets sufficient to ensure adequate financial support in old age.

Capital markets

Households may desire to increase the productivity of their assets, but to do so they may also need to acquire capital to make the necessary investments. Farm families, for example, may seek to irrigate their fields, apply fertilizers, buy scientifically improved seeds, or acquire machinery, but lack the money to purchase these inputs. Non-farm families may seek to invest in the education or training of household members, or to acquire capital goods that can be used to produce goods for sale on consumer markets, but again they may lack money to cover these costs. In developed countries, of course, such investments are funded either through savings or borrowing, both of which are greatly assisted by access to a sound and efficient banking system.

In many developing countries, however, savings institutions are unreliable or underdeveloped, and people are reluctant to entrust their savings to them. The needed funds may also be difficult to borrow because the family lacks collateral to qualify for a loan, because there is a scarcity of lending capital, or because the banking system provides incomplete coverage, serving mainly the needs of affluent families or large firms. For poor families, the only real access to borrowing is often from local moneylenders who charge high interest rates, making transaction costs prohibitive. Under these circumstances, migration again becomes attractive as an alternative source of capital to finance improvements in productivity, and the family has a strong incentive to send one or more workers abroad to accumulate savings or to transfer capital back in the form of remittances.

Credit markets

Whenever households lack access to a sound and efficient banking system, for whatever reason, they not only lose the ability to capitalize new productive activities; they also lose the ability to finance large consumer purchases such as appliances, cars, and homes. In most developed countries, consumers have instantaneous access to credit through universal bank cards such as Mastercard and Visa, which in effect provide an immediate loan for any purpose up to a pre-set amount and subject to a contractual rate of interest. Thus, when a refrigerator suddenly expires and a family does not have the income or savings to replace it immediately, it can nonetheless purchase the appliance by charging it to a credit card and then repaying the debt over a period of months. Naturally, credit limits and interest rates vary with the creditworthiness of the consumer, but in most developed countries even people of very modest means can qualify for credit of some sort. The credit limit may be $500 and the interest rate high, but credit is nonetheless there and available for emergencies. The absence of consumer credit can create a strong motivation for short-term migration, given a sudden need to make a large purchase.

A demand for consumer credit need not require a household emergency, of course. As markets expand into domains formerly governed by non-market or pre-market mechanisms, consumers in developing countries often find themselves filled with a range of new material aspirations acquired from the mass media, but without access to the credit mechanisms that make mass consumption possible. Like their counterparts in wealthier countries, residents of the Third World want to own televisions, CD players, stereos, and video cassettes, and they increasingly find these goods for sale in local markets, but they do not have the ready cash to pay for them and can only borrow the money at exploitive rates of interest. As international markets penetrate developing countries, therefore, nascent demands for consumer goods create another motivation for temporary migration abroad.

Perhaps the most important consumer purchase is a home. In many developed countries, home ownership is financed through bank mortgages that enable borrowers to make a small down payment and then cover the balance of the purchase price with a long-term bank loan, which is paid off gradually in monthly instalments. In this way, home ownership is put within reach of a large share of families of relatively modest means. In the USA, for example, thirty-year mortgages requiring as little as 10 per cent down have been widely available to families since the 1940s, giving that country one of the highest rates of home ownership in the world.

Within most developing countries, in contrast, mortgages are uncommon or non-existent, requiring families to amass the entire cost of a home in cash before making a purchase. Under these circumstances, international migration becomes attractive as a means of financing home ownership. Foreign earnings saved or remitted back to family members may be put directly into the purchase, expansion, or construction of a home. Often new homes are acquired through a gradual process of construction financed by repeated foreign trips. In migrant-sending communities throughout the developing world, it is common to see homes stalled at various stages of construction, as migrants run out of funds and return abroad to accumulate more cash. The acquisition or improvement of a home is probably the single most important motivation for international migration prevailing in the world today. Remittance use studies consistently reveal it to be the most common target for migrant spending and investment (see Chapters 8 and 9). Failures in consumer credit markets thus constitute an extremely important, if unrecognized, cause of international migration.

Relative deprivation

A key proposition in the foregoing discussion is that income is not a homogeneous good, as assumed by neoclassical economics. The source of the income really matters, and households have significant incentives to invest scarce family resources in activities and projects that provide access to new income sources, even if these activities do not increase total income. The new economics of migration also questions the assumption that income has a constant effect on utility across socio-economic settings, i.e. that a $100 real increase in income means the same thing to a person regardless of community conditions and irrespective of his or her position in the local income distribution.

The new economic theorists argue that households send workers abroad not only to improve their incomes in absolute terms, but also to increase them *relative* to other households, and, hence, to reduce their *relative* deprivation compared with some reference group (see Stark *et al.* 1986, 1988; Stark and Yitzhaki 1988; Stark and Taylor 1989, 1991*a*; Stark 1991). A household's sense of relative deprivation depends on the incomes of which it is deprived in the reference-group income distribution. If $F(x)$ is the cumulative income distribution and $h[1 - F(x)]$ represents the dissatisfaction felt by a household with income x from not having an income that is slightly higher than x (i.e. in the range from x to $x + \Delta x$, where $\Delta x \rightarrow 0$), then the relative deprivation of a household with income x can be expressed conceptually as:

$$RD(x) = \int_{x}^{xmax} h[1 - F(x)]dx \qquad (2)$$

where *ymax* is the highest income found in the community. In the simple case where $h[1 - F(x)] = 1 - F(x)$, this expression is equivalent to the product of two terms: the share of households with income greater than x, and the average difference between these higher household incomes and x (Stark and Taylor 1989, 1991).

To illustrate this concept of relative income, consider an increase in the income of affluent households. If poor households' incomes are unchanged, then their relative deprivation increases. If household utility is negatively affected by relative deprivation, then even though a poor household's absolute income and expected gains from migration remain unchanged, its incentive to participate in international migration increases if, by sending a family member abroad, it can hope to reap a relative income gain in the community. The likelihood of migration thus grows because of the change in *other* households' incomes. Market failures that constrain local income opportunities for poor households may also increase the attractiveness of migration as an avenue for effecting gains in relative income.

The theoretical models growing out of the 'new economics' of migration yield a set of propositions and hypotheses that are quite different from those emanating from neoclassical theory, and they lead to a very different set of policy prescriptions:

1. Families, households, or other culturally defined units of production and consumption, not the autonomous individual, are the appropriate units of analysis for migration research.
2. A wage differential is not a necessary condition for international migration to occur; households may have strong incentives to diversify risks or accumulate capital through transnational movement even in the absence of wage differences.
3. International migration and local employment or local production are not mutually exclusive possibilities. Indeed, there are strong incentives for households to engage in both migration and local activities. An increase in the returns to local economic activities may even *increase* the attractiveness of migration as a means of overcoming capital and risk constraints on investing in those activities. Thus, economic development within sending regions need not reduce the pressures for international migration; it may intensify them.
4. International movement does not necessarily stop when wage differentials have been eliminated between different national labour markets. Incentives for migration will continue to exist if other markets within sending countries (insurance, futures, capital, and consumer credit) are absent, imperfect, or in disequilibrium.
5. The same expected gain in income may not have the same effect on the probability of migration for households located at different points in the income distribution, or even on households with identical incomes but located in communities with different income distributions.
6. Governments can influence migration rates not only through policies that influence labour markets, but also through those that shape insurance markets, capital markets, consumer credit markets, and futures markets. Government insurance programmes, particularly unemployment insurance, retirement, and loan programmes, can significantly affect the incentives for international movement.

7. Government policies and economic changes that shape the income distribution will change the relative deprivation of some households and thus alter their incentives to migrate.

8. Government policies and economic changes that affect the distribution of income will influence international migration independently of their effects on mean income. In fact, government policies that produce a higher mean income in migrant-sending areas may *increase* migration if relatively poor households do not share in the income gain. Conversely, policies may reduce migration if relatively rich households do not share in the income gain.

Segmented Labour Market Theory

Although neoclassical theory and the new economics of migration lead to divergent conclusions about the origins and nature of international migration, both are essentially micro-level decision models. What differ are the units assumed to make the decision (the individual or the household), the entity being maximized or minimized (income, capital, or risk), assumptions about the economic context of decision-making (complete and well-functioning markets versus missing or imperfect markets), and the extent to which the migration decision is socially contextualized (whether income is evaluated in absolute terms or relative to some reference group). Standing distinctly apart from these models of rational choice, however, is segmented labour market theory, which sets its sights away from decisions made by individuals and argues that international migration stems from the intrinsic labour demands of modern industrial societies.

Piore (1979) has been the most forceful and elegant proponent of this theoretical viewpoint, arguing that international migration is caused by a permanent demand for immigrant labour that is inherent to the economic structure of developed nations. According to Piore, immigration is not caused by push factors in sending countries (low wages or high unemployment), but by pull factors in receiving countries (a chronic and unavoidable need for foreign workers). This built-in demand for immigrant labour stems from four fundamental characteristics of advanced industrial societies and their economies.

Structural inflation   *especially*
└ Lead to outsourcing (?) b/c of Labour unions

Wages not only reflect conditions of supply and demand; they also confer status and prestige, social qualities that inhere to the jobs to which the wages are attached. In general, people believe that wages should reflect social status, and they have rather rigid notions about the correlation between occupational status and pay. As a result, wages offered by employers are not entirely free to respond to changes in the supply of workers. A variety of informal social expectations and formal institutional mechanisms (such as union contracts, civil service rules, bureaucratic regulations, company job classifications) ensure that wages correspond to the hierarchies of prestige and status that people perceive and expect.

If employers seek to attract workers for unskilled jobs at the bottom of an occupational hierarchy, they cannot simply raise wages. Raising wages at the bottom of the hierarchy would upset socially defined relationships between status and remuneration. If wages are increased at the bottom, there will be strong pressure to raise wages by corresponding amounts at other levels of the hierarchy. If the wages of waiter's assistants are raised in response to a shortage of entry-level workers, for example, they may overlap with those of waitresses, thereby threatening their status and undermining the accepted social hierarchy. Waitresses, in turn, demand a corresponding wage increase, which threatens the position of cooks, who also pressure employers for a raise. (Those unfamiliar with the status hierarchies typical in restaurants should read George Orwell's *Down and Out in London and Paris*.) Workers may be aided in their efforts by union representatives or contracts.

Thus, the cost to employers of raising wages to attract low-level workers is typically more than the cost of these workers' wages alone; wages must be increased proportionately throughout the job hierarchy in order to keep them in line with social expectations, a problem known as structural inflation. Attracting native workers by raising entry wages during times of labour scarcity is thus expensive and disruptive, providing employers with a strong incentive to seek easier and cheaper solutions, such as the importation of migrant workers who will accept low wages.

Hierarchical constraints on motivation

Occupational hierarchies are also critical for the motivation of workers, since people work not only for income, but also for the accumulation and maintenance of social status. Acute motivational problems arise at the bottom of the job hierarchy because there is no status to be maintained and there are few avenues for upward mobility. The problem is inescapable and structural because the bottom cannot be eliminated from the labour market. Mechanization to eliminate the lowest and least desirable class of jobs will simply create a new bottom tier composed of jobs that used to be just above the bottom rung. Since there always has to be a bottom of any hierarchy, motivational problems are inescapable. What employers need are workers who view bottom-level jobs simply as a means to the end of earning money, and for whom employment is reduced solely to income, with no implications for status or prestige.

For a variety of reasons, immigrants satisfy this need, at least at the beginning of their migratory careers. Most migrants begin as target earners, seeking to earn money for a specific goal that will improve their status or well-being at home—building a house, paying for school, buying land, acquiring consumer goods. Moreover, the disjuncture in living standards between developed and developing societies means that even low wages abroad appear to be generous by the standards of the home community; and even though a migrant may realize that a foreign job is of low status abroad, he does not view himself as being a part of the receiving society. Rather he sees himself as a member of his home community, within which foreign labour and hard-currency remittances carry considerable honour and prestige.

Economic dualism

Bifurcated labour markets come to characterize advanced industrial economies because of the inherent duality between labour and capital. Capital is a fixed factor of production that can be idled by lower demand but not laid off; owners of capital must bear the costs of its unemployment. Labour is a variable factor of production that can be released when demand falls, so that workers are forced to bear the costs of their own unemployment. Whenever possible, therefore, capitalists seek out the stable, permanent portion of demand and reserve it for the employment of equipment, whereas the variable portion of demand is met by adding labour. Thus, capital-intensive methods are used to meet basic demand, and labour-intensive methods are reserved for the seasonal, fluctuating component. This dualism creates distinctions among workers, leading to a bifurcation of the labour force.

Workers in the capital-intensive primary sector get stable, skilled jobs working with the best equipment and tools. Employers are forced to invest in these workers by providing specialized training and education. Their jobs are complicated and require considerable knowledge and experience to perform well, leading to the accumulation of firm-specific human capital. Primary-sector workers tend to be unionized or highly professionalized, with contracts that require employers to bear a substantial share of the costs of their idling (in the form of severance pay and unemployment benefits). Because of these costs and continuing obligations, workers in the primary sector become expensive to let go; they become more like capital.

In the labour-intensive secondary sector, however, workers hold unstable, unskilled jobs; they may be laid off at any time with little or no cost to the employer. Indeed, the employer will generally lose money by retaining workers during slack periods. During down cycles the first thing secondary-sector employers do is cut their payroll. As a result, employers force workers in this sector to bear the costs of their unemployment. They remain a variable factor of production and are, hence, expendable.

Thus, the inherent dualism between labour and capital extends to the labour force in the form of a segmented labour market structure. Low wages, unstable conditions, and the lack of reasonable prospects for mobility in the secondary sector make it difficult to attract native workers, who are instead drawn into the primary, capital-intensive sector, where wages are higher, jobs are more secure, and there is a possibility of occupational improvement. To fill the shortfall in demand within the secondary sector, employers turn to immigrants.

Ethnic enclaves Blends Low status (2nd Sec.) jobs w/primary sec. job possibilities

In their analysis of the process by which Cuban immigrants were incorporated into the USA, Portes and Bach (1985) uncovered evidence of a third employment sector that blends features of primary and secondary labour markets. Like the secondary sector, ethnic enclaves contain low-status jobs characterized by low pay, chronic instability, and unpleasant working conditions, jobs that are routinely shunned by natives. Unlike the secondary sector, however, the enclave provides immigrants with significant economic returns to education and experience, as well as the very real prospect of upward socio-economic mobility, thus replicating features of the primary sector.

Not all immigrations produce ethnic enclaves, however, and studies suggest they are rather hard to create (Logan *et al.* 1994). Indeed, the ethnic enclaves identified to this point have formed under rather unusual circumstances of geographic concentration and distinctively timed, class-selective immigration (Wilson and Martin 1982; Portes and Stepick 1993). In general, an enclave economy emerges when an initial wave of élite immigrants possessing significant amounts of financial, human, social, and/or cultural capital concentrates disproportionately in one urban area and, after becoming established there and founding new business enterprises, employs successive waves of lower-status but aspiring immigrants from the same country.

The existence of a large, concentrated population of co-ethnics creates a demand for specialized cultural products and ethnic services that immigrant entrepreneurs are uniquely qualified to fill. In addition, their privileged access to a growing pool of low-wage immigrant labour gives them an advantage when competing with firms outside the enclave. Immigrants working in the enclave trade low wages and the acceptance of strict discipline upon arrival for a greater chance of advancement and independence later on (Portes and Bach 1985). The implicit contract between employers and workers stems from a norm of ethnic solidarity (a form of cultural capital), which suffuses and supports the enclave (Portes and Manning 1986; Portes and Rumbaut 1990). At the same time, social networks and personal linkages to other entrepreneurs (a form of social capital) launch new immigrants on independent careers in small business, and once established, these new entrepreneurs are expected to help and promote other immigrants in return (cultural capital again). The prospects for enclave formation are especially enhanced if the initial immigrants are well educated and possess organizational or business skills (human capital), or if they have access to savings, credit, or government assistance (financial capital).

Although it may begin with the immigration of entrepreneurs, in order to function effectively over time, an ethnic enclave requires a steady stream of new workers willing to trade low initial wages for the possibility of later mobility, yielding an independent structural source of labour demand for immigrant workers, complementing that emanating from the secondary sector. As immigrant entrepreneurs arrive, concentrate geographically, and establish new business enterprises that rely upon immigrant labour for their survival, immigration can, quite literally, generate its own demand.

Demography of labour supply

The problems of motivation and structural inflation inherent to modern occupational hierarchies, together with the dualism intrinsic to market economies, create a permanent demand for workers who are willing to labour under unpleasant conditions, at low wages, with great instability, and facing little chance for advancement. In the past, this demand was met partially by three sets of people with social statuses and characteristics conducive to these sorts of jobs: women, teenagers, and rural-to-urban migrants.

Historically, women have tended to participate in the labour force up to the time of their first birth, and to a lesser extent after children have grown. They sought to earn supplemental income for themselves or their families. They were not primary breadwinners and their principal social identity was that of a sister, wife, or mother. They were willing to put up with the low wages and instability because they viewed the work as transient and the earnings as supplemental; the positions they held were not threatening to their main social statuses, which were grounded in the family.

Likewise, teenagers historically have moved into and out of the labour force with great frequency in order to earn extra money, to gain experience, and to try out different occupational roles. They do not view dead-end jobs as problematic because they expect to get better jobs in the future, after completing school, gaining experience, or settling down. Moreover, teenagers derive their social identities from their parents and families of orientation, not their jobs. They view work instrumentally as a means of earning spending money. The money and the things that it buys enhance their status among their peers (by giving them clothes, cars, music, etc.); the job is just a means to an end.

Finally, rural areas of developed nations for many years provided industrial cities with a steady supply of low-wage workers. Movement from a social and economic backwater to the dynamism and excitement of the city created a sense of upward mobility and personal improvement regardless of the modesty of the circumstances at the place of destination; even menial unskilled jobs in cities provided access to housing, food, and consumer goods that represented a real step up in the world for impoverished migrants from the countryside. As long as large reserves of rural population existed, new industrial nations could look internally to satisfy the emerging demand for unskilled, low-wage labour.

In advanced industrial societies, however, these sources of entry-level workers have shrunk over time because of four fundamental sociodemographic trends: the rise in female labour force participation, which has transformed women's work into a career pursued for social status as well as income; the rise in divorce rates, which has transformed women's jobs into a source of primary income support; the decline in birth rates and the extension of formal education, which have produced very small cohorts of teenagers entering the labour force; and the urbanization of society, which has eliminated farms and rural communities as potential sources for new migrants to the city. The imbalance between the structural demand for entry-level workers and the limited domestic supply of such workers has generated an underlying, long-run demand for immigrants in developed countries.

Segmented labour market theory neither posits nor denies that actors make rational, self-interested decisions, as predicted by microeconomic models. The negative qualities that people in industrialized countries attach to low-wage jobs, for example, may open up employment opportunities to foreign workers, thereby raising their expected earnings, increasing their ability to overcome risk and credit constraints, and enabling households to achieve relative income gains by sending family members abroad. Recruitment by employers helps to overcome informational and other constraints on international movement, enhancing migration's value as a strategy for family income generation or risk diversification.

Although not in inherent conflict with neoclassical economics, segmented labour market theory does carry implications and corollaries that are quite different from those emanating from micro-level decision models:

1. International labour migration is largely demand-based and is usually initiated through recruitment by employers in developed societies, or by governments acting on their behalf.
2. Since the demand for immigrant workers grows out of the structural needs of the economy and is expressed through recruitment practices rather than wage offers, international wage differentials are neither a necessary nor a sufficient condition for labour migration to occur. Indeed, employers have incentives to recruit workers while holding wages constant.
3. Low-level wages in immigrant-receiving societies do not rise in response to a decrease in the supply of immigrant workers; they are held down by social and institutional mechanisms and are not free to respond to shifts in supply and demand.
4. Low-level wages may fall, however, as a result of an increase in the supply of immigrant workers, since the social and institutional checks that keep low-level wages from rising do not prevent them from falling.
5. Under certain circumstances of geographic concentration and timed,

class-selective migration, ethnic enclaves form as a third sector of the labour market to generate an independent structural demand for foreign workers that complements that emanating from the secondary sector.

6. Governments are unlikely to influence international migration through policies that produce small changes in wages or employment rates; immigrants fill a demand for labour that is structurally built into modern, post-industrial economies, and influencing this demand requires major changes in economic organization.

Historical-Structural Theory and World Systems

The historical-structural approach to social theory emerged during the 1950s in response to functionalist theories of social change and development, which held that countries developed economically by progressing through an orderly series of evolutionary stages culminating in modernization and industrialization. In contrast, historical-structural theorists argued that because political power is unequally distributed across nations, the expansion of global capitalism acted to perpetuate inequalities and reinforce a stratified economic order. Rather than experiencing an inexorable progression towards development and modernization, poor countries in reality were trapped by their disadvantaged position within an unequal geopolitical structure, which perpetuated their poverty.

Historical-structural theory reached its peak of influence during the 1960s and 1970s and it gained particular currency among social scientists in Latin America. Theorists such as Furtado (1965, 1970) and Cardoso and Faletto (1969, 1979), observing a deterioration in the terms of trade between wealthy capitalist countries and poor nations in the years after the Second World War, concluded that developing nations were being forced into dependency by structural conditions dictated to them by powerful capitalist countries. According to Andre Gundre Frank (1969) global capitalism acted to 'develop underdevelopment' within the Third World.

This line of historical-structural thinking became known as dependency theory and ultimately embraced a diverse group of scholars who drew inspiration from the work of Baran (1957, 1973) and his conceptualization of the ideas of Marx and Lenin. Although they may have agreed on fundamental concepts, however, dependency theorists argued frequently about the details, and particularly about the political means by which barriers to economic development might be overcome. Whereas Frank (1969) held that capitalism was not a viable strategy for economic development under any circumstances, Amin (1974, 1976) argued that peripheral countries could achieve self-sustaining and autonomous economic growth if they could only disconnect themselves from the global market economy.

A second line of historical-structural theory emerged somewhat later and drew on the work of the dependency theorists, as well as the historiography of the French social historian Fernand Braudel (1981, 1982). Its leading exponent was Emmanuel Wallerstein (1974, 1980), who undertook a comprehensive analysis of the global expansion of the capitalist system from the sixteenth century onwards. He sought to reconstruct the historical processes by which unequal political/economic structures were created and extended throughout the world, and the mechanisms by which non-capitalist or pre-capitalist regions were incorporated into the global market economy. He classified countries according to the degree of their dependency on the dominant capitalist powers, which he termed 'core' nations. 'Peripheral' nations were the most dependent, whereas 'semi-peripheral' countries were somewhat wealthier and had slightly more independence in the global market place. Nations in the 'external arena' remained isolated and largely outside the global capitalist system. Given the scope of this work and its sweeping vision of an expanding global capitalism, this line of thought eventually became known as 'world systems theory' (Simmons 1989).

At first, neither world systems theory nor dependency theory had much interest in international migration. During the 1960s and 1970s, historical-structural theorists tended to focus on the consequences of rural population growth, the displacement of agrarian workers by the penetration of market forces, the spatial concentration of population in cities, the rapid growth of large urban agglomerations, and the rise of an informal urban economy. Given these concerns, researchers working in the historical-structural tradition tended to be interested in internal migration, and particularly in rural-to-urban migration.

In contrast to economic theorists such as Todaro (1969, 1976) and sociological theorists such as Lee (1966), who viewed migration as a rational calculation made by individuals to secure their material improvement, historical-structural theorists linked migration to the macro-organization of socio-economic relations, the geographic division of labour, and the political mechanisms of power and domination. Singer (1971, 1975) and other investigators who applied historical-structural principles to the study of internal migration (see Muñoz *et al.* 1977; Raczynski 1983; Stern 1988) sought to link rural-to-urban movements to specific historical contexts and particular transformations in the economic structure of rural and urban areas.

Throughout the 1970s, the subject of international migration rarely engaged the interest of theorists working in the historical-structural tradition. Even as the volume of emigration from the developing world grew during the 1960s and 1970s, investigators were slow to appreciate the significance of the phenomenon. It was only after the economic recessions of the mid-1970s that observers began to understand that international flows were not just a 'temporary' aberration, and that international migration also might be linked to structural changes that accompanied a nation's insertion into the global market place.

One exception to the general lack of interest in international migration shown by historical-structural theorists was their fascination with the 'brain drain' (see Khoshkish 1966; Kannappan 1968; Adams 1969; Watanabe 1969; Glaser 1978). The brain drain referred to the selective migration of talented and educated people from poor to wealthy nations, which emerged as a key point of contention between the First and the Third Worlds in the years following decolonization. Although relatively small in quantitative terms, dependency theorists argued that the emigration of skilled and educated workers decisively undermined the prospects for development in poor countries by depriving them of essential human capital. They saw it as yet another manifestation of the unequal terms of trade between developed and developing countries and one more means by which global capitalism 'developed underdevelopment'. By attracting, and at times even recruiting, the most productive workers from developing countries, core nations siphoned off a critical resource for future economic growth. Worse than that, because developing nations covered the costs of feeding, clothing, educating, and maintaining the emigrants until they reached productive age, the brain drain actually constituted a *subsidy* of wealthy nations by the poor.

The fascination of historical-structural theorists with the brain drain reflected less of an interest in labour migration than in capital flight. Although the capital was attached to people in this case, it was capital nonetheless, and for the most part historical-structural theorists were not very interested in the international movement of labour. This situation changed dramatically in the late 1970s when widespread economic stagnation throughout the industrialized world made explicit the fact that the various migratory 'guests' were not going home and that virtually all developed nations now faced the prospect of integrating ethnically diverse populations of permanent immigrants.

As the absorption of foreigners emerged as a potent political issue throughout the developed world, scholars there finally began to apply the precepts of historical-structural theory to analyse the salient flows of labour they were suddenly observing with new eyes. Like their intellectual forebearers, theorists such as Portes and Walton (1981), Petras (1981), Sassen (1988), and Morawska (1990) sought to explain international migration not as a product of individual or household decisions, but as a structural consequence of the expansion of markets within a global political hierarchy. Although their propositions up to now have not formed a coherent theory so much as a general approach to the study of international migration, here we attempt to synthesize historical-structural explanations under the general rubric of 'world systems theory'.

In essence, world systems theory argues that the penetration of capitalist economic relations into non-capitalist or pre-capitalist societies creates a mobile population that is prone to migrate. Driven by a desire for higher profits and greater wealth, owners and managers of capitalist firms in core countries enter poorer nations on the periphery of the world economy in search of land, raw materials, labour, and consumer markets. In the past, this market penetration was assisted by colonial regimes that administered poor regions for the benefit of economic interests in colonizing societies. Today it is made possible by neocolonial governments and multinational firms that perpetuate the power of national élites who either participate in the world economy as capitalists themselves, or offer their nation's resources to global firms on acceptable terms.

International migration thus emerges as a natural outgrowth of disruptions and dislocations that inevitably occur in the process of capitalist development. As capitalism has expanded outwards from its core in Western Europe, North America, Oceania, and Japan, ever-larger portions of the globe and growing shares of the human population have been incorporated into the global market economy. As land, raw materials, and labour within peripheral regions come under the influence and control of global markets rather than local communities or national bureaucracies, migration flows are inevitably generated, some of which have always moved abroad (Massey 1988).

Land

In order to achieve the greatest profit from existing agrarian resources and to compete within global commodity markets, capitalist farmers in peripheral areas seek to consolidate landholdings, mechanize production, introduce cash crops, and apply industrially produced inputs such as fertilizer, insecticides, and high-yield seeds. Land consolidation destroys traditional systems of land tenure based on inheritance and common rights of usufruct. Mechanization decreases the need for manual labour and makes many agrarian workers redundant to production. The substitution of cash crops for staples undermines traditional social and economic relations based on subsistence (Chayanov 1966); and the use of modern inputs produces high crop yields at low unit prices, which drives small, non-capitalist farmers out of local markets. All of these forces contribute to the creation of a mobile labour force displaced from the land with a weakened attachment to local agrarian communities.

Raw materials

The extraction of raw materials for sale on global markets requires industrial methods that rely on paid labour. The offer of wages to former peasants undermines traditional forms of social and economic organization based on norms of reciprocity and fixed role relations and creates incipient labour markets based on new conceptions of individualism, private gain, and social change. These trends likewise promote the geographic mobility of labour in developing regions, often with international spillovers.

Labour

Firms from core capitalist countries enter developing countries to establish assembly plants that take advantage of low wage rates, often within special export-processing zones created by sympathetic governments. The demand for factory workers strengthens local labour markets and weakens traditional productive relations. Much of the labour demanded is female, however, and the resulting feminization of the workforce limits opportunities for men; but since the new factory work is demanding and poorly paid, women tend only to work a few years, after which time they leave to look for new opportunities. The insertion of foreign-owned factories into peripheral regions thus undermines the local economy by producing goods that compete with those made locally; by feminizing the workforce without providing factory-based employment opportunities for men; and by socializing women for industrial work and modern consumption, albeit without providing a lifetime income capable of meeting these needs. The result is the creation of a population that is socially and economically uprooted and prone to migrate.

The same capitalist economic processes that create migrants in peripheral regions simultaneously attract them into developed countries. Although some people displaced by the process of market penetration move to cities, leading to the urbanization of developing societies, inevitably many are drawn abroad because globalization creates material and ideological links to the places where capital originates. The foreign investment that drives economic globalization is managed from a small number of global cities, whose structural characteristics create a strong demand for immigrant labour.

Material links

In order to ship goods, deliver machinery, extract and export raw materials, coordinate business operations, and manage expatriate assembly plants, capitalists in core nations build and expand transportation and communication links to the peripheral countries where they have invested. These links not only facilitate the movement of goods, products, information, and capital, they also promote the movement of people by reducing the costs of movement along certain international pathways. Because investment and globalization are inevitably accompanied by the build-up of a transportation and communication infrastructure, the international movement of labour generally follows the international movement of goods and capital in the opposite direction.

Military links

The creation and perpetuation of a global trading regime requires an underlying system of international security. Core capitalist nations have both an economic interest in and the military means of preserving geopolitical order, and most of the leading powers maintain relatively large armed forces to deploy as needed to preserve the integrity of the global capitalist system. Threats to the stability of that system are often met by military force projected from one or more of the core nations. After 1945, for example, the threat of communist expansion in Europe presented such a threat to a weakened capitalism that Britain, France, and the USA stationed large numbers of troops permanently in bases throughout the Continent. They also periodically dispatched military forces to various hot spots that cropped up in Africa, the Middle East, Asia, and Latin America in the course of a forty-year Cold War with the Soviet Union.

As the leading economic and political power in the post-war capitalist world, of course, the USA has played the most important role in preserving international peace and security in the post-war world, maintaining a uniquely large military establishment and frequently dispatching its armed forces to counter leftist insurgencies, turn back communist invasions, or quell outbreaks of violence that threaten the capitalist order. In the years since 1945, the USA has intervened covertly or overtly in at least a dozen countries: Iran, Guatemala, Nicaragua, Cuba, the Dominican Republic, Haiti, Grenada, Chile, Somalia, and, of course, Vietnam, Cambodia, and Korea. Most recently, it led a multinational force to restore order (and the flow of oil) in Kuwait. In order to retain its capacity to project military power whenever and wherever it is needed, the USA maintains numerous large military bases in far-flung areas throughout the world.

Each military base and armed intervention, however, creates a range of social and political connections that promote the subsequent movement of immigrants. Soldiers often acquire local spouses who seek to accompany them home when their tour of duty ends, and in the USA (and many other countries), spouses have a privileged claim on entry by virtue of their marriage to a citizen. Spouses, in turn, may seek to sponsor the immigration of their brothers, sisters, mothers, fathers, and minor children. These people have their own claims on entry by virtue of their kinship with a legal resident, and if the spouse ultimately naturalizes, by virtue of their kinship with a citizen.

Large-scale military operations also involve the hiring of numerous support personnel from the local civilian population, creating personal relationships, political debts, and moral obligations that may be invoked to gain access to immigrant visas when the military departs, or to obtain refugee status in the event the client State collapses. If the military presence is long term, moreover, a host of commercial and service establishments inevitably grow up around the base, further expanding the range of personal interactions and social debts, and transmitting new linguistic codes and cultural conventions into the local population. Intensive contact with US troops not only increases the odds of matrimony, it also inculcates a knowledge of English and US culture that raises the potential rewards of working in the USA and increases the motivation to do so. For these reasons, therefore, significant military deployments are typically accompanied by sizeable return flows of immigrants (Jasso and Rosenzweig 1990; Donato 1991; Schmeidl 1997).

Ideological links

The process of economic globalization creates cultural links between core capitalist countries and their peripheries through other means besides military intervention. In many cases, these cultural links are longstanding, reflecting a colonial past in which core countries established administrative and educational systems that mirrored their own in order to govern and exploit a peripheral region. Citizens of Senegal, for example, learn French, study at lycées, and use a currency directly tied to the French franc in economic transactions. Likewise, Indians and Pakistanis learn English, take British-style degrees, and join with others in a transnational union known as the British Commonwealth. Even in the absence of a colonial past, the influence of economic penetration can be profound: Mexicans increasingly study at US universities, speak English, and follow American consumer styles closely.

These ideological and cultural connections are reinforced by mass communications and advertising campaigns directed from the core countries. Television programming from the USA, France, Britain, and Germany transmits information about lifestyles and living standards in the developed world, and commercials prepared by foreign advertising agencies inculcate modern consumer tastes within peripheral peoples. The diffusion of core country languages and cultural patterns and the spread of modern consumption patterns interact with the emergence of a transportation/communication infrastructure to channel international migration to particular core countries.

Global cities

The world economy is managed from a relatively small number of urban centres in which banking, finance, administration, professional services, and high-tech production tend to be concentrated (Castells 1989; Sassen 1991). In the USA, global cities include New York, Chicago, Los Angeles, and Miami; in Europe, they include London, Paris, Frankfurt, and Milan; and in the Pacific, Tokyo, Osaka, and Sydney qualify. Within these global cities, a great deal of wealth and a highly educated workforce are concentrated, creating a strong demand for the services of unskilled workers (gardeners, waiters, waiter's assistants, hotel workers, domestic servants). At the same time, the shifting of heavy industrial production overseas; the growth of high-tech manufacturing in electronics, computers, and telecommunications; and the expansion of service sectors such as health and education create a bifurcated labour market structure with strong demand for workers at both the upper and lower ends, but with relatively weak demand in the middle.

Poorly educated natives resist taking low-paying jobs at the bottom of the occupational hierarchy, creating a strong demand for immigrants. Meanwhile, well-educated natives and skilled foreigners dominate the lucrative jobs at the upper tier of the occupational distribution, and the concentration of wealth among them helps to fuel the demand for the type of services immigrants are most willing to meet. Native workers with modest educations cling to jobs in the declining middle, migrate out of global cities, or rely on social insurance programmes for support.

World systems theory thus argues that international migration follows the political and economic organization of an expanding global market, a view that yields six distinct hypotheses:

1. International migration is a natural consequence of capitalist market formation in the developing world; the penetration of the global economy into peripheral regions is the catalyst for international movement.
2. The international flow of labour follows international flows of goods and capital, but in the opposite direction. Capitalist investment foments changes that create an uprooted, mobile population in peripheral countries while simultaneously forging strong material and cultural links with core countries, leading to transnational movement.
3. International migration is especially likely between past colonial powers and their former colonies, because cultural, linguistic, administrative, investment, transportation, and communication links were established early and were allowed to develop free from outside competition during the colonial era, leading to the formation of specific transnational markets and cultural systems.
4. Since international migration stems from the globalization of the market economy, the way for governments to influence immigration rates is by regulating the overseas investment activities of corporations and controlling international flows of capital and goods. Such policies, however, are unlikely to be implemented because they are difficult to enforce, tend to incite international trade disputes, risk world economic recession, and antagonize multinational firms with substantial political resources that can be mobilized to block them.
5. Political and military interventions by governments of capitalist countries to protect investments abroad and to support foreign governments sympathetic to the expansion of the global market, when they fail, produce refugee movements directed to particular core countries, constituting another form of international migration.
6. International migration ultimately has little to do with wage rates or employment differentials between countries; it follows from the dynamics of market creation and the political structure of the global economy.

The Perpetuation of International Movement

Immigration may begin for a variety of reasons—a desire for individual income gain, an attempt to diversify risks to household income, a programme of recruitment to satisfy employer demands for low-wage workers, an international displacement of peasants by market penetration within peripheral regions, or some combination thereof. But the conditions that initiate international movement may be quite different from those that perpetuate it across time and space. Although wage differentials, relative risks, recruitment efforts, and market penetration may continue to cause people to move, new conditions that arise in the course of migration come to function as independent causes themselves: migrant networks spread, institutions supporting transnational movement develop, and the social meaning of work changes in receiving societies. The general thrust of these transformations is to make additional movement more likely, leading to the perpetuation of international migration across time and space.

Social Capital Theory

The economist Glenn Loury (1977) introduced the concept of social capital to designate a set of intangible resources in families and communities that help to promote social development among young people, but Bourdieu (1986) pointed out its broader relevance to human society. According to Bourdieu and Wacquant (1992: 119), 'social capital is the sum of the resources, actual or virtual, that accrue to an individual or a group by virtue of possessing a durable network of more or less institutionalized relationships of mutual acquaintance and recognition.'

The key characteristic of social capital is its convertibility—it may be translated into other forms of capital, notably financial capital, in this case foreign wages and the remittances they permit (Harker *et al.* 1990). People gain access to social capital through membership in networks and social institutions and then convert it into other forms of capital to improve or maintain their position in society (Bourdieu 1986; Coleman 1990). Although Portes and Sensenbrenner (1993) point out that social capital may have negative as well as positive consequences for the individual, theorists generally have emphasized the positive role it plays in the acquisition and accumulation of other forms of capital (see Coleman 1990, 1988), an emphasis that has been particularly strong in work on migrant networks.

Migrant networks

Migrant networks are sets of interpersonal ties that connect migrants, former migrants, and non-migrants in origin and destination areas through ties of kinship, friendship, and shared community origin. They increase the likelihood of international movement because they lower the costs and risks of movement and increase the expected net returns to migration. Network connections constitute a form of social capital that people can draw upon to gain access to various kinds of financial capital: foreign employment, high wages, and the possibility of accumulating savings and sending remittances.

Beginning in the 1920s, sociologists recognized the importance of networks in promoting international movement (see Thomas and Znaniecki 1918–20; Gamio 1930). Drawing on social ties to relatives and friends who have migrated before, non-migrants gained access to knowledge, assistance, and other resources that facilitated movement (Cholden 1973). Tilly and Brown (1967) referred to these ties as the 'auspices' of migration; others have labelled them 'migration chains' (MacDonald and MacDonald 1974); and Levy and Wadycki (1973) have called them a 'family and friends effect'. Taylor (1986, 1987) characterizes them as a form of economic 'migration capital'. Massey *et al.* (1987: 170) appear to have been the first to identify migrant networks specifically as a form of social capital.

Following Coleman's (1990: 304) dictum that 'social capital . . . is created when the relations among persons change in ways that facilitate action,' Massey and his associates identified migration itself as the catalyst for this change in the nature of social relations. Everyday ties of friendship and kinship provide few advantages, in and of themselves, to people seeking to migrate abroad. Once someone in a personal network has migrated, however, the ties are transformed into a resource that can be used to gain access to foreign employment and all that it brings. Each act of migration creates social capital among people to whom the new migrant is related, thereby raising the odds of their migration (Massey *et al.* 1987, 1994).

The first migrants who leave for a new destination have no social ties to draw upon, and for them migration is costly, particularly if it involves entering another country without documents. After the first migrants have left, however, the potential costs of migration are substantially lowered for friends and relatives left behind. Because of the nature of kinship and friendship structures, each new migrant creates a set of people with social ties to the destination area. Migrants are inevitably linked to non-migrants, and the latter draw upon obligations implicit in relationships such as kinship and friendship to gain access to employment and assistance at the point of destination.

Networks make international migration extremely attractive as a strategy for risk diversification or utility maximization. When migrant networks are well developed, they put a destination job within easy reach of most community members and make emigration a reliable and secure source of income. Thus, the growth of networks that occurs through the progressive reduction of costs may also be explained theoretically by the progressive reduction of risks. Every new migrant expands the network and reduces the risks of movement for all those to whom he or she is related, eventually making it virtually risk-free and costless to diversify household labour allocations through emigration.

Migrant-supporting institutions

Once international migration has begun, private institutions and voluntary organizations also tend to arise to satisfy the demand created by a growing imbalance between the large number of people who seek entry into capital-rich countries and the limited number of immigrant visas these countries typically offer. This imbalance, and the barriers that core countries erect to keep people out, create a lucrative economic niche for entrepreneurs and institutions dedicated to promoting international movement for profit, yielding a black market in migration. As this underground market creates conditions conducive to exploitation and victimization, voluntary humanitarian organizations also arise in developed countries to enforce the rights and improve the treatment of legal and undocumented migrants (Hagan and Gonzalez Baker 1993).

Goss and Lindquist (1995) point to migrant institutions as a structural complement to migrant networks, arguing that interpersonal ties are not the only means by which international movement is perpetuated. Building on ideas put forth by Giddens (1990), they argue that:

international migration is best examined not as a result of individual motivations and structural determinations, although these must play a part in any explanation, but as the articulation of agents with particular interests and playing specific roles within an institutional environment, drawing knowledgeably upon sets of rules in order to increase access to resources. (Goss and Lindquist 1995: 345)

For-profit organizations and private entrepreneurs provide a range of services to migrants in exchange for fees set on the underground market: surreptitious smuggling across borders; clandestine transport to internal destinations; labour-contracting between employers and migrants; counterfeit documents and visas; arranged marriages between migrants and legal residents or citizens of the destination country; and lodging, credit, and other assistance in countries of destination (Prothero 1990). Humanitarian groups help migrants by providing counselling, social services, shelter, legal advice about how to obtain legitimate papers, and even insulation from immigration law enforcement authorities (Christiansen 1996). Over time, individuals, firms, and organizations become well known to immigrants and institutionally stable, constituting another form of social capital that migrants can draw upon to gain access to foreign labour markets. Recruiting agents can at times be active in creating new flows of migration from areas of labour surplus to areas of labour scarcity.

The recognition of a gradual build-up of institutions, organizations, and entrepreneurs dedicated to arranging immigrant entry, legal or illegal, yields hypotheses that are once again quite distinct from those emanating from micro-level decision models. The theory of social capital accepts the view of international migration as an individual or household, but argues that acts of

Handwritten annotations:
Social capital = Migrant Networks Theory
& For-profit/entre. S
then → Humanitarian groups

migration at one point in time systematically alter the context within which future migration decisions are made, greatly increasing the likelihood that later decision-makers will choose to migrate. The conceptualization of migration as a self-sustaining diffusion process has implications and corollaries that are quite different from those derived from the general equilibrium analyses typically employed to study migration:

1. Once begun, international migration tends to expand over time until network connections have diffused so widely in a sending region that all people who wish to migrate can do so without difficulty; then migration begins to decelerate.
2. The size of the migratory flow between two countries is not strongly correlated to wage differentials or employment rates, because whatever effects these variables have in promoting or inhibiting migration are progressively overshadowed by the falling costs and risks of movement stemming from the growth of migrant networks over time.
3. As international migration becomes institutionalized through the formation and elaboration of networks, it becomes progressively independent of the factors that originally caused it, be they structural or individual.
4. Governments can expect to have great difficulty controlling flows once they have begun, because the process of network formation lies largely outside their control and occurs no matter what policy regime is pursued.
5. Certain immigration policies, however, such as those intended to promote reunification between immigrants and their families abroad, work at cross-purposes with the control of immigration flows, since they reinforce migrant networks by giving members of kin networks special rights of entry.
6. As organizations develop to support, sustain, and promote international movement, the international flow of migrants becomes more and more institutionalized and independent of the factors that originally caused it.
7. Governments have difficulty controlling migration flows once they have begun because the process of institutionalization is difficult to regulate. Given the profits to be made by meeting the demand for immigrant entry, police efforts only serve to create a black market in international movement, and stricter immigration policies are met with resistance from humanitarian groups.

Cumulative Causation

The theory of cumulative causation argues that over time international migration tends to sustain itself in ways that make additional movement progressively more likely, a process first identified by Myrdal (1957) and later reintroduced to the field by Massey (1990b). Causation is cumulative in the sense that each act of migration alters the social context within which subsequent migration decisions are made, typically in ways that make additional movement more likely. So far, social scientists have discussed eight ways that migration is affected in this cumulative fashion: the expansion of networks, the distribution of income, the distribution of land, the organization of agriculture, culture, the regional distribution of human capital, the social meaning of work, and the structure of production. Feedbacks through other variables are also possible, but have not been systematically treated.

Expansion of networks

As just discussed, once the number of network connections in an origin area reaches a critical threshold, migration tends to become self-perpetuating because each act of migration creates the social structure needed to sustain it. Every new migrant reduces the costs and risks of subsequent migration for a set of friends and relatives, and some of these people are thereby induced to migrate, which further expands the set of people with ties abroad, which, in turn, reduces costs for a new set of people, causing some of them to migrate, and so on. Over time, migratory behaviour spreads outward to encompass broader segments of the sending society (Hugo 1981; Taylor 1986; Massey and García España 1987; Massey 1990a, 1990b; Gurak and Caces 1992; Massey *et al.* 1994).

Distribution of income

The new economics of migration argues that people may be motivated to migrate not only to increase their absolute income or to diversify their risks, but also to improve their income relative to other households in their reference group. As a household's sense of relative deprivation increases, so does the motivation to migrate. Before anyone has migrated from a community, income inequality within most poor, rural settings is not great because nearly all families live close to the subsistence level with minimal outside incomes. After one or two households have begun participating in foreign wage labour, however, remittances increase their incomes greatly. Given the costs and risks associated with international movement, moreover, the first households to migrate are usually located in the middle or upper ranges of the local income hierarchy (Massey *et al.* 1994).

Seeing some families vastly improve their income through migration makes families lower in the income distribution feel relatively deprived, inducing some of them to migrate, which further exacerbates income inequality and increases the sense of relative deprivation among non-migrants, inducing still more families to migrate, and so on. Income inequality and relative deprivation go through a series of phases, being low at first, then high as the rate of out-migration accelerates, then low again as a majority of households participate in the migrant workforce, reaching a minimum when practically all families are involved in foreign wage labour (Stark *et al.* 1986; Stark and Taylor 1989; Stark 1991; Taylor 1992).

Distribution of land

An important spending target for migrants from rural communities is the purchase of land. But land is often purchased by migrants abroad for its prestige value or as a source of retirement income rather than as a productive investment. International migrants are likely to use their higher earnings to purchase farmland, but they are more likely than non-migrants to let the land lie fallow since foreign wage labour is more lucrative than local agrarian production. This pattern of land use lowers the demand for local farm labour, thereby increasing the pressures for out-migration. The more out-migration, the more people have access to the funds necessary to buy land, leading to additional purchases by migrants and more land withdrawn from production, creating still more pressure for out-migration (Rhoades 1978; Reichert 1981; Mines 1984; Wiest 1984).

Organization of farm production

When migrant households do farm the land they own, moreover, they are more likely than non-migrant families to use capital-intensive methods (machinery, herbicides, irrigation, fertilizers, and improved seeds) since they have access to capital to finance these inputs. Thus migrant households need less labour per unit of output than non-migrant households, thereby displacing local workers from traditional tasks and again increasing the pressures for out-movement (Massey *et al.* 1987). The more migration, the greater the capitalization of agriculture and the greater the displacement of agrarian labour, leading to still greater migration.

Culture of migration

As migration grows in prevalence within a community, it changes values and cultural perceptions in ways that increase the probability of future migration. Among the migrants themselves, experience in an advanced industrial economy changes tastes and motivations (Piore 1979). Although migrants may begin as target earners seeking to make one trip and earn money for a narrow purpose, after migrating they acquire a concept of social mobility and a taste for consumer goods and styles of life that are difficult to attain through local labour. Once someone has migrated, therefore, he or she is very likely to migrate again, and the odds of taking an additional trip rise with the number of trips already taken (Massey 1986).

At the community level, migration becomes deeply ingrained into the repertoire of people's behaviour, and values associated with migration become part of the community's values. For young men, and in many settings young women as well, migration becomes a rite of passage, and those who do not attempt to elevate their status through international movement are considered lazy, unenterprising, and undesirable (Reichert 1982). Eventually, knowledge about foreign locations and jobs becomes widely diffused, and values, sentiments, and behaviour characteristic of the core society spread widely within the sending region (Brettell 1979; Massey *et al.* 1987; Rouse 1989, 1991; Alarcón 1992; Smith 1992; Goldring 1996*a*).

Distribution of human capital

Migration is a selective process that often tends, initially, at least, to draw relatively well-educated skilled, productive, and highly motivated people away from sending communities (although as pointed out earlier, migration tends to become less selective over time as the costs and risks fall because of network formation), although this selectivity depends critically on the characteristics of migrant labour markets (Taylor 1987). Sustained out-migration thus may lead to the depletion of human capital in sending regions and its accumulation in receiving areas, enhancing the productivity of the latter while lowering that of the former. Over time, therefore, the accumulation of human capital reinforces economic growth in receiving areas while its simultaneous depletion in sending areas exacerbates their stagnation, thereby further enhancing the conditions for migration (Myrdal 1957; Greenwood 1981, 1985; Greenwood *et al.* 1987). Programmes of school construction and educational expansion in sending areas reinforce this cumulative migration process because raising educational levels in peripheral rural areas increases the potential returns to migration and gives people a greater incentive to leave for urban destinations at home or abroad.

Social labelling

Within receiving societies, once immigrants have been recruited into particular occupations in significant numbers, those jobs become culturally labelled as 'immigrant jobs' and native workers are reluctant to fill them, reinforcing the structural demand for immigrants. Immigration changes the social definition of work, causing a certain class of jobs to be stigmatized and viewed as culturally inappropriate for native workers (Böhning 1972, 1984; Piore 1979). The stigma comes from the presence of immigrants, not from the characteristics of the job. In most European countries, for example, jobs in car manufacturing came to be considered 'immigrant jobs', whereas in the USA they are considered 'native jobs'.

Limits to cumulative causation

In any finite population, of course, processes of cumulative causation cannot continue *ad infinitum*. If migration continues long enough, networks eventually reach a point of numerical saturation within any particular community (Massey *et al.* 1994). More and more community members reside in branch

Migration as wide
Curve = n.t. n. dist. occurs
or "HUMP"

settlements overseas and virtually all those at home are connected to someone living abroad or having substantial foreign experience. When networks reach such a high level of elabouration, the costs of migration do not fall as sharply with each new migrant and the process of migration loses its dynamic momentum for growth. The prevalence of migration in the community approaches an upper asymptote and migratory experience becomes so diffused that the stock of potential new migrants gets very small and is increasingly composed of women, children, and the elderly.

If migration continues long enough, local labour shortages and rising wages in the home community may further dampen the pressures for emigration, causing the rate of entry into the international migrant workforce to trail off (Hatton and Williamson 1994a). Observed at the national level, this asymptotic trend may be difficult to detect because new communities are continuously incorporated into the migratory stream. As the rate of out-migration decelerates in places with longer histories of migration, new areas are drawn into transnational circuits and their rates of migration begin to accelerate. As a result, the total outflow from the nation as a whole may continue to grow as migration spreads from place to place.

Nevertheless, migratory experience eventually becomes widely diffused even across communities, and observers have identified the historical emergence of a characteristic 'migration curve' in national populations that have made the transition from emigration to immigration. According to Ackerman (1976), this curve follows an inverted U-shape that starts at low levels and rises to a peak before declining, yielding what Martin and Taylor (1996) have called a 'migration hump' that countries experience in the course of economic development. Hatton and Williamson (1994c: 9–10) note that 'the upswing of the emigration cycle usually coincide[s] with industrialization and rising real wages at home [as] demographic forces, industrialization, and the mounting stock of previous emigrants abroad all serve to drive up the emigration rate. . . . As these forces weakened [historically], the narrowing gap between home and foreign wages began to dominate and emigration receded,' yielding a U-shaped density function and an S-shaped cumulative density function, with the total stock of migratory experience approaching an upper asymptote over time.

Viewing international migration in dynamic terms as a cumulative social process yields a set of propositions broadly consistent with those derived from social capital theory:

1. Social, economic, and cultural changes brought about in sending and receiving countries by international migration give the movement of people a powerful internal momentum resistant to easy control or regulation, since the feedback mechanisms of cumulative causation largely lie outside the reach of government.

2. During times of domestic unemployment and joblessness, governments find

it difficult to curtail labour migration and to recruit natives back into jobs formerly held by immigrants. A value shift has occurred among native workers, who refuse the 'immigrant' jobs, making it necessary to retain or recruit more immigrants.

3. The social labelling of a job as 'immigrant' follows from the concentration of immigrants within it; once immigrants have entered a job in significant numbers, whatever its characteristics, it will be difficult to recruit native workers back into that occupational category.

4. As networks expand and the costs and risks of migration fall, the flow becomes less selective in socio-economic terms and more representative of the sending community or society.

5. Over the long term, countries experiencing mass emigration undergo a migratory transition in which the rate of emigration follows an inverted U-shape, starting low, rising to a peak, and then falling off. Cumulative migratory experience in the population follows an S-shaped curve, starting slowly and rising rapidly before reaching an upper asymptote.

Evaluation of Theories

Because theories proposed to explain the origins and persistence of international migration posit causal mechanisms at many levels of aggregation, the various explanations are not necessarily contradictory unless one adopts the rigid position that causes must operate at one level and one level only. We find no a priori grounds for such an assertion. As stated earlier, it is entirely possible that individuals engage in cost-benefit calculations; that households act to minimize risk and overcome barriers to capital and credit; and that the socio-economic context within which these decisions are made is determined by structural forces operating at the national and international levels (Papademetriou and Martin 1991). Thus, we are sceptical both of atomistic theories that deny the importance of structural constraints on individual decisions, and of structural theories that deny agency to individuals and families.

Rather than adopting the narrow argument of theoretical exclusivity, we adopt the broader position that causal processes relevant to international migration might operate on multiple levels simultaneously, and that sorting out which of the explanations are useful is an empirical and not only a logical task. Each model must be considered on its own terms and its leading tenets examined carefully to derive testable propositions. Only then can we clearly specify the data and methods required to evaluate them empirically.

The neoclassical economic model yields a clear empirical prediction that, in principle, should be readily verifiable: that the volume of international migration is directly and significantly related, over time and across countries, to the

neoclassical = employment possibilities
= higher wages
Migration ends as = equil. is reached

Theories of International Migration   51

size of the international gap in wage rates. Regression analyses based on this model should therefore contain transnational wage differentials as the leading predictor, controlling, of course, for the costs of movement.

Later refinements of the neoclassical model, however, suggest that the pertinent factor in migration decision-making is the *expected* earnings gap, not the absolute real-wage differential (Todaro 1969, 1976; Todaro and Maruszko 1987). At any point in time, expected earnings are defined as real earnings in the country under consideration multiplied by the probability of employment there. Although typically estimated as one minus the unemployment rate, the likelihood of employment is probably more appropriately measured as one minus the underemployment rate (Clogg and Schockey 1984), given the pervasiveness of sporadic, part-time employment in low-skill jobs within developing regions. The key predictor of international migratory flows is thus an interaction term that cross-multiplies wages and employment probabilities. A statistical test for the significance of this interaction term, compared to a regression model where real wages and/or unemployment rates appear alone or as separate direct effects, constitutes a critical test comparison between the Ranis-Fei and the Todaro versions of neoclassical theory (see Todaro (1980) and Greenwood (1985) for reviews of the substantial empirical research literature testing the Todaro model).

A logical corollary of both models, however, is that international movement should not occur in the absence of an international gap in either observed or expected wages, and that movement between countries should cease when wage differentials have been erased (net of the costs of movement, both monetary and psychological). International flows that occur in the absence of a wage gap, or that end before a gap has been eliminated, represent anomalous conditions that constitute prima-facie evidence challenging the assumptions of neoclassical economic theory.

At the individual level, the Todaro model and its successors predict that individual and household characteristics that are positively related to the rate of remuneration or the probability of employment in destination areas will increase the probability of migration by raising the expected returns to international movement. Hence, the likelihood of emigration is predicted to be reliably related to such standard human capital variables as age, experience, schooling, marital status, and skill. The propensity for international migration is also expected to vary with a household's access to income-generating resources at home (such as owning land or supporting a business enterprise), since these will affect the *net* return to movement.

Since human capital variables that affect rates of employment and remuneration in destination areas also tend to affect wage and employment rates in places of origin, a key empirical issue is whether the rewards to human capital are greater at home or abroad. Given the fact that international migration involves a change of language, culture, and economic system, human capital acquired at home generally transfers abroad imperfectly (see Chiswick 1979). In this case, international migrants may be *negatively* selected with respect to variables such as education and job experience.

Among rural Mexicans, for example, the economic returns to schooling historically have been greater in urban areas of Mexico than in the USA. Whereas an undocumented migrant with a secondary education gets the same minimum-wage job in Los Angeles as one with no schooling at all, that education would qualify the same person for a clerical or white-collar job in Mexico City, thereby raising the likelihood of rural–urban migration and lowering the probability of international movement (Taylor 1987).

This pattern of negative selectivity cannot be hypothesized universally, however, since selection on human capital variables depends on the transferability of the skill or ability under consideration, which itself is determined by social, economic, and historical conditions specific to the countries involved, as well as on the relative rates of remuneration in sending and receiving areas. In general, any social change that influences the market value of human capital in either society has the potential of shifting the size and direction of the relationship between independent variables and the likelihood of international movement.

Thus it is nearly impossible, a priori, to predict the direction of the relationship between a specific individual background variable and the probability of migration, and it is consequently difficult to derive a convincing test of neoclassical economic theory at the micro-level in a reduced-form regression—that is, one in which the probability of migration is modelled directly as a function of individual and household variables. In general, the only universal prediction that can be offered is that human capital should somehow be reliably related to the likelihood of international movement, but the strength and direction of the relationship is impossible to know in the absence of historical information about the countries involved. Only after the historical circumstances have been clearly specified and their influence on the returns to specific forms of human capital clarified, can a critical test of the neoclassical microeconomic model be formulated.

A more formal alternative is to model the probability of migration structurally as a function of the expected income differential, and simultaneously model the expected-income differential as a function of individual and household variables. In this way, the effects of individual background variables on migration through their influence on the expected-earnings differential can be tested explicitly. In addition, the possible effects of these variables on migration independent of their influence on expected earnings can be rejected (Taylor 1986). In the absence of structural tests, it is difficult to falsify the human capital model by examining individual regressions. The only evidence that could conceivably cast serious doubt on the validity of the human capital theory of migration would be the complete absence of a relationship between human capital and migration.

In contrast to neoclassical economic theory, the new economics of migration focuses on the household or family, rather than the individual, as the relevant decision-making unit; and it posits that migration is a response to income risk and to failures in a variety of markets (insurance, capital, and credit), which together constrain local income opportunities and inhibit risk-spreading. The most direct test of this theory would be to relate the presence or absence of such market imperfections to households' propensities to participate in international migration. If the new economics of migration is correct, households confronted by the greatest local market imperfections should be most likely to adopt an international migration strategy, other things being equal.

Unfortunately, other things generally are not equal. Typically there is a high correlation between market imperfections and other variables (namely low wages and incomes) that are the focus of the neoclassical (human capital) migration model. The greatest challenge of this direct test, then, is to isolate the influence of market imperfections and risk on international migration from the role of other income and employment variables.

One of the most distinctive contributions of the new economics of migration is its integration of migration decision-making with migrants' remittance behaviour and households' remittance use—aspects of migration that hitherto have been treated separately in the literature. If risks to income and a desire to overcome local constraints on production are the driving forces behind migration, then the outcomes of migration (e.g. the patterns and uses of remittances) should reflect this fact. A number of indirect tests of the new economics model are available.

If risk diversification is the underlying motivation, then migrant remittances should be greatest in households most exposed to local income risks and in periods when this risk is most acute (e.g. during a severe drought, as demonstrated by Lucas and Stark (1985)). If a primary motivation of migration is to overcome risk and credit constraints on local production stemming from market failures, then migration and remittances should positively influence local income-generating activities (Lucas 1987; Taylor 1992). Such findings would provide evidence in favour of the new economics of migration, because positive effects of migration on local production activities are ruled out by neoclassical economic theory, as are risk effects. Neoclassical theory focuses on an individual's maximization of expected income and assumes that markets are complete and well functioning.

The new economics of migration also places migration within a broader community context, specifically linking a household's migration decision to its position in the local income distribution. The theory of relative deprivation predicts that a household's odds of sending migrants abroad are greater the larger the amount of income earned by households above it in the reference income distribution, and more generally, the greater the income inequality in the reference community. A systematic test of this proposition requires a multilevel statistical model that not only contains the usual individual and household-level predictor variables, but also incorporates the community characteristic of income inequality, or an operational measure of relative income. Stark and Taylor (1989) found that relative income was more significant than absolute income in explaining international labour migration within a sample of rural Mexican households, except at the two extremes of the income distribution.

The new economic model can also be tested at the aggregate level. Unlike the neoclassical model, risk diversification allows for movement in the absence of international differences in wages or employment rates, because it links migration not just to conditions in the labour market but to failures in the capital, credit, and insurance markets as well. In order to test this conceptualization, regressions predicting international population movements should contain, as independent variables, indicators of the presence or absence of insurance programmes (e.g. crop insurance and unemployment insurance), the presence or absence of key markets (e.g. futures, capital, and consumer credit markets), levels of market coverage (per capita measures of market participation), and transaction costs (e.g. insurance and interest rates). In general, deficiencies in these ancillary markets are predicted to increase the size of international flows and to raise the likelihood that particular households send migrants abroad, holding constant conditions in the labour market.

Although segmented labour market theory posits a bifurcated occupational structure and a dual pattern of economic organization for advanced industrial societies, in practice it has proved difficult to verify this segmented market structure empirically (Cain 1976; Hodson and Kaufman 1982). Usually the distinction between 'primary' and 'secondary' sectors is arbitrary, leading to great instability in empirical estimates and a high degree of dependency of results on the decision rule chosen to allocate jobs to sectors (Tolbert *et al.* 1980; Hodson and Kaufman 1981; Horan *et al.* 1981; but see Dickens and Lang 1985, for an exception to this criticism).

Rather than attempting to verify the empirical structure of the labour market, therefore, a more efficacious strategy might be to focus on the theory's predictions regarding patterns of international movement, which are quite specific and objectively testable. Piore and others argue that immigration is driven by conditions of labour demand rather than supply. In statistical models that regress secular trends in international migration on changing market conditions in sending and receiving countries, one should therefore observe a higher degree of explanatory power among receiving-country indicators compared with those for sending countries. If real wages and employment conditions are entered into an equation predicting movement between Turkey and Germany, for example, German indicators should dominate in terms of predictive power.

Being demand-based, the segmented labour market approach also predicts that international flows of labour begin through formal recruitment mechanisms rather than individual efforts. In principle, it should be easy to verify this proposition simply by listing the major international migration flows that have emerged since 1950 and documenting which ones were initiated by formal recruitment procedures, either public or private. If most or all of the flows are traceable to some sort of recruitment programme, then a key prediction of segmented labour market theory will have been sustained. In his book, Piore does not undertake this exercise; he refers only to several cases that happen to be consistent with his theory (for an example of such an exercise, however, see Massey and Liang 1989).

One last prediction of segmented labour market theory is that secondary-sector wages are flexible downward, but not upward. Over time, therefore, fluctuations in wage rates in jobs filled by immigrants should not be strongly related to fluctuations in labour supply and demand. During periods of low labour immigration and high labour demand, wages in receiving countries should not rise to attract native workers because of institutional rigidities, but during periods of high immigration and low demand there is nothing to prevent wages from falling in response to competitive pressure. We thus expect an interaction between changes in wage rates and whether or not immigration was expanding or contracting during the period: the effect is expected to be zero in the former case and negative in the latter. We also expect a widening wage gap between these jobs and those held by native workers over time.

Although world systems theory constitutes a complex and at times diffuse conceptual structure, it yields several relatively straightforward and testable propositions, the first of which is that international flows of labour follow international flows of capital, only in the opposite direction. According to Sassen and others, emigrants are created by direct foreign investment in developing countries and the disruptions that such investment brings. Thus, we should observe that streams of foreign capital going into peripheral regions are accompanied by corresponding outflows of emigrants.

This basic migratory process should be augmented by the existence of ideological and material ties created by prior colonization as well as ongoing processes of market penetration. If one were to specify a model of international migration flows to test world systems theory, therefore, one would want to include indicators of prior colonial relationships, the prevalence of common languages, the intensity of trade relations, the existence of transportation and communication links, and the relative frequency of communications and travel between the countries.

Finally, world systems theory specifies not only that international migration should flow from periphery to core along paths of capital investment, but also that it is directed to certain 'global cities' that channel and control foreign investment. Although the theory does not provide specific criteria for defining a 'global city', a set of operational criteria have been developed from information about capital assets and corporate headquarters (see Friedmann 1986). Having identified global cities, one could then examine the relative frequency of movement to them, as opposed to other places within developed nations.

Social capital theory leads to a series of eminently testable propositions about migrant networks. Controlling for a person's individual migrant experience, the probability of international migration should be greater for individuals who are related to someone who has prior international experience, or for individuals connected to someone who is actually living abroad. Moreover, the likelihood of movement should increase with the closeness of the relationship (i.e. having a brother in Germany is more likely to induce a Turk to emigrate than having a cousin, a neighbour, or a friend); and it should also rise with the quality of the social capital embodied in the relationship (having a brother who has lived in Germany for ten years is more valuable to a potential emigrant than having one who has just arrived, and having one who is a legal resident is better than having one who lacks residence documents).

Another hypothesis stems from the recognition that international movement requires migrants to overcome more barriers than does internal movement. In addition to the normal costs of travel and searching for work are the costs of learning and adapting to a new culture, the costs of acquiring appropriate documentation, and, if acquiring legal papers is impossible, of evading arrest and deportation. In general, the greater the barriers to movement, the more important should network ties become in promoting migration, since they reduce the costs and risks of movement. We should thus observe that network connections are systematically more powerful in predicting international migration than internal migration (Taylor 1986).

Within households, we should also be able to detect the effect of social capital on individual migration behaviour. In general, members of households in which someone has already migrated abroad should display higher probabilities of movement than those from households that lack migratory experience. If social capital theory is correct, for example, a common vector by which migratory behaviour is transmitted is from parents to children (Massey *et al.* 1987). For example, dependent sons whose fathers who are active or former international migrants should be more likely to emigrate than those whose fathers lack foreign experience.

At the community level, one should also be able to observe the effect of the prevalence of network ties. People should be more likely to migrate abroad if they come from a community where many people have migrated and where a large stock of foreign experience has accumulated than if they come from a place where international migration is relatively uncommon (Massey and García España 1987). Moreover, as the stock of social ties and international migrant experience grows over time, migration should become progressively less selective and spread from the middle to the lower segments of the socioeconomic hierarchy. In general, then, individual or household migration decisions need to be placed within a local setting, suggesting the need for multilevel analytic models incorporating indexes of network connections within the community.

Social capital theory also argues that disparities between the supply of and the demand for entry visas into core receiving societies creates a lucrative niche for entrepreneurs to create social structures to promote licit and illicit entry services. The establishment and growth of institutions dedicated to facilitating immigration constitutes another form of social capital that persists over time and increases the volume of international population movements.

Although it may be feasible through case studies to document such institutional development and its effect on immigration, it is more difficult to link institutions to aggregate population flows or micro-level migration decisions in an analytically rigorous fashion. On special surveys, migrants and non-migrants might be asked whether they are aware of social institutions or groups providing support to immigrants, including smuggling and recruiting organizations, and responses to this question may be used to predict the likelihood of movement. Or the presence of such organizations might be documented across communities and used to predict the rate of out-migration at the community level, or, in a multilevel model, the probability of emigration at the individual or household level.

Finally, the theory of cumulative causation states the general hypothesis that migration sustains itself in such a way that migration tends to create more migration. This hypothesis follows from the proposition that individual and household decisions are affected by the socio-economic context within which they are made, and that acts of migration at one point in time affect the context within which subsequent decisions are made. Migration decisions made by families and individuals influence social and economic structures within the community, which influence later decisions by other individuals and households. On balance, the changes at the community level increase the odds of subsequent movement, leading to migration's cumulative causation over time (Massey *et al.* 1987; Massey 1990*b*).

The theory of cumulative causation is readily testable using individual-level data. According to a variety of theorists, once someone has migrated internationally, he or she is very likely to do so again, leading to repeated movements over time. Thus the likelihood of an additional trip should increase with each trip taken; the probability of transnational migration should be greater among those with prior international experience than among those without it; and the likelihood of additional migration should increase as the amount of foreign experience rises.

The systematic testing of the theory at the aggregate level poses more substantial data demands. In order to test for cumulative causation using cross-sectional data, complicated recursive systems of structural equations must be specified, and these typically require instrumental variables that are difficult to define and identify, especially in international data sets. Ideally, the theory should be tested using multilevel longitudinal data, which contain variables defined at the individual, household, community, and perhaps even national levels, all measured at different points in time (see Massey and

Espinosa 1997). Only with such a dataset can the reciprocal feedback effects of individual or household decisions on social structure be discerned and measured.

The theory of cumulative causation, while in many ways still rudimentary in its development, does point to several factors as particularly important in channelling the feedback between individual behaviour and community structure. The first factor is migrant networks, suggesting the need to gather detailed information about kin and friendship ties between migrants and non-migrants. A second factor is income equality, which requires the accurate measurement of household income. A third is land distribution, which requires detailed data on land tenure and ownership. A fourth, pertaining only to rural areas, is the nature of agrarian production, which requires information on the use of irrigation, machinery, hired labour, herbicides, pesticides, and improved seeds by both migrant and non-migrant families. The last and perhaps most difficult factor to measure in testing for cumulative causation is culture, which requires information about beliefs, values, and normative practices.

Ideally, all of these factors should be measured longitudinally, although in some cases—culture, for example—this would be next to impossible. Given the difficulty of securing longitudinal information on changes in the prevalence of migrant networks, the degree of income inequality, the unevenness of land distribution, and the capital intensiveness of agricultural production, an alternative strategy might be to rely on geographic diversity in these factors across communities, specifying simultaneous structural equation systems to model the feedbacks, but this approach raises serious technical issues with respect to identification and instrumentation.

In sum, theories developed to understand contemporary processes of international migration posit causal mechanisms that operate at widely divergent levels of analysis. Although the propositions, assumptions, and hypotheses derived from each perspective are not inherently contradictory, they nonetheless carry very different implications for policy formulation. Depending on which model is supported and under what circumstances, a social scientist might recommend that policy-makers attempt to regulate international migration by changing wages and employment conditions in destination countries; by promoting economic development in origin countries; by establishing programmes of social insurance in sending societies; by reducing income inequality in places of origin; by improving futures or capital markets in developing regions; or by some combination of these actions. Or one might advise that all of these programmes are fruitless given the structural imperatives for international movement growing out of global market relations.

Whatever the case, given the size and scale of contemporary migration flows, and the potential for conflict and misunderstanding inherent in the diverse, multi-ethnic societies now forming around the world, political decisions about international migration will be among the most important made over the next two decades. Sorting out the degree of empirical support for each of the theoretical schemes and integrating them in light of that evaluation will be among the most important tasks carried out by social scientists in ensuing years. In order to lay the groundwork for that larger enterprise, the succeeding chapters evaluate the propositions of each theory by undertaking a systematic review of empirical research in each of the world's principal international migration systems, beginning with the largest and oldest: North America.

3 Understanding the North American System

We begin our review of the global research literature by examining the North American international migration system, concentrating primarily but not exclusively on the post-1945 period. After briefly discussing what we mean by an international migration 'system', we describe the evolution and structure of that which prevails in North America. We go on to review the rather voluminous literature on migration into Canada and the USA to determine how well the various theoretical propositions are borne out by empirical reality in North America. We conclude with a reappraisal of how well each theoretical model holds up under close scrutiny in the world's largest and oldest migration system, describing the kinds of studies and data that will be needed in the future to address the core theoretical questions and conceptual issues before the field.

The Meaning of Migration Systems

The idea of 'migration systems' can be traced to the work of Mabogunje (1970), who argued that migration must be recognized fundamentally as a spatial process with a clear geographic form and structure. His work focused on rural–urban migration within Africa, but Kritz *et al.* (1992) generalized his insights to the case of international migration generally, building on the prior work of Fawcett and Arnold (1987) and Portes and Borocz (1989). They argued that any 'consideration of the causes or impacts of international migration from a sending or a receiving country perspective fails to convey the dynamics associated with the evolution of the flow, from its origins, through the shifts in its composition and volume as it matures' (Kritz *et al.* 1992: 2).

Although international migration systems fundamentally consist of countries that exchange relatively large numbers of migrants, they are also characterized by certain feedback mechanisms that connect movements of people (immigrants, students, tourists, and employees) to concomitant flows of goods, capital, ideas, and information. Economic, cultural, and political links form a network of relationships holding international migration systems together (Fawcett 1989; Gurak and Caces 1992).

To a great degree, migration systems are international labour markets. This internationalization stems from a variety of factors: the global reach of multinational firms (Salt 1992); the worldwide demand for certain specialities (academics, managers, engineers, scientists, programmers); and formal treaty arrangements enacted explicitly to create supranational jobs, such as the European Economic Community and to a lesser extent the North American Free Trade Agreement, the Gulf Cooperation Council, the forum for Asia Pacific Economic Cooperation, and Mercosur, the trade block recently enacted in South America's Southern Cone (Miller 1992).

The movement of people within international migration systems is reinforced by the formation and expansion of networks of personal and family ties, which, once established, become conduits for additional migration. Migrant networks operate independently of government policies and often in spite of them, although they may be encouraged by immigration policies that allocate visas for purposes of family reunification. Mabogunje (1970) refers to migrant networks and other spontaneous institutions created and maintained by migrants as 'informal control subsystems'.

Mabogunje also identifies certain 'formal control subsystems', which include actions carried out by policy-makers, planners, legislators, and bureaucrats, as well as those undertaken by recruiters, lawyers, agents, shippers, and assorted other middle men and women who together comprise what might be termed the 'international migration industry', a set of institutional arrangements with both legal and illegal dimensions (see Prothero 1990).

These formal and informal subsystems operate to perpetuate and reinforce the systemic nature of international flows by encouraging migration along certain pathways, and discouraging it along others. The end result is a set of relatively stable exchanges of people between certain nations, complemented by parallel flows of goods, capital, ideas, and information, yielding an identifiable geographic structure that persists across space and time. Although migration systems may originate in colonial ties established under imperialistic regimes (Rumbaut 1991, 1992; Kritz *et al.* 1992), a colonial past does not guarantee a migratory flow, nor does its absence preclude it.

In identifying migration systems for this book, we adopt the general approach of Kritz *et al.* (1992), who argued that an international migration system exists whenever 'a network of countries [is] linked by migration interactions whose dynamics are largely shaped by the functioning of a variety of networks linking actors at different levels of aggregation. The attention given to the role of institutional and migrant networks in channelling and sustaining migration is a key aspect of the systems approach' (Kritz *et al.* 1992: 15). In attempting to characterize systems empirically in this and subsequent chapters, we rely on data for the decade of the 1980s, which at the time we were working were reasonably complete although by no means entirely accurate. Although the distinguishing features of the various systems have continued to evolve and change in the 1990s—sometimes quite rapidly—their basic structure and organization, and the patterns of movement within them, were established in the 1980s.

The North American System

The North American migration system is the best documented of all contemporary international migration systems (see Bouvier and Gardiner 1986; Papademetriou 1988, 1991*a*, 1991*b*; Portes and Rumbaut 1990; Freeman and Jupp 1992; Zlotnik 1992). Its principal destination countries, Canada and the USA, are traditional immigrant-receiving societies that have long supported research and data-collection efforts related to international migration. Although Canada takes in a larger number of immigrants relative to its size than the USA, the latter has always absorbed the lion's share of the world's immigrants. In fact, the state of California *by itself* takes in more permanent immigrants than any other *nation* in the world (except the USA itself—see Winsberg 1993). Between 1980 and 1989 the USA received roughly a third of all of the world's international migrants (Zlotnik 1993).

As of 1990, the USA had 19.8 million foreign-born residents comprising 8 per cent of its total population, compared with Canada's 4.2 million foreign-born residents representing 16 per cent of its population. The foreign-born percentage has been increasing in both countries in recent decades as a result of a sharp upsurge in immigration that began in the mid-1960s. By the end of the 1980s, immigration into North America had come to exceed the record levels observed during the first decades of the century (see Massey 1995). For example, the average number of permanent immigrants admitted to the USA each year rose from 385,000 during the period 1970–4 to 603,000 during 1985–9. By 1991, it was running at 1.4 million per year, owing partly to the implementation of a legalization programme for undocumented migrants. In Canada, annual immigration grew from an average of 159,000 in 1970–4 to 221,000 during 1990–2 (United Nations 1992).

These increases in international migration have been accompanied by a pronounced shift in immigrant origins away from historical sources in Europe towards new sources in Asia, Latin America, and the Caribbean. Although Europeans still constitute a majority of Canada's foreign-born population (54 per cent in 1991), the percentage was falling rapidly (down from 67 per cent in 1981) and a crossover probably occurred sometime during the early 1990s. In the USA, the percentage of Europeans among the foreign born had already reached low levels in 1991 (about 25 per cent—see Rumbaut 1994).

Table 3.1 suggests the reason for this remarkable shift; it presents the regional origins of permanent immigrants to the USA and Canada during the 1980s. Zlotnik (1992: 25) has observed that these two countries 'are at the core of a single migration system that encompasses strong migration interactions with countries all over the world.' Virtually every country in the world sends *at least some* immigrants to Canada, the USA, or both. During the 1980s, 8.7 million people entered North America as legal immigrants, 85 per cent going the USA and 15 per cent to Canada. Were United Nations definitions to be employed rather than counts of persons admitted for permanent legal resi-

Table 3.1 Regional composition of legal immigration to the USA and Canada, 1981–1990

Source region	USA Number	Percent	Canada Number	Percent	North America Number	Percent
Europe	761.6	10.4	351.5	26.4	1,113.1	12.8
Britain	159.2	2.2	81.5	6.1	240.7	2.8
Portugal	40.4	0.6	38.6	2.9	79.0	0.9
France	32.3	0.4	15.3	1.1	47.6	0.5
Greece	38.4	0.5	6.9	0.5	45.3	0.5
Italy	67.3	0.9	11.2	0.8	78.5	9.1
Poland	83.2	1.1	81.4	6.1	164.6	1.9
Other	340.8	4.6	116.7	8.7	457.5	5.3
Africa	176.9	2.4	72.9	5.5	249.8	2.9
Asia	2,738.2	37.3	619.1	46.5	3,357.3	38.7
Hong Kong	98.2	1.3	97.0	7.3	195.2	2.3
India	250.8	3.4	90.1	6.8	340.9	3.0
China	346.7	4.7	74.2	5.6	420.9	4.9
Philippines	548.8	7.5	67.7	5.1	616.5	7.1
Middle East	183.7	2.5	91.0	6.8	274.7	3.2
Other	1,310.0	17.9	199.2	15.0	1,509.2	17.4
North America	2,280.8	31.1	114.1	8.6	2,394.9	27.6
Canada	156.9	2.1	—	—	156.9	1.8
USA	—	—	63.1	4.7	63.1	0.7
Central America	2,123.9	29.0	51.0	3.8	2,174.9	25.1
Caribbean	872.0	11.9	89.1	6.7	961.1	11.1
South America	461.8	6.3	67.9	5.1	529.7	6.1
Oceania	45.2	0.6	15.9	1.2	61.1	0.7
Other	1.5	0.0	0.4	0.0	1.9	0.0
TOTAL	7,338.0	100.0	1,330.9	100.0	8,668.9	100.0

Sources: US Immigration and Naturalization Service (1994); Statistics Canada (1995).

dence, long-term immigration into the USA would be at least 5 per cent higher (Kraly and Warren 1991).

Although sources for this new immigration are diverse, the most important countries of origin are found in Asia, Latin America, and the Caribbean. Together these three regions contribute 85 per cent of all immigrants to the USA and 67 per cent of those to Canada. In both nations, Asian migration arose from virtually nothing in the 1960s to become a pre-eminent source by the 1980s, representing 47 per cent of all Canadian immigrants and 37 per cent of those to the USA (see Table 3.1). Average annual immigration from Asia into North America increased from just 18,000 persons during 1960–4 to 132,000 during 1970–4 and reached 305,000 during 1980–4; by the late 1980s it was running at about 308,000 persons per year (Zlotnik 1993).

This remarkable shift away from European sources was facilitated in both countries by the repeal, during the 1960s, of racist immigration laws that explicitly favoured northern and western Europeans, and which barred the entry of Asians. These laws were replaced by immigration systems that allocated visas to reunify families, attract skilled labour, and offer refuge to persons fleeing persecution and violence, procedures that, in theory at least, were neutral with respect to national origins (see Keely 1979; Kubat 1979; Jasso and Rosenzweig 1990). During the 1980s, 69 per cent percent of all immigrants who entered the USA came as relatives of citizens or legal residents, 18 per cent came as refugees, and 9 per cent were workers; in Canada the respective percentages were 52 per cent, 16 per cent, and 33 per cent. The relative importance of family reunification in both countries underscores the importance of kinship networks in promoting and sustaining international migration.

A growing avenue of entry into both Canada and the USA, as in other developed countries, has been political asylum. In contrast to refugees, who are granted the right to enter a country based on a fear of political persecution acknowledged in advance by the receiving country, asylees enter as tourists, students, visitors, or undocumented migrants and then attempt to get the receiving country to acknowledge their claim of political persecution. In Canada, the annual number of asylum applications grew from 5,000 to 30,000 between 1983 and 1991, while in the USA it rose from 20,000 to 70,000 (Barrett 1993).

Much of the movement within the North American system is circular. Warren and Kraly (1985) estimate that 1.2 million former immigrants left the USA during the 1970s, and Woodrow (1988) found that 1.2 million left between 1980 and 1987. Hugo (1994a) suggests that emigration from Canada, if accurately measured, would offset about a quarter of annual entries. Circularity is also indicated by the growing number of visitors. From 1981 to 1993, for example, the number of temporary visitors to the USA nearly doubled, going from 11.8 million to 21.4 million per year (US Immigration and Naturalization Service 1994). Unlike permanent immigrants, however, temporary visitors come mainly from other developed nations, notably Britain, Germany, and Japan (Papademetriou 1991a).

Despite similarities in their immigrant streams, Canada and the USA display certain contrasts that reflect differences between them in terms of size, economic power, and geopolitical influence. Compared with the USA, for example, Canada continues to retain stronger links to Europe, which still accounts for 26 per cent of its immigrants compared with only 10 per cent of those to the USA. In addition, although the Caribbean represents an important source of immigrants for both countries (see Table 3.1), Canada has stronger ties to French- and English-speaking, islands whereas the USA has stronger connections to the Spanish Caribbean. Thus, the most important Caribbean sources for Canada are Haiti and Jamaica, whereas Cuba and the Dominican Republic predominate among the origins of Caribbean immigrants to the USA.

This contrast in Caribbean origins is even sharper than just indicated, for it does not take account of the large number of Puerto Ricans who annually migrate to the USA. From 1950 to 1990, a net figure of more than one million Puerto Ricans moved from the island to the US mainland (Maldonado 1976; Rivera-Batiz and Santiago 1994). As US citizens, Puerto Ricans are classified as internal rather than international migrants; but their movement has contributed to the growing Caribbean presence in eastern cities of the USA.

The close articulation between the USA and the Spanish-speaking world is also evident in the emergence, during the 1980s, of large migration streams from Central America. Whereas nations such as Mexico, El Salvador, Guatemala, and Nicaragua contribute few migrants to Canada, they account for nearly 30 per cent of all immigrants to the USA (see Table 3.1), reflecting the latter's deeper history of economic and political entanglement in the region (see Vázquez and Meyer 1985). During the period 1981–90, Mexico by itself sent 1.7 million legal immigrants to the USA (US Immigration and Naturalization Service 1994).

The foregoing data do not include a large number of undocumented immigrants, who further accentuate the US connection to Latin America. According to Warren (1995), 3.4 million illegal migrants lived in the USA in 1992, 40 per cent of whom were from Mexico and another 24 per cent of whom came from elsewhere in Latin America. Passel (1995) estimates that illegal migrants arrived at the rate of 300,000 per year during the 1990s, with 53 per cent coming from just three Latin American countries (Mexico, El Salvador, and Guatemala). Although illegal migration is also significant in Canada, it is smaller and composed more of Asians and Caribbeans than Latin Americans (Employment and Immigration Canada 1992). Estimates prepared for 1983 put the number of undocumented immigrants in Canada at approximately 50,000 persons (Robinson 1984).

As a result of the greater volume of Latin American immigration into the USA, the fraction of Asians among new arrivals is lower in the USA (37 per cent) than in Canada (47 per cent). The two countries also differ with respect to the origins of Asian immigrants. Principal US sources include the Philippines, South Korea, Taiwan, and Indo-China. In contrast, the principal Canadian sources are Hong Kong, India, and Pakistan. The Canadian pattern reflects the importance of ties established under the British Commonwealth, whereas the US pattern reflects its history of colonialism and military intervention (Rumbaut 1991, 1994).

The basic structure of the North American system is summarized schematically in Figure 3.1, which uses data on flows observed during the

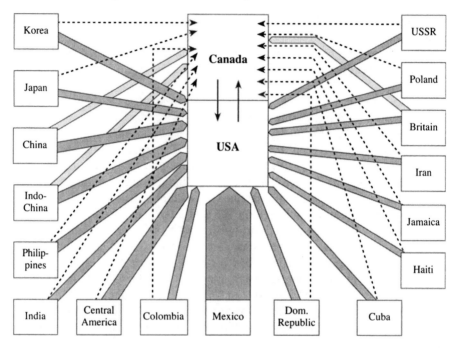

Fig. 3.1   International migration in the North American system, 1980–1990

1980s. The diagram includes all countries or regions that sent more than 100,000 migrants to either country during the period under study (75 per cent of those to the USA and 60 per cent of those to Canada). The absolute size of the flow is proportional to the width of the arrow, and flows less than 100,000 persons are indicated with a dashed line.

For the USA, we measured immigration as the change in the size of the foreign born population (from Rumbaut 1994) to include at least a partial accounting for undocumented migration. For Canada, we used the count of immigrants who entered the country between 1980 and 1990 (from Statistics Canada 1995). In the figure, immigrants from Hong Kong, the People's Republic of China, and Taiwan are grouped together as 'China', while Vietnam, Cambodia, and Laos are grouped together as 'Indo-China'; El Salvador, Guatemala, and Nicaragua are combined with Panama, Honduras, and Costa Rica to comprise the category 'Central America'.

A quick glance at the figure reveals the salient features of the North American migration system. First, the diversity of sources is notable: significant immigration into North America (in excess of 100,000 persons) occurs from seventeen subareas located in six world regions: East Asia (Korea, Japan, and China), South Asia (Indo-China, the Philippines, and India), Latin America (Mexico, Colombia, and Central America), the Caribbean (Cuba, the Dominican Republic, Jamaica, and Haiti), the Middle East (Iran), and Europe (Britain, Poland, and the former countries of the Soviet Union). A second salient feature of the system's structure is the region that is omitted from the list of sending regions: Africa. At present, African nations appear to be marginal participants in the North American migration system.

Another important aspect of the system that is immediately obvious is the dominance of the USA: while most of the arrows leading to that country are thick, those going to Canada tend to be thin or dashed, indicating the smaller scale of its immigration flows (which are nonetheless larger in proportional terms). Only three flows into Canada exceeded 100,000 immigrants—those from China, Indo-China, and Britain. The greater size and diversity of the streams into the USA indicate the greater reach of its culture, institutions, and geopolitical interests. Countries that send large numbers of migrants to the USA tend to be those that are linked to it via strong economic, political, or military ties (Rumbaut 1994).

By far the largest flow in the North American system is from Mexico to the USA. Despite vast differences between these countries with respect to wealth, power, and standards of living, their fates are closely intertwined. The USA has invaded Mexico three times; it annexed one-third its territory; it is the primary source of capital for Mexican investment; it is Mexico's largest trading partner and Mexico is the second most important trading partner for the USA (Hart 1987; Sheahan 1991; Centeno 1994); and currently economic integration between Mexico and the USA is occurring under the terms of the North American Free Trade Agreement (Lustig *et al.* 1992; Belous and Lemco 1995).

Other countries sending large numbers of immigrants to the USA also tend to have a history of US political intervention, economic penetration, or both. Many have been invaded or occupied by US troops (Haiti, Cuba, the Dominican Republic, Japan, Nicaragua); some house large military bases (Korea, Japan, Indo-China, the Philippines, Cuba, Britain, Panama); others were the scenes of wars in which the USA was a prominent combatant (Korea, Japan, Indo-China); several were targets of operations by the US Central Intelligence Agency (Central America, the Dominican Republic, Cuba, Iran, Poland, the USSR); most are significant US trading partners (Korea, Japan, China, the Philippines, Mexico, Britain); and one nation (the Philippines) is a former US colony and another (Cuba) a near-colony whose original constitution gave the USA the right to intervene militarily at will. In no small way, then, the North American migration system is a *political* economy that reflects the interests of the superpower at its core.

Policies in North America have moved in contradictory directions with respect to international migration. On the one hand, Canada, Mexico, and the USA have sought to integrate their markets more closely and are reaching out to other nations in the western hemisphere as possible partners in an expanded free trade agreement. The creation of an integrated market generally accelerates the movement of economic factors within it, including labour. On the other hand, Canada and the USA have sought to impose restrictive immigration policies in response to a growing public backlash against immigrants from precisely those countries with which they are integrating economically, notably Mexico (see Lamm and Imhoff 1985; Espenshade and Calhoun 1993; Brimelow 1995).

Whether policy-makers can simultaneously limit the movement of labour while encouraging the movement of goods, capital, and information is an open question, particularly in light of expanding migrant networks, growing pressures for family reunification, the increasing use of asylum as a vehicle for entry, and rising political and economic instability in important source countries. The inherent contradiction between economic integration and limited international movement yields a great deal of uncertainty in predicting the course of migration within the North American System.

The State of Research in North America

The number of studies focusing on North American immigration is vast. A review of twenty-five social science journals over the past ten years turned up more than 300 references on US or Canadian immigration. Most of this work, unfortunately, is not relevant to the task of evaluating theory. The number of studies that bear directly on theoretical propositions is rather small, and the number that critically compare competing theoretical models is even smaller. A good deal of the literature is not even empirical: it consists of polemic arguments or theoretical perorations that are merely illustrated with a few convenient facts. The studies that are empirical, moreover, tend to be descriptive and of limited use in sorting out the various claims and counter-claims of competing theories.

Among the empirical studies that purport to be analytic, a lamentably large proportion are flawed in one way or another. The statistical methods they employ are often rudimentary or biased, the models are simplistic, and appropriate controls are lacking. Often no particular issue—theoretical or substantive—is addressed, and in many cases, unreliable survey designs offer little basis for hypothesis testing or generalization. Non-random samples of migrants from one sending community, one receiving area, one job site, or one social service agency are common.

There are two basic reasons for this unfortunate state of affairs. The first is simply a lack of good, representative data (Bilsborrow *et al.* 1997). A sizeable share of the immigrant flow into North America is undocumented, and thus outside of national statistical systems. Even for legal immigrants, however, the quantity and quality of information is generally inadequate. Statistics on immigrant entries are mired in legal concepts rather than demographic realities (Kraly and Warren 1991, 1992); the amount of information gathered from legal arrivals is minimal (Levine *et al.* 1985); and neither

Canada nor the USA maintains a useable record of immigrant departures (Warren and Kraly 1985).

In addition, unlike other fields of study, international migration has never evolved a specialized survey dataset (Bilsborrow *et al.* 1997). There is no equivalent of the World Fertility Survey, the Demographic and Health Survey, or the US National Longitudinal Surveys, which were developed to provide information on fertility, mortality, and stratification, respectively. Although national censuses provide some information about the foreign born, these data have their own problems and limitations (see Bean *et al.* 1984; Borjas 1985, 1987; Passel 1985; Lindstrom and Massey 1994). In particular, they underenumerate undocumented migrants, they provide no information on legal status, and they are ill-suited to the study of immigration as a process rather than an event (Passel 1985).

As a result of these and other difficulties, a great deal of the North American research literature is devoted to methodological and measurement issues: how to measure undocumented migration; how to count the number of emigrants; how to study patterns of immigrant assimilation; how to analyse the social and economic consequences of immigration. Although these questions are important, the answers to them do not advance theoretical understanding of the forces that shape and control international migration.

Even allowing for difficulty of measurement, however, a second and more fundamental reason for the scarcity of good, incisive studies of immigration is the lack of a commonly accepted theoretical framework. As the prior chapter revealed, social scientists do not approach the study of immigration from a shared paradigm, but from a variety of competing theoretical viewpoints fragmented across disciplines, regions, and ideologies. As a result, research on the subject tends to be narrow, inefficient, and characterized by duplication, miscommunication, reinvention, and bickering about fundamentals. Only when researchers accept common theories, concepts, tools, and standards will knowledge begin to accumulate (see Kuhn 1962).

At this juncture, then, population scientists are little closer to achieving a solid understanding of the powerful forces responsible for the remarkable resurgence of immigration into North America. Through this empirical review, we hope to begin building a framework for accumulating such knowledge. We start by evaluating theories that account for the initiation of international migration and move on to consider those that explain the persistence of transnational movements across space and time.

The Initiation of International Migration

Neoclassical Economics

According to neoclassical theory, flows of labour move from low-wage to high-wage countries, and capital (including human capital) moves in the opposite direction. As a result, migration is expected to exert downward pressure on wages in destination countries and upward pressure on wages in sending nations until an equilibrium is reached. At equilibrium, the international wage gap exactly equals the cost of migration between the countries (including psychic costs), and net migration ceases. Thus, labour migration should theoretically continue until this equilibrium is achieved and should not stop until the gap in expected wages (minus migration costs) has been closed. Emigrants should also go to the destination country in which they expect the highest net gain.

Despite the familiarity of this argument and its widespread use by scholars, policy-makers, and the public, it has not been rigorously tested in explaining international migration. Although various attempts have been made to relate immigration flows and individual emigration propensities to differentials in wages and incomes, studies generally have not examined *expected* wages (the product of wages and employment rates), which since the time of Todaro (1969) have been accepted theoretically as the relevant determinant of migration flows. Measures of employment (or unemployment), when they are included in regression analyses of migration flows, are typically entered additively rather than multiplicatively, as specified by the Todaro model.

Although Puerto Rico is not an independent country, movement between it and the US mainland replicates many of the features of international movement, and it provides a unique laboratory to test the propositions of neoclassical economics. As with migration from independent nations in the Caribbean region, movement out of the Commonwealth of Puerto Rico entails crossing significant cultural, linguistic, and geographic boundaries, but unlike migration from places such as the Dominican Republic, it occurs without legal restriction. In the absence of legal barriers, movement between Puerto Rico and the US mainland should closely follow the predictions of neoclassical theory, since there are no legal impediments to the functioning of the 'transnational' labour market.

The earliest analysis of Puerto Rico–US migration was conducted by Fleisher (1963), who estimated a series of regression models to predict annual net movement from the island to the mainland for the period 1947–8. The small number of observations limits the reliability of Fleisher's findings, however, and creates problems for hypothesis testing. In order to conserve degrees of freedom, he fit a basic model predicting net migration from an 'unemployment ratio' that expressed the difference between Puerto Rican and US unemployment rates as a proportion of the US rate; then he added in other predictors and observed their effect on the baseline model's explanatory power.

His analysis revealed a strong relationship between Puerto Rican unemployment and the volume of migration to the USA ($R^2 = 0.61$). The higher the relative unemployment on the island, the greater the outflow of migrants to the mainland. Including the ratio of hourly manufacturing earnings in Puerto

Rico to those in New York added no explanatory power to the model, and this wage ratio only weakly predicted the volume of out-migration when it was regressed on migration by itself. The relative cost of air transportation to New York did, however, improve the model's fit significantly (raising the R^2 to 0.83). As expected, the higher the costs of transportation, the lower the volume of net migration to the mainland.

These results were updated by Maldonado (1976) using annual data from 1947 to 1973. The additional years of observation allowed her to enter more explanatory variables and to carry out more reliable statistical tests. She regressed total net out-migration on three ratios that measured economic conditions in Puerto Rico relative to those in the four leading states of destination: New York, New Jersey, Connecticut, and Illinois. The three conditions she examined were unemployment, hourly wages in manufacturing, and average monthly welfare payments.

Unlike Fleisher (1963), she found that differentials in both unemployment and wages were significant in determining the volume of migration between Puerto Rico and the mainland ($R^2 = 0.57$). As Puerto Rican unemployment increased relative to that in the USA, the volume of out-migration rose significantly; and as average wages in Puerto Rico increased relative to those on the mainland, the volume of out-migration fell. The size of the outflow was marginally related to the relative size of welfare payments on the island and the mainland. Estimates of the model for the period 1947 to 1967, when Maldonado judged economic motivations to be paramount, yielded a tighter fit ($R^2 = 0.80$) and the effect of relative employment increased while that of relative wages declined.

From 1950 to 1970, a net figure of 643,000 Puerto Ricans emigrated to the US mainland and the percentage of all Puerto Ricans living on the mainland grew from 9 per cent to 23 per cent (Maldonado 1976). According to neoclassical theory, this large outflow should have put substantial upward pressure on island wages, and in fact from 1950 to 1970 average wages in Puerto Rican manufacturing rose from $0.42 to $2.33 while the ratio of mainland to island wages dropped from 3.4 to 1.9 (Castillo-Freeman and Freeman 1992). As migration proceeded, therefore, the wage gap was indeed closing. Thus, research on Puerto Rico–US migration broadly supports the postulates of neoclassical economic theory, at least through the early 1970s.

After this time, the Puerto Rican case provides an interesting natural experiment, since in 1974 the island was suddenly brought into conformity with the minimum wage laws of the USA. Prior to 1974, local wage boards had exempted many of the island's industries from US standards and set substantially lower minimum wages on an industry-by-industry basis. These boards were abolished by the US Congress in 1974, and over the following several years Puerto Rican industries were brought up to US minimum wage standards. By 1977 the island had achieved the same average minimum wage and the same level of industrial coverage as the US mainland.

Given the relatively lower wage rate that prevailed on the island before 1974, the new wage policy caused a sudden and sharp increase in the average wage rate. It also reduced the variance of the Puerto Rican wage distribution and produced a substantial compression of wages around the legal minimum. As wages rose, however, so did unemployment, because a growing number of industries no longer found it profitable to engage in production on the island (Castillo-Freeman and Freeman 1992). According to neoclassical theory, this exogenous wage shock should have been followed by a change in patterns and levels of labour migration to the USA, since shifts in employment levels and wages must have altered the distribution of expected wages on the island.

In a series of studies, Santiago (1991, 1993) has examined the effect of Puerto Rican wage policy on migration. Working with monthly data from January 1970 to June 1987, he related net migration rates to changes in four measures of the minimum wage: the nominal change in the minimum wage; the real change in the minimum wage; the change in the ratio of the minimum to the average wage; and the change in the ratio of the minimum to the average wage weighted by the percentage of industries covered. He derived migration elasticities using a first-order autoregressive model with moving averages and seasonal differencing estimated using the Akaike Information Criterion (Amemiya 1985). His computations suggest that raising the minimum wage in Puerto Rico significantly slowed the volume of emigration to the mainland. Although the island continued to experience net out-migration in most years, at the margins the new policy reduced the outflow below what it might otherwise have been.

Santiago's estimates have been criticized by Castillo-Freeman and Freeman (1992), however, for not including any other control variables, for not considering the displacement effect of unemployment on the island, for employing a complex, non-standard model, and for the fact that Santiago's zero-order correlations yielded coefficients with signs opposite those achieved using his more complex model. They developed an alternative specification that expressed the rate of annual net migration as a function of the US gross national product (GNP), the Puerto Rican GNP, and the Puerto Rican minimum wage (all variables logged). They found that whereas out-migration was positively related to US GNP and negatively related to Puerto Rican GNP, it was not significantly affected by the minimum wage itself. Although the effect was positive, as in Santiago's estimates, the standard error was too large to place much confidence in the result.

Castillo-Freeman and Freeman (1992) argue that no strong conclusion can be drawn about the effect of the minimum wage hike on the *volume* of Puerto Rican out-migration. Instead, they focused on changes in the *selectivity* of migration. Because of the sharp increase in island wages, employment levels fell in low-wage industries and a large number of unskilled and blue-collar workers were displaced. Because of high capital/labour ratios on the US mainland, these workers could expect a higher likelihood of employment and higher wages there than in Puerto Rico, inducing them to emigrate. At the same time, however, higher average wages on the island might induce mainland Puerto Ricans with skills and education to depart for the island.

Consistent with earlier descriptive work by Ortiz (1987), both Castillo-Freeman and Freeman (1992) and Ramos (1992) find a pattern of shifting migrant selectivity over time. After 1974, migration from the island to the mainland became more prevalent among the unemployed and by 1980 was highly selective of those with little schooling. At the same time, migration from the mainland to the island became more selective of those with more education. As a result, post-1975 arrivals earned the lowest wages among Puerto Ricans on the mainland, while US-born Puerto Ricans earned the highest wages among those on the island.

These findings highlight the selective nature of migration, which is implicit in human capital models but frequently ignored in empirical applications based on aggregate data. A recent study by Melendez (1994) shows that Puerto Rican migrants are not only selected in terms of education, but also occupation. During 1982–8, he found that farmworkers, labourers, and crafts workers were overrepresented among migrants to the mainland, and that this pattern of occupational selectivity was explained by two factors: unemployment in Puerto Rico and having a job offer from the USA; relative wages appeared to play no role in selecting who migrated to the USA.

Migration between Mexico and the USA—clearly the largest sustained flow of migrant workers in the contemporary world—also has been studied intensively. Between 1940 and 1992, some 1.2 million Mexicans were admitted into the USA as legal immigrants (US Immigration and Naturalization Service 1993); another 4.6 million came temporarily as contract workers (also known as *braceros*—see Calavita 1992); and a net figure of around 4 million entered without documents (Passel 1985; Passel and Woodrow 1987). Some 2.3 million of the latter were later legalized under the 1986 Immigration Reform and Control Act (US Immigration and Naturalization Service 1992). As a result of the massive entry of migrants and their subsequent natural increase, by 1990 people of Mexican origin comprised 6 per cent of the total population of the USA.

In neoclassical terms, the incentives for migration between Mexico and the USA are large. Average wages rates differ by a factor of five between the two countries (Conroy 1980); and even after adjusting for the costs of transportation, entry, and foreign living, most Mexican workers can expect to earn three times what they would at home (Cuthbert and Sterns 1981; Massey and Espinosa 1997). The absence of a direct count of undocumented Mexican migrants, however, causes serious problems for analysis, and most investigators have been forced to rely on government apprehensions statistics as a crude indicator of the gross inflow.

These data are simply totals of the number of Mexicans caught trying to enter the country illegally and subsequently deported by the US Immigration and Naturalization Service (INS). It is a tally of enforcement actions and not people: the same person may be caught once, twice, several times, or not at all (see Espenshade 1990; Donato *et al.* 1992; Massey and Singer 1995), causing a variety of potential biases.

The first systematic investigation of Mexico–USA migration using INS data was carried out by Frisbie (1975). He estimated the rate of illegal migration as the annual number of Mexican apprehensions divided by the mid-year population of Mexico. He regressed yearly changes in this rate on annual changes in six factors: farm wages, agricultural productivity, and agricultural commodity prices in Mexico; and US farm wages, US agricultural productivity, and the rate of US capital investment in Mexico.

Overall, his model explained about half of the yearly variation in illegal migration to the USA. The two most important predictors were farm wages and agricultural productivity in Mexico—as they rose, illegal migration to the USA fell. Almost as important were US farm wages, which worked in the opposite direction: as they rose so did migration. Also significant was agricultural productivity in the USA, with the direction again being positive: as US farm productivity increased, more undocumented workers were attracted from Mexico. Together, these four variables accounted for 61 per cent of the explained variance. Changes in Mexican commodity prices and shifts in the rate of US investment in Mexico were less important.

Jenkins (1977) expanded Frisbie's analysis by increasing the range of years, adding several new variables as predictors, and estimating their effect on *bracero* as well as illegal migration. *Braceros* were Mexican agricultural workers contracted through a binational labour programme administered by the US government from 1942 through 1964 (Calavita 1992). In addition to the variables considered by Frisbie, Jenkins also included the rate of capital investment in Mexican agriculture, the rate of seasonal farm employment in the USA, the level of US agricultural unemployment, US agricultural commodity prices, and the Mexico–USA wage differential.

He carried out a lagged regression of first differences for the period 1948 through 1972 and reported standardized partial correlations. His estimates showed that the Mexico–USA wage differential had a positive effect on the rate of both *bracero* and illegal migration, and was particularly strong in predicting the total rate of Mexican out-migration (*bracero* plus illegal migration). As suggested by neoclassical theory, the rate of migration to the USA rose as the wage differential widened. The result was the same whether the wage gap was measured as a difference or as a ratio between Mexican and US wages.

In general, Jenkins found that push factors in Mexico, taken together, were stronger than pull factors in the USA in predicting the rate of out-migration. As Mexican wages, commodity prices, farm productivity, and levels of investment in agriculture rose, out-migration to the USA fell. In contrast to Frisbie, however, Jenkins found that the rate of Mexican emigration was *negatively* related to changes in US farm wages and agricultural productivity (although he did replicate Frisbie's positive correlation between Mexican emigration and US commodity prices).

Blejer *et al.* (1978) further extended research on Mexico-USA migration by considering legal as well as illegal migrants. They focused on the fifteen-year period from 1960 to 1975 and employed models that assessed the effects of only two variables on migration levels: wage differentials and unemployment ratios. They estimated a series of models to predict the yearly *number* of legal immigrants and undocumented apprehensions from the ratio of Mexico/USA unemployment, the ratio of Mexico/USA industrial wages, and the ratio of Mexico/USA agricultural wages. All variables were expressed as logs to improve the model's statistical fit.

The model performed better for undocumented ($R^2 = 0.71$) than for legal immigrants ($R^2 = 0.35$), and the explanatory power of the employment variable exceeded that of wages, whether or not the model considered agricultural or industrial wages, and whether or not it examined legal, undocumented, or total migration. Most of the explanatory power captured by the unemployment ratio came from variation in Mexican unemployment levels. Indeed, the log of the Mexican unemployment rate by itself performed *better* than the Mexico/USA employment ratio. As Mexican unemployment increased, whether absolutely or in relation to rates in the USA, the volume of both legal and undocumented migration from Mexico rose. Relative wages contributed no additional explanatory power once the effect of Mexican unemployment was controlled.

Probably the best study to examine the economic determinants of Mexico–USA migration arose not as an explicit attempt to test theory, but, tellingly, as an effort to evaluate public policy. The passage of the Immigration Reform and Control Act (IRCA) in 1986 brought demands from policy-makers and the public to evaluate its effects in deterring illegal Mexican migration to the USA. In response, Bean *et al.* (1990) studied trends in the number of monthly apprehensions of Mexicans along the southern US border. They regressed the log of monthly apprehensions from 1977 through 1988 on a set of independent variables that included dummy variables for periods before and after the implementation of IRCA.

Of greatest theoretical interest are the substantive variables they included as controls in their policy evaluation. In addition to IRCA-related indicators, the investigators also included the size of the Mexican population aged 15 to 34, the ratio of US to Mexican male unemployment rates, and the ratio of US to Mexican non-agricultural wages. They also controlled for the number of hours spent by US immigration agents patrolling the border (linewatch hours) and the amount of capital spent on enforcement by the INS (enforcement capital).

The estimated model—summarized in White *et al.* (1990) and reported fully in Bean *et al.* (1990)—yielded a remarkably good fit to the data ($R^2 = 0.941$)

and its coefficients were generally consistent with predictions derived from neoclassical theory. The effect of the unemployment ratio was strong and negative, while that of the wage ratio was strong and positive. As wages in the USA rose relative to those in Mexico, the monthly flow of undocumented migrants increased; and as unemployment in the USA rose relative to that in Mexico, it decreased. The level of undocumented migration also rose as the supply of young Mexican workers increased, and, not surprisingly, the number of apprehensions was positively related to linewatch hours and enforcement capital. The same basic pattern of effects was found when investigators considered interior apprehensions, adult male apprehensions, or the apprehensions of women and children.

Espenshade (1990) argued, however, that the number of apprehensions is not a good indicator of the gross inflow of undocumented migrants. The correspondence between apprehensions and illegal entrants depends on the probability of apprehension, and if this parameter changes over time it could bias the analysis performed by Bean *et al.* (1990). Drawing on probability theory, he developed a 'repeated trials model' to estimate the likelihood of apprehension at any point in time and then applied this estimate to the number of apprehensions recorded by the INS. In this way, he derived a new estimate of the gross inflow of undocumented migrants from Mexico to the USA. When he replicated the analysis of Bean *et al.* (1990), however, he found virtually the same pattern of results as before.

In addition to these aggregate-level analyses, three studies have employed individual-level data to evaluate propositions derived from neoclassical theory. Taylor (1987) estimated a structural probit model to predict the likelihood that residents of two Mexican communities migrated to the USA during the year prior to the survey. In addition to variables such as age, sex, headship, migrant experience, family size, kinship ties, and total household income, Taylor developed an indicator of the difference in family members' expected contributions to household income in the USA and Mexico—precisely the factor that would be identified by neoclassical economists as the principal determinant of migration in a household-decision framework.

This quantity was estimated using instrumental variable techniques. Taylor examined contributions to household income by individuals as migrants in the USA and as workers in Mexico and regressed these figures on selected individual and household characteristics correcting for self-selection into the USA or Mexican workforce. These equations were then used to predict the income each person could expect to earn working in the USA and Mexico during the year prior to the survey. These predictions provide estimates of 'expected income' that correspond closely to the concept defined in neoclassical theory, and the difference between them yields an unbiased estimate of the expected net gain to Mexican households from sending a family member abroad.

If neoclassical theory is correct, we expect this factor to play the predominant role in the decision to migrate, and to account for most of the variation in likelihood of migration. Although expected income is indeed positive and significant in predicting the likelihood of international movement, it does not explain the bulk of the variation nor is it even the strongest effect in the model.

Massey and Espinosa (1997) undertook a similar analysis using survey data gathered in twenty-five Mexican communities and their US destination areas between the years of 1987 and 1992. They estimated a series of discrete-time event history models to predict the odds of undertaking a first trip to the USA, the odds of undertaking an additional US trip given that at least one had occurred, and the odds of returning to Mexico given a prior entry into the USA. Among the many independent variables they considered was the ratio in expected wages between Mexico and the USA.

As with Taylor's analysis, expected wages were estimated using instrumental variable techniques. Massey and Espinosa first estimated a selectivity-corrected regression equation that expressed Mexican wages (measured in constant US dollars) as a function of selected background variables; then they repeated the same exercise for US wages (also measured in constant dollars). By inserting a respondent's changing background characteristics into these wage equations, they were able to estimate expected wages in Mexico and the USA during each year of the event history.

When the authors formed the ratio of wages expected in the USA and Mexico and included it as an independent variable in their analyses, they found that it was positively related to the odds of taking a first illegal trip to the USA, but that it was unrelated to the odds of taking additional US trips, either legal or illegal; it was also unrelated to the likelihood of returning home to Mexico. Moreover, even though the wage ratio was significant in predicting first trips by undocumented migrants, its effect was relatively weak compared to other variables in the model. Thus, neoclassical theory is clearly supported by the work of both Taylor and Massey and Espinosa, but results suggest that, by itself, the wage differential does not constitute a complete explanation of the migration decision.

A third micro-analysis employed survey data from El Salvador gathered during the mid-to-late 1980s. Funkhouser (1992) estimated regression equations to predict wages that individuals could expect to earn in the USA and El Salvador given their personal characteristics. Rather than estimating instrumental variables, however, he simply demonstrated the existence of a differential in expected earnings between the USA and El Salvador, and then showed that educated, urban workers could expect a substantially larger earnings gain from US migration than poorly educated rural dwellers, especially when the fixed costs of movement were subtracted. Emigration was thus a more viable strategy for the urban middle class. He then presented survey evidence to support this conclusion: US migrants were differentially selected from the middle classes.

This conclusion is consistent with the results of an aggregate-level analysis by Jones (1989), who related levels of emigration from different Salvadorean provinces to various indicators of political violence and economic disruption. He found that political violence produced emigration only indirectly, by causing economic setbacks—sabotage, land disputes, strikes, abandonment, and disinvestment—which themselves promoted movement. As a result of the economic dislocations, poor rural villagers from the northern and central provinces migrated internally or to neighbouring countries, and better-off urban dwellers from the eastern provinces and the capital city of San Salvador migrated to the USA.

Funkhouser buttressed his neoclassical interpretation of the data with additional estimates showing that Salvadorean households were less likely to have members working locally when they had one or more members remitting money from the USA, and that the likelihood of withdrawing from the local labour force increased as the size of US remittances grew. Given the large direct effect of US migration in reducing the Salvadorean labour force (somewhere between 10 per cent and 15 per cent of the entire country had emigrated by 1988), the upward pressure on wages must have been substantial. He estimated aggregate and individual regressions to show that people living in areas with a high prevalence of US migrants could expect to earn significantly higher wages (4 per cent to 8 per cent higher) than those living elsewhere.

Given the scale of Mexican emigration to the USA, neoclassical theory would predict substantial upward pressure on wages in Mexico as well. According to Corona (1993), by 1990 at least 5 per cent of all people born in Mexico were living in the USA. Consistent with the upward pressure postulated by neoclassical theory, Gregory (1986) found a steady increase in Mexican real wages through the late 1970s in both rural and urban areas. During this time, the volume of emigration to the USA was growing, but the Mexican economic crisis of the 1980s had not yet begun. By the late 1970s, in fact, the Bank of Mexico was reporting rural labour shortages in core sending regions.

Thus, the accumulated empirical evidence generally supports neoclassical theory's fundamental proposition that immigration is tied to international differences in wage rates. In El Salvador, the people who migrated most frequently were people least affected by the political violence who could expect the greatest income gain from working in the USA. In Mexico, aggregate-level studies consistently find that transnational wage differentials strongly predict the volume and rate of emigration to the USA; and individual-level studies show that the probability of US emigration rises as expected income gains increase. In Puerto Rico, studies generally find a significant relationship between the volume of emigration and mainland–island wage differentials. There is also evidence, albeit inconclusive, of a migratory response to Puerto Rico's minimum wage hike in 1974.

It seems clear, therefore, that transnational migration is sensitive to gaps in wage rates between countries of origin and destination. It is also clear, however, that international migration is not fully explained by wage gaps alone. At the most general level, countries with the lowest wages relative to those in the USA are not necessarily the largest senders of migrants; and even after wage differentials are controlled, significant variation in the aggregate volume or individual likelihood of emigration remains unexplained.

Although migration decisions may be sensitive to international wage differentials, the accumulated empirical evidence suggests that they may not be the most important factor in determining migration decisions. Whereas wage variables are occasionally found to be insignificant in migration models (see Fleisher 1963), employment variables are *always* significant. In the studies we have reviewed, the effects of employment-related variables generally equalled or exceeded those of wage-related indicators.

As an example, Maldonado (1976) found that unemployment differentials completely dominated wage gaps in explaining migration between Puerto Rico and the US mainland. A neoclassical economist might argue that shifts in employment rates alter the distribution of expected wages and, hence, the distribution of expected net gains from migration, and that Maldonado's model simply captures this effect additively. But when we re-estimated Maldonado's model using the ratio of expected wages (wages times employment probabilities) rather than the ratio of absolute wages, the pattern of results remained the same: unemployment ratios still dominated expected wage ratios in predicting the flow of out-migrants to the mainland.

This result lends credence to the conclusions of Ramos (1992) and Castillo-Freeman and Freeman (1992), who argue that Puerto Rican migration is driven more by displacement arising from structural economic change than from yearly fluctuations in the wage gap. An alternative explanation advanced by Hatton and Williamson (1992) with respect to historical immigration to the USA is that unemployment rates determine the timing of migration and thus account for much of the year-to-year fluctuation in migration rates, but that wage differentials determine the underlying propensity to migrate and drive long-term trends. Unfortunately, no analyst has yet examined contemporary immigration patterns with the care and analytic skill that these analysts have devoted to the study of historical immigration flows.

The New Economics of Migration

DOES NOT ASSUME > COMPLETE WELL FUNC. MARKET LIKE NEO-

The new economics of migration argues that international migration stems from market failures that threaten the material well-being of households and create barriers to their economic advancement. Unlike the neoclassical model, the new economic model does not posit complete and well-functioning markets. Indeed, it recognizes that in many settings, particularly in the developing world, markets for capital, futures, and insurance may be absent, imperfect, or inaccessible. In order to self-insure against risks to income, production, and property, or to gain access to scarce investment capital, households send one or more workers to foreign labour markets. Given relatively high wages in developed countries, international migration offers an attractive and effective strategy for minimizing risks and overcoming capital constraints.

This theoretical view is consistent with a growing body of circumstantial evidence from the North American migratory system suggesting that poor households use international migration in a deliberate way to diversify their labour portfolios. The combination of foreign wage labour with local work and other economic activities has been documented for the Dominican Republic (Bray 1984; Georges 1990; Portes and Guarnizo 1990; Grasmuck and Pessar 1991), Puerto Rico (Jackson 1984; Hernández Cruz 1985, 1986; Rodríguez 1988), the English-speaking Caribbean (Palmer 1974; Rubenstein 1982*a*, 1983; Wood and McCoy 1985; Hope 1986; Levine 1987; Maingot 1991; Simmons and Guiengant 1992), Central America (Poitras 1980; Funkhouser 1992; United Nations 1991*b*), the Philippines (Griffiths 1979; McArthur 1979; Root and DeJong 1991) and, of course, Mexico (Reichert 1979, 1981, 1982; Mines 1981; Dinerman 1982; Roberts 1982; Massey *et al.* 1987; Grindle 1988; Durand and Massey 1992; Fletcher and Taylor 1992).

In these countries, it is clear that rural communities are not isolated, economically autonomous entities, if they ever were. Rather, they are closely connected to national and international markets and rely heavily on migrant earnings to support local investment and consumption. Adelman *et al.* (1989) found that inhabitants of one Mexican community consumed 37 per cent more goods and services than they produced, and that this 'trade deficit' was covered entirely by migrant remittances: 56 per cent from the USA and 44 per cent from the rest of Mexico. Massey and Parrado (1994) found that in some Mexican communities, the annual flow of remittances from the USA was greater than the yearly total of locally earned income. In other words, there were more US dollars circulating locally than the dollar equivalent of pesos.

Such linkages between families in sending regions and migrants working in foreign settings contradict the assumptions of the neoclassical human capital model. According to this model, individuals relocate permanently in whatever sector yields the highest expected lifetime income and play little role in the economic life of the community thereafter. Out-migration only influences the local economy through its effects on prices and incomes, shifting the supply of labour inward or outward and, hence, raising or lowering wages. Income transfers in the form of remittances are outside the realm of the traditional neoclassical framework.

In addition, neoclassical household models (such as those specified in Singh *et al.* 1986) do not allow income transfers to have non-unitary effects on the income of farm households: each additional dollar sent from abroad should increase household income by just one dollar. Because risk is disregarded and all markets are assumed to be complete and well functioning, production decisions are presumed to be independent of household budget constraints and other sources of income (Taylor 1992*a*). Migrant remittances increase the utility of households by loosening the budget constraint on consumption by the amount of the remittances; but unless relative prices change, they should not influence other income-generating activities. The increase in income simply produces a greater consumption of 'normal goods', given the household-farm budget constraint.

Leisure is one kind of normal good consumed by rural households, and farm families may employ hired labour (presumed to be a perfect substitute for family labour) in order to generate more leisure time for family members. But remittances should not affect the household's use of total labour or other inputs in production. As profit maximizers, farmers should use inputs only up to the point where the value of their marginal product equals their cost. Under neoclassical theory, migrant remittances do not alter this calculus unless they alter prices, which is generally ruled out in static models.

Recent work in rural Mexico suggests that these conditions do not hold. A detailed analysis of survey data from two communities in Michoacán by Taylor and colleagues shows that remittances increase the *productive use* of machinery, land, and hired labour by households (Fletcher and Taylor 1992). In addition, they promoted the *acquisition* of income-producing assets such as livestock, equipment, and education (Taylor and Wyatt 1996). As a result, remittances from the USA raised household income by more than the value of the remittances themselves, something not allowed under neoclassical theory (Taylor 1992*a*).

When Taylor (1992*a*) regressed household income on remittances, controlling for asset ownership, the resulting coefficient was 1.85, suggesting that each dollar remitted eventually brought in $1.85 in additional household income. This non-unitary effect occurred because a significant portion of the money was not spent on normal consumption goods (as allowed under neoclassical assumptions), but on income-producing assets (as predicted by new economic theory). Remittances are likely to be used for investment rather than consumption when access to capital is limited and when risk is a factor in family production decisions. Although they have not employed such detailed economic data or sophisticated analytic methods, several other investigators have likewise shown that Mexican households with US migrants channel a significant portion of their remittances into the accumulation of income-producing assets (Massey *et al.* 1987; Trigueros and Rodríguez 1988; Escobar and Martínez 1990; Massey and Parrado 1994; Durand *et al.* 1996).

High wages available in the USA thus offer Mexicans an incentive to migrate not only because they yield higher expected lifetime earnings, but also because they offer poor families a way to loosen liquidity constraints and manage risks. By migrating internationally, poor families are able to gain access to scarce capital and initiate new productive enterprises at low risk.

The new economics of migration has also challenged the neoclassical assumption that higher income has a uniform effect in promoting migration at all socio-economic levels. In the neoclassical view, individuals migrate to achieve an *absolute gain* in lifetime earnings: $100 in extra income means the same to each actor regardless of his or her position in the socio-economic hierarchy. Theorists of the new economics argue, in contrast, that households migrate not only to improve absolute income, but also to increase their incomes *relative* to others in the community. Through international migration, in other words, households attempt to ameliorate their sense of *relative deprivation*.

Relative deprivation depends on where a household is located in the income distribution: the greater the share of income earned by households above it, the greater the sense of relative deprivation. As a result, households located towards the bottom of the income distribution are more likely to migrate than those situated towards the top, and places with unequal distributions are more likely send out migrants than those where income is equally distributed. In other words, $100 in additional income provides more of an incentive to migrate for poor households located in skewed income distributions compared to poor households in equal distributions. The effect of a given expected income gain on behaviour is not uniform across socio-economic settings.

Stark and Taylor (1989) operationalize relative deprivation for a given household as the proportion of households in the income distribution with income greater than that of the household times the average amount by which these incomes exceed the household's income. When they included this measure of relative deprivation in a structural probit model predicting the probability of undocumented migration to the USA from the Pátzcuaro region of Michoacán, they found that it had a very strong and positive effect. Their analysis controlled for absolute household income, the income gain expected from US migration, and other individual and household variables.

Stark and Taylor (1991) also examined the degree to which relative deprivation predicted internal migration within Mexico. They hypothesized that internal migration should not be as effective in reducing relative deprivation because of the phenomenon of 'reference group substitution'. People who migrate to a Mexican urban area may generate remittances to improve their relative standing in the community, but they will also tend to compare themselves to urban Mexicans and to feel relatively deprived. Because Mexican rural and urban areas lie within a similar social, cultural, and economic setting, internal migrants end up substituting one reference group for another.

By migrating to the USA, however, migrants not only gain access to high wages and remittances capable of shifting their position in the local income distribution, they also move into a different society that constitutes a radically different frame of social and cultural reference. At least initially, they do not see themselves as part of the destination society and they view their menial work instrumentally as a tool, a means of earning money to enhance their status at home (see Piore 1979). Even though they understand that the jobs may be demeaning and poorly paid by US standards, they do not see those standards as applying to them because they do not imagine themselves to be part of US society; reference group substitution is minimized.

When Stark and Taylor (1991) estimated a multinomial logit model to predict the relative odds of migrating internally, internationally, or not at all, they found that relative deprivation significantly raised the likelihood of US migration but had no effect on the probability of internal migration, consistent with their line of reasoning. Even though absolute income had a significant effect, in accordance with neoclassical theory, the index of relative deprivation provided additional explanatory power to improve the model's overall predictability.

Thus, although wage differentials may provide one incentive for international migration, systematic tests suggest that wage gaps are not the only factor behind international movement. Holding constant the effect of expected income, international migration reduces the risks faced by households, it reduces the capital constraints they face in inaugurating production, and it offers a way to ameliorate feelings of being relatively deprived. Based on the evidence available to date, therefore, the new economics of migration and the neoclassical model appear to complement one another in explaining international migration; both models are 'correct' and either one by itself would constitute an incomplete explanation of international migration.

Segmented Labour Market Theory

In contrast to neoclassical and new economic theory, both of which view international migration as originating in rational calculations made by individuals and families responding to market forces, segmented labour market theory sees immigration as demand-driven, built into the economic structure of advanced industrial societies. Inherent tendencies in modern capitalism lead to a bifurcated labour market, creating a primary sector that produces jobs with secure tenure, high pay, generous benefits, and good working conditions, and a secondary sector typified by instability, low pay, limited benefits, and unpleasant or hazardous working conditions. Employers recruit immigrants to fill secondary sector positions because they are rejected by natives.

Although segmented labour market theory has received considerable attention in the research literature, most studies have not addressed the issue of immigration *per se*. For many years, social scientists worked to identify primary and secondary sectors empirically by factor analysing job and worker characteristics, or by comparing wage equations estimated across occupational and industrial categories (Dickens and Lang 1985). Although some studies found results consistent with segmented labour market theory (Osterman 1975; Buchele 1976; Wright 1979; Carnoy and Rumberger 1980; Tolbert *et al.* 1980), others did not (Bibb and Form 1977; Zucker and Rosenstein 1981) and by the early 1980s segmented labour market research ground to an inconclusive halt.

A serious problem with these early studies was the *ad hoc* way that sector membership was operationalized, leading to instability in empirical estimates and charges that the definition of sector membership usually made the 'finding' of lower returns to human capital in the secondary sector tautological (Hodson and Kaufman 1981). Some critics advocated discarding segmented labour market theory entirely (Cain 1976; Hodson and Kaufman 1982), but in the mid-1980s Dickens and Lang (1985) developed a novel methodological approach that overcame the logical flaws of earlier studies. Rather than attempting to operationalize sector membership in advance using a set of *ad hoc* criteria and complicated definitions, they specified a 'switching model' that simultaneously estimated an equation for sector attachment and two sector-specific wage equations.

Their estimates revealed that two wage equations defined by an estimated switching equation fit the data considerably better than a single wage equation estimated using ordinary least squares (Dickens and Lang 1985). Consistent with segmented labour market theory, the equation for the primary sector was characterized by significant returns to experience, schooling, and metropolitan residence, whereas the secondary sector equation showed no apparent returns to human capital. They also found that primary and secondary sector jobs were allocated largely on the basis of race, with blacks being excluded from the latter on the basis of non-economic criteria. Since the publication of this study, segmented labour market theory has gained new credibility (Dickens and Lang 1988) and dual-sector models have increasingly appeared in mainstream economics journals (McDonald and Solow 1985; Bulow and Summers 1986; Heckman and Hotz 1986).

Relatively few analysts have attempted to apply the segmented labour market model to the study of North American immigration. In general, the immigration policies of the USA and Canada reinforce labour market segmentation by creating barriers to mobility for unauthorized migrants (Taylor 1992*b*). Some indirect evidence comes from studies of wage attainment estimated for various groups of immigrants, but it is generally inconclusive. If immigrant workers were recruited into the secondary labour market to work at unstable, poorly paid jobs with few mobility prospects, as hypothesized by segmentation theorists, then we would expect to observe lower returns to education, skills, and work experience compared with natives.

Chiswick has carried out a series of studies using cross-sectional data on legal and illegal immigrants and has consistently found significant positive returns to human capital factors and a clear trajectory of rising wages with time spent in the USA (Chiswick 1978, 1979, 1984, 1988), a pattern observed also in Canadian data (see Chiswick and Miller 1988; Bloom and Gunderson 1991). In some cases, the rate of return exceeds that of natives. Although these findings appear to challenge segmented labour market theory, Borjas (1982, 1985, 1987) has criticized Chiswick's work on methodological grounds. Because he relies on cross-sectional data, his estimates confound the effects of human capital and time since arrival with trends in the quality of immigrant cohorts and changes in the pattern of selective emigration.

When data not subject to these limitations are employed to estimate wage regressions, studies have found attenuated effects of past labour market experience, education, and skills on US wage rates among Mexican immigrants working in the USA, consistent with the predictions of segmented labour market theory (Massey 1987*a*; Donato *et al.* 1992*a*; Donato and Massey 1993; Lindstrom and Massey 1994). The same studies, however, do find significant returns to improvements in English language ability and US experience.

These results are consistent with other studies showing that Mexican immigrants to the USA are negatively selected with respect to indicators of human capital, particularly education (Taylor 1986, 1987; Massey 1987*b*; Massey and García España 1987; Stark and Taylor 1991*a*). Because human capital is not rewarded in the US secondary labour market, Mexicans with skills and education have tended to migrate internally rather than internationally. This historical pattern, however, was disrupted in the 1980s by Mexico's economic crisis, which drastically reduced the returns to education in Mexico's economy. As a result, internal migrants are no longer positively selected with respect to education, and skilled Mexican workers have increasingly moved to the USA rather than to urban Mexico (Cornelius 1992; Fletcher and Taylor 1992).

The most direct and systematic test of segmented labour market theory was carried out by Portes and Bach (1985), who analysed the experience of Mexican and Cuban immigrants in the USA. The investigators interviewed respondents as they arrived in 1973–4, and then twice again in 1976 and 1979. They defined primary-sector workers as those working for non-Hispanic white (Anglo) employers in settings where the majority of other workers were also non-Hispanic and white. Secondary-sector workers were defined as those working for Anglo employers in places where the majority of the workers were Hispanic or black.

Mexican immigrants were generally incorporated into the secondary-sector after entry and remained there for the next six years with little intersector mobility. Those Mexicans who did manage to acquire primary-sector jobs did so on the basis of US experience and English language ability gained prior to entry in 1973 or 1974 (i.e. on earlier trips as undocumented migrants). Sector of employment was not related to education, but those Mexicans who worked in the primary sector earned significantly higher incomes than their counterparts in the secondary sector. Nonetheless, they experienced few returns to education, experience, or prior US residence. Immigrants in the secondary sector, in contrast, experienced gains in income from their work experience and prior US residence, but not from education.

Portes and Bach (1985) also analysed changes in occupational status within each sector, and the trajectory of occupational mobility conformed more closely to the predictions of segmented labour market theory. As work experience, education, and occupational aspirations rose among immigrants in the primary sector, so did the socio-economic status of their job; but only education predicted occupational status in the secondary sector and the rate of return to schooling was half that observed in the primary sector.

When they turned to analyse patters of wage and occupational attainment among Cuban immigrants, Portes and Bach (1985) had to modify dual labour theory to incorporate a third sector: the ethnic enclave. This sector includes Cubans who worked for a Cuban boss or owner, usually in a company where most workers were also Cuban immigrants. Consistent with the predictions of segmented labour market theory, the researchers found that Cubans employed in the primary sector experienced significant returns to English ability, education, and experience, but that the secondary sector provided few rewards for skills, experience, or education. The enclave sector, in contrast, replicated many of the features of the primary sector and provided Cuban immigrants with significant returns to education and experience.

The Cuban enclave consists of businesses located in and around Miami that are owned and operated by Cuban entrepreneurs (Wilson and Martin 1982; Portes and Stepick 1993). The existence of a large, concentrated Cuban population creates a demand for specialized cultural products and services that Cuban entrepreneurs are uniquely qualified to fill. In addition, their privileged access to the pool of low-wage immigrant labour gives them an advantage when competing with firms outside the enclave.

Immigrants working in the enclave are apparently willing to trade low wages upon arrival for a greater chance of advancement and independence later on (Portes and Bach 1985). This implicit contract between employers and workers stems from the norm of ethnic solidarity, which suffuses and supports the enclave (Portes and Manning 1986; Portes and Rumbaut 1990). Social networks and contact with other entrepreneurs launch new immigrants on independent careers in small business, and once established, these new entrepreneurs are expected to help and promote other immigrants in return. Since the existence of the enclave requires a steady stream of new immigrant workers willing to trade low initial wages for the possibility of later mobility, immigrant enclaves constitute another source of demand for immigrants stemming from the process of labour market segmentation.

Sanders and Nee (1987) attempted to apply enclave theory to Chinese immigrants in the San Francisco Bay Area. They defined the enclave to include Chinese living in the city of San Francisco and found that whereas entrepreneurs received higher returns to human capital in the enclave than outside of it, manual workers did not, causing the investigators to question, or at least modify, the enclave version of segmented labour market theory. But Portes and Jensen (1987) countered that enclave membership could not be defined on the basis of residence; rather it depends on the ethnicity of one's employer. As they point out, many Cubans live in Miami (the home of the Cuban enclave) but work for Anglo employers alongside Anglo workers (in the primary sector) or for Anglo employers alongside minority workers (in the secondary sector).

When Portes and Jensen (1989) re-estimated the three-sector model and incorporated data on the most recent wave of post-1980 Cuban immigrants, they replicated the earlier findings of Portes and Bach. They found that enclave membership conferred a different pattern of benefits for Cuban men and women, however. Although ethnic enterprise provided an effective path of economic mobility for Cuban males, there was no such path for Cuban females, although they did receive higher net earnings compared to women working in other sectors.

Zhou and Logan (1989) examined Chinese immigrants in New York City and sought to avoid the definitional problems of Sanders and Nee; they used three alternative definitions of enclave membership: employment-based, residence-based, and industry-based. When they compared the experience of Chinese men and women, they found that females received no returns to human capital characteristics within the enclave, whether as entrepreneurs or workers, but that male immigrants working in the enclave were able to covert human capital into earnings at a rate comparable with those in the non-enclave economy, and that male entrepreneurs achieved significantly greater returns to human capital in the enclave than elsewhere.

Research thus suggests that urban labour markets in the USA are, in fact, segmented, but in cities with large immigrant populations they may be divided into three sectors rather than two, as originally hypothesized by Piore (1979). Logan *et al.* (1994) have recently attempted to identify other ethnic enclaves in cities throughout the USA. They examined five Asian and three Hispanic groups in seventeen metropolitan areas and found that enclaves were confined to a few low-wage industries with low capitalization, low levels of unionization, and large numbers of female workers. The typical immigrant enclave consisted of a combination of apparel manufacturing and ethnic food-processing; but three enclaves stood out for their unusual size and diversity: the Cuban economy of Miami, the Japanese economy of Honolulu, and the Korean economy of Los Angeles.

The accumulated evidence thus appears to indicate that US labour markets are indeed segmented, that immigrants are selectively excluded from the primary labour market and found disproportionately in the secondary labour market where they earn limited returns to education, skills, and experience, and that immigrant enclaves provide significant returns to human capital and an alternative mobility ladder for immigrants in some cities, especially for male entrepreneurs. Confidence in these conclusions must be guarded, however, because most studies have not distinguished between primary and secondary labour markets in comparing the enclave with the mainstream economy and none has employed the switching regression model of Dickens and Lang (1985). In addition, none has attempted to apply the enclave model to the largest immigrant group in the USA, Mexicans, despite the fact that Los

Angeles, San Diego, El Paso, Houston, San Antonio, and Chicago all carry the demographic potential for enclave formation.

One area of extensive Mexican employment is US agriculture (see Mines *et al.*, 1992), but recent research casts doubt on whether enclave theory applies to the agrarian economy at all. In the USA, Mexican immigrant farmworkers increasingly are hired not by the growers themselves, but through labour contractors who are almost all Mexican. As employers in their own right, Mexican labour contractors might be considered to constitute an ethnic enclave nested within US agriculture. Rather than constituting an enclave, however, Mexican labour contractors appear to function as a niche in the secondary labour market of US rural areas (Vandemann *et al.* 1991; Taylor 1992*b*).

In general, contractors serve as revolving-door employers of new immigrants, paying significantly lower wages, offering fewer benefits, and providing less security compared to workers hired directly by growers, who are primarily Anglos. Rather than providing a mobility ladder for fellow immigrants, Mexican labour contractors are more likely to exploit the workers they employ than to offer opportunities for advancement. This state of affairs stems from the sharp asymmetry in market power between contractors and growers. As a result, the former are forced to extract a nearly invisible profit margin by exploiting a steady flow of new, undocumented workers from abroad (Taylor 1992*b*). Mexican farm labour contractors are the agents through which growers secure access to workers to fill the lowest-skilled, seasonal farm jobs at low cost.

The use of farm labour contractors was given impetus by the passage of the 1986 Immigration Reform and Control Act, which enacted penalties against employers who 'knowingly' hire undocumented workers. Contractors serve as an effective buffer between the growers and US immigration authorities (Martin and Taylor 1991; Taylor and Thilmany 1993). Since the contractors are usually legal immigrants, and the growers hire the contractors and not the farmworkers, farmers are protected from legal sanctions even though they may rely exclusively on an undocumented workforce. Labour contractors absorb the risk of sanctions, and for this service they extract a portion of the undocumented migrants' wages in compensation. In the same way, the contractors also shield growers from the requirements of US labour law.

Another failure of segmented labour market research is that it has not clearly linked immigration to a demand for unskilled workers arising from the intrinsic characteristics of the secondary labour market. According to Piore (1979), the principal means by which this demand is expressed is through foreign labour recruitment. Although some US immigrant flows clearly began in this way—including those from Mexico (Galarza 1964; Kiser and Woody 1979; Reisler 1976; Calavita 1992), the Philippines (McArthur 1979; Wong 1986), and Puerto Rico (Piore 1977)—others appear to have arisen spontaneously without the substantial involvement of labour recruiters (such as Korea, the Dominican Republic, and Colombia); and several other important immigrant flows (from Cuba, Vietnam, and Russia) began not through labour recruitment, but through refugee movements (see Zolberg *et al.* 1989; Schmeidl 1997).

A weaker statement of Piore's (1979) theory is that immigration is largely demand-driven, whether or not recruitment actually occurred. In statistical analyses that include variables defined for both sending and receiving nations, therefore, the latter should dominate in explanatory power; but this generally has not been the case. Frisbie (1977) found that farm wages and agricultural productivity in Mexico had a greater effect on illegal migration to the USA than farm wages and productivity in the USA. Likewise, Jenkins (1977) found that push factors in Mexico, taken together, were stronger than pull factors in the USA; and Blejer *et al.* (1977) found that most of the variation in size of immigrant flow between Mexico and the USA was explained by the rate of Mexican unemployment. Holding constant economic conditions in both countries, Bean *et al.* (1991) showed that the size of the undocumented flow was strongly predicted by the number of Mexicans of labour-force age, but Massey and Espinosa (1997) found that employment growth, while positively related to the odds of undertaking initial and repeated illegal trips to the USA, was not very strong in its effect.

In summary, although US labour markets generally appear to be divided into primary and secondary sectors as predicted by Piore (1979), and while under rather special conditions some urban labour markets may be further segmented into an immigrant enclave as posited by Portes and Bach (1985), it is not clear that labour market segmentation explains all or most of the demand for immigrants. Recruitment represents one of several possible inducements to migrate, but immigration flows are also related to wage differentials, capital constraints, and risk diversification, as discussed above. While segmented labour market theory complements the neoclassical and new economic models of migration, it clearly does not supplant them.

World Systems Theory

World systems theory argues that international migration follows directly from the globalization of the market economy. As capitalism extends outwards from core nations in Europe, North America, Oceania, and Japan, and as market relations penetrate countries of the developing and former communist world, non-capitalist patterns of social and economic organization are disrupted and transformed. In the process of market penetration, however, large numbers of people are displaced from secure livelihoods as peasant farmers, family artisans, and employees of state-owned industries, creating a mobilized population prone to migrate, both internally and internationally.

The expansion of the market economy into ever-farther reaches of the globe is directed and coordinated from a relatively small number of global cities (Castells 1989; Sassen 1991). These sites manage production processes that are increasingly decentralized and scattered, with labour-intensive operations being located in low-wage countries and capital-intensive processes being allocated to high-wage areas. This geographic division of labour emerged gradually after the Second World War, but accelerated after 1973, when profit margins fell and capital accumulation stagnated as a result of recession and inflation in core capitalist nations (Harvey 1990). The globalization of production, in turn, put downward pressure on wages, working conditions, and employment levels among workers with limited skills and educations.

Although low-skill workers saw their prospects dim as a result of economic globalization, those of high-skill workers brightened. Managing a global economy generates a strong demand for expertise in electronics, education, telecommunications, banking, finance, insurance, law, government, and science, and highly educated workers migrate to global cities to fill this demand. The congregation of high-income workers and wealthy capitalists in global cities creates a demand for ancillary workers in restaurants, hotels, construction, maintenance, and personal services. Since natives are reluctant to accept onerous jobs at low pay, and since service jobs cannot easily be shifted overseas, employers recruit immigrants into these positions. Once immigrant communities become established, they create their own jobs that further accentuate the demand for immigrant labour.

Although immigrants are drawn to global cities because of a demand that is built into the structure of the international economy, their movement is facilitated by lines of transportation and communication that arise to connect global cities to production sites and markets overseas, and by cultural links that stem from the penetration of capitalist cultural products and social attitudes into peripheral societies. Thus, processes of economic globalization at once creates a pool of mobile workers in developing countries and simultaneously connects them to labour markets in particular cities where their services are demanded.

The functioning of a global market economy is predicated on the existence of a stable international system conducive to capitalist social and economic relations. The process of capital accumulation that drives economic growth in core nations benefits greatly from unhindered access to markets and natural resources scattered around the globe. In the past, this need for access and stability led European powers to impose colonial regimes on much of Asia, Latin America, and Africa. More recently, Europe, and especially the USA, have pursued diplomatic and military means to preserve the integrity of the international system, and thereby to protect overseas investments, ensure continued access to natural resources, defend lanes of transportation and communication, support political allies, and maintain sympathetic pro-capitalist regimes (Zolberg *et al.* 1989; Rumbaut 1991, 1992).

The colonial systems established by Europe in the eighteenth and nineteenth centuries proved not to be politically viable after 1945, and in the ensuing wave of decolonization, international migrants were created in large numbers (Zolberg *et al.* 1989). Some of these migrants were colonialists and their descendants who returned to Europe; others were refugees who sought to escape sectarian violence and ethnic persecution by fleeing to a neighbouring country; and still others were colonial subjects who sought to settle in the core power because of close ties stemming from prior military service, government employment, foreign education, or intermarriage.

Although decolonization and national consolidation were particularly disruptive and prone to the production of immigrants, other political events associated with the preservation and maintenance of the global political economy have also contributed to the international flow of migrants. Foreign policies and military interventions frequently go awry, leading to new flows of refugees directed to core capitalist nations. Even in the absence of military or political setbacks, the deployment of military personnel around the world creates social and economic connections that promote immigration to core countries (Rumbaut 1991, 1992).

Although considerable empirical information has been presented in association with world systems theory, the data marshalled to date tend to be illustrative rather than analytic. Theorists have presented facts consistent with the world systems model, yet key propositions generally have not been subject to systematic tests against competing hypotheses. With a few exceptions, analysts have not sought to link the ebbs and flows in the volume of immigration across time or between countries to indicators of market penetration in developing regions, nor to the emergence of world cities in industrial nations, nor to military or political entanglements overseas.

Although their study is rooted in neoclassical economics, Hatton and Williamson (1994*a*) carry out an analysis that is relevant to hypotheses derived from world systems theory. They analysed data from eleven European countries during the late nineteenth and early twentieth centuries and examined the relationship between annual emigration and four theoretical variables: the share of each country's male labour force working in agriculture (an indicator of industrialization); the ratio of real wages at home and in destination countries (an indicator of the size of the wage gap); the rate of natural increase two decades earlier (an indicator of demographic pressure); and the relative number of emigrants already in the destination country (an indicator of network effects).

They found that most European countries experienced an 'emigration cycle' characterized by an upswing in out-migration rates followed by a levelling off and then a downswing (see Ackerman 1976). Different variables predominated in explaining emigration at different phases of the cycle. Out-migration early in the cycle was caused by industrialization acting upon large cohorts of new workers. As out-migration grew, this effect was reinforced by a rising stock of migrants living abroad (the network effect discussed below). During the plateau and downswing phases of the cycle, the forces of industrialization and demography weakened and fluctuations in the flow of emigrants became linked to the size of wage gap between sending and receiving countries.

Additional evidence linking economic development to emigration comes from contemporaneous studies carried out in Mexico. Roberts (1982) examined four agrarian communities located in different regions and found that the effects of agricultural development depended on the distribution and quality of farmland. When commercial crops and capital-intensive methods were introduced into areas with good soil, irrigated land, and an even distribution of farmland, rural incomes rose, risks to household income fell, and out-migration decreased; but when market-oriented development was introduced into regions with poor soil, irregular rainfall, and an unequal distribution of farmland, rural incomes fell and risks rose, leading families to diversify their incomes through international migration.

Arroyo and colleagues likewise showed that the introduction of commercial agriculture into poorly developed rural areas of the Mexican state of Jalisco promoted out-migration, whereas its insertion into well-developed rural areas and semi-urban areas did not (Arroyo 1989; Arroyo *et al.* 1990). Thompson *et al.* (1986) similarly found that the development of a fresh export tomato industry in the state of Sinaloa was not sufficient to reduce undocumented emigration to the USA, and that unless there were a shift in development policies, the liberalization of Mexico's agrarian sector could be expected to increase the pressures for out-migration. Zabin and Hughes (1995) argue that the employment of Mexicans in export agriculture lowers the costs and risks of US migration in two ways: by exposing them to more diverse social networks and information about the USA, and by providing stable, albeit low-wage employment to women and children, thereby allowing male household heads to migrate with lower risk to the family.

One study has examined the effect of agricultural modernization on out-migration in the Philippines. Findley (1987) demonstrated that the extent of agricultural commercialization had a significant positive effect on the likelihood of out-migration to Hawaii or Manila, but that it interacted with a community's general level of infrastructure. The relationship was strongest in communities with a high degree of social and economic infrastructure (many shops, stores, petrol stations, hospitals, clinics, and family-planning units), weaker in areas with a medium level of infrastructure development, and negative in communities with little infrastructure to offer.

The available evidence thus suggests that industrialization and agricultural development (indicators of capitalist market penetration) are instrumental in initiating migratory flows, as predicted by world systems theory, particularly when they occur under unfavourable demographic and agrarian conditions and near communities that are well connected to the larger world. The displacement of workers through development sets off a process whereby individuals and families search for higher wages and more diverse sources of income, and over time, fluctuations in the size of the outflow become more strongly connected to international differentials in wage rates.

Ricketts (1987) has studied the process of market penetration more directly by examining the effect of US direct foreign investment on the rate of out-migration to the USA from eighteen Caribbean nations. Direct foreign investment was named by Sassen (1988) as a leading indicator of capitalist market penetration and the principal cause of emigration. Ricketts found that the annual rate of out-migration to the USA from 1970 to 1979 was strongly related to the growth in US investment from 1966 to 1977. This strong relationship persisted when he controlled for size of country, per capita income, and the rate of population growth, and the relationship was not significantly affected by the inclusion or exclusion of outliers from his sample of nations.

Massey and Espinosa (1997) found, however, that annual rates of growth in direct foreign investment in Mexico were *negatively* related to the likelihood of first or repeat migration to the USA; but while they measured out-migration at the individual level, they could only measure investment trends for the nation as a whole. Foreign investment, however, is often targeted to export-processing zones that offer exemptions from tariffs on goods produced for export, such as the maquila zones established in Mexico before the ratification of the North American Free Trade Agreement (Wilson 1992). Owing to the absence of data, the Massey and Espinosa study did not assess the effects of such regionally targeted investment. In keeping with world systems theory, however, they did find that out-migration was greatest from communities with high wages and high levels of female employment in manufacturing (i.e. those that were most developed), and not poor, economically marginal communities.

Sassen (1988) and other world systems theorists have argued that the establishment of export-processing zones contributes to international migration by producing goods that compete with those made locally; by feminizing the workforce without providing factory-based employment opportunities for men; and by socializing women for industrial work and modern consumption without providing a lifetime income capable of meeting these needs. The result is the creation of a population that is socially and economically uprooted and prone to migration. When Davila and Saenz (1990) examined the effect of maquiladora employment on the monthly flow of Mexican undocumented immigrants to the USA, however, they found a *negative* relationship: employment growth in the maquila sector was followed by a reduction of undocumented migration one month later.

None of the foregoing studies has examined the theoretical notion of global cities, a key element of world systems theory. Friedmann (1986) has put forth a set of theoretical criteria by which such cities might be identified empirically: the existence of a major financial centre, the presence of a transnational corporate headquarters, the presence of an international organization, the rapid growth of business services, the importance of the city as a manufacturing centre, its importance as a transportation node, and its population size. When he applied these criteria to the USA, he identified three primary global cities (New York, Chicago, and Los Angeles) and three secondary global cities (Miami, Houston, and San Francisco).

Circumstantial evidence clearly suggests a strong link between these six global cities and immigration to the USA. According to the US Immigration and Naturalization Service (1993), New York received more immigrants in 1992 than any other metropolitan area in the USA, followed in rank order by Los Angeles, Miami, Chicago, San Francisco, Washington, and Houston. In other words, the three primary global cities identified by Friedmann were ranked 1, 2, and 4 in terms of immigration, and the three secondary global cities were ranked 3, 5, and 7. The flow of immigrants into these six metropolitan areas averaged 14,000 during 1992, but the average number of immigrants going to the remaining metropolitan areas was under 2,300. In the USA, therefore, immigration is overwhelmingly directed to global cities.

The only global city that Friedmann (1986) identified in Canada was Toronto, which he classified as a secondary global city. According to Statistics Canada (1992), Toronto attracted some 30 per cent of the nation's 214,230 immigrants. After Toronto, the next largest cities are Montreal and Vancouver, which attracted 12 per cent and 11 per cent of all immigrants, respectively. Thus, roughly a third of all immigrants go to Canada's only recognized global metropolis, and another third go to the second- and third-ranked cities. Obviously, Canadian immigration is directed towards those urban areas most strongly linked to the international economy.

Walker *et al.* (1993) analysed patterns of internal and international migration to the USA in an effort to confirm the labour market dynamics hypothesized by world systems theorists. If high-paying blue-collar jobs are being reallocated to low-wage regions abroad, and labour markets within global cities are bifurcating into low-wage and high-wage sectors, then we should observe immigrants and white-collar workers entering global cities in large numbers as blue-collar workers depart. Further down the urban hierarchy, we should observe the entry of blue-collar workers and the out-migration of white-collar workers combined with little or no immigration.

This pattern is essentially what Walker and his colleagues observed in their analysis of internal and international migration from 1975 to 1980 across urban areas of the USA. Immigration flows were directed towards metropolitan areas that were experiencing a rapid growth in value-added (i.e. global cities), but the arrival of immigrants and the rapid growth in high value-added production were associated with a strong out-migration of blue-collar workers. The migration of white-collar workers was, in turn, linked to a high growth in value added but was not strongly affected by the rate of immigration. Comparable results were obtained by White and Imai (1992) using a simpler model, and by Wright *et al.* (1997) in their analysis of 1985–90 flows. The latter concluded that the out-migration of native workers and the in-migration of foreign workers both stemmed from the same underlying factor: industrial restructuring.

These patterns correspond closely to state-level results reported by Frey (1994), who found that six key US states—California, New York, Texas, New Jersey, Illinois, and Massachusetts—attracted large numbers of international migrants and skilled native white workers but lost poor whites. Florida contradicted the general pattern of immigrant-receiving states by attracting all kinds of movers, immigrants as well as white- and blue-collar native workers.

As Rumbaut (1991) has pointed out, there is also strong circumstantial evidence linking US immigration to American military and foreign policy entanglements overseas. Of the top fifteen US immigrant-sending countries in 1992, five of the flows could be tied to a military presence, a political misadventure, or a military defeat: Vietnam, the Philippines, El Salvador, Korea, and Iran; and three more could be linked in some fashion to US foreign policy concerns: the Soviet Union, Poland, and China (US Immigration and Naturalization Service 1993). Arrivals from these eight countries comprised 37 per cent of all immigrants to the USA.

Geopolitical concerns apparently played a key role in the initiation of migration between the Dominican Republic and the USA. Before 1961 annual emigration from that country averaged only a few hundred people per year, but afterwards it mushroomed to over 10,000. In his memoirs, Ambassador John B. Martin (1966) relates how top US officials asked that he speed up visa-processing and loosen restrictions to allow more emigration after 1961. Fearing political instability and gains by left-wing political factions in the wake of dictator Rafael Trujillo's assassination, the US government sought to reduce political tensions by using emigration as a 'safety valve' (Georges 1990; Grasmuck and Pessar 1991). This intervention was followed in 1965 by a full-scale invasion and occupation by US armed forces, and by 1966 the Dominican Republic was receiving more US aid per capita than any country but Vietnam (Black 1986).

Several statistical analyses have sought to quantify the connection between immigration and the presence of a US military base. Jasso and Rosenzweig (1990) estimated a multivariate model across a variety of countries to demonstrate that the presence of a base significantly increases the number of persons admitted as wives and husbands of US citizens, the proportion of females among immigrants admitted as spouses of US citizens, and the size of a country's visa backlog. Likewise, Donato (1991) has shown that the number of men stationed in a country strongly predicts the proportion of women in the immigrant flow.

Thus, the limited empirical research that has been carried out to date is generally supportive of world systems theory, but its theoretical propositions generally have not received sufficient analytic attention and it is difficult to draw firm conclusions at this time. Although the paradigm yields clear and researchable hypotheses, with the exception of studies by Ricketts (1987),

Walker *et al.* (1993), Massey and Espinosa (1997), and Wright *et al.* (1997), relatively little has been done to test these propositions systematically, and even less has been done to contrast them with competing theoretical models.

The Perpetuation of International Migration

Social Capital Theory

Social capital emanates from migrant networks. These are interpersonal ties that link migrants, former migrants, and potential migrants in origin and destination areas through the connections of kinship, friendship, and shared community origin. The existence of these ties is hypothesized to increase the likelihood of emigration by lowering the costs, raising the benefits, and mitigating the risks of international movement. Networks thus constitute a valuable source of social capital that people draw upon to gain access to foreign employment and the economic benefits it brings (Choldin 1973; MacDonald and MacDonald 1974; Boyd 1989; Gurak and Caces 1992; Ho 1993).

The effect of social ties on rates and probabilities of emigration has been convincingly demonstrated by many analysts using a variety of datasets and methodologies. Students of historical migration between Europe and the USA have long recognized a 'family and friends effect', whereby the concentration of particular nationality groups in certain cities or regions dramatically increases the probability that other members of the same group will migrate there (Levy and Wadycki 1973). Whenever the number of prior immigrants or co-ethnics has been included as a regressor in aggregate models of immigration flows, analysts have found that it strongly predicts the rate of migration to the country, region, or city in question (Nelson 1959; Gallaway and Vedder 1971; Dunlevy and Gemery 1977, 1978; Dunlevy 1992; Hatton and Williamson 1994*a*).

One study has examined settlement patterns among contemporary immigrants to Canada and two others have done so for recent immigrants to the USA. In the Canadian case, Simmons (1989) regressed a variety of independent variables on the number of immigrants who arrived in Canada from sixty-six countries between 1980 and 1982. He found that the number of immigrants sent by a country in this period was very strongly and positively predicted by the size of the national-origin community already present in Canada by 1980. In his analysis of the USA, Dunlevy (1991) estimated a different sort of model: he sought to predict the State of destination for immigrants from eleven Caribbean and Latin American nations in 1987. In addition to the stock of each country's immigrants already resident in the State, he also measured each State's average income, urbanization, black percentage, mean temperature, distance to sending country, population, and border location. For most groups, the size of the migrant stock was the most important predictor of immigrant location, and once this variable was included in the equation, the effects of other variables fell to insignificance or were markedly reduced.

Walker and Hannan (1989) undertook a similar analysis, but their model was dynamic rather than static and allowed the effect of the migrant stock to change over time. They estimated a pooled cross-section time-series model for eleven nationality groups across fifty metropolitan areas from 1970 through 1979. Their model specified time-varying effects for income, employment, migrant stock, and lagged migration. Not only did they find strong evidence of a friends and family effect; they also determined that it varied over time and across countries. For three new immigrant groups—Mexico, Jamaica, and the Dominican Republic—the effect of migrant stock grew stronger over time while the sensitivity of the streams to prior conditions diminished, thereby confirming the dynamic self-perpetuating nature of network migration.

This dynamic pattern of results is consistent with individual-level results developed by Massey (1987*b*). Using data gathered in four Mexican communities, he found that the likelihood of undertaking a first trip to the USA was increased by having a father with US migrant experience, but that it was also related to landlessness and to personal characteristics such as age, sex, education, and occupational status. The probability of undertaking subsequent trips, however, was unrelated to these individual or household characteristics; it depended entirely on the migratory experience of the individual and his social connection to other migrants. Over time, therefore, the migration decision became increasingly disconnected from social and economic conditions in the community and determined more by the accumulation of migration-related human capital and social capital in the form of network connections.

A number of other studies from Mexico, the Caribbean, and Central America suggest that having a social tie to someone living in the USA, or to someone with prior US migrant experience, dramatically increases the probability of international movement. Many investigators have presented case studies documenting the growth and formation of migrant networks and their role in promoting international migration, including Weist (1973, 1979, 1984), Mines (1981, 1984), Dinerman (1982), Fjellman and Gladwin (1985), López (1986, 1988), Massey *et al.* (1987), Chavez (1988, 1990), Georges (1990), Grasmuck and Pessar (1991), Vega *et al.* (1991), Hagan (1994), and Kyle (1995). One study has documented how private community-based organizations may also constitute a source of social capital for undocumented migrants seeking to perpetuate their stay in the USA (Hagan and Gonzalez Baker 1993). Fewer researchers have demonstrated the importance of migrant networks quantitatively using representative data and multivariate models that include appropriate statistical controls.

Massey and García España (1987) employed a national sample of rural Mexican communities to show that the probability of emigration to the USA was strongly elevated by living in a household containing a prior US migrant or in a community where a large proportion of the people had been to the

USA. These two network indicators were the strongest effects in their model, dominating all other social and economic indicators.

Kossoudji (1992) did not seek to establish a link between networks and migration *per se*, but using a national sample of returned US migrants, she documented that the existence of network connections changed migratory behaviour. Specifically, she found that migrants with access to networks returned home sooner than those without such access. Being confident of their ability to come and go with ease, and to gain access to US employment whenever they needed it, migrants with strong network connections tended to take shorter and more frequent trips.

Taylor and colleagues documented the powerful effect of network connections directly using survey data from two communities in Michoacán, Mexico. Taylor defined a US network connection to exist whenever a close relative was living in the USA at the beginning of the observation period. He found that the possession of such a tie strongly increased the odds of migrating to the USA during this period, controlling for the expected US–village earnings differential, household income, family size, age, sex, and prior migrant experience (Taylor 1987). When he examined the effects of US versus Mexican network ties, he found that US network connections strongly predicted international migration while Mexican ties predicted internal migration, again controlling for household size, number of workers, income, wealth, sex age, education, and past migratory experience (Taylor 1986). This finding also held up when an additional control for relative deprivation was added to the model (Stark and Taylor 1991*b*).

In their event history analysis of out-migration from twenty-five Mexican communities, Massey and Espinosa (1997) found that social ties to people with prior migrant experience were among the most important factors in predicting whether or not a respondent decided to migrate to the USA in the first place, or to undertake repeated trips, and that the size of the network effects greatly exceeded what would be predicted by neoclassical economics (the differential in expected wages) or segmented labour market theory (US employment growth).

Even after controlling for the leading predictors of other theories, therefore, network connections strongly predict the likelihood of international movement. In a related paper, Espinosa and Massey (1997) carried these analyses one step further by defining networks as continuous variables rather than dichotomous connections. They conceptualized networks as a form of social capital and found that as the quality and quantity of social ties to US migrants increased, US wages and hours of work rose among Mexican immigrants, thereby increasing the potential returns from undocumented migration. Consistent with this fact, they found that the odds of making an initial US trip rose strongly as the amount of social capital increased.

Other studies also suggest that network connections carry the potential to increase significantly the economic benefits of foreign wage labour, and hence to raise the incentives for migration. Massey (1987*a*) found that having a social tie to a migrant family member significantly increased wage rates among immigrants from four Mexican communities; and using a larger random sample of ten Mexican communities, Donato *et al.* (1992*a*) discovered that family connections in the USA not only raised immigrants' wages, but also their hours of work and total monthly incomes. Greenwell *et al.* (1997) found that having kin contacts in the workplace increased the wages of male Salvadoreans and Filipinos in Los Angeles, but not females. Within the secondary sector, however, women's wages were higher and men's lower when working with relatives. They also found that network connections mediated the effect of human capital among men: those with good English skills earned more when they had social ties in the USA but those with poor skills earned less. In her study of Latin American domestic workers in Los Angeles, Hondagneu-Sotelo (1994*a*) found that network connections permitted women to exert more leverage in negotiating jobs with their employers.

Several investigators have examined the effect of migrant networks in the Philippines using a household survey of Ilocos Norte, a region with a long history of out-migration to Manila and Hawaii. DeJong *et al.* (1983) found that having family members in Hawaii strongly increased respondents' stated intentions of migrating there; and Findley (1987) showed that people in families with prior migrant experience were much more likely to make a trip to Manila or Hawaii than people in families without such experience. She also found that families living in communities with a high prevalence of former migrants were more likely to send out migrants themselves than families in places with few migrants. Finally, Root and DeJong (1991) found that households in direct contact with relatives living outside the community were more likely to export migrants than households not in direct contact with non-resident relatives.

In the USA, a literature on the 'immigrant multiplier effect' has recently developed. US law allocates most immigrant visas on the basis of a family tie to someone already in the USA (see Jasso and Rosenzweig 1990). People who are legal resident aliens of the USA gain the right to petition for the entry of spouses and children, subject to certain numerical restrictions; and immigrants who naturalize to US citizenship gain the right to petition for the entry of their spouses, unmarried children, and parents without numerical restriction, and for the entry of their married children and siblings (and their spouses and children) subject to numerical restriction.

By allocating visas along family lines, US law thus reinforces and formalizes the operation of migrant networks. Studies show that each new immigrant creates a large pool of potential immigrants, but that much of the potential is not realized (Arnold *et al.* 1989; Teitelbaum 1989; Jasso and Rosenzweig 1990; Liu *et al.* 1991). The gap between the theoretical number of relatives who might enter and the number who actually do enter occurs for several reasons: low rates of naturalization in many groups, the fact that some family members are already in the USA, and the fact that not all family members seek to exercise their rights of US entry.

Although family chaining may not be as great as theoretically possible, however, it is nonetheless significant. Jasso and Rosenzweig (1986) estimate the immigrant multiplier is around 1.2 for each immigrant worker. That is, for each new immigrant admitted as a labourer rather than a relative, 1.2 additional immigrants can be expected to arrive within ten years. Arnold *et al.* (1989) calculate that for each new Filipino immigrant, one additional family member will arrive in the future, and for each Korean immigrant, 0.5 family members will eventually come. As a result, even though immigrant flows often begin selectively with skilled workers, over time they tend to broaden out, become less selective, and ultimately become dominated by relatives making use of family reunification provisions.

The potential for future immigration through such multiplier effects is suggested by the long backlog for legal entry visas from many countries. This backlog includes people who qualify for legal entry as family members, but who must wait their turn until a numerically restricted visa becomes available. As of 1985, the visa backlog was 362,395 from the Philippines, 142,434 from India, 134,778 from Korea, and 112,843 from China (Jasso and Rosenzweig 1990). In all of these countries the backlog was growing, not declining. The potential for network-based emigration is particularly strong in Mexico: its 1985 visa backlog stood at 366,820 and one-half of all respondents to a 1989 national survey said they had relatives living in the USA (Camp 1993: 45).

The evidence accumulated so far is thus strong and consistent in confirming the powerful role played by migrant networks in structuring individual and household migration decisions, and in promoting and directing aggregate flows of immigrants. Indicators of migrant stock consistently predict settlement patterns of immigrants to the USA in both historical and contemporary data, and the possession of a kinship connection to a current or former international migration increases the odds that individuals or families will become involved in international migration themselves. Nonetheless, results thus far have come from a relatively small number of community case studies and a small number of quantitative analyses from a limited range of countries and datasets. In particular, more and better research on non-Mexican samples is clearly needed to confirm the generality of findings.

Cumulative Causation

Cumulative causation refers to the tendency for international migration to perpetuate itself over time, regardless of the conditions that originally caused it. At the individual level, this self-perpetuation stems from the fact that each act of migration alters motivations and perceptions in ways that encourage additional migration. Migrants are changed by the experience of living and working in an advanced industrial economy. The knowledge and skills they acquire increase their productivity and raise their value to employers, and thereby elevate their expected wages. Through migration, they also gain valuable information about how to arrive, get around, and find work, thereby reducing the costs and risks of movement. In addition, they acquire tastes for modern consumer goods and new aspirations for socio-economic mobility, thus changing their motivations. As a result of these changes, people who migrate once are quite likely to do so again. Although international migration may begin as a short-term strategy for income generation, one trip leads to another and, over time, the duration of trips grows and foreign experience accumulates (Piore 1979). *Cumulative Causation*

This line of reasoning is consistent with data from the Philippines, which shows that the probability of migration is strongly increased by having prior migrant experience (DeJong *et al.* 1983; Findley 1987; Root and DeJong 1991). In addition, a variety of studies from Mexico show that the odds of US migration rise sharply as the amount of prior US experience grows (Taylor 1986, 1987; Massey 1987*b*; Massey *et al.* 1987; Stark and Taylor 1991*a*, 1991*b*). Massey (1985) has also shown that once Mexican men have migrated internationally, the odds are very high—at least 60 per cent—that they will migrate again, and that the probability of making an additional trip rises with each trip already taken (Massey *et al.* 1987; Massey and Liang 1989; Donato *et al.* 1992*b*; Espinosa and Massey 1997).

Thus, the more US trips one has taken and the more international experience one has accumulated, the more one is likely to continue migrating. As the number of trips multiplies and their length increases, migrants also acquire more social and economic ties to the destination country and display a growing tendency towards settlement (Massey 1985; Massey *et al.* 1987). Proclivities for cumulative causation at the individual level thus lead to changes at the social structural level—the formation of branch communities at points of destination—sowing the seeds for the emergence of an ethnic enclave to act as an additional magnet for future immigration (Portes and Bach 1985; Portes and Manning 1986). *C.C. = Network Formation*

Processes of cumulative causation at the individual level lead to other mechanisms of self-perpetuation at the social structural level, one of the most important being network formation. According to social capital theory, each act of migration creates the social structure necessary to sustain additional movement. Migrants are linked to non-migrants through social ties that carry reciprocal obligations for assistance based on shared understandings of kinship, friendship, and common community origin. Non-migrants draw upon these ties to gain access to employment abroad. Every new migrant reduces the costs and risks of migration for a set of friends and relatives, and with these lowered costs and risks, they are induced to migrate, which further expands the set of people with ties abroad, which, in turn, reduces the costs and risks of movement for a new set of people, causing some of them to migrate, and so on. *S.C. Theory = C.C. = Net. Form.*

Illustrative data consistent with this model have been presented in a series of descriptive studies by Massey and colleagues (Massey 1986; Massey *et al.* 1987, 1994); but the specific linkages underlying the hypothesized cumulative causation have yet to be convincingly demonstrated. Although Massey *et al.* (1994) show that the stock of migratory experience and the density of network connections expands as communities move from lower to higher levels of migratory prevalence, they did not sort out the causal ordering of network expansion and migration. In fact, to date no study has examined the interplay between individual actions and network growth that is hypothesized to build a dynamic momentum into international migratory flows. Although cumulative causation through network formation remains a plausible hypothesis that is consistent with circumstantial evidence, its base of empirical support is tenuous at this point.

A second mechanism of cumulative causation that has been hypothesized occurs through community income distributions. According to the new economics of migration, households engage in international labour not only to improve their absolute income, but also to increase income relative to others in the community; but in remitting earnings back home to family members, migrants also affect the distribution of income, thereby changing the relative deprivation experienced by others, which, in turn, affects their propensities to migrate. Through remittances, migrants change the socio-economic context within which future migration decisions are made, creating a feedback loop. If foreign remittances allow migrant households to skip over others as they advance up the income distribution, then the relative deprivation of households below them will increase and these households will, in turn, become more likely to send workers abroad.

Stark *et al.* (1986) compared two Mexican communities characterized by different levels of US migratory participation. They found that when individuals from relatively few households migrated internationally, remittances had an unequalizing effect on the local income distribution; but when many households participated in migration, remittances had an equalizing effect. Georges (1990) found comparable results when she compared two communities in the Dominican Republic. These results suggest that income inequality is low initially and then increases as a few households began sending out migrants and gaining access to high US incomes; but eventually it moderates when a majority of households became involved in US migration; and in the end, the distribution of income becomes more equal as nearly all households come to participate in international labour.

Since relative deprivation varies directly with income inequality, its cumulative effect in causing US migration is low initially, then high, and then low once again. A reanalysis of the data revealed, however, that this tendency towards diminishing relative deprivation is substantially mitigated if greater weight is given to households at the lower end of the income distribution (Stark *et al.* 1988). If barriers to migration persist for low-income households, preventing them from achieving full access to US employment, then relative deprivation remains a significant cause of out-migration even at high levels of migratory prevalence.

Recent work by Taylor (1992*a*) also suggests that the direct effect of remittances on income distributions may understate their true unequalizing effect. Remittances have strong indirect effects because they put low-income households in a position to acquire income-producing assets. In a longitudinal analysis of data collected in two Mexican communities, Taylor (1992*a*) showed that a significant share of migrant remittances were invested in productive enterprises, and that these enterprises later produced income that exacerbated income inequality (see also Taylor and Wyatt 1996).

In other words, remittances not only drive up income inequality directly; they also increase it by promoting investment in assets, the income from which further accentuates income inequality indirectly. Evidence from Mexico, therefore, strongly suggests that international migration is caused cumulatively through feedback mechanisms operating via the local income distribution: migration brings remittances, which increase income inequality, which raises relative deprivation, which brings more migration.

Some researchers have argued that inequality in landholding constitutes another mechanism by which migration is cumulatively caused. Many field studies suggest that land is an important spending goal of international migrants (Reichert 1981; Mines 1984; López 1986; Massey *et al.* 1987; Grasmuck and Pessar 1991; Taylor and Wyatt 1996). In most communities, however, the available land base is quite limited, and migration-induced demand leads to a rapid inflation of land values. Dependency theorists such as Wiest (1984) and Rubenstein (1983, 1992) point out that by gaining early access to high incomes, the first migrant families are able to gain privileged access to land; but as more households send migrants abroad and channel their remittances into such purchases, prices escalate out of reach. As a result, landownership becomes concentrated in the hands of a few successful migrants.

The concentration of landownership carries a potential for cumulative causation for three reasons. First, to the extent that it indicates more landlessness, it means that a growing number of families are deprived of a means of support, thereby increasing the pressure for out-migration. Second, migrant households often use land less intensively than non-migrants, purchasing it as an investment or as a token of prestige and letting it lie fallow or using it for less-intensive activities such as cattle-grazing. To the extent that land is withdrawn from crop production, local demand for farm labour is reduced, once again increasing the pressure for out-migration. Finally, although some migrant families do continue active farming, they tend to use more capital-intensive methods, substituting machines, irrigation equipment, high-yield seeds, insecticides, and herbicides for hand labour, and thus lowering once again the demand for hand labour.

Although circumstantial evidence linking migration to land inequality is available from several field studies in Mexico (Mines 1984; López 1986; Massey *et al.* 1987), the Dominican Republic (Georges 1990; Grasmuck and Pessar 1991), and the English Caribbean (Rubenstein 1983), the degree of empirical support for the hypothesis of cumulative causation is weak. Most of these studies are compromised by a lack of longitudinal or comparative data; inferences about growing inequality are based on the reports of informants or on observed differences in rates of landholding between migrant and non-migrant families. From cross-sectional data, however, it is difficult to sort out which came first, landownership or migration. An exception is provided by Reichert (1981), who traces land acquisition back to the point of initial US migration and then moves forward to document its concentration in the hands of a few legal migrants to the USA.

Unfortunately, no study has undertaken the kind of careful quantitative analysis of landholding that Taylor and colleagues have carried out to analyse the interplay between migration and income inequality (Stark *et al.* 1986, 1988; Taylor 1992*a*; Taylor and Wyatt 1996). The only study even to report a Gini index of land inequality is that of Georges (1990), and she concludes that international migration simply exacerbated a trend towards land concentration already under way because of government agricultural policies and national market conditions. Considerably more (and better) research is needed to establish the existence and extent of the causal link between international migration and land inequality.

The second link in the hypothesized chain of cumulative causation through land distributions is that migrant families use farmland less intensively, leading to the constriction of local labour opportunities and greater pressures for out-migration. Massey *et al.* (1987) documented a clear decline in farming among inhabitants of two rural Mexican communities as they became more involved in the migratory process. Taylor and Wyatt (1996) and Taylor (1992*a*) also record in considerable detail the ongoing shift to cattle-raising by migrant households in Michoacán, Mexico. The association of international migration with cattle-raising has also been documented in other communities of Mexico (Reichert 1981) and the Dominican Republic (Georges 1990; Grasmuck and Pessar 1991). But Griffith (1986) reports no differences between US migrants and non-migrants in Jamaica with respect to land owned, land cultivated, or involvement in livestock production.

The last link in the chain of cumulative causation involves the use of capital-intensive methods among migrants who do farm. Both Massey *et al.* (1987) and Jones (1992) show that migrant households are more likely than non-migrant households to make productive agricultural investments, and that the propensity to use inputs such as machines, fertilizers, and insecticides rises as families become more involved in international migration. But Massey *et al.* (1987) also show that while the use of family labour falls with greater involvement, the employment of non-family labour rises. Fletcher and Taylor (1992) likewise found a shift away from family-intensive farming towards a greater use of tractors, herbicides, and hired labour—all family-labour substitutes. In addition, Griffith (1986) reported a greater use of hired labour by migrant households in Jamaica, and Wood and McCoy (1985) found a marginal increase in the use of labour by migratory households on five Caribbean islands.

In summary, the hypothesis of cumulative causation through land inequality must be regarded as plausible and broadly consistent with the evidence, but still unproven. The various links in the causal chain are, on the whole, tenuously connected to empirical evidence, and no study has yet demonstrated a quantitative connection between land inequality and an elevated propensity for international migration among households.

One final avenue of cumulative causation that has been discussed in the theoretical literature is culture. According to post-modern theorists, the circulation of people, goods, and ideas creates a new transnational culture that combines values, behaviours, and attitudes from sending and receiving societies to create a new, largely autonomous social space that transcends national boundaries (Rouse 1989, 1990, 1991, 1992; Georges 1990; Goldring 1992, 1996a, 1996b). This transnationalization of culture changes the context within which migration decisions are made.

Although the new culture is complex and multifaceted, it is characterized by several distinct features that reinforce and perpetuate international movement. First, migrants evince a widely admired lifestyle that others are drawn to emulate. Materially successful migrants provide a powerful demonstration effect, especially for the young, based on their elevated ability to consume goods and purchase property, and they are instrumental in spreading the values of consumerism throughout the community. Second, although some of migration's attractiveness is material, it also acquires a strong normative component. Over time, foreign labour becomes integrated into the structure of values and expectations, and young people contemplating entry into the labour force, don't consider other options: they expect to migrate internationally in the normal course of events. Third, as migration assumes a greater role in the community, it becomes increasingly important as a rite of passage for young men, providing an accepted means of demonstrating worthiness, ambition, and manhood. Finally, as women come to participate in the migration process, they gain greater power and influence within the family through their contributions to family income (Hagan 1994; Hondagneu-Sotelo 1994). While abroad they come into contact with more egalitarian gender relations and push for greater equality. Realizing that patriarchal constraints on female autonomy are lower in modern industrial societies, they encourage activities that cement ties to the receiving society, such as the purchase of homes in destination communities, and actively work to promote settlement abroad.

Over time and with extensive movement back and forth, therefore, a 'culture of migration' emerges that is distinct from the culture of both sending and receiving nations. Although cultural effects are difficult to measure and quantify, elements of this culture have been widely observed in field studies carried out in a variety of national and community settings. Many observers have commented on the expansion of consumerism in migrant communities, including fieldworkers in Mexico (Wiest 1973, 1979; Mines 1981; Reichert 1981, 1982; Dinerman 1982; López 1986; Massey *et al.* 1987; Alarcón 1992; Fletcher and Taylor 1992; Goldring 1992; Smith 1992), the Dominican Republic (Georges 1990; Grasmuck and Pessar 1991), and the English Caribbean (Rubenstein 1979, 1983; Wood and McCoy 1985). Field investigators have also mentioned the emergence of social norms promoting international movement, especially as a rite of passage for young men (Mines 1981; Reichert 1982; Massey *et al.* 1987; Georges 1990; Rouse 1990, 1992; Alarcón 1992; Goldring 1996*b*). Finally, several analysts have reported shifts in gender roles and a stronger emphasis on foreign settlement as a result of the incorporation of women into the migratory process (Georges 1990; Grasmuck and Pessar 1991; Goldring 1992, 1996*a*, 1996*b*; Hondagneu-Sotelo 1994*b*, 1995). Although the hypothesized effect of cultural change in cumulatively promoting migration may be difficult to quantify and objectively assess, the large number of field reports documenting this phenomenon suggest there is something to it.

Theory and Evidence in North America

Our systematic review of empirical studies of international migration in the North American system has not turned up substantial evidence that would lead to the rejection of any of the theoretical models we have surveyed. On the contrary, each model has received at least some empirical support, suggesting that each theory captures some element of truth. Although the base of empirical research is more convincing for some theories than others, we rarely encountered negative evidence. Rather, the characteristic defect in the base of empirical research was an absence of evidence, not contrary evidence.

What is unclear is how well the various models perform against each other, and how much of an *independent* contribution to explanatory power each model might retain in a simultaneous examination of theoretical propositions. For the most part, world systems theory, dual labour market theory, and the theory of cumulative causation have not been systematically compared against competing models. Extensive comparisons have been conducted to evaluate the relative efficacy of neoclassical economics, the new economics, and network theory, and when all is said and done, all three theories display their relevance in direct comparisons with the others. Controlling for relative deprivation and expected wage differentials, networks retain their importance; controlling for network connections and wage differentials, relative deprivation is still found to predict international movement; and controlling for relative deprivation and network connections, wage differentials strongly predict the odds of migration.

Despite a great deal of supportive circumstantial evidence, the specific mechanisms underlying cumulative causation have not been modelled or compared with the predictions of other models, with the partial exception of those mechanisms operating through income distributions. Principal goals of future research should be to integrate segmented labour market theory and world systems theory with the other theoretical models; to carry out comprehensive empirical tests that systematically test the validity of competing propositions; and to specify more clearly and quantify the feedback loops by which migration comes to be cumulatively caused.

Our review uncovered other deficiencies in the research literature. Far too much of the research is centred in Mexico, which because of its unique relationship to the USA may be unrepresentative of broader patterns and trends. Even within Mexico, a great deal has been generalized from a rather small set of studies from a handful of sending communities and relatively few investigators. Within Mexico, new researchers need to become involved and to gather information from a broader sample of communities. Within the field generally, more attention needs to be devoted to other prominent sending countries, such as the Philippines, the Dominican Republic, Jamaica, Colombia, El Salvador, Korea, and China. Research on these countries should include analyses of individual sending communities as well as studies of aggregate rates and flows.

Research within each paradigm can also be improved. Studies carried out under neoclassical economics should employ expected wages (wages times employment rates) as the leading explanatory factor, not observed wages as has been done to this point. Research on the new economics of migration should relate migration decisions directly to indicators of market failures, such as high interest rates, the absence of insurance coverage, or a lack of credit. Research on segmented labour market theory should attempt to adapt the switching regression model of Dickens and Lang (1985) to the three-sector model developed by Portes and Bach (1985), and it should broaden the study of enclaves beyond Cubans in Miami to consider other possible enclaves, beginning with those identified by Logan *et al.* (1994). Investigators of world systems theory should expand the analysis of Ricketts (1986) to a broader sample of countries and dates using a better-controlled study, and they should replicate the study of Hatton and Williamson (1994*a*) for the modern period. Network theory should move beyond dichotomous indicators of network connections to measure networks as a form of social capital that varies continuously with respect to quality and quantity (Espinosa and Massey 1997). Finally, greater effort must be made to compile multilevel longitudinal data files, which ultimately will be needed to model linkages specified under the theory of cumulative causation.

4 Coming to Terms with European Migration

In a few short years, the foreign-born percentage of Europe has come to rival that of older immigrant-receiving societies such as the USA, Australia, or Canada. Ardittis (1990) estimates that in 1985 some 12 million foreigners legally resided in Western Europe, about half from nations outside the European Union (EU), plus around 2–3 million additional illegal non-EU immigrants. Haskey (1992) puts the total number of immigrants, legal and illegal, at around 16 million in 1990, and Fassmann and Münz (1992) estimate it at 16.6 million. Official tabulations prepared by SOPEMI (1992) indicate that 15.5 million foreign nationals lived in the countries Western Europe in 1990, representing around 7 per cent of its total population.

According to Ardittis (1990), the evolution of European immigration is characterized by five broad, overlapping phases. The first extends from the beginning of the century into the early 1950s (and a little bit later in some countries). During this period, Europe continued to be a major region of emigration, sending a significant number of migrants to the rest of the world, especially the Americas. The second phase began in the early 1950s and lasted until 1973; it coincided with Europe's emergence as a region of labour-importation.

Shortly after 1950, several nations, notably Germany and Switzerland, began to experience serious labour shortages (as a result of rapid economic expansion coupled with low population growth) and initiated the recruitment of workers from abroad. The need for labour was initially met by migrants from Southern Europe, first from Italy; then from Spain, Portugal, and Greece; and finally from Yugoslavia. During this time, Southern Europe not only sent emigrants to Western Europe, but also to Australia and the Americas. Eventually, however, Southern Europe could not provide enough workers to satisfy demand in the north, so governments began recruiting labour from the countries of the Mediterranean basic and North Africa, and over time these immigrants came to dominate the flows.

The third phase of European immigration began with the oil boycott of 1973, which ushered in an economic recession that led to a round of industrial restructuring and labour displacement. As domestic unemployment rose, European governments terminated their labour recruitment programmes and instituted new, more restrictive immigration policies. They also enacted policies that attempted to stabilize the number of foreigners and promote the return of guestworkers. During this phase, the countries of Southern Europe—Italy, Spain, Greece, and Portugal—shifted from the exportation to the importation of labour (Fakiolas 1995; Solé 1995), and countries in Northern and Western Europe—notably France, Germany, Switzerland, and Belgium—shifted from the recruitment of workers to the accommodation of growing numbers of spouses, children, and dependants of former guestworkers who had decided to settle permanently abroad (Hoffmann-Nowotny 1995; Van Amersfoort 1995).

The fourth phase began in the mid-1980s and was characterized by a sporadic and largely uncontrolled influx of migrants from Eastern Europe, North Africa, and other developing nations. Waves of new immigrants arrived in Germany from Eastern Europe to claim citizenship on the basis of German ethnicity and large numbers of people entered France from North Africa to exercise historical claims on French nationality. Asylum applications rose everywhere, but especially in Germany, owing to the liberal provisions of its post-war constitution (now amended). Within most countries of Western Europe, a second generation of immigrants progressed through the educational system and began to enter the labour market.

The final phase of European migration emerged only in the 1990s and is still evolving. It is characterized by the consolidation of Western Europe as a free, internal market with unrestrained movement of EU citizens between member States, combined with tighter controls on entry from outside the Union. Citizenship laws are now being amended throughout Western Europe to forestall growing immigration from former colonies. At the same time, the criteria for asylum are being tightened (Joly 1995). As a result of these restrictive policies and the resulting scarcity of entry visas, illegal migration is growing (Castles and Miller 1993; Miller 1995).

Zlotnik (1992) argues that the countries of Western Europe comprise the core of a single system because there is: (i) congruence among their immigration policies; (ii) close economic and political ties among them; (iii) comparable levels of economic development; (iv) similar cultural backgrounds; (v) geographical proximity; and (vi) a common change-over from emigration to immigration within recent memory. To Zlotnik's list, one might also add a common worry about high levels of immigration and a degree of public concern greater than that displayed in other parts of the world (United Nations 1992).

Some observers argue, however, that the European system is composed of several distinct subsystems. Southern European nations, for example, have followed a very different migration trajectory from those in the North and West, experiencing substantial emigration until the early 1970s. Baldwin-Edwards (1991) identifies four subsystems linked to different policy regimes: a semi-peripheral Mediterranean regime; a mainland continental regime; a Scandinavian regime; and a United Kingdom–Ireland regime. Zlotnik (1992) also sees the British Isles as lying outside the main European system, along with Scandinavia. Excluding Ireland, only 13 per cent of all foreigners in Britain are from the European Union, whereas roughly half are from countries of the British Commonwealth (Haskey 1992). Likewise, one-third of all foreign nationals in Sweden are from Finland, compared to just 14 per cent from the European Union.

Despite these differences, we feel there are sufficient similarities among the nations of Western Europe to consider them as a single international migration system organized under the Treaty of Rome and united in a common economic and political order that now embraces twelve core countries. Although this system has been described before (Zlotnik and Hovey 1990; Haskey 1992; Zlotnik 1992; Stalker 1994), we undertake a fresh characterization based on data from the 1980s.

The European Migration System

Western Europe has been a major destination of international migrants only for the past three decades. Lacking a long history of immigration, most European countries have been slow to acknowledge their new status as immigrant-receiving societies and have failed to establish effective procedures to count immigrants or study their effects. Measuring the stocks and flows of immigrants is especially difficult because no two countries use the same categorization of origin nations, and because they differ with respect to rules of citizenship and naturalization, which determine who gets counted as an 'immigrant' and who does not.

Differences in the rules of citizenship cause especially serious problems because most European nations tabulate data by *nationality* rather than birthplace. In countries where naturalization is difficult and citizenship hard to achieve (as in Switzerland), a count of foreign nationals provides a reasonably accurate approximation of the size of the immigrant population, and changes in this number provide a serviceable indicator of the volume of recent flows; but in countries where naturalization occurs frequently (as in France), or where some foreign-born persons are able to claim citizenship upon entry (in both Germany and France), counts of foreign nationals yield estimates of immigration that are biased downward.

The central difficulty is that the number of foreign nationals in a country at any point in time not only represents a balance between immigrant arrivals, departures, and deaths, but also *naturalizations and citizen claimants*. Thus, changes in the number of foreign nationals accurately mirror net flows of immigrants only when the number of naturalizations is low and relatively constant across time, and when few among arriving foreigners can claim citizenship upon entry.

Each country in Europe classifies immigrants according to its own peculiar history, legal imperatives, political needs, and national interests. As a result, it is impossible to create a single table that shows the national origins of immigrants for all receiving countries. Instead, we must present a series of tables that group countries with similar reporting conventions and histories and then simplify them to derive the data for a summary sketch of the entire European migration system.

Table 4.1 reports stocks and flows of foreigners by nationality for Europe's two leading ex-colonial powers, Britain and France. Using data from SOPEMI (1992), we show the number of foreign nationals in 1990 and use the change in this number since 1980 as a rough indicator of the size of recent flows. In these and subsequent tables, we estimate counts for missing national origins by applying the proportionate distribution of immigrants reported to the United

Table 4.1   Foreign population by nationality in 1990 and change in foreign population between 1980 and 1990: Britain and France ('000s)

Source region	United Kingdom		France	
	1990	1980–90	1990	1980–90
European Union				
Italy	75.0	−13.0	253.7	−121.6
Portugal	21.0	18.0	645.6	−119.3
Spain	25.0	−2.0	216.0	−159.9
Other	768.0	316.0	193.6	36.3
Eastern Europe				
Poland			46.3	26.8
Yugoslavia	57.0	13.0	51.7	−13.0
Other			11.0	11.0
Middle East				
Turkey	75.0	21.0	201.5	99.6
Other			32.9	0.3
Africa				
North	0.0	0.0	1,421.1	197.8
Sub-Saharan	90.0	−5.0	11.5	0.1
Asia				
Bangladesh	38.0	28.0	0.0	0.0
India	155.0	12.0	6.6	0.1
Pakistan	63.0	13.0	2.1	0.1
Americas				
Caribbean	70.0	−102.0	113.0	0.9
Other	247.0	36.0	75.9	0.6
Other	191.0	−61.0	325.1	171.1
TOTAL	1,875.0	274.0	3,607.6	28.9
% Foreign national	3.3		6.4	

Sources: Organization for Economic Cooperation and Development (1992); United Nations (1991*a*).

Nations (1991*a*). We also estimate Britain's 1980–90 flow by extending average annual levels observed during 1984–90 to the entire decade.

The top panel of Table 4.1 shows that immigration into Britain and France from Southern Europe has generally declined. Although Italy, Spain, and Portugal still comprise a sizeable share of foreign nationals in each country, especially France, their numbers fell over the decade. Only Portuguese nationals in the United Kingdom showed an increase. Thus, characterizing the contemporary structure of British and French immigration by using stocks rather than flows would greatly overstate the importance of Southern European sending nations.

Nor are other European Union members contributing many migrants to these countries. The number of other EU nationals in France increased by only 36,000 during the 1980s. Although the number rose by 316,000 in Britain, 145,000 of these migrants were from Ireland, for centuries an integral part of the British economy. While international migration within the European Union was on the wane during the 1980s, however, migration from Eastern Europe and the Middle East was notably on the rise, particularly from Poland and Turkey (at least in France, where detailed breakdowns are available).

The pattern of migration into Britain and France clearly reflect each nation's colonial past. The largest stocks and flows observed in France are not from Europe, but from former colonies in North Africa, notably Algeria, Tunisia, and Morocco. Likewise, the principal contemporary flows into Britain are from former colonies in Asia, notably Bangladesh, India, and Pakistan, whose numbers were augmented by the arrival of numerous people of South Asian origin displaced from East Africa (Hall 1988: 286).

The apparent decline in the number of Caribbean nationals within Britain reflects processes of naturalization and mortality rather than out-migration. Although the number of Caribbean *nationals* stood at just 70,000 in 1990, the number of Afro-Caribbean *ethnicity* was some 474,000 (Stalker 1994). Likewise, the number of North Africans in France is substantially understated by the nationality figures tabulated by SOPEMI. According to the latest figures on place of birth reported to the United Nations (1991*a*), Algerian nationals represent only 56 per cent of all foreign-born Algerians living in France, while Tunisian nationals constitute just 53 per cent of persons born in Tunisia. Thus, although nationality statistics appear to suggest an outflow of Algerians during the 1980s (the number of Algerian nationals declined by some 158,000), information on long-term arrivals reported to the United Nations (1991*a*) reveals that 529,000 Algerians arrived in 1988 alone. The ongoing flow of migrants from North Africa to France is camouflaged by the use of nationality rather than birthplace statistics.

Table 4.2 continues the assessment of migration patterns within the European system by showing stocks and flows of foreign nationals for the principal German-speaking countries of Central Europe: Austria, Germany, and Switzerland (the latter also contains French- and Italian-speaking areas, of course).

Table 4.2 Foreign population by nationality in 1990 and change in foreign population between 1980 and 1990: Austria, Germany, and Switzerland ('000s)

Source region	Austria 1990	Austria 1980–90	Germany 1990	Germany 1980–90	Switzerland 1990	Switzerland 1980–90
European Union						
Greece	0.6	0.2	314.5	17.0	8.3	−0.5
Italy	2.4	−0.7	548.3	−69.5	378.7	−42.0
Portugal	0.0	0.0	84.6	−27.7	85.6	74.9
Spain	0.0	0.0	134.7	−45.3	116.1	18.9
Other	13.1	1.0	351.6	−114.8	171.5	32.7
Eastern Europe						
Bulgaria	1.4	0.8	11.4	7.3	0.3	0.0
Czechoslovakia	21.7	13.3	33.0	18.7	5.7	−8.2
Hungary	13.8	8.5	35.1	14.0	4.5	−1.5
Poland	28.1	17.3	241.3	219.6	5.0	1.3
Romania	5.8	3.6	53.1	43.5	0.6	0.0
Soviet Union	0.2	0.1	9.3	4.0	0.0	0.0
Yugoslavia	209.9	23.6	625.5	20.7	140.7	96.8
Middle East						
Iran	5.0	3.1	89.7	72.9	1.2	0.1
Turkey	95.9	50.1	1,675.0	212.6	64.2	26.1
Africa						
Algeria	0.0	0.0	6.7	1.7	0.0	0.0
Morocco	0.0	0.0	67.5	31.6	0.0	0.0
Tunisia	0.0	0.0	25.9	3.3	0.0	0.0
Other	15.5	9.8	907.6	378.9	117.9	8.9
TOTAL	413.4	130.7	5,241.8	788.5	1,100.3	207.5
% Foreign national	5.3		8.2		16.3	

Sources: Organization for Economic Cooperation and Development (1992); United Nations (1991*a*).

During the 1960s, these countries generally implemented the largest and most extensive labour recruitment programmes in the European system (see Castles and Kosack 1973; Krane 1979; Power 1979), which in two cases (Germany and Switzerland) produced foreign percentages comparable to those observed in the traditional immigrant-receiving societies such as the United States and Canada (8 per cent and 16 per cent, respectively).

Austria and Germany display the same pattern of zero or declining migration from Southern Europe observed in Britain and France. The drop in the number of Italians, Portuguese, and Spaniards was particularly sharp in Germany. Although Portuguese and Spanish immigrants continued to flow into Switzerland during the 1980s, the number of Greeks and Italians in that country fell.

Replacing these departing Southern Europeans were new migrants from Eastern Europe. Austria experienced a strong surge in migration from the bordering nations of Czechoslovakia, Hungary, and Yugoslavia. In each Germanic country, there was also an influx of migrants from the Middle East, notably Turkey, the largest supplier of guestworkers to Germany before the end of labour recruitment (see Martin 1991). Although guestworker migration may have ceased, however, the population of Turkish nationals continues to grow as family members migrate to join their kin living abroad. During the 1980s, the number of Turkish nationals rose by 213,000 in Germany, 50,000 in Austria, and 26,000 in Switzerland. A large number of Iranians also entered Germany during the 1980s, with the population growing from 17,000 to 90,000 over the decade. At the same time, a significant number of North Africans arrived, including a net increment of 32,000 Moroccans, further augmenting the Muslim presence in Germany.

In total, the foreign population of Germany grew by some 789,000 persons during the 1980s, an increase of 15 per cent. Yet even this substantial figure understates the true increase in the number of immigrants, as the German constitution continues to recognize the right of 'ethnic Germans' living in former territories of pre-war Germany to enter the country as returning citizens who are not counted as immigrants. According to Bade (1993), during the period 1988–91 about 1.2 million ethnic Germans 'returned' to Germany from areas of the Soviet Union, Poland, and Romania, with some 398,000 arriving in 1990 alone, more than doubling the official total of immigration from Eastern Europe (which showed a net increase of only 328,000 foreign nationals).

Table 4.3 presents immigration figures for the Benelux countries of Belgium, the Netherlands, and Luxembourg. Once again the familiar pattern of return migration to Southern Europe is evident, particularly in Belgium; but unlike the Central European States of Germany, Switzerland, and Austria there is relatively little in-migration from Eastern Europe. Rather, the Benelux countries generally experience strong inflows from the Middle East and North Africa, especially from Turkey and Morocco. As in the rest of Western Europe, therefore, the Benelux nations are characterized by declining migration within Europe and growing entry from developing areas.

We observe similar patterns in the Scandinavian countries, Norway and Sweden, shown in Table 4.4. Migration from Western Europe and the EU either fell in absolute terms (as in Sweden) or ran at modest levels (as in Norway). Sweden experienced a large influx of immigrants from Iran and Turkey, while inflows from these countries into Norway were more modest. Norway experienced a large influx of Asians while Sweden did not. Neither country took in many Africans, but both countries experienced small but significant immigration from Latin America, specifically from Chile. The latter

Table 4.3 Foreign population by nationality in 1990 and change in foreign population between 1980 and 1990: Belgium, the Netherlands, and Luxembourg ('000s)

Source region	Belgium		Netherlands		Luxembourg	
	1990	1980–90	1990	1980–90	1990	1980–90
European Union						
Greece	20.9	−57.1	4.9	0.8	1.2	1.0
Italy	241.1	−41.3	16.9	−4.2	20.4	−0.7
Portugal	16.5	6.0	8.3	−1.1	35.3	12.5
Spain	52.2	−7.0	14.2	−6.0	2.3	0.1
Other	219.7	−13.9	121.1	8.2	31.5	3.0
Eastern Europe						
Poland	11.4	2.4	3.1	6.0	0.4	0.1
Yugoslavia	5.8	−0.1	13.5	−0.6	1.7	0.2
Middle East						
Turkey	84.9	20.9	203.5	65.0	0.2	0.1
Africa						
Algeria	10.7	−0.2	1.0	0.7	0.1	0.1
Morocco	141.6	34.9	156.9	73.5	0.2	0.1
Tunisia	6.3	−0.6	2.6	0.2	0.2	0.1
Zaire	12.0	3.1	4.5	3.5	0.2	0.1
Other	81.4	17.6	142.4	25.5	12.5	−0.7
Total	904.5	20.9	695.9	171.5	105.5	15.0
% Foreign national	9.1		4.6		28.0	

Sources: Organization for Economic Cooperation and Development (1992); United Nations (1991*a*).

migration began with political exiles in the 1970s and expanded into a more sustained immigrant flow during the 1980s.

The newest immigrant-receiving countries in the system are those of Southern Europe, notably Italy and Spain. As recently as 1968–70, Italy was still sustaining a net out-migration of more than 250,000 people; but this centuries-old pattern of Italian emigration suddenly reversed itself in the 1970s, and by 1976–80 more people arrived than left for the first time in that country's history (Barsotti and Lecchini 1990; Stalker 1994: 204–5; Fakiolas 1995). Spanish immigration is even more recent (Muñoz-Pérez and Izquierdo Escribano 1989; Blanco Fernández de Valderrama 1993; Solé 1995), and there are still more Spaniards outside of Spain than foreigners within it; but immigration began to rise dramatically after 1980, with the number of foreigners growing from under 200,000 in that year to around 400,000 by 1993 (Stalker 1994: 206–7).

Table 4.4   Foreign population by nationality in 1990, and change in foreign population between 1980 and 1990: Norway and Sweden ('000s)

Source region	Norway		Sweden	
	1990	1980–90	1990	1980–90
Europe				
European Union	40.6	7.7	67.7	−10.2
Western Europe	11.7	3.3	163.2	−48.2
Eastern Europe	7.1	4.7	65.3	12.6
Middle East				
Iran	5.9	5.8	39.0	36.1
Turkey	5.5	3.0	25.5	7.2
Africa				
North	2.3	1.0	5.6	0.7
Sub-Saharan	10.2	4.3	21.9	2.8
Asia				
India	3.5	1.9	0.5	0.1
Pakistan	11.4	4.9	3.2	0.4
Philippines	2.3	1.6	0.3	0.0
Sri Lanka	5.2	4.9	0.5	0.1
Vietnam	6.9	4.6	3.1	1.1
Americas				
Chile	5.4	4.5	19.9	12.7
USA	9.5	−1.2	8.0	2.2
Other	15.8	9.7	60.0	44.4
TOTAL	143.3	60.7	483.7	62.0
% Foreign national	3.4		5.6	

Sources: Organization for Economic Cooperation and Development (1992); United Nations (1991*a*).

Immigration into Southern Europe is so new that governments have not established reliable statistical systems for reporting the flows; and being closer to the Third World than other European nations, illegal migration has assumed larger proportions. Calvaruso (1987) estimates that between 600,000 and 1 million illegal immigrants reside in Italy, from diverse sources such as North Africa, the Middle East, Senegal, Eritrea, the Cape Verde Islands, the Philippines, and Thailand. Likewise, Spain is estimated to house some 300,000 illegal immigrants, mainly from North Africa (Stalker 1994). Champion and King (1993) put the total in Italy, Spain, and Portugal at 2–3 million in 1990.

A rough idea of recent immigration trends in Italy and Spain can be gleaned from statistics on registered foreigners, which are summarized in Table 4.5.

Table 4.5   Number of foreigners registered in Italy and Spain and change in that number between 1980 and 1990 ('000s)

Source region	Italy		Spain	
	1990	1980–90	1990	1980–90
Europe	267.4	108.3	174.3	56.8
Africa	238.6	208.8	61.8	56.8
Americas	128.4	65.7	77.7	22.7
Asia	140.4	98.4	28.2	18.2
Other	1.1	0.0	0.0	0.0
TOTAL	775.9	481.2	342.0	154.5
% Foreign national	1.4		0.9	

Sources: Organization for Economic Cooperation and Development (1992); Stalker (1994).

Unlike more established labour-importing countries such as Germany, France, Switzerland, Belgium, or Sweden, these countries of Southern Europe are still taking in a substantial number of migrants from elsewhere in the continent, in addition to absorbing many returning citizens who are not counted in these figures. During the 1980s, the number of European nationals living in Italy rose by 68 per cent to reach 267,000, and the number in Spain grew by 48 per cent to reach 174,000. These European immigrants include workers and businessmen, but also a large number of retirees seeking warmer climates and easier living in Europe's sunbelt. In Italy, another important source of immigration has been the Balkan region. During March of 1991, for example, some 21,000 Albanians arrived in Italy as refugees and were dispersed throughout the country (SOPEMI 1992).

Despite the importance of immigration from Europe, the most explosive growth has been in migration from the Third World, notably Africa (Campani 1989; Bodega *et al.* 1995). The number of Africans in Italy rose from just 30,000 in 1980 to 209,000 ten years later, a sevenfold increase; likewise the number of Africans in Spain grew by a factor of 11 to reach 62,000 in 1990. These figures do not include the presumably large number of illegal immigrants, who further bolster the African presence in Southern Europe.

At the same time, the descendants of former Italian and Spanish emigrants to the Americas have taken advantage of liberal entry provisions to gain access to the European Union (Champion and King 1993). Until 1985, Latin Americans of Spanish ancestry did not need permits to enter Spain, and immigrants from its former colonies still receive preferential treatment in gaining visas (Stalker 1994). Likewise, the children and grandchildren of Italian emigrants to the Americas are still able to exercise historical claims on citizenship to gain entry to Italy.

Through these means, the number of immigrants to Italy from the Americas rose by 66,000 to reach 128,000 in 1990, while the number of Americans in Spain rose by 23,000 to reach 78,000. A salient source in both of these flows is Argentina (Clavaruso 1987; Chozas 1993). Over the same period, migration from Asia also rose precipitously in both Italy and Spain. The number of Asians roughly doubled in each place during the 1980s to reach 140,000 in Italy and 28,000 in Spain.

As with their wealthier neighbours to the north, therefore, Italy and Spain have become magnets for immigrants from the developing world, in particular those from North Africa, Latin America, and in the case of Italy, the Balkan region. The figures reported in Tables 4.1–4.5 are conservative, however, in that they generally do not incorporate illegal migrants or asylum seekers. As avenues for legal entry in to Western Europe have grown scarcer and immigration and labour policies more restrictive, applications for asylum have grown very rapidly.

According to Oberg and Wils (1992) Western Europe took in more than 2 million asylum applicants between 1980 and 1990, with roughly half (47 per cent) going to Germany (Baldwin Edwards (1991) puts the percentage at 60 per cent and Kuijsten (1994) at 44 per cent). Other important asylum countries are Britain (11 per cent of all applicants), France (9 per cent), and Switzerland (8 per cent). In addition, Austria, Italy, and Sweden each account for around 5 per cent of asylees within Europe (Oberg and Wils 1992).

Of the roughly 430,000 asylum cases that were filed in Western Europe during 1990, 14 per cent were from Romania, 11 per cent were from Turkey, and 7 per cent each were from Yugoslavia and Lebanon (Baldwin-Edwards 1991). Other important sources include India, Sri Lanka, Iran, Poland, and Somalia. Thus, asylum migration generally reinforces the shift in immigrant origins away from Southern Europe towards new sources in Eastern Europe, the Middle East, Africa, and Asia.

The main features of the European international migration system are summarized in Figure 4.1, which shows 1980–90 flows into six core zones of Western Europe: Britain, France, Central Europe, Benelux, Scandinavia, and Southern Europe. The figures for France have been adjusted upward by dividing the recorded 1980–90 change in the number of North Africans by the ratio of foreign nationals to foreign-born among immigrants from Algeria, Morocco, and Tunisia (0.631), thereby correcting for the underestimation that stems from the use of nationality data. We also added flows of ethnic Germans to the recorded flows of Eastern Europeans to Germany (using figures from Kuijsten (1994) and Stalker (1994)). Owing to a lack of data, however, we are unable to include asylum seekers in the estimated flows.

The figure makes clear that Britain and Scandinavia are minor and peripheral players in the European migration system. Not only are the flows much smaller in absolute terms than those into other parts of the system, they also tend to be from regions that are quite different from the principal source countries for the rest of Western Europe.

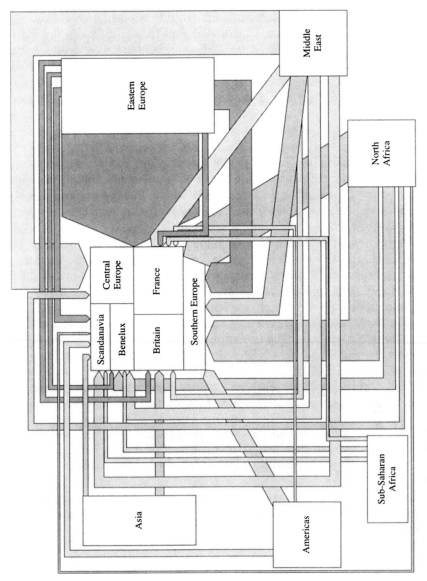

Fig. 4.1 International migration in the European system, 1980–1990

In general, the European system is dominated by two major receiving areas and their respective immigrant streams. By far the largest flow in the entire system consists of Eastern Europeans moving into the Central European States of Germany, Switzerland, and Austria. The next largest flows are those of North Africans moving to France and Middle Easterners (mainly Turks) moving into Central Europe. A smaller flow of Middle Eastern immigrants goes into France.

The Benelux and Southern European countries occupy a middle position between the peripheral nations of Britain and Scandinavia, on the one hand, and the core nations of Germany, Switzerland, and France, on the other. Belgium, the Netherlands, Italy, and Spain all receive substantial inflows of migrants from the Middle East and North Africa; but in Southern Europe these flows are augmented by substantial inflows from other regions as well, notably Eastern Europe, Asia, and the Americas.

In coming years, the importance of immigration from Eastern Europe, the Middle East, and Africa is likely to grow for several reasons. First, the demographic gap between Western Europe and the poor countries of the Mediterranean littoral is even sharper than that between Mexico and the USA. The rate of population growth among countries located on the southern and eastern rim of the Mediterranean Sea is 3.3 times that in Western Europe, and the former are projected to increase their population by 58 million between 1990 and 2000, compared to only 4.5 million in Western Europe (Champion and King 1993).

Second, during the late 1980s most countries in Eastern Europe and the former Soviet Union relaxed travel and emigration restrictions, yielding a sharp upswing in emigration that totalled some 800,000 during 1990–91. Of these, some 200,000 were estimated to be undocumented migrants and most of the remaining 600,000 were ethnic descendants of former settlers (United Nations 1992). By far the largest number (nearly 400,000) were ethnic Germans returning from historical areas of German expansion. Ardittis (1990) estimates that of the 3.5 million ethnic Germans remaining in Eastern Europe, 2 million will emigrate westward by the end of the century, mostly into Germany itself.

Although ethnic Germans constitute the largest portion of the flow from the east, they are not the only stream of ethnic migrants moving westward. According to Oberg and Wils (1992), nearly 50,000 were ethnic Greeks leaving the former territories of the USSR, with 30 per cent going to Greece, 20 per cent to Scandinavia, and the rest to Switzerland. In May of 1990 another exodus was sparked when the Albanian Parliament passed a law granting its nationals the right to travel abroad for the first time in decades. Shortly thereafter, in March of 1991, 21,300 Albanians arrived in Italy, and in August of the same year another 17,000 came (SOPEMI 1992). Although the first wave was accepted and dispersed throughout Italy, the second was turned back. Since then the flow has gone underground.

Third, governments of former colonial powers have found it necessary to open their doors (at least partially) to immigrants from former colonies. Britain was forced to accept Asian refugees from East Africa during the 1970s and 1980s, and in anticipation of the reversion of Hong Kong to China, the United Kingdom arranged for the entry of 50,000 of its inhabitants to enter Britain through a special point system (United Nations 1992). Likewise, 100,000 residents of Macao will be offered Portuguese residence when that colony reverts to China in 1999. Meanwhile, the descendants of earlier waves of emigrants from Italy, Spain, and Portugal continue to draw on historical ties and generous immigration policies to remigrate back to their mother countries in Europe (Champion and King 1993).

Fourth, the disintegration of Yugoslavia has generated a new stream of migrants from Eastern Europe into the West. According to *The Economist* (19 September 1992), there were 532,000 refugees outside the former Yugoslavia in 1992 and more than 2 million displaced persons within it. As with other Eastern European migrants, Yugoslavs tend to settle in Central Europe, with 41 per cent going to Germany, 13 per cent to Switzerland, and 11 per cent to Austria. The spread of political disorder and social chaos to other countries in the former Eastern block could trigger similar or even larger outflows.

Finally, despite public posturing and tough talk, the governments of Western Europe have not been any more successful in stopping illegal immigration than those of Canada and the USA. Indeed, according to Champion and King (1993), the Mediterranean has proved to be less of a barrier to undocumented migration than the Rio Grande. Despite several regularization campaigns, Baldwin-Edwards (1992) estimates that Europe still houses 2.6 million illegal migrants, a quarter of whom are in Germany, 23 per cent in Italy, 12 per cent in Spain, and 8 per cent in France. Movement from Francophone North Africa into Spain, Italy, and France is particularly strong, and once inside these EU countries, the lack of internal border inspections facilitates movement throughout the European system.

Presently few Western European nations are willing to face up to the fact that they have become countries of immigration. All house sizeable and rapidly growing foreign populations, and in the receiving nations of longest standing (notably Britain, France, Germany, Sweden, Belgium, and Switzerland) a second generation born or raised abroad is coming of age and beginning to demand political and economic rights. In some cases, the ratio of immigrants to total population exceeds that observed in the USA or Canada.

These new immigrants enter a European economy characterized by unusually high levels of unemployment, with some 20 million people currently out of work (Witznitzer 1993), and societies gripped by rising xenophobia. According to a report in *Le Monde* (21 May 1993), 'xenophobia in Western Europe has reached unprecedented levels. In France and Britain, many immigrants have been knifed or clubbed to death. In Germany, neo-Nazi skinheads have burned down Turkish homes murdering women and children. Government figures show that more than 6,000 anti-foreigner offences were committed in Germany this year.' Whether the combination of an inhospitable economic climate, an anti-foreign social climate, and restrictive immigration policies will be able to slow the flow of immigrants into Western Europe remains to be seen.

The European Research Literature

Compared with the research literature of North America, the range of studies available for Europe provides a rather limited basis upon which to judge the efficacy of theoretical explanations put forth to account for the initiation and perpetuation of international migration. The rudimentary state of knowledge is not for want of scholarly attention. On the contrary, the number of empirical studies on European immigration is quite large. Our systematic review of sources uncovered more than 150 publications over the past ten years, and new data and findings are constantly being added to the literature.

The problem is not a lack of research so much as a scarcity of theoretically relevant research, and a general disarticulation between theory and study design. Unlike traditional immigrant-receiving societies, the nations of Western Europe lack a strong heritage of data collection and dissemination with respect to international migration. Indeed, many governments have difficulty accepting the fact that they have become immigrant-receiving societies, despite mounting evidence to the contrary. In keeping with this reluctance to acknowledge immigration as a demographic fact, national statistical agencies often tend to be secretive and rather defensive about the publication and dissemination of information on immigration.

European governments, for example, do not customarily release public-use data files on the characteristics of the foreign born enumerated in national censuses and surveys. Neither do they routinely prepare and distribute databases on the characteristics of arriving immigrants. Such files have constituted two principal sources for research on immigration in Australia, Canada, and the USA. In many European nations, not even aggregate tabulations from censuses or surveys are published.

While government agencies have resisted accepting immigration as a demographic process, European investigators have been slow to generate alternative sources of data on the topic. In the USA, Canada, and Australia, useful data have been developed by investigator-initiated surveys of specific sending communities or regions, but such initiatives are sadly lacking in Europe.

Even when field surveys have been conducted, moreover, they have not been guided very strongly by theory, and analysis of available government statistics also tends to be relatively atheoretical. As a result, much of the European research literature is purely descriptive, and to the extent that the data are connected to theory, they tend to be used to illustrate rather than to test and question. Nevertheless, a small but growing number of studies provide some information relevant to the task of examining contemporary theories of international migration.

Neoclassical Economics

Standard economic theory links migration flows to wage differentials between countries, and Western Europe offers some of the highest wages in the world. For potential migrants in Africa or the Middle East, the expected benefits of working in countries such as Germany, France, and Switzerland can be substantial. Kolan (1976), for example, used data gathered from a survey of returning Turkish guestworkers to calculate the expected gain in earnings that would result from a period of temporary labour in Germany. In 1964, he estimated that urban-origin Turks could expect to earn 145 per cent per year more in Germany than at home; and for rural-origin migrants, the potential gains were even greater: a 523 per cent yearly increase in expected earnings. A more recent (1991) survey of Hungarians found that 51 per cent mentioned a higher standard of living as a reason for potentially emigrating westward (Szoke 1992).

Although the potential gains to be had from migrating to Western Europe are substantial, the evidence linking wage differentials to actual population movements is mixed. Peach (1968), for example, studied patterns of movement between the Caribbean and the United Kingdom during the 1950s, and, consistent with neoclassical assumptions, found that high emigration tended to occur from countries with low incomes; but he also found that *changes* in migration rates were not strongly related to *changes* in average incomes. Indeed, changes in Caribbean emigration flows were more strongly connected to seasonal shifts in British *employment*. His analysis was limited, however, by the small number of cases and the lack of formal statistical modeling.

Böhning (1970) proceeded more systematically by regressing annual counts of foreign workers entering Germany on annual employment and wage rates. For the years 1957 through 1968, he examined migration flows into Germany from Austria, Belgium, France, Britain, Greece, Italy, the Netherlands, Spain, and Switzerland. Among the nine country-specific regression equations, wage differentials predicted migration significantly in just two cases, France and Britain, whereas employment differentials predicted the level of movement in seven cases. As with Peach's earlier study, however, Böhning's analysis was limited by the small number of cases, yielding just nine degrees of freedom and a consequent lack of statistical power and considerable unreliability in the estimated regression coefficients.

Straubhaar (1986) improved this situation by examining annual flows of migrants from 1962 through 1983 and estimating a two-parameter model, yielding 20 degrees of freedom. He studied movement out of five countries

(Italy, Spain, Greece, Portugal, and Turkey) into a composite destination area that included Germany, France, the Netherlands, and Belgium, which together were taken to represent 'Western Europe'. Following the well-known Todaro model (Todaro 1969; Harris and Todaro 1970), Straubhaar created an index that multiplied the employment rate in Western Europe by the ratio of per capita income there to that in the origin country. He found that this index, which corresponds closely to Todaro's conception of expected wages, very strongly and significantly predicted the rate of movement out of Spain, Greece, Portugal, and Turkey; and for Italy, the relationship was in the expected direction (positive) but not statistically significant.

Straubhaar (1986) added another variable to the model, however, that diminished the apparent importance of the expected wages. This second variable was the relative change in Western Europe's employment rate over the prior year. He found that the faster the relative increase in employment, the larger the number of migrants from Spain, Greece, Portugal, and Turkey. In a side-by-side comparison within a single equation, moreover, fluctuations in employment proved to be stronger in predicting international movement than expected wage gains, although the latter remained significant. These results led him to conclude that labour demand was the dominant force explaining immigration into Western Europe, not wage differentials.

Walsh (1974) carried out a similar analysis for Ireland, regressing net emigration between Ireland and Britain from 1951 to 1971 on indicators of employment and wages in the two countries. As with Böhning and Straubhaar, he found a significant relationship between migration and wage rates, just as predicted by neoclassical economic theory. The higher the wages in the United Kingdom relative to those in Ireland, the larger the number of Irish emigrants to Britain. Although statistically significant, however, the wage differential was rather weakly related to emigration, yielding an R^2 of just 0.24. In contrast, when the difference in employment rates was regressed on emigration rates, the squared correlation was more than twice as large (0.62); and when the two indicators were included at the same time, the squared correlation reached 0.79. Like Straubhaar, Walsh found that employment clearly dominated over wages when both factors were included in the same model.

O'Gráda (1986) re-analyzed microdata originally gathered from rural Irish teenagers by Hannan (1970) in the 1960s and found results generally consistent with Walsh's estimates. Specifically, he estimated a multivariate logit model that predicted the odds of emigrating to Britain between 1965 and 1968 among 271 young people interviewed in 1965. He found that neither frustration with income nor father's 1965 income significantly predicted the likelihood of emigration by 1968, which was more strongly related to occupational factors such as the number of prior jobs held and father's occupational status. It was also positively related to education.

In sum, the available evidence garnered from a few studies confirms the central proposition of neoclassical economics, but in a rather narrow sense.

Although rates of international migration are positively related to wage differentials between sending and receiving nations, wage gaps by themselves do not provide sufficient explanatory power to account fully for yearly fluctuations in migration rates, and generally they are less powerful than employment differentials in accounting for yearly variations in the flow of international migrants.

The most revealing analysis is probably that of Straubhaar (1986), who includes both Todaro's index of expected wages (wages times the employment probability) and an indicator of employment demand in the same model. According to neoclassical theory, employment should affect the migration decision only to the extent that it influences expected wages, but controlling for this effect (through the Todaro index), fluctuations in employment still exert a powerful independent effect.

One final indication that wage differentials are not the driving force behind European migration comes from the European Union itself. When Spain, Portugal, and Greece entered the Union, some observers feared that the large disparity in wage rates between Northern and Southern Europe might prompt a surge of migration into countries such as Germany, Belgium, and Denmark from the new Union members. For the most part, however, this expected migration never materialized. Indeed, as we have seen, countries in Northern and Western Europe have experienced a net *out-migration* of Southern Europeans during the 1980s, with large numbers of Italians, Spaniards, Greeks, and Portuguese going back to their home countries, despite the persistence of sizeable wage differentials between North and South.

The New Economics of Migration

According to theorists of the new economics of labour migration, international migration is a strategic behaviour undertaken by families and households, not individuals; and the primary motivation for movement is not the reaping of higher lifetime earnings at the place of destination, but the management of risk and the overcoming of market failures at home. By migrating internationally, poor families seek to secure scarce capital so they can finance large consumer purchases and initiate new productive enterprises at low risk. Whereas circular migration, remittances, and investments undertaken by migrants in home communities are anomalous under neoclassical economics, they are explicitly predicted under the new economic model.

There is considerable circumstantial evidence in the European system to suggest that international migration is employed strategically by families to finance consumption and investment at home and to manage risk. As in the North American system, a variety of field studies document the propensity of migrant households to diversify their sources of income through foreign wage labour, which is typically combined with local production and work in the home community. Such a pattern has been documented for Spain (Rhoades 1978, 1979), Yugoslavia (Baucic 1972), Turkey (Kaysar 1972; Abadan-Unat *et al.* 1975; Pennix and Van Renselaar 1978), North Africa (Baddou 1983; Lazaar 1987, 1993; Simon 1990; Bencherifa *et al.* 1992), and the Sahel (Condé *et al.* 1983). By combining foreign labour with local employment and production, families are able to achieve a higher level of consumption and investment with fewer risks to household income.

Beyond this circumstantial evidence, however, there are few systematic empirical tests of propositions derived from the new economic model. Indeed, our survey of the literature uncovered only two studies germane to this body of theoretical work. Kumcu (1989) estimated a multivariate regression model to predict the savings behaviour of Turkish guestworkers in Germany. He found that migrants who owned property in Turkey and who had articulated a plan to return home before retirement saved considerably more money than other migrants, suggesting that employment in Germany was being used as a means of accumulating capital for use at home (in accordance with the new economic model) rather than as a means of achieving higher income and consumption abroad (as assumed by neoclassical economics).

Huntoon (1995) analysed the behaviour of guestworkers returning to Spain after a period of work in Germany. Her multivariate model showed that, other things equal, migrants with savings went to regions with high interest rates to buy a house, indicating that they were sensitive to interregional variation in mortgage interest rates, which in turn suggests that they were using wage labour in Germany as a means of overcoming barriers to capital (i.e. the high cost of home mortgages) in Spain.

Thus, although the European evidence generally supports the new economic perspective, findings remain suggestive rather than definitive. Most studies were not designed to test propositions derived from this theoretical model and they provide few results germane to its hypotheses. This situation reflects the greater demands on data made by the new economic model compared with neoclassical theory: whereas the latter can be tested using aggregate data tabulated across space or time, the new economics of migration generally requires microdata on the behaviour of households and individuals.

The current empirical vacuum with respect to the new economic model can only be filled when European investigators begin implementing surveys of sending communities that ask detailed questions about migration, remittances, income, spending, and investment. Only then will analysts be able to test for non-unitary effects of remittances on household income in the manner of Taylor (1992*a*); document the effect of foreign earnings on income distributions in the manner of Stark and Taylor (1989, 1991); reveal the effect of migration on local production in the manner of Adelman *et al.* (1988); or show the connection between interest rates and emigration in the manner of Massey and Espinosa (1996). Until the right data are collected, the leading hypotheses of the new economics of migration will remain untested in Europe.

Segmented Labour Market Theory

Segmented labour market theory holds that post-industrial economies are characterized by a dual economic structure that generates a built-in demand for immigrant labour, so that immigration occurs in response to shifts in employment rather than changes in wage rates. Once a critical mass of immigrants in a receiving city is reached, moreover, immigrant enclaves may form to create another economic sector demanding immigrant labour, augmenting the dual post-industrial structure of primary and secondary labour markets to create a trichotomous structure of an immigrant enclave plus primary and secondary sectors.

As discussed earlier, the European literature offers ample evidence that labour demand plays a dominant role initiating international migration into Western Europe. Peach (1968) found that fluctuations in the rate of West Indian emigration during the 1950s were tied more closely to changes in British employment than to variation in wage differentials. Likewise, Böhning (1970) found that job vacancies significantly predicted migration from seven of nine countries into Germany, but that wage rates predicted the flows in just two cases. Likewise, Straubhaar (1986) showed that changes in employment were more powerful than wage differentials in predicting out-migration from five countries to Western Europe, a finding confirmed by Walsh (1974) in his study of migration between Ireland and Britain.

These quantitative findings simply confirm what is obvious from the post-war history of European immigration. As shown by Kindleberger (1967), Castles and Kosack (1973), Tapinos (1975), Salt (1976), Martin and Miller (1980), Korte (1985), and Castles (1986), flows of immigrants into Western Europe were initiated, virtually without exception, by labour recruitment programmes established by European governments for the express purpose of covering shortfalls in the supply of workers during an era of rapid economic expansion. As predicted by Piore (1979) and other segmented labour market theorists, therefore, the migration of foreigners into Western Europe was demand-led. In addition, the distribution of workers across economic sectors displayed a clear pattern of segmentation, at least initially. Certain sectors were reserved for natives while others were dominated by immigrant workers (see Böhning 1972, 1984; Castles and Kosack 1973; Tapinos 1975; Berrier 1985; Salt 1986).

The European system thus provides clear and rather compelling evidence to support the hypothesis that international migration originates in the dual labour market structure that characterizes mature capitalist economies. Given the large number of immigrants now in Europe, however, and their high concentration in many cities, it is surprising that European investigators have not sought to identify and study emerging immigrant enclaves. As far as we can determine, social scientists have not attempted to document the existence of immigrant economic enclaves in European cities, nor have they examined patterns of socio-economic mobility within them. In Europe, there is nothing like the empirical research of Portes and his colleagues (Portes and Bach 1985; Portes and Manning 1986; Portes and Jensen 1987, 1989) or his more recent successors (Sanders and Nee 1987; Zhou and Logan 1989; Logan *et al.* 1994). The closest thing to a study of immigrant enterprise was that of Ma Mung and Guillon (1986) who examined the penetration of immigrants into the commercial sector of Paris.

World Systems Theory

A comparable scarcity of research characterizes world systems theory, which argues that international migration stems from the penetration of capitalist economic relations into peripheral countries where non-market or pre-market social and economic structures prevail (see Sassen 1988). Led by direct foreign investment and fomented by the creation of export-processing zones, the emerging market economy displaces people from traditional livelihoods and creates a mobile population prone to migrate. At the same time, the formation of ideological and material links to global cities in the developed world channel a large share of these workers abroad, where they are employed in secondary labour markets created by the remarkable accumulation of capital and wealth in those world centres.

Although Sassen (1991) has documented London's status as a global city and discussed the role that immigrants play in its post-industrial economy, we could not find any systematic tests of the propositions of world systems theory (such as that carried out by Rickets (1987) for the North American system). We uncovered no efforts to link emigration to variation in the level of direct foreign investment, to the establishment of export-processing zones, to shifts in class structure in leading European destination cities; or to the effect of colonial or military entanglements in sending regions.

Despite a relative lack of formal analyses pertaining to the world systems model, scattered evidence exists in support of the theory. Baletic (1982) argues that emigration from Yugoslavia during the 1960s and 1970s stemmed partly from capital-intensive development in agriculture, although he rejects the view that this stems from *capitalist* penetration, since it was a product of Yugoslavia's socialist planners. Park (1992) carried out a quantitative analysis of emigration from Morocco's thirty-five districts and showed that market penetration into the country's least developed region (composed of districts around Marrakesh) produced a significant increase in migration, whereas expansion of the market within districts in the more developed northern region (around Tangiers) yielded significantly lower emigration.

Friedman (1986), in his analysis of global cities, identified London, Paris, Rotterdam, Frankfurt, and Zurich as Europe's primary global cities, with Brussels, Milan, Vienna, and Madrid as secondary centres. Although no investigator has demonstrated that these places attract a disproportionate share of European immigrants (as world systems theory would suggest), all house large immigrant populations, lending prima-facie validity to Sassen's (1988) theory. Garson (1988) also gives a clear and convincing historical and documentary account of how old colonial ties structure the migration flows between Africa and France.

In 1994, the Economic Commission for Europe of the United Nations sponsored a round of 'ethnosurveys' in Poland (Okolski *et al.* 1995; Jazwinska and Okolski 1996), Ukraine (Pyrozhkov *et al.* 1995), and Lithuania (Sipaviciene *et al.* 1995) modelled on similar surveys undertaken in Mexico by Massey and colleagues (Massey 1987c; Massey *et al.* 1987, 1994). These surveys document very clearly the initiation of emigration to the West as a direct response to market penetration.

Eastern European nations such as Poland, Lithuania, and Ukraine offer a kind of natural experiment in the effects of market penetration. Before 1989 they were largely cut off from the capitalist West, shielded from the forces of competition, and protected from the effects of economic globalization. With the fall of the Berlin Wall and the collapse of the Soviet Union, these nations were suddenly exposed to the forces of an international capitalist economy for the first time in many decades. Each country-specific report to the European Economic Commission documents a clear upsurge in international migration during the transition to a market economy.

During the era of Soviet domination, mobility was low and dominated by military moves and other state-sponsored activities. With the collapse of the Soviet system, mobility immediately rose. The first migrants tended to be traders making successive circular trips back and forth to purchase goods in the West and resell them at home. They were followed by labourers who worked seasonally in the West before returning home with savings to finance consumption and investment there (as predicted under the new economics). Seasonal foreign labour was especially common among Poles, who like Mexicans, took advantage of a common border with an advanced industrial society.

Most recently, settled communities of Eastern Europeans have begun to form in Western cities, creating a new social infrastructure capable of sponsoring the arrival and integration of later waves of emigrants (as specified under social capital theory). In general, the more integrated a country is into Western markets, the higher the rate of out-migration, so that mobility is greatest in Poland, followed by Lithuania, and finally Ukraine. Judging from these early studies, therefore, additional out-migration to the West can be expected to occur as market forces penetrate more deeply—geographically, socially, and economically—into the former non-market societies of Eastern Europe.

Social Capital Theory

Social capital theory argues that, however initiated, migration is perpetuated by networks of kinship and friendship, and by social organizations devoted to the entry and circulation of migrants, both of which constitute sources of social capital that potential migrants can draw upon to reduce the costs and risks and raise the benefits of international movement. In the North American literature, the effect of network ties has been demonstrated in two ways: by showing a 'family and friends effect' at the aggregate level (documenting that immigrants tend to go to places and settle in cities where prior immigrants from the same country have concentrated); and at the micro-level, by showing how the possession of a social tie to someone living abroad or with prior migrant experience raises the odds of international out-migration.

The positive effect that a large stock of prior immigrants has in promoting additional migration was demonstrated by Walsh (1974) in his analysis of net migration between Ireland and Britain. According to his results, the larger the number of Irish emigrants in one year, the greater the flow in the next year, controlling for wage and employment differentials between the two countries and making appropriate statistical adjustments for serial autocorrelation. At the individual level, O'Gráda (1986) demonstrated that having a sibling in Britain in 1965 significantly increased the likelihood that Irish teenagers would emigrate by 1968. Aside from these two studies, however, we could find no other quantitative tests of social capital theory in the European system.

More common are qualitative analyses that document the existence and operation of migrant networks, community associations, and other institutional forms involved in the migration process. In Britain, Joly (1987) has described the structure and operation of Pakistani community associations, while Josephides (1987) has done the same for Greek Cypriots and Philpott (1973) has accomplished this task for West Indians. Hily and Poinard (1987) show how networks operate among Portuguese migrants to France to channel jobs and resources and to provide a platform for the entry of new arrivals. Campani and Catani (1985) and Campani et al. (1987) carried out parallel analyses among Italian immigrants in France. Lelièvre (1987), however, shows how migration can influence the constitution of families in France, and that it is not only family ties that influence migration.

Several studies have documented the role that networks play in promoting movement between Finland and Sweden (Jaakkola 1987; Pohjola 1991), and Cammaert (1986) has documented the existence of a migrant network linking sending communities in Morocco to specific neighbourhoods in Brussels, while Tarrius (1987) has done the same for Tunisian migrants in Marseilles. Probably the largest number of network studies have focused on the role that social networks play in facilitating the arrival, adaption, and integration of Turkish guestworkers in Germany (see Kudat 1975; Kiray 1976; Wilpert 1984, 1988, 1992; Gitmez and Wilpert 1987).

Although these case studies and field reports clearly demonstrate the existence of migrant networks and their importance in the migration process, the European literature yields little in the way of quantitative analysis documenting the effect of network ties in promoting and sustaining international movement, studies that have become increasingly common in the North American literature. Once again, such an analysis awaits the collection and compilation of appropriate data.

Cumulative Causation

The theory of cumulative causation argues that migration changes the social and economic context within which individual and household decisions are made, specifically in ways that make subsequent migration more likely. In North America the process of cumulative causation has been most convincingly demonstrated through quantitative analyses of how network ties and income inequality change over time in response to migration, and how these changes feed back onto the household decision process to promote additional migration. Unfortunately, we did not encounter similar studies for any nation in the European system.

In Europe, the principal evidence on cumulative causation once again comes from qualitative reports suggesting the emergence of a pattern of dependent development in sending regions and a growing reliance on immigrants in receiving societies. Böhning (1984) offers data to show how immigrants enter receiving societies within a narrow and well-defined economic niche, but then spread outward to other economic sectors as employers become dependent on their services and forego structural adjustments within their firms that might attract native workers, improve efficiency, and eliminate the demand for immigrants.

More common is the argument that large-scale emigration leads to a pattern of dependent development in sending communities. According to Böhning (1984), for example, migration allows a higher standard of living than can be supported through local labour, causing people to continue migrating in order to support the level of consumption to which they have grown accustomed, which makes it less likely they will invest locally to generate economic growth that might preclude the need for migration. As a result, communities become locked into a self-perpetuating cycle of migration and stunted development.

Such a feedback process has been discerned in fieldwork undertaken by a variety of researchers working in several distinct sending regions, including Yugoslavia (Baucic 1972; Bennett 1979; and Baletic 1982); Spain (Rhoades 1978, 1979); Morocco (Lebon 1984; Lazaar 1987); Italy (Vivolo 1984); and most of all for Turkey (Abadan-Unat *et al.* 1975; Kolan 1975; Pennix and Van Renselaar 1978; and Heckmann 1985). As will be discussed in the chapters on migration and development, however, there are serious problems with the design, methodology, and data of these studies that render their conclusion of cumulative causation somewhat suspect.

One other feedback process is better supported in the research literature, but again only in qualitative analyses. Some theorists have suggested that international migration is associated with the emergence of a 'culture of migration', where migration becomes so well established in a community that social pressures and expectations are brought to bear to encourage additional out-movement. Such a state of affairs has been mentioned by fieldworkers in Spain (Rhoades 1978, 1979), Portugal (Brettell 1979), the West Indies (Philpott 1973; Rubenstein 1979), Yugoslavia (Baucic 1972), and Turkey (Abadan-Unat *et al.* 1975; Pennix and Van Renselaar 1978), but again the data are rather impressionistic.

Conclusion

The research literature on international migration into Western Europe offers a much weaker and more limited basis for testing theory than the extensive and more theoretically directed empirical literature of North America. Aside from several studies conducted in the neoclassical tradition, the most salient feature of research on European immigration, aside from a scarcity of good data, is the *lack* of connection to theory. When studies bear on theoretical issues of concern to the field, it is usually by accident rather than by design. Nonetheless, a few studies yield relevant findings that permit initial generalization.

Despite vast differences in history, culture, and policies concerning international migration, the ultimate conclusion we reach in Europe is remarkably similar to that we derived from an extensive review of studies in North America: all theoretical paradigms receive some measure of support. The neoclassical prediction of a positive relationship between wage differentials and international migration flows is sustained, but as in North America wage gaps are by no means the strongest predictor of migration levels in the quantitative analyses that have been done.

Moreover, European studies, like their American counterparts, yield evidence suggesting that migration is connected to risk and market failures in sending regions (as expected under the new economic model) and to the formation and expansion of network ties connecting migrants and potential migrants (as specified under social capital theory), although the evidence adduced in each case is nowhere near as systematic or rigorous as in North America. We also find circumstantial evidence in support of world systems theory's leading proposition that migration emanates from capitalist development and is directed to global cities in core capitalist States, particularly in the round of ethnosurveys recently conducted by the UN Economic Commission for Europe in Poland, Lithuania, and Ukraine; but the data on cumulative causation, although consistent, are relatively weak and circumstantial.

The European and North American research literatures both yield one very clear and telling contrast with respect to the predictions of segmented labour market theory. Although labour demand continues to play a significant role in the initiation of migration into North America, active recruitment has not been a major factor since 1960, when the US Bracero Program began to be phased out. Even during the Bracero period (1942–64), recruitment efforts were principally confined to one country and since then they have played at most a supplementary role, taking a back seat to more the powerful forces described by the new economics of migration, world systems theory, and social capital theory (see Massey and Espinosa 1997).

In contrast, the initiation of European immigration was connected very directly and forcefully to recruitment programmes that began in the 1950s and lasted until 1973, and fluctuations in the volume of immigration continue to be quite strongly connected to variations in labour demand. In direct comparisons, European employment rates always predict immigration rates more strongly than international wage differentials.

European labour markets also seem to be more highly segmented than their American counterparts, reflecting tighter government controls on immigration and citizenship, and more limited access to employment extended to non-nationals within the EU. Growing out of guestworker programmes, immigration in most countries was explicitly organized by European governments to segment foreign workers off from the rest of society, housing and employing them in locations and sectors that were distinct from those of natives. As a result, segmented labour market theory carries more weight in Europe as an explanation for international migration, compared with North America where social capital theory, world systems theory, and the new economics of migration tend to predominate.

Despite the historical importance of labour demand and labour market segmentation in Europe, and the stronger role played by government policies in controlling the arrival, incorporation, and settlement of immigrants, it is not clear whether European governments will be any more successful in regulating immigration and preventing future entry than officials in North America. The process of immigrant settlement is already well advanced in many European countries, suggesting a growing role for the forces described by social capital theory and cumulative causation. Likewise, the potential for immigration arising from the penetration of capitalist markets into the former socialist economies of Eastern Europe to date remains largely unrealized. Eastern Europe thus constitutes an ever-present possibility for future growth in the number of immigrants, probably a more serious possibility than the much poorer and less economically developed in Africa and the Middle East. Whatever happens, Western Europe has arrived at a crossroads with respect to international migration.

5 Labour Migration in the Gulf System

During the post-war era, nations in both Europe and North America implemented recruitment programmes designed to facilitate the entry of foreigners as workers but to minimize their participation in society as human beings. The Bracero Program in the USA (Calavita 1992) and various guestworker programmes implemented in Germany and elsewhere (Castles and Kosack 1973; Martin 1991*a*) sought to extract labour from people without engaging them fully as social or political actors. In both nations, regulations sought to limit the length of stay, promote segregation in housing, tie the right of residence to employment, restrict the right of entry by family dependants, limit access to permanent resident visas, and, at least in Germany, discourage naturalization.

As subsequent research and practical experience have shown, however, these restrictive policies ultimately failed, and in both regions the temporary 'guests' of the 1950s and 1960s became the permanent settlers of the 1970s and 1980s (Martin and Miller 1980; Reichert and Massey 1982; Castles 1984, 1986; Massey and Liang 1989; Castles and Miller 1993). In the relatively open, democratic societies of Western Europe and North America, migrant networks flourished, institutions to promote clandestine immigration emerged, and organizations to defend the rights of immigrants arose. Employers, meanwhile, actively worked to circumvent the restrictive policies of the State and the migrants themselves shifted from sojourners to settlers. As earlier chapters have demonstrated, these processes occurred in a manner broadly consistent with hypotheses advanced by social capital theory and the theory of cumulative causation. What happened is summarized by the oft-quoted remark of Max Frisch that 'we called for workers and got human beings instead'.

International migration into the Middle East arose under very different circumstances. The countries of the Gulf Cooperation Council (GCC) achieved high per capita incomes not through autonomous processes of economic growth and industrial development, but from the historical accident of being located atop immense petroleum reserves during a period of rapid price inflation (Seccombe 1988). By the mid-1970s, the Gulf nations had amassed huge reserves of capital, which officials then deployed to construct a modern industrial infrastructure that they hoped would be capable of sustaining economic growth after the oil was gone. Rather than generating wealth through industrialization, therefore, the Gulf States sought industrialization through wealth (Ibrahim 1982).

In the early 1970s, countries in the GCC were themselves relatively undeveloped, with low levels of education, high rates of fertility, low rates of female labour force participation, a low degree of industrial and service employment, and little infrastructure for modern transportation, communications, or production (Birks and Sinclair 1980). Building an industrial base and constructing a developed economy required more labour at higher skill levels than the Gulf countries could supply domestically, and their political leaders turned to labour migration as the only feasible way to resolve this fundamental imbalance (Weiner 1982; Birks *et al.* 1988; Seccombe 1988).

As in the West, governments in the GCC sought to implement programmes that would extract labour from people without engaging them fully as human beings (Choucri 1978; El-Mallakh 1982; Ismael 1986; Nagi 1986*b*; Sell 1988). Unlike Germany and the USA, however, countries such as Saudi Arabia, Kuwait, Bahrain, Qatar, Oman, and the United Arab Emirates were not open, secular, pluralist democracies, but homogeneous Islamic societies led by hereditary monarchs who presided over centralized, non-democratic States. Officials in the Gulf States were thus in a stronger position than their counterparts in Germany or the USA to enforce a separation of the economic and social selves of the migrants.

Laws and regulations governing migration and labour within the GCC are consequently much stricter than those prevailing in Europe or North America (Halliday 1984; Dib 1988; Sell 1988; Abella 1992*a*). None of the Gulf nations recognizes any right to asylum, for example, and none allows residence without a job. In addition, no GCC country recognizes a right of family reunification; none guarantees legal access to housing, social benefits, or medical care; none offers migrants any rights of appeal with respect to decisions about their status; and all permit deportation at any time by simple administrative decree (Dib 1988). In short, whereas migrants are incorporated into the economic organization of the Gulf nations, they are explicitly excluded from social and political structures (Weiner 1982).

Within the GCC, residence permits are granted to foreign workers only for periods of one year, subject to renewal, except in Saudi Arabia, where the period is two years, and Kuwait, where it is five. In all cases, residence permits cannot be obtained without first having a job, and loss of job automatically leads to cancellation of the permit. Access to social benefits, health care, and housing is determined entirely by the migrant's employment contract. Although such contracts have been standardized and now include an allowance for housing, medical care for accidents at work, forty-five days of home leave per year, and a return ticket upon termination, aliens have few avenues of redress if these obligations are not honoured (Abella 1984; Halliday 1984; Dib 1988; Sell 1988).

Interior ministers within GCC nations have nearly unlimited discretionary power to expel foreign workers at any time without showing cause. In addition, foreign workers must submit a separate application for the entry of each family member, which the minister may approve or deny without explanation. Most GCC countries do not permit naturalization, and even though those that do permit foreign workers to acquire citizenship under restrictive conditions (Kuwait and the United Arab Emirates) do not grant naturalized immigrants the same rights as natives (Dib 1988).

The labour-importing nations of the Gulf thus sponsor strict labour migration regimes designed to maximize the economic potential of migrants as workers but to minimize their social participation as human beings. In this chapter, we undertake a critical review of data and research available in English, French, and Arabic to assess how well theories of international migration perform in explaining patterns within this unusual migration system. A key theoretical issue is whether the remarkable plenary powers exercised by Gulf authorities have been successful in neutralizing the forces that have led to the perpetuation of migration in Europe and North America. We also seek to determine how well migration into the Gulf region conforms to predictions derived from neoclassical economics, segmented labour market theory, world systems theory, and the new economics of labour migration. First, however, we begin with a description of the migration system that emerged in the oil-rich nations of the GCC over the past twenty years.

The Gulf Migration System

A small set of capital-rich, oil-producing countries in the Middle East form the core of a coherent, identifiable international migration system. Migratory flows converge on six wealthy States that border the Persian Gulf along the Arabian peninsula and are linked together politically through the Gulf Co-operation Council: Saudi Arabia, Kuwait, Bahrain, Qatar, Oman, and the United Arab Emirates. While these nations are rich in oil and capital, they are poor in labour reserves. Together their 18 million inhabitants constitute only 7 per cent of the Middle East's entire population; but they earn 81 per cent of its total income.

These six countries satisfy Zlotnik's (1992) criteria for system identification: they are connected by a formal agreement; they share a common history of immigration; they have similar cultures, religions, and economic structures; their immigrants display common occupational profiles; and they share a common policy of encouraging temporary labour migration while making permanent settlement difficult to arrange and citizenship nearly impossible (Birks and Sinclair 1980, 1992).

Throughout the 1950s and 1960s, labour migration occurred in association with the development of oil resources under British and American company domination (Seccombe and Lawless 1986; Seccombe 1998). The year 1973 was pivotal in transforming migratory patterns within the Gulf. Early in that year, the non-aligned nations held a conference in Algiers to push for a reevaluation of raw materials prices, including oil. The conference yielded a historic reconciliation between Iran and Iraq and created a new solidarity among oil-producing countries. Egyptian successes in the 1973 Yom Kippur War encouraged Arab nations to resist Israel's Western allies along a variety of fronts, including the formation of an oil cartel to drive up prices. Within a year oil prices had quadrupled, and even staunch Western allies such as the Shah of Iran found themselves unable to resist the lure of higher oil prices.

The rapid inflation in the price of oil after 1973 created massive accumulations of capital within the GCC that were then employed to finance large-scale economic development. The labour demand associated with this development led directly to the importation of workers, initially from other Arab nations that had large and growing populations and a relative surplus of workers over jobs. During the initial phases of Gulf migration, for example, Egypt supplied around 60 per cent of all workers to the Gulf States, while Jordan, Yemen, and Sudan accounted for most of the rest (Adams 1991; Feiler 1991; Omran and Roudi 1993).

Although labour migration from India dates to the 1930s, when the British imported South Asians to manage and control oil exploitation in the region, the entry of Indians was subordinate to that of Arabs during the initial phases of system development (Seccombe and Lawless 1986). During late 1970s and 1980s, however, recruitment in India expanded and then spread to other Asian nations. This diversification was facilitated by the fact that the rise in oil prices created serious foreign exchange problems for many Asian nations, giving them strong incentives to cooperate in labour migration as a means of securing (through migrant remittances) the currency they needed to pay their fuel bills. Over time, the origins of labour migrants therefore shifted and diversified, and by the outbreak of the Gulf War in 1990, Kuwait employed workers from some forty-eight different nations (Russell 1992*a*).

Although it is easy to designate the Gulf States as the core of a migration system conceptually, it is more difficult to measure flows empirically because data are once again limited and plagued by inconsistencies between sources. Birks and Sinclair (1980, 1992) combed available statistics to compile a picture of stocks and flows, as have Omran and Roudi (1993). Table 5.1 draws on a recent report by the UN Economic and Social Commission for Western Asia (1993), which builds on this earlier work, to show the number of foreign workers in countries of the Gulf Cooperation Council in 1990, along with changes in the number of foreign workers between 1980 and 1990.

This table reveals the large size of contemporary migration flows into the Gulf States, in both relative and absolute terms, and the extraordinary dependence of the GCC countries on immigrant labour. During the 1980s the population of foreign workers nearly doubled to reach 5.2 million, and in all countries immigrants constituted a majority of workers in the labour force in 1990. The lowest percentage of foreign workers was observed in Bahrain, where 'only' 51 per cent of all workers were foreign; in Oman the figure was 70

Table 5.1   Number of foreign workers in countries of the Gulf Cooperation Council (GCC) in 1990, and changes between 1980 and 1990 ('000s)

GCC country	1990	1980–90	Percent of workers foreign in 1990
Bahrain	132	54	51
Kuwait	731	338	86
Oman	442	272	70
Qatar	230	124	92
Saudi Arabia	2,878	1,144	80
United Arab Emirates	805	334	89
TOTAL	5,218	2,266	68

Source: United Nations (1993).

per cent. In Kuwait, Qatar, Saudi Arabia, and the United Arab Emirates, the percentage ranged upwards of 80 per cent. In the tiny state of Qatar (population 413,000) a remarkable 92 per cent of all workers were foreign, and across all GCC countries, 68 per cent of the workforce and 40 per cent of the population was of foreign nationality (Birks and Sinclair 1992). The share of foreign workers has risen steadily over the years in most GCC countries. In Saudi Arabia, for example, it went from 27 per cent in 1970 (Shah 1993) to 32 per cent in 1975 (Omran and Roudi 1993), to 53 per cent in 1980, to 79 per cent in 1985, and finally reached 80 per cent in 1990 (Birks and Sinclair 1992).

Table 5.2 shows the distribution of foreign workers within GCC countries by nationality along with estimated changes between 1980 and 1990. The structure of the system is shown graphically in Figure 5.1, where once again the width of the streams are drawn proportional to the estimated size of the flows. These displays reveal the growth and diversification of international migration into the Gulf region during the 1980s.

Although Egypt was the predominant sending nation during the early phases of Gulf migration, by the early 1990s first place had been captured by India, which accounted for 20 per cent of all foreign residents within GCC States. Egypt occupied the second spot with about 16 per cent of all foreign residents, but its growth over the decade lagged behind that of India. Whereas 779,000 Indians entered GCC countries as migrants between 1980 and 1990, only 537,000 Egyptians did so.

These contrasting trends between India and Egypt are part of a broader trend away from dependence on Middle Eastern sources. Although the Gulf system continued to experience significant growth in migration from Lebanon and Sudan, it experienced a substantial *out-migration* of Iranians, Palestinians, Moroccans, Tunisians, and Yemenis. The latter population, in particular, de-

Table 5.2 Foreign population of nations in the Gulf
Cooperation Council by nationality, 1990

Source region	1990	1980–90
Middle East		
Egypt	1,105.4	537.0
Iran	71.2	−4.6
Jordan/Palestine	602.7	−132.1
Lebanon	203.4	83.1
Morocco and Tunisia	11.2	−2.5
Sudan	257.7	119.9
Syria	111.7	8.5
Yemen	87.6	−285.9
Other Arab	292.7	151.8
Asia		
India	1,426.4	779.1
Bangladesh	507.9	296.5
Pakistan	828.2	
Sri Lanka	453.0	
Philippines	428.9	1,246.2
South Korea	97.2	
Thailand	80.8	
TOTAL	7,075.9	

Sources: Birks and Sinclair (1980 and 1992).

clined drastically after the Gulf War, when restrictions were placed on Yemenis working in the region. According to Birks and Sinclair (1992), the number of Yemeni workers in Saudi Arabia declined from 850,000 before the crisis to less than 60,000 afterwards.

In total, migration from Middle Eastern countries to the Gulf States rose by only 475,000 during the 1980s, representing just 17 per cent of the net increase in the number of foreigners. The bulk of the growth in the Gulf system's foreign population occurred through the migration of Asians, who by 1990 comprised a majority of all foreigners within the GCC. In addition to India's contribution of nearly 780,000 migrants, Bangladesh sent 297,000 and other Asian nations (mainly Pakistan, Sri Lanka, the Philippines, South Korea, Thailand) contributed another 1.25 million persons.

Over time there has also been a gradual shift eastward in the origins of Asian migrants. In the 1970s, South Asian countries were the main suppliers of workers, but since 1980 South-East Asia, and to a lesser extent East Asia, have become increasingly important. Whereas India and Pakistan contributed 97 per cent of all Asian workers to the Gulf in 1975, by 1989 the figure had

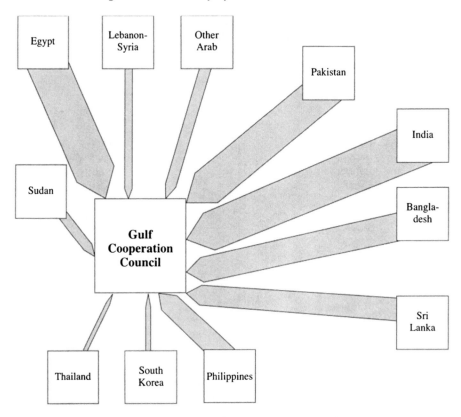

Fig. 5.1   International migration in the Gulf system, 1980–1990

dropped to just a third. Meanwhile, Indonesia, Korea, the Philippines, and Thailand, which collectively only accounted for just 2 per cent of Gulf migrants in 1974, represented 51 per cent by 1989 (Shah 1993).

The increase in the stock of Asian migrants within Gulf countries accounts for only a fraction of the total number of people involved because of the constant coming and going of workers. According to the United Nations (1992), nearly 1 million people leave eight Asian nations each year through legal channels to perform seasonal work in the Middle East, with 87 per cent coming from India, Pakistan, the Philippines, and Korea. By the early 1990s, the Philippines had come to dominate this circular flow of workers, and in 1992 alone, some 370,000 Filipinos worked in Saudi Arabia (Birks and Sinclair 1992). At the same time, the migration of South Korean workers declined from 151,000 in 1982 to just 21,000 in 1988 (Birks and Sinclair 1992). During the late 1980s and early 1990s, moreover, migration from Indonesia appears to have gained ground. According to unpublished statistics from the Indonesian

Ministry of Manpower (made available to Graeme Hugo), the number of emigrants to the Middle East rose from 11,000 during 1980–1 to 98,000 in 1992–3.

The growing involvement of Asian countries in the Gulf system reflects an explicit desire on the part of GCC nations to deter the permanent settlement and social integration of labour migrants. The ethnic, linguistic, and religious backgrounds of Asians set them apart from the local population more than workers from neighbouring Arab nations, thereby minimizing the propensity to settle. In addition, GCC nations are very selective in granting nationality to outsiders, and even when rights are granted they are different from those of native-born citizens (Dib 1988; Sell 1988; Russell 1989).

While in the Gulf, foreign workers participate in a hierarchical labour system that allocates different nationalities to different statuses subject to different conditions. At the top are a small number of Western professional experts, who earn the highest salaries and enjoy the most extensive array of benefits and privileges, followed in descending order by local citizen workers, Arab migrants, and finally Asian migrants. In Saudi Arabia, Asian workers are paid half what their Arab counterparts get for the same work (Omran and Roudi 1993).

These differentials originate in practices implemented by US and British petroleum companies during the 1930s and 1940s. As British subjects, Indian workers were easily imported into a territory controlled by the colonial power, and they quickly organized themselves into relatively autonomous communities that provided for their own needs and whose relations with local Arabs were mediated by the British. These arrangements persisted after independence under concessions granted to the oil companies that permitted them to recruit their workforces. These concessions continued through 1973 and British and American companies routinely paid lower wages to Asians than to their own nationals. Seccombe (1992) notes social tensions between Arabs and Asians dating back to the 1930s and 1940s owing to the fact that foreign companies generally preferred Asian to Arab labour even during periods of high local unemployment.

During 1990–91 the Gulf War produced a major upheaval in the international migration system and demonstrated how vulnerable its foreign workers were to shifts in immigration policy, and how reliant sending nations were on remittances as a source of foreign exchange. According to Russell (1992*a*: 721), 'the mass dislocations following Iraq's invasion of Kuwait are among the most far-reaching in recent history. Altogether, in the space of twelve months, it is estimated that between 4 and 5 million people were uprooted.' Some migrants were used as human shields against attack, others were stranded without assets or the ability to pay their return fares. Some Pakistani workers are reported to have walked all the way home, and in the aftermath of the war, Palestinians and Yemenis were deported en masse from both Kuwait and

Saudi Arabia. Russell (1992*a*) estimates that the loss in remittances to countries of origin exceeded $5 billion.

The Gulf War, following close on the heels of a long and bloody conflict between Iran and Iraq, broke the solidarity of Arab oil producers and undermined their ability to maintain high prices. With the drop in oil prices in the mid-1980s, many observers expected labour migration into the Gulf to diminish (Russell 1992*a*). Despite the slackening of labour demand, however, the declines in migration failed to materialize. Indeed, the drop in labour migration from Arab nations was more than counterbalanced by an acceleration of migration from Asia. This acceleration has also been accompanied by a shift in the *nature* of the labour demanded. Construction work has given way to service employment, and the involvement of migrant women has increased. Females now dominate the outflow of migrants from Sri Lanka and Indonesia (see Spaan 1988; Eelens *et al.* 1990; Hugo 1992). The shift towards services has also produced greater variety of immigrant occupations, which range from unskilled labourers, through semi-skilled operatives and skilled craftsmen, to highly educated professionals (Birks and Sinclair 1992).

The continuation of massive labour migration into the Gulf region depends crucially on the persistence of oil revenues. Since oil is a non-renewable and ultimately finite resource, at some point earnings from petroleum will begin to dwindle, and unless current investments in infrastructure and industry have borne fruit by then, the flows of migrants will inevitably slacken. In the interim, fluctuations in the price of oil will largely determine the capacity of the GCC countries to absorb migrants, but the potential for political shocks adds a significant element of uncertainty to the system.

The small populations of GCC countries virtually guarantee that labour migration will continue for the foreseeable future, despite Kuwait's announced intention of reducing its dependence on foreign workers. Rather than reducing labour importation, GCC governments will be more likely to diversify their sources by recruiting more workers from Asia while limiting their intake from the Arab world (Omran and Roudi 1993). In doing so, they hope to reduce their dependence on unstable, politically volatile labour sources; avoid an overreliance on any single nation; and minimize the likelihood of long-term settlement through the selection of culturally and religiously dissimilar migrants.

Will the GCC countries succeed in preventing permanent settlement where European and North American governments have failed? Only time will tell. In some countries, established Arab workers have already become *de facto* permanent residents, and some migrant groups have formed well-developed cultural associations in Saudi Arabia (Omran and Roudi 1993). Women are also increasingly being employed as migrant workers, increasing the odds of family formation and settlement. Whether or not individual migrants stay or go, however, international migration itself has become a permanent feature of social and economic life in the Gulf region.

The Economics of Gulf Migration

Segmented Labour Market Theory

The theory of segmented labour markets was developed by Michael Piore (1979) and others to explain migration into advanced industrial societies, and as originally envisaged, immigrants would constitute only a small fraction of the total labour force. In mature capitalist economies, so the theory goes, the labour market bifurcates into a primary, capital-intensive sector of high-paying, stable jobs with multiple avenues for advancement, and a secondary, labour-intensive sector of unstable, low-wage jobs with few paths of upward mobility. Since it is difficult to recruit natives into the latter sector without costly changes in the social organization and the cultural meaning of work, employers look abroad to find workers to fill these positions, yielding a persistent demand for immigrant labour.

The oil-exporting nations of the Gulf obviously do not replicate the economic conditions originally envisioned by segmented labour market theorists. The GCC states are not wealthy, industrialized societies seeking to attract foreign workers to overcome structural employment problems; they are pre-industrial nations seeking to use a windfall of capital to construct, maintain, and operate a new industrial base. Rather than importing workers to fill a small number of positions in a narrow segment of the economy, they recruit massive numbers of foreigners to occupy most of the jobs in fledgling industrial systems.

The Gulf countries thus constitute a special case of market segmentation in which immigrants dominate the labour force, and in which the industrial base is still in the process of construction. Although foreign workers in the Gulf were initially concentrated in the construction industry—building roads, bridges, ports, telecommunications facilities, power plants, transmission networks, and factories—over time they shifted to maintaining and operating this new infrastructure (Shaw 1979, 1983; Ecevit 1981; Nagi 1986*a*; Birks *et al.* 1988).

Throughout the process of industrialization, GCC citizens have been concentrated in government and the top echelons of the private sector, a concentration that has only increased over time. In Kuwait, the best-documented case, 75 per cent of native males were employed as professionals, administrators, service workers, or clerical employees in 1970, with only 23 per cent employed in production and 11 per cent in sales (Shah 1986). By 1980, only 16 per cent of Kuwaiti men worked in production and 6 per cent in sales, and by 1993 these numbers had dropped to just 10 per cent and 3 per cent (Shah 1995). Thus, very few Kuwaiti men play a direct role in economic production; and although Kuwaiti women have entered the labour force in significant numbers in recent years, 93 per cent are employed in professional or clerical positions (ibid.).

In contrast, 58 per cent of non-Kuwaiti men worked in production in 1993, and 74 per cent of non-Kuwaiti women worked in services, primarily as domestics (Shah 1995). All told, foreign workers outnumbered natives in the labour force by a margin of more than 4 to 1 among men, and nearly 3 to 1 among women. Even when non-Kuwaitis work in the same occupations as Kuwaitis, moreover, they put in more hours and longer labour. Among professional workers, for example, Kuwaitis averaged 35 hours per week compared with 40 hours among non-Kuwaitis. Among managers and administrators the differential was 38 hours for natives compared with 48 hours for foreigners; among service workers the figures were 45 hours and 60 hours; and among production workers 41 hours and 51 hours (ibid.).

Thus, rather than a bifurcation between capital- and labour-intensive sectors of an advanced industrial economy, labour market segmentation within the Gulf States is between privileged natives in government and the upper tiers of private enterprise and immigrants in the rest of the economy, including nearly all material production (done by foreign men) and domestic service (done by foreign women). In the words of one observer, the Gulf States thus constitute 'a social order divided between a consumer-oriented native population and a productivity-oriented migrant population' (Weiner 1982: 3), which is managed and controlled by a 'sinecurist public sector' reserved for natives (Seccombe 1988). Oil wealth thus transformed 'onto a higher plane through "modern" means. . . . the Emir's traditional role as dispenser of wealth and assistance', yielding a highly paid, lavishly supported, and relatively unproductive public sector of citizen-employees (Benton 1979: 4).

In this segmented system, a traditional cultural institution, the *kafala*, has been adapted in the effort to generate privileged opportunities for natives (Beauge 1986) through a postmodern blending of folk and modern forms (Harvey 1990). Any foreigner who wishes to do business in GCC countries must find a *kafil*, or guarantor, who for a fee will act as a link to the host society. The kafala originates in the Bedouin practice of requiring outsiders to have a sponsor, or kafil, for safe passage through a clan's territory. In the modern Gulf, any citizen may serve as kafil for a foreign entrepreneur. A kafil is necessary because foreigners, by themselves, are prohibited from owing property and engaging in trade. Kafils thus provide access to licences, government contracts, indirect property ownership, markets, and banking services. Foreign firms and entrepreneurs compete with one another to find influential kafils, the most powerful of which belong to the royal family.

Not only do natives have privileged access to public sinecures and private business opportunities; even when they perform the same work as foreigners, they typically earn more money. Throughout the Gulf, there is a widespread pattern of wage discrimination in favour of natives and against foreign workers. In Saudi Arabia, for example, citizens in 1989 were paid 3.6 times more than Asians in the same jobs; and a 1987 survey of Saudi firms employing more than 100 workers revealed that the wages of natives were 40 per cent higher than those of other Arabs (Arab Population Conference 1993). The severity of wage discrimination follows a rough national origins hierarchy, with Europeans and Americans at the top, Asians at the bottom, and non-GCC Arabs in-between.

The best-documented case is again that of Kuwait. Al-Qudsi and Shah (1991) estimated wage regressions to predict the log of monthly earnings for male workers using a set of predictor variables that included standard human capital indicators: years of education, years of pre-migration labour market experience, years of post-migration labour market experience, sector of employment, proficiency in Arabic, and marital status. A set of dummy variables measured the independent effect of national origins while controlling for these background factors. Consistent with wage regressions estimated in other countries, Al-Qudsi and Shah (1991) found that earnings rose sharply with education and with labour market experience accumulated both before and after migration. They also found that fluency in Arabic conferred a substantial earnings premium and that married men earned more than those without spouses. Other things equal, moreover, earnings were about 12 per cent lower in the public than the private sector.

Holding constant these background factors, however, foreign men received substantially lower earnings than Kuwaiti men. The deficit was 81 per cent for Bangladeshis, 72 per cent for Indians, 67 per cent for Egyptians, 60 per cent for Iraqis, 59 per cent for Palestinians and Jordanians, 44 per cent for Syrians and Lebanese, and 37 per cent for Iranians. These differences are very large compared to differentials between blacks and whites in the USA, which has an unusually long history of harsh racial discrimination (Farley 1984; Farley and Allen 1987; National Research Council 1989).

When Al-Qudsi and Shah (1991) estimated the regressions separately by occupational category, they found that discrimination against foreigners was most severe in services, less severe but still quite strong in blue-collar occupations, and least severe but still detectable in white-collar occupations. Only men in the residual 'Other' category earned more than Kuwaiti men (they were mainly Europeans and Americans); all other origin groups in all other occupations earned less than Kuwaitis. By way of summary, Al-Qudsi and Shah (1991: 163) concluded that 'the dominant feature of the Kuwait migrant earnings differentials is, therefore, the relative importance of potential wage discrimination in favour of Kuwaitis', which indicated to them 'that the labour market of Kuwait is segmented along ethnicity lines'.

Shah *et al.* (1991) carried out a separate analysis of wage discrimination against foreign women in Kuwait. They estimated separate earnings regressions for Kuwaiti, Arab, and Asian women in 1977–9 and compared results with the same regressions estimated in 1986–7. Their analysis, which controlled for education, experience, and family size, showed that the earnings gap between Kuwaiti and non-Kuwaiti women had widened over time, and that in the late 1980s most of the gap was explained by apparent discrimination.

Among Asian women, in particular, there were no returns to experience in the Kuwaiti labour market whatsoever. Although both Arab and Asian women possessed more human capital than Kuwaiti women, the mitigating effect of human capital in reducing the wage differential was overwhelmed by rampant discrimination in favour of Kuwaiti women.

Kuwait is in many ways the most progressive of the Gulf States, so discrimination in wages and hours worked is probably more severe elsewhere in the GCC. The existence of sharp wage differentials suggests that policymakers deliberately manipulate the national origins of the migrant workforce to sharpen the separation between the economic and social selves of foreign workers, and in so doing to extract labour more efficiently from immigrants.

GCC officials publicly express a preference for Arab migrants and laud the goal of 'Arabizing' their workforce (Russell 1989; Looney 1992). In addition, scholars in the GCC worry about the cultural effects of having so many non-Arab, non-Islamic migrants in their midst (Ibrahim and Mahmoud 1983; Fergany 1984; Ibrahim 1984). Despite these protestations, however, the Gulf States have steadily shifted recruitment away from Arabia and towards Asia, and within Asia away from the Indian subcontinent towards more distant nations in East and South-East Asia (Seccombe 1988; Birks and Sinclair 1992; Shah 1993). The shift from South to East Asia also entails a movement from Islamic to non-Islamic migrants. In making these shifts, GCC officials have come to rely more on formal contracts between consortia of employers and large recruitment organizations than on private agreements between individual employers and migrants (Ling 1984; Seccombe and Lawless 1985; Shah and Arnold 1986; Eelens and Speckmann 1990).

The way that Arabization programmes have worked out in practice is illustrated by the case of Kuwait, whose government launched a 'Kuwaitization' programme during the late 1980s and early 1990s. This effort sought to replace highly qualified (and expensive) migrant workers (usually Arabs, but also Europeans and Americans) with educated young Kuwaitis, who, owing to the decline in oil prices, could not be absorbed so readily into the usual government sinecures (Addleton 1991). Although the policy was successful in generating jobs for the small number of young Kuwaitis who before the programme had faced constricted employment opportunities, it did not fulfil the manifest goal of 'Arabizing' the workforce, since the departing Arabs were typically replaced by less qualified but cheaper and less politically threatening Asian workers (Looney 1992).

In sum, there is rather clear evidence of a broad pattern of labour market segmentation within the Gulf States; but unlike the situation in Western Europe and North America, where segmentation is between a numerically dominant, capital-intensive sector of natives and a small, labour-intensive sector of immigrants, the split in the Gulf is between a native élite who occupy privileged sinecures in government and business and a much larger, numerically dominant workforce of foreigners who do most of the productive work for longer hours and lower pay.

This segmented structure was manufactured deliberately by GCC political leaders, who through rules and regulations sought to undermine the bargaining position of migrants in the workforce. At the same time, by shifting the national origins of workers away from high-wage Muslim Arabs with a moral claim on justice toward low-wage, non-Islamic Asians unable to exercise such a claim, they were able to create a labour market in which open discriminatory practices could be more easily sustained. Now, as in the past, 'the Gulf governments . . . decide how many migrants to admit, what qualifications they must have, how long they can stay, what wages should be paid, what rights and benefits should be provided, and whether or not they should be imported from India, Pakistan, and other parts of Asia, or from Arab countries' (Weiner 1982: 7).

Labour migration within the Gulf system thus appears to be demand-led, brought about by the massive build-up of capital within the GCC after 1973 and its strategic deployment to foster rapid industrialization and development. Consistent with key predictions of segmented labour market theory, this development led to the emergence of a dual labour market and to the establishment of labour recruitment programmes designed to procure immigrants for jobs shunned by natives. Unlike the situation imagined by theorists such as Piore, however, migrants are not confined to a narrow segment of the economy, but occupy most of the Gulf s productive economic positions.

Neoclassical Economics

Although labour demand and market segmentation may predominate in explaining migration into the Gulf, this fact does not gainsay the validity of other explanations of labour migration, such as that offered by neoclassical economics. Even though migrants may be recruited to satisfy a demand for foreign workers created through labour market segmentation, the migrants themselves may be motivated to increase their incomes and be responsive to fluctuations in the international wage gap.

Consistent with the predictions of neoclassical economics, migrants to the Gulf region appear to be selected on traits likely to bring economic returns within Gulf labour markets. Elnajjar (1993) demonstrates that Palestinian emigrants from Gaza are better educated, more skilled, and more predominantly white-collar than people who remain behind, and Mahmoud (1983) found a similar pattern of selectivity for migrants from Sudan. Likewise Adams (1989) shows that the likelihood of out-migration from three Egyptian villages increases with education and prior employment experience. He also shows that income has a curvilinear effect on out-migration, yielding the highest probability of movement in the middle ranges (Adams 1993). Birks and Sinclair (1980) found that emigrants from Arab countries into Kuwait were drawn primarily from the technical, skilled, and semi-skilled sectors of their home societies.

Demery (1986) shows that emigrants from Asian countries are better educated than their non-migrant counterparts at home, and that they are highly concentrated in the middle ranges of the occupational distribution, mainly in the skilled blue-collar trades. According to the results of both Peerathep (1982) and Kanok and Uitrakul (1985), moreover, emigrants from rural Thailand are likewise drawn disproportionately from households with educated members. Once in the Gulf, Eelens (1988) shows that Sri Lankan migrants who earn high incomes are much less likely to return home than those with low incomes.

Thus, people who choose to migrate to the GCC tend to have characteristics that will be remunerated in Gulf labour markets. Drawing on the earlier work of Phuaphongsakorn (1982), Pongsapich (1989) presents cost/benefit ratios and rates of return to Gulf employment for Thai workers in different occupational categories. According to his figures, the cost/benefit ratio always exceeds 1 (the average is 1.69), indicating that immigrants consistently experience a net benefit from labour migration to the Gulf. The average rate of return per year of prior labour-force experience is 2.2 per cent above that in Thailand. Thus, a person with ten years of work experience could expect to earn a salary that was 22 per cent greater in the Gulf than in Thailand.

The returns are generally greatest for migrants with specialized skills. Thus, mechanics had a cost/benefit ratio of 4.4 and a net rate of return on experience of 4 per cent; electricians had a ratio of 3.2 and a net return rate of 3.7 per cent; and for drivers, the respective figures were 4.1 and 3.2 per cent. Despite the restrictive conditions of entry and employment within the Gulf Cooperation Council, therefore, and despite pervasive wage discrimination against them, Thai migrants can expect to receive clear and substantial economic returns from a period of paid labour in the Gulf States.

Although the net return to Gulf labour may be quite large for potential immigrants, it does not automatically follow that the volume of migration into the Gulf is related to fluctuations in international wage differentials, as predicted by the neoclassical model. The only study to examine this issue directly was conducted by Kandil and Metwally (1992), who regressed the rate of migration from Egypt to the Gulf on the relative size of the Egyptian population, the rate of Egyptian inflation, and the ratio of per capita income in the Gulf to that in Egypt (i.e. the wage differential).

Over the twenty-year period from 1966 to 1986, the investigators found that all three indicators displayed strong positive effects on the rate of Egyptian out-migration, with the effect of inflation being lagged. In general, migration into the Gulf accelerated about two years after a burst of inflation. The strongest effect in the model, however, was the per capita income ratio, suggesting that widening wage differentials after 1973 do help to explain the upsurge in Egyptian migration towards the Gulf. When the investigators re-estimated the model using data only on the flow of migrants between Egypt and Saudi Arabia, results were similar but the effect of the income ratio was even stronger.

Despite the apparent salience of labour demand in accounting for migration into the Gulf, therefore, neoclassical theory appears to have some explanatory validity: over time migration has tended to rise when the expected returns to Gulf labour increase and to fall when they decline. Kandil and Metwally's model, however, did not include an indicator of labour demand, which is likely to be correlated with per capita income, since the increase in Gulf income coincides with the mushrooming of labour demand. Thus, it is not clear how much of an effect wages would have if the effect of labour demand were held constant.

In addition, Kandil and Metwally focus on a rather unusual case. Migrants from Egypt probably correspond more closely the assumptions of neoclassical theory than do those from Asia. Whereas Egyptians (and Arab migrants in general) tend to obtain jobs as individuals through personal networks and direct contact with employers, Asians more often enter the region through intermediaries, after being recruited at home by a government corporation, private recruitment agent, or labour-contracting firm (Al-Moosa and McLachlan 1985; Birks *et al.* 1988; Seccombe 1988). Egyptians, therefore, correspond more closely to the assumptions underlying neoclassical theory (autonomous individuals acting freely in open markets) than do Asians. Very different results might have been obtained were the analysis to have been carried out for migration from India, Pakistan, or Korea.

The New Economics of Migration

Neoclassical economics has a hard time explaining the widespread practice of remitting money back to countries of origin. If migrants are utility maximizers moving to reap higher lifetime earnings, then logically they should endeavour to settle abroad permanently, cut economic ties with their home communities, and cease remitting their earnings. Yet many investigators have shown that the flow of migrant remittances from the countries of the GCC is truly massive (Gilani *et al.* 1981; Birks *et al.* 1986; Russell 1986, 1992*b*; Eelens and Speckmann 1990; Adams 1991*b*; Feiler 1991; Addleton 1991; Arnold 1992). In 1989, for example, Egypt alone received $US3.5 billion in remittances; India received $2.8 billion, Pakistan $1.9 billion, and Bangladesh $771 million (Russell and Teitelbaum 1992). The importance of remittances is such that during the 1990–1 Gulf War their interruption caused a major financial crisis in many migrant-sending nations (Addleton 1991; Russell 1992*a*).

Although remitting may be anomalous under neoclassical assumptions, it is theoretically expected under the new economics of labour migration, which predicts that migrants will send money home to diversify risks to household income and overcome failures in capital and credit markets. The observation of substantial, ongoing flows of remittances from the Gulf region into migrant-sending countries, and their use at home for consumption and investment purposes, thus provides strong prima-facie evidence in favour of the new economic model (see Chapters 8 and 9 for a complete review of the literature on remittances and their use).

A few studies offer more direct evidence on hypotheses derived from the new economics. Lefebvre (1990) undertook a case study of emigration from two Pakistani villages. He found that a lack of access to credit was a major problem for local farmers, especially those seeking to participate in Pakistan's ongoing Green Revolution, as such participation required them to buy expensive seeds, fertilizers, and equipment. According to Lefebvre (1990: 79), 'a vacuum in the rural credit facilities appeared' and as a result, 'new sources of credit were innovated . . . after the start of the "Green Revolution."' One of these 'innovations' was labour migration to the Gulf, which permitted migrants to channel remittances into productive investments once more basic needs had been satisfied. As a result, the rate of out-migration was highest among the landowning castes, who had the greatest need for capital by being in the best position to participate in the Green Revolution.

In his study of international migration from three Egyptian villages, Adams (1989 1991b) likewise found a high rate of out-migration among landowners, but only among those who were relatively poor. Non-poor households possessed resources that permitted them to self-finance production, so emigration was not necessary. Adams (1991b) also demonstrated that migrants did not spend excessively large amounts on consumption; indeed, migrants displayed a higher propensity to invest than non-migrants, other things equal.

World Systems Theory

There is very little in the research literature on the Gulf that supports the precepts of world systems theory, which hypothesizes, among other things, that migration is initiated by the penetration of capitalist socio-economic relations into traditional societies. There is no evidence, for example, that capital invested from the Gulf has played any role in fomenting emigration. Moreover, none of the countries of the GCC appears to contain an urban agglomeration that satisfies the criteria of a global city, which Sassen (1991) hypothesizes to attract immigrants. Of the thirty global cities identified empirically by Friedmann (1986), none was located in the Gulf region, even though twelve of the thirty were in other countries of the developing world.

The only evidence we could uncover in support of world systems theory comes from Lefebvre's (1991) observation that the arrival of the Green Revolution in rural Pakistan led to a desire for capital that was partially satisfied through out-migration to the Gulf. The penetration of capitalist agriculture into a traditional agrarian society thus disrupted longstanding social and economic relations and initiated a process of out-migration; but there is little evidence that the penetration of the market into Pakistan was in any way directed or financed from the Gulf.

The Sociology of Gulf Migration

While the forces that instigate international migration tend to be economic, those that perpetuate it across time and space tend to be social; and in Western Europe and the USA, it has been the social forces that have prevailed in the long run, yielding a influx of migrants after the initial conditions of demand have subsided. At issue in the present review is whether the centralized governments of the GCC have been successful in limiting migrants to the economic sphere and in precluding the emergence of social processes that have tended to perpetuate and sustain international migration in the West.

Social Capital Theory

The theory of social capital argues that networks of interpersonal ties and other social institutions created in the process of international migration have a life of their own that serves to promote additional movement by lowering the costs and risks of migration. In their study of Sri Lanka, Eelens and Speckmann (1990) identified several modes by which workers entered the Gulf States, which we reduce to four categories: government agencies, private companies, recruitment organizations, and personal networks. As these institutions come into existence and expand over time, migrants draw upon the social capital contained in their structures to support further international movement.

The first category identified by Eelens and Speckmann includes government bureaux and government-owned corporations in sending countries that sponsor the international movement of migrants for purposes of employment, and the second category includes private companies that undertake the same activities, often with government encouragement but not ownership. In both cases, a company or government agency signs a contract with an employer in the Gulf to supply a set quantity of workers at a fixed price to perform a well-defined task over a specified period of time, such as building a road, constructing a power plant, or staffing a factory. The number of workers, as well as their housing, salaries, and working conditions, are worked out in advance and administered directly by the company or bureau, which receives a contractual fee for providing the labour.

Private companies obviously find labour contracts attractive as a source of profit. Governments in sending countries find such arrangements attractive as a means of securing access to foreign exchange from workers' remittances (Amjad 1989), and a secondary motivation is the protection of migrants' rights (Shah and Arnold 1986; Abella 1992a). Thus, many governments, particularly those in East Asia, have been active in founding agencies and in subsidizing companies to promote the international movement of their citizens to the Gulf as contract workers (Arnold and Shah 1984; Abella 1992*a*).

During its phase of active participation in world labour markets, the Korean government was probably most assertive in promoting the out-migration of workers, founding a variety of institutions to facilitate the exportation of Korean workers for profit, including the Trade Promotion Corporation, which has employment centres throughout the region; the Korea Foundation for Middle East Studies, which advises firms on employment opportunities in the Gulf; and the Korean Overseas Construction Corporation, which assembles and coordinates construction companies for work in the Gulf. During the period 1979–81, twelve private Korean companies were also active in the Gulf region (Ling 1984).

Similar ventures were launched in other countries. Thailand created the Labour Management Organization to facilitate labour exports, and the governments of both the Philippines and Indonesia have established consortia to promote the export of workers. The Taiwanese government founded BES Engineering Corporation explicitly to secure contracts in the Middle East, and together with other large Taiwanese firms have established operations throughout the Middle East during the 1970s (Ling 1984).

Receiving countries find labour contracts with government agencies and private companies attractive because they limit the social and political costs of labour migration and are conducive to an 'enclave' style of development, whereby foreign workers are sequestered in special work camps that supply all their needs. In this way, contact with natives is minimized and potential social and political consequences from labour migration are muted (Ling 1984; Nagi 1986*a*; Shah and Arnold 1986). Camps effectively confine migrants to their roles as economic actors rather than allowing them to become full social beings, thus minimizing the risks of settlement and network formation (Abella 1992*a*).

In addition to government bureaux and private companies, labour migration into the GCC is facilitated by private recruitment agencies, which serve as a third source of social capital for aspiring migrants. These agencies generally act as middlemen, matching the needs of Gulf employers with the characteristics and abilities of workers identified in sending countries through recruitment agents. Private agencies may be authorized and regulated by officials in both countries, or unauthorized and largely working outside of the law, supplying workers on the international black labour market (Singhanetra-Renard 1992).

Eelens and Speckmann (1990: 306) argue that recruitment agencies entail 'an exchange relationship with capital, labour, information, and relations as resources'. According to Houben (1987), success in the business of labour recruiting requires the cultivation and maintenance of contacts with employers and bureaucrats in the Gulf, contacts that must be defended in a highly competitive international labour market. The existence of labour recruitment organizations has been well documented throughout South Asia in Bangladesh, India, Pakistan, Sri Lanka, Philippines, and Thailand (see Shah and Arnold 1986; Athukorala 1990; Eelens and Speckman 1990), but their use appears to be much less common in Arab countries.

The number of recruitment agencies has been growing throughout Asia. In Bangladesh, for example, the number of recruitment agencies increased from fifty-five in 1977 to 300 in 1980, and in Sri Lanka the count went from four to 544; in India it rose from 850 in 1980 to 1,119 in 1985, and in the Philippines it went from 650 to 964; by 1985 more than 300 specialized labour agencies were operating in Thailand (Abella 1992a).

The last category of social capital accessible to migrants comes in the form of migrant networks—webs of interpersonal connections linking migrants and potential migrants to employers in the Gulf. The existence of such networks and their use to acquire jobs in the Gulf have been documented in Lebanon (Azzam and Sahib 1989), Jordan (Kamiar and Ismail 1992), Yemen (Swanson 1979a), and throughout the Arab region generally (Al-Moosa and McLachlan 1985). Migrant networks have been found to play a role in promoting labour emigration from India (Weiner 1982; Kuthiala 1986), Pakistan (Burki 1991), Thailand (Singhanetra-Renard 1992), and Sri Lanka (Eelens and Speckmann 1990). Mostly this documentation consists of field reports or illustrative case studies; there is virtually no analytic work that quantifies the effect of networks on the likelihood of individual international movement.

The relative importance of government bureaux, private companies, recruitment agencies, and social networks in promoting migration to the Gulf appears to vary across time and space. Migrant networks seem to predominate as the principal mode of job acquisition for Arabs (Nagi 1986a), for in spite of at least seventeen bilateral agreements between nations in the Arab world, Arabs generally move as individuals (Ibrahim and Mahmoud 1983). Arab recruitment firms generally have difficulty competing with Asian companies, which are often government subsidized, so few Arab organizations exist to promote labour export. In their sample of migrants to Kuwait, for example, 89 per cent of whom were Arabs, Al-Moosa and McLachlan (1985) reported that half got their job through a relative, and another 45 per cent got it through direct contact with their employer.

Among Asian migrants to the Gulf, in contrast, the use of recruitment agencies seems to predominate. On their last trip to work in the Gulf, only 27 per cent of the Sri Lankans surveyed by Eelens and Speckmann (1990) reported getting their job through relatives or through personal contacts with the employer; 71 per cent reported using a recruitment agency and another 1 per cent went through a government employment bureau. Overall, specialized agencies account for around 28 per cent of Asian entries into the Gulf (Abella 1984), and nearly 90 per cent of all entries in the case of Thais (Singhanetra-Renard 1992).

Shah (1996) recently surveyed 800 Asian migrant workers in one district of Kuwait, selecting 200 male respondents from each of four key sending countries: Bangladesh, India, Pakistan, and Sri Lanka. About half of the migrants reported securing a work visa through a recruiting agent, but the percentage varied widely between nations, going from just 26 per cent among Indian migrants to 79 per cent among those from Sri Lanka. Among Pakistanis the share was 41 per cent and among Bangladeshis it was 53 per cent. In contrast to other migrants, those from Pakistan tended to secure their visa through a friend or relative: 56 per cent reported getting their visa in this fashion, compared with 39 per cent among Bangladeshis, 31 per cent among Indians, and just 13 per cent among Sri Lankans. A rather large share of the migrants from India (42 per cent) got their visas directly from the government without going through any intermediary, but this mode of entry was rare in other countries.

No matter how a visa was actually obtained, however, Asian workers generally reported that their move was facilitated by friends in Kuwait. The percentage reporting such a friend was 69 per cent among Bangladeshi respondents, 67 per cent among those from India, and 71 per cent among those from Pakistan. The average number of friends reported ranged from 3.1 among Indians to 4.7 among Pakistanis to 5.4 among Bangladeshis, and the percentage saying that they learned of their job through a friendship tie ranged from 53 per cent to 70 per cent across the same countries. Only migrants from Sri Lanka were relatively unlikely to have friends living in Kuwait before the move or to be helped by them afterwards: just 20 per cent reported such friends, only 17 per cent heard about their job from them, and the average number of friendships reported was just 1.7 (Shah 1996).

In addition to being helped by friends, a significant plurality of respondents reported helping other migrants in turn. Over a third of all Pakistani migrants (36 per cent) helped someone else to migrate, compared to about a quarter of the workers from Bangladesh and India (22 per cent and 29 per cent, respectively) and 10 per cent among those from Sri Lanka. Given these results, Shah (1996: 9) concluded that

migration through networks of friends and relatives has been described as a self-sustaining and self-perpetuating phenomenon. The experience from Kuwait suggests that despite the differences in setting, and the active efforts at regulating migration by the sending and receiving country governments, [the migrant] network has gained a lot of significance [and that it constitutes] a very important dimension of social integration of temporary migrant workers in the host country.

As migration flows develop and mature over time, there appears to be a gradual shift from the use of government and private agencies to a greater reliance on personal networks and direct connections (Singhanetra-Renard 1992). Thus, during the early years of Pakistani labour migration (1971–6), virtually all migrants to the Gulf region went through agencies (13 per cent public and 87 per cent private). After 1976, however, the share of migrants using personal networks rose substantially, with the percentage obtaining their job in this fashion averaging 29 per cent overall and 36 per cent of cases by 1983 (Burki 1991).

Once a migration flow has begun through one of these mechanisms, interest in labour migration tends to spread rapidly within sending regions and demand for a means of emigration to the Gulf escalates, bringing about an inflation in recruitment fees (Singhanetra-Renard 1992). The profit potential in the black market for international migrants leads to a proliferation of unauthorized recruitment agents (Singhanetra-Renard 1992). According to Eelens and Speckmann (1990), 9 per cent of Sri Lankan migrants used an unauthorized agent on their last trip to the Gulf.

Illegal migration to the Gulf appears to be on the rise. In 1979, Saudi Arabia rounded up and deported some 88,000 illegal residents, and in 1980 Kuwait expelled 18,000 unauthorized foreigners (Seccombe 1988). By the mid-1980s, the number of deportations had risen sharply to nearly 300,000 per year in Saudi Arabia and 27,000 per year in Kuwait. In 1986, some 73,000 cases of illegal entry were investigated by Kuwait's Interior Ministry (Birks *et al.* 1986).

As these figures on deportation suggest, Gulf country governments have not been entirely successful in preventing the emergence of social processes that promote migration and settlement outside of official channels. Despite stringent efforts to regulate the labour market and control the supply of foreign workers, social connections promoting unofficial immigration appear to have taken hold in the Gulf, prompting officials constantly to shift recruitment to new sources.

The strategy of switching to new labour sources just as the emergence of social processes threatens to undermine control of the prior source explains the progressive shift from a reliance on Arab migrants from Egypt, Palestine, and Yemen, to Indians and Pakistanis, to Taiwanese and Koreans, and finally to Thais, Filipinos, and Indonesians. In addition to shifting recruitment towards regions that are more geographically distant and culturally dissimilar from the Gulf, policy-makers have also found it necessary to engage in periodic sweeps and police actions to arrest and summarily deport undocumented migrants.

Yet even these measures have been insufficient to preclude the formation of established communities of settled immigrants in most countries of the Gulf (Weiner 1982; Seccombe 1988). As the earliest entrants to the region, Palestinians, Yemenis, and Egyptians by 1990 had established the longest relationships with employers and other citizens, social ties they were able to mobilize to secure more a more permanent legal status and the entry of family members (Addleton 1991).

Yemenis in Saudi Arabia, in particular, have historically enjoyed a range of privileges that the regime found difficult to revoke, owing to the bonds of religion, proximity, and tradition. Unlike other migrants to the kingdom,

Yemenis were not required to obtain visas or permits to live and work in Saudi Arabia, and they could operate shops and businesses without kafils (Addleton 1991). Eliminating such deeply rooted Arab communities proved difficult until the Gulf War offered a unique political opening to officials in Kuwait and Saudi Arabia.

The war created rival camps among the Arabs—those siding with Iraq and those with Kuwait and Saudi Arabia. Nations that chose the latter were compensated not only by the nullification of debts, but by a more tolerant attitude towards labour migration, whereas migrants from countries siding with Iraq were systematically penalized. In the wake of the Iraqi invasion, migrants streamed out of Kuwait as refugees, mainly back to Jordan, the West Bank, and Egypt. Addleton (1991) estimated that up to one million foreign workers and their families left Kuwait by the end of the war. With the liberation of Kuwait, however, officials did not renew invitations to former Arab workers, who constituted the bulk of foreign residents before 1990 (Birks *et al.* 1988). Indeed, many Palestinians and Jordanians, whose leaders had sympathized with the Iraqis, were forcibly deported soon after the restoration of Kuwaiti authority.

The removal through flight or deportation of most of Kuwait's pre-1990 workforce offered policy-makers an unusual opportunity to control the national origins composition of the nation's migrant workforce. Historically, Kuwaiti élites had been divided between three competing groups (Russell 1989). One faction advocated a 'Kuwaiti Kuwait' reserved only for descendants of the original families who established the State; another argued for an 'Arab Kuwait' that would welcome migrants from the Arab world; and a third sought to create an 'Islamic Kuwait' that would give preferential treatment to migrants from Muslim countries, including Pakistan, India, and Indonesia.

The traumatic experience of the Iraqi invasion strengthened the position of the first faction, yielding a policy of recruiting replacement workers from more distant and culturally dissimilar lands: 'In the early weeks of its recovery, the Government of Kuwait placed a heavy emphasis on Kuwaiti nationalism at the expense of Arab or Islamic nationalism, publicly stating that it intends to impose and enforce more restrictive migration policies. This in turn points to a small migrant workforce that is more Asian and less Arab than in the past' (Addleton 1991: 517). As a result, the labour needed to rebuild Kuwait from the devastation of the Gulf War will probably come from Asia.

The exodus of Egyptian, Palestinian, and Jordanian migrants from Kuwait was followed closely by the expulsion of Yemeni workers from Saudi Arabia (Addleton 1991). As official and popular support for Iraq within Yemen became clear, the Saudi government angrily revoked privileges that heretofore had been accorded to Yemenis within the kingdom. Historically, Yemenis did not need permits to work in Saudi Arabia or kafils in order to reside or do business there. During September of 1990 some 800,000 Yemenis were forced to return home, many to camps near the city of Hodeibah, making them refugees in their own land. According to Addleton (1991: 514), 'in the span of only a few weeks, much of the Yemeni migrant community built up in Saudi Arabia over the preceding decades simply disappeared.' In addition, 'smaller numbers of Jordanians and Palestinians are also believed to have been forced home throughout the fall of 1990, not only from Saudi Arabia but also from the smaller GCC States' (Addleton 1991: 515). Thus the expulsion of migrants became a political tool that the GCC governments used to achieve their national objectives.

In summary, even the strict controls on immigration and foreign employment imposed by Kuwait and Saudi Arabia were unable to prevent the formation of permanent immigrant settlements, and it took rather drastic actions, made possible only by the unusual political circumstances of the Gulf War, to extirpate them once they had formed. Once they come into existence, either through the actions of government, the profit-seeking behaviour of firms, or the agency of migrants themselves, networks and various migrant-supporting institutions arose to provide a social infrastructure that promoted the additional migration of settlement of foreign workers despite the wishes of Gulf societies and the best efforts of their governments (Fawcett 1989).

Cumulative Causation

Recruitment organizations and social networks thus constitute valuable sources of social capital accessible to aspiring migrants seeking to reap the rewards of Gulf labour. As outlined in earlier chapters, the endurance of social networks and recruitment organizations over time has been found to promote a process of cumulative causation within other migration systems. At present, however, virtually no research conducted in the Gulf system demonstrates analytically the operation of cumulative causation through network formation. The only direct evidence on this hypothesis comes from studies of income inequality.

Adams (1989, 1991*b*) undertook a very careful analysis of how labour migration to the Gulf affected the distribution of income in three Egyptian villages. His decomposition clearly showed that migrant remittances had a strong negative effect on community income structure, pushing it towards greater inequality. Because migrants were selected from the middle-to-upper ranges of the pre-migration income distribution, foreign earnings went to households that were already relatively well off. The arrival of the remittances pushed them further up the income hierarchy and generated additional inequality. Similar findings have been reported in Pakistan (Gilani *et al.* 1981).

According to the new economics of migration, such increase in inequality will elevate the sense of relative deprivation experienced by people situated below migrant households in the distribution of income, and this greater sense of relative deprivation will itself constitute an independent motivation for international migration, apart from the desire to maximize net income, manage risks, or gain access to capital. Labour migration to the Gulf thus increases the sense of relative deprivation among people in sending communities, which motivates additional households to send migrants abroad, which further skews the income distribution and creates more relative deprivation, yielding more migrants, and so on.

The effect of networks, social institutions, and other mechanisms promoting the cumulative causation of migration can be observed in the economic downturn that occurred in the Gulf from 1982 to 1989 as a result of the fall in oil prices (Birks *et al.* 1986; Feiler 1991). Before the downturn, observers had expected the constriction in labour demand to be followed by repatriation and a decline in the number of foreign workers. Kuthiala (1986: 445) predicted that 'once the construction boom is over, almost 40 per cent of the migrant workers will not be needed', and Seccombe and Lawless (1985: 142) argued that 'future employment levels in the Middle East depend primarily on the length of the construction phase in the development programmes of the Arab oil exporters.'

Contrary to expectations, the economic slowdown of the mid-1980s and the dwindling of construction needs were not accompanied by the end of recruitment or the repatriation of foreigners. Although the inflow of migrants to Kuwait fell as government spending declined, labour migration continued on a smaller scale as construction workers were replaced by maintenance workers and factory operatives (Birks *et al.* 1986; Shah 1986; Feiler 1991). Although the number of new work permits declined, the drop was offset by a sharp increase in work-permit renewals (Birks *et al.* 1988). By the late 1980s, therefore, the immigrant workforce had stabilized and was once again growing.

In a scenario remarkably similar to what happened in Europe when guestworker recruitment was terminated, Kuwait's foreign workers endeavoured to hang on to their jobs rather than rotating home as they normally would have. Arab migrant communities, in particular, began to deepen their roots in the Gulf and petition for the entry of spouses and dependants (Seccombe 1988: 203). The process of settlement was particularly marked in the case of Egyptians, who followed the 'classic social process which starts with a *homo economicus* phase, advances into a goal reorientation phase, and ends with the establishment of diaspora communities in destination societies' (Sell 1988: 87). Although the Gulf War provided the GCC governments with an unusual opportunity to root out settled communities of Jordanians, Palestinians, and Yemenis, owing to the Egyptian President's strong support for Saudi Arabia and Kuwait against Iraq, the Egyptian community was able to remain and it continues to deepen its social roots throughout the Gulf region (Addleton 1991).

What We Learn from the Gulf System

As with our reviews of other migration systems, this analysis suggests that no single theory is adequate to account completely for patterns of international migration into the Middle East, a conclusion that concords with that of Findlay and Stewart (1986). Nonetheless, two theoretical models stand out as more relevant than others in understanding levels and trends in international migration to the Gulf region since 1973: segmented labour market theory and social capital theory.

Migration into countries of the Gulf Cooperation Council clearly originates in a chronic labour demand expressed through formal recruitment mechanisms tightly regulated by the State. Through stringent regulations, GCC officials have sought to incorporate migrants as a factor of production but to exclude their full participation in society as social and political beings, yielding labour markets that are highly segmented between a native élite occupying sinecures in business and government and foreigners occupying most of the productive economic positions in society. This segmentation is reinforced by an intentional manipulation of the national origins composition of migrants, shifting recruitment away from the Arab world and towards Asian countries whose migrants can be more effectively exploited through policies of deliberate discrimination.

Despite these rather draconian labour market and immigration policies, migrant networks and social institutions have nonetheless arisen to promote the perpetuation of migration and the emergence of settled communities, especially among migrants from the Arab world. The shift of recruitment to Asia constitutes implicit recognition that policies intended to preclude permanence were failing, and even this policy was not enough to stop processes identified under social capital theory. It took the trauma of the Gulf War and the unusual political circumstances it provided to unleash policies of mass deportation, and even these were more effective in extirpating long-standing communities of Jordanians, Palestinians, and Yemenis than of Egyptians. But illegal migration into the Gulf continues, and the Egyptian community continues to grow while more permanent Asian communities appear to be forming, especially among Indians and Pakistanis.

Against this larger theoretical backdrop, there is scattered evidence that forces anticipated by neoclassical economics and the new economics of labour migration play ancillary roles in accounting for trends. One study has linked variation in the volume of Egyptian–Saudi migration to fluctuations in the binational income differential, and a case study in Pakistan traced international migration to the failure of local credit markets. A third study showed that Gulf migration increases income inequality among rural villages in Egypt, thus inculcating a sense of relative deprivation among those left behind. We could find little evidence, however, that the forces hypothesized by world systems theory were relevant to the initiation or perpetuation of international migration to the oil-rich nations of the Gulf.

6 Theory and Reality in Asia and the Pacific

Over the past two decades geographic mobility within the Asia Pacific region has grown dramatically and the outlines of a new system of international migration have emerged, one that is quite different from the systems prevailing in North America, Western Europe, and the Persian Gulf. Perhaps the most salient feature of the system is its newness. The Asia Pacific system only assumed form during the 1980s, and its structure is still very much evolving. Our description is thus tentative and subject to likely modification by rapidly changing social, economic, and demographic circumstances throughout the region.

The Asia Pacific Migration System

Although international migration in Asia was significant during the colonial era, when Europeans deployed workers throughout the region under the 'contract-coolie' system (see Hugo 1980, 1981), during the three decades between the Second World War and the mid-1970s the movements were small in both scale and impact. Two exceptions were the massive redistribution of population that accompanied the partition of India in 1947, and the migration of relatively skilled workers to the USA that began in the mid-1960s from nations such as the Philippines, South Korea, Taiwan, and India.

The Asia Pacific migration system emerged gradually in the 1970s and early 1980s as a result of four notable transformations: a shift in the national origins of immigrants to Japan and Australia (the latter enabled by a fundamental change in immigration policy); the sudden termination of net-migration into New Zealand, a traditional immigrant-receiving society; the onset of significant labour migration into rapidly growing, newly industrialized nations such as Hong Kong, Korea, Taiwan, Malaysia, and Singapore; and the emergence of South-East Asia as a major source of political refugees.

During the 1980s immigration into Japan moved decisively away from its traditional origins on the Korean peninsula to incorporate new sources in Asia and the Americas, growing in volume as it diversified (Sassen 1991, 1993). Somewhat earlier, Australian immigration had also moved sharply away from traditional sources in the British Isles and Europe towards new origins in Asia and the Pacific (see Appleyard 1988; Stalker 1994; Wooden et al. 1994). The precipitating event for Australia's transformation was the 1965 Immigration Act, which replaced the country's 'whites only' immigration policy with a new law that allocated visas according to labour market skills and family reunification criteria (Price 1979; Zubrzycki 1981; Castles 1988). This shift in Australian policy paralleled similar changes in US and Canadian policies passed at roughly the same time (Kubat 1979). After decades of demographic isolation, the new legislation suddenly and decisively connected Australia to the rest of Asia and the Pacific.

As immigration to Australia rose, that into New Zealand withered. The entry of the United Kingdom into the European Union eliminated New Zealand's privileged access to British markets, and the consequent drop in primary exports (mutton and wool) caused severe economic dislocations throughout the country. New Zealand suddenly found itself cut off from its historical international patron and newly isolated within a rapidly globalizing Pacific economy.

After years of steady immigration from Britain, Ireland, and Australia, New Zealand began to experience net outflows of population after 1976. From a population of only 3.1 million, the country lost 191,000 people through net emigration between 1977 and 1987, a 6 per cent population loss in just ten years (New Zealand Department of Statistics 1990). As immigration from Europe dried up, that from the Pacific islands increased, but not enough to offset the large losses through emigration. Only during the 1990s has net immigration revived and turned positive again, and it is now composed pre-dominantly of Asians and Pacific Islanders.

With the withdrawal of US armed forces from Vietnam and the subsequent collapse of US-backed governments in South Vietnam, Laos, and Cambodia, South-East Asia in the late 1970s and 1980s emerged as a major source of refugees (Mingot 1995). The largest number ended up in the USA, of course, with smaller concentrations in Canada and Europe; but a significant number of South-East Asians stayed within the region as refugee migration ex-panded into Japan, Hong Kong, Taiwan, and, especially, Australia. Smaller streams of refugees have originated in other political trouble spots, such as Sri Lanka.

The foregoing transformations have produced an unusual system structure that is distinguished in several ways from the systems prevailing elsewhere. First, the receiving nations of Asia and the Pacific are not spatially contiguous, but clustered around four geographically dispersed nodes: Australia, Japan, Singapore-Malaysia, and Hong Kong-Taiwan-Korea. (Although Thailand be-come a major destination in the 1990s, throughout the 1980s it remained a net exporter of migrants.) Moreover, these countries are still in the process of developing political and economic ties with one another, principally through the Association of South-East Asian Nations (ASEAN). There is still no comprehensive framework to promote integration, however, comparable to the North American Free Trade Agreement, the Treaty of Rome, or the Gulf Cooperation Council, although the forum for Asia Pacific Economic Cooperation (APEC) moves in that direction.

In addition, immigrant-receiving nations in Asia and the Pacific are just beginning to move towards a common immigration policy, and they have not yet achieved full economic parity. Japan is clearly the region's dominant economy, followed by the 'Asian Tigers' (Singapore, Hong Kong, Taiwan, Korea) and Australia, with Malaysia lagging significantly behind the others. Nonetheless, economies throughout Asia and the Pacific boomed during 1980s and living standards moved significantly closer to those prevailing in Japan and Australia, the system's two developed nations.

In short, the Asia Pacific system is inchoate, and its principal receiving societies are only just beginning to satisfy the criteria for system status adumbrated by Zlotnik (1992). A relatively stable and identifiable structure has nevertheless emerged, and sizeable numbers of legal immigrants flow into the wealthiest countries of the Asia Pacific region, accompanied by parallel streams of illegal migrants whose volume is also rising rapidly (see Brennan 1984; Spencer 1992; Selya 1994; Wooden *et al.* 1994).

The most serious problem encountered in attempting to identify the Asia Pacific System is empirical rather than conceptual, owing to a scarcity of data. Several receiving countries have so recently shifted from exporting to importing labour that statistical systems for the enumeration and classification of immigrants do not really exist, and with the exception of Australia, most have yet to face up to the fact that they have become immigrant-receiving societies. Finally, clandestine movements occur throughout the region and present strong barriers to accurate measurement. Hugo (1995a) estimates that the illegal flows are at least as large as the documented flows, and possibly larger.

Table 6.1 uses statistics on foreigners residing in Australia and Japan to approximate recent flows of immigrants into those countries. In the former country, we present 1991 counts of the foreign born by nationality and the change in the number of foreign born observed over the prior ten years; in the latter nation we use counts of registered foreigners in 1990, and changes in this number between 1980 and 1990.

In both countries, the historical legacy of past immigration is clearly visible in the distribution of foreigners by nationality. The largest number of foreign-born persons in Australia come from Britain and Ireland, who at 1.2 million, together make up 28 per cent of those born abroad; 1.1 million immigrants are from elsewhere in Europe and add another 27 per cent to the total. Thus, over half (55 per cent) of all immigrants living in Australia in 1991 were of European origin. Foreigners in Japan are similarly dominated by its traditional source: Korea. Of the 1.1 million foreigners living in Japan in 1990, some 688,000 or 64 per cent were Korean (Statistics Bureau of Japan 1995).

Despite the dominance of Europeans and Koreans among foreigners in Australia and Japan, when we examine recent flows, their salience diminishes considerably. Although the number of British, Irish, and Southern Europeans continued to rise in Australia during the 1980s, the number of other Europeans declined sharply. As a result, the total number of Europeans grew by

Table 6.1 Foreign populations of Australia and Japan *c.*1990 and changes over the prior decade, by nationality

Source region	Foreign born in Australia		Registered foreigners in Japan	
	1991	1981–91	1990	1980–90
Europe				
UK and Ireland	1,174.9	42.3	10.2	5.2
Southern Europe	662.3	114.5	2.2	0.5
Other Europe	462.5	−145.6	12.6	3.5
Americas				
North America	75.1	19.9	43.9	19.6
Latin America	72.0	27.5	70.7	68.9
Asia				
Southern Asia	110.5	38.9	8.5	5.6
East Asia	199.5	158.8	838.3	120.9
South-East Asia	377.8	227.5	72.7	59.8
Middle East	167.6	72.1	5.1	3.6
Other				
Oceania	351.5	127.6	5.4	3.8
Africa	99.1	8.9	2.1	1.3
TOTAL	4,125.1	692.4	1,071.7	238.7
per cent Foreign	24.5 per cent		0.9 per cent	

Sources: Australian Bureau of Statistics (1995); Statistics Bureau of Japan (1995).

just 11,000 over the decade. Likewise, although the number of East Asians in Japan displayed a sharp increase during the 1980s, most of this growth did not come from the entry of Koreans. Indeed, of the 121,000 new East Asian migrants in Japan, only 23,000 came from Korea.

In both Australia and Japan, the dwindling of migration from traditional sources was accompanied by a rapid expansion of entry from new sources scattered throughout Asia. Of the 692,000 additional foreign-born Australians, 61 per cent were from East, South, or South-East Asia, with another 10 per cent coming from the Middle East. The largest increases were observed among immigrants from South-East Asia (228,000), followed by East Asia (159,000) and South Asia (39,000). Likewise, in Japan 97,000 of the 121,000 new East Asians came from China (41 per cent of the total). In addition, the number of South-East Asians in Japan grew by 60,000 (25 per cent of the total) and the number of South Asians by 6,000 (2 per cent of the total).

In both Australia and Japan, therefore, a substantial majority of recent immigrants (over 60 per cent) come from non-traditional sources in Asia.

Unlike Australia, however, Japan also takes in a significant number of immigrants from the Americas. During the 1980s, 69,000 immigrants from Latin America accounted for 29 per cent of the total increase in its foreign residents.

The strong demand for low-wage labour in Japan, combined with a wealthy, ageing population, created a serious dilemma for Japanese government officials: how to find workers willing to take jobs rejected by citizens without violating Japanese preferences for racial uniformity and cultural homogeneity (see Awanohara 1986; Spencer 1992). The solution was to recruit temporary workers from the Japanese diaspora in Latin America, seeking to entice back to Japan the grandchildren of emigrants who had left Japan earlier in the century to seek their fortunes in Peru, Brazil, and Colombia (Takenaka 1996).

Statistical systems in other countries of the Asia Pacific system are generally weaker than those prevailing in Australia and Japan. It is therefore more difficult to compile accurate data on the number of foreign residents and the size of recent flows. We rely on data compiled by Stahl *et al.* (1993), who estimated stocks of foreign labour migrants in various Asian nations. In Table 6.2 we reproduce their data for key receiving States in Asia: three East Asian NICs (Hong Kong, Korea, and Taiwan) and two South-East Asian NICs (Singapore and Malaysia).

Table 6.2   Stocks of labour migrants in the newly industrializing countries of Asia *c.*1990 ('000s)

Source	East Asian NICs			Southeast Asian NICs		
	Hong Kong	Korea	Taiwan	Malaysia	Singapore	Total
South Asia						
Bangladesh	—	—	—	20	10	30
India	—	—	—	—	10	10
Sri Lanka	—	—	—	—	20	20
South-East Asia						
Indonesia	—	5	—	350	30	385
Malaysia	—	5	20	—	60	85
Philippines	75	10	10	110	40	245
Thailand	15	10	10	10	30	75
East Asia						
China	25	40	—	—	—	65
TOTAL	115	70	40	490	200	1,015
% Foreign	2.0	0.2	0.2	2.6	7.1	

Source: Stahl *et al* (1993).

These figures must be regarded as approximate rather than exact, and they differ from those shown in Table 6.1 in three respects: they refer to workers rather than all foreigners, they pertain to stocks rather than flows, and they include an estimate of undocumented as well as documented migrants. Since immigration into these NICs is so recent, however, stocks provide a reasonable approximation of flows during the 1980s; and because migrants tend to be labourers rather than dependants during the early stages of migration, counts of workers provide a good indication of the size of total stocks of immigrants.

As the row totals reveal, by the end of the 1980s Indonesia and the Philippines had emerged as the two largest sending nations in this portion of the Asia Pacific system. The vast majority of Indonesian workers (some 350,000) are found in Malaysia but about 30,000 are employed in Singapore. Although few Indonesians migrate to Japan, a substantial number have entered Australia in recent years. Between 1981 and 1991 the number of Australian residents born in Indonesia rose by around 20,000 (Australia Bureau of Statistics 1995). There is also a significant migration of Indonesians into the Netherlands, its former colonial ruler.

Whereas Indonesians concentrate in a few countries, Filipino migrants are found in virtually all receiving countries of the Asia Pacific system. Of the 245,000 migrants that Stahl *et al.* (1993) estimate to be working in Asian NICs *circa* 1990, the largest number (110,000) were in Malaysia, but 75,000 were in Japan and 40,000 were in Singapore, with around 10,000 each in Korea and Taiwan. When these stocks of out-migrant Filipinos are added to the 73,000 living in Australia, the 49,000 in Japan, the 429,000 in the countries of the Gulf, the 90,000 in Canada, and the 913,000 in the USA, it is clear that the Philippines is one of the most important sources for emigrants in the entire world, and that the Asia Pacific migration system overlaps considerably with those in North America and the Gulf.

Although Thailand's outflow appears to be smaller than that of the Philippines, Thai workers are found in all of the NICs, and in modest but significant numbers in the USA, Australia, Canada, Japan, and the Gulf. Emigrant Thais are fairly evenly scattered across NIC destination areas, but with significant concentrations in Singapore and Hong Kong. Although not indicated in our data *circa* 1990, by the mid-1990s, Thailand had probably also become a net importer of workers, even though it continued to send out significant numbers of emigrants.

Malaysia (as well as several of the Asian Tigers) is both a sender and receiver of immigrants, reflecting the recency of its economic development and the newness of the shift to labour importation. Although emigrant Malaysians are found in Korea and Taiwan, they are mainly concentrated in Singapore, its island neighbour and the most developed economy outside of Japan and Australia. The South Asian countries of Bangladesh, India, and Sri Lanka mostly send to Singapore, but large numbers are found Britain, the USA, Canada, and the Gulf States, once again underscoring the overlap between the Asia Pacific system and other migration systems throughout the world.

Chinese emigrants to NICs are found mainly in Hong Kong and Korea. In addition to the 25,000 Chinese estimated to be working in Hong Kong and the 40,000 in Korea, however, some 150,000 Chinese were in Japan as of 1990, and by 1993 this figure had risen to 210,000. Moreover, like the Philippines, China is strongly connected to the North American system. During the 1980s, 73,000 Chinese entered Canada and 345,000 entered the USA; a significant number also entered Europe. China, the Philippines, and India thus send emigrants to a diverse array of destinations in several migration systems.

Figure 6.1 graphs the principal flows within the Asia Pacific system drawing on the data summarized in Tables 6.1 and 6.2. The system is dominated by a few very large flows, the largest of which are those out of South-East Asia into Australia, Japan, and both sets of NICs. The largest single flow in the system occurs within South-East Asia, however: between the origin countries of Indonesia, Thailand, and the Philippines and the destination countries of Malaysia and Singapore. Other large flows occur between East Asia, principally China, and Australia, Japan, and the East Asian NICs of Taiwan, Korea, and Hong Kong. There are also large flows from Oceania and the Middle East into Australia, and from the Americas into both Australia and Japan, which judging from the diversity of their sources, represent the most mature nodes in the system.

A key facet of the Asia Pacific system that differentiates it from other migration systems in the world is the vast size of the populations involved. China, for example, is presently estimated to have 200 million more workers than it can productively employ; and Indonesia's workforce of 80 million has an underemployment rate of about 40 per cent (Hugo 1993*a*). Although not measured with the same precision, India, Pakistan, Bangladesh, and Vietnam likewise have large reserves of under-used labour. Despite rapid economic growth and local increases in labour demand, the increasing volume of international labour migration has not exhausted the vast reserves of surplus labour in the region.

The geographic imbalance between labour supply and demand that prevails in Asia is expected to become more acute in future years, exacerbating the impetus for migration within the system. According to projections by Stahl (1992), labour-sending nations will be able to employ only a fraction of the growth in their labour forces between now and the year 2000, while in labour-importing nations, there will be two to three jobs created for every native worker. Whatever migration results from this imbalance will most likely be augmented significantly by refugee movements. Of the world's refugees, some 40 per cent, or 7 million people, originate in Asia, principally in Indochina, Afghanistan, and Iran.

Thus, immigration within the Asia Pacific system is likely to grow and become more routinized as networks expand and begin channelling immi-

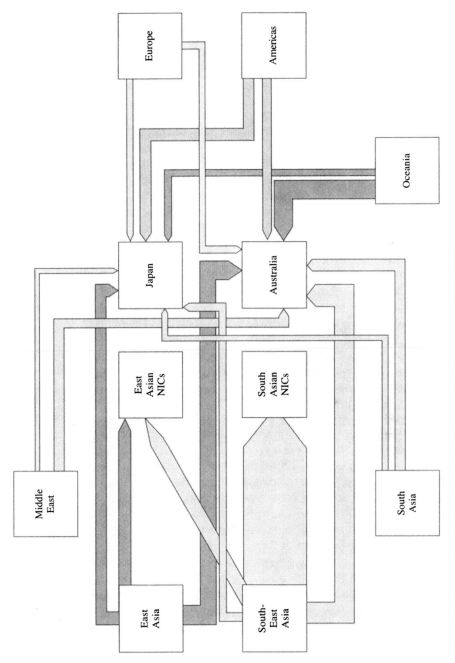

Fig. 6.1 International migration in the Western Pacific system, 1980–1990

grants to places where beachheads have already been established. Moreover, the economic forces that promote immigration show no signs of declining, particularly in Japan. Severe labour shortages continue to plague the Japanese economy, with job vacancies exceeding job-seekers by 46 per cent, on average, and the construction industry being short of some 100,000 workers at the last count (see Stahl *et al.* 1993).

Although Japan's legal foreign population now exceeds 1.3 million, and legal immigration has been growing at 60,000 persons per year since 1985 (an annual growth rate in excess of 5 per cent), this movement has not been sufficient to meet labour demand. Hence, a large number of Asian migrants are allowed to enter Japan as 'trainees' in 'exchange programmes', which are really thinly—veiled guestworker programmes of the European mould (Stahl *et al.* 1993). Japan recently expanded the number of job categories within which foreign 'trainees' could be accepted for up to three years (Sassen 1993); and despite an economic downturn in the early 1990s, the Tokyo Chamber of Commerce lobbied for a legal quota of 600,000 temporary foreign workers (Prasai 1993).

At the lower end of the labour market, demand is met largely through illegal migration. According to Prasai (1993: 23), 'the number of illegals in Japan and the newly Industrialized Countries of East Asia has skyrocketed in the last decade, going from less than 200,000 in 1980 to as many as 2–3 million today, with most of these illegal workers being supplied by their less well-off neighbors.' The imposition of sanctions on employers of illegal workers in Japan has been ineffective and has not lowered the demand for unskilled workers (Sassen 1993). According to the *Japan Times* (25 February 1993), official estimates of the number of visa overstayers in Japan approached 300,000 by the end of 1992, an increase of 35 per cent over the prior year. Of these overstayers, 18 per cent were Thai, 13 per cent were South Korean, 12 per cent were Malaysians, 12 per cent were Filipinos, and 10 per cent were Chinese. A sample of illegal migrants apprehended in Japan during 1989 revealed that 19 per cent were from Pakistan, 23 per cent were from the Philippines, 14 per cent were from Bangladesh, 19 per cent were from Korea, and 11 per cent were from Malaysia (Spencer 1992).

Until the last decade, South Korea was a net exporter of labour, supplying large numbers of contract workers to the Gulf States and substantial numbers of permanent settlers to the USA. By the late 1980s, however, the Korean Labour Ministry announced a shortage of 570,000 workers (Stahl *et al.* 1993). Despite mounting pressure from employers, immigration laws remain quite strict and illegal migration has consequently flourished. Filipinos appear to be the largest group of illegal migrants in Korea, supplemented by substantial numbers from Pakistan, Sri Lanka, Bangladesh, and Nepal (*Philippine Daily Register*, 25 May 1993).

Taiwan likewise experienced a shortfall of some 200,000 workers in 1989, and in 1990 the government for the first time allowed 30,000 contract workers into the country. Legal migration, however, is still insufficient to meet the demand, and once again an influx of clandestine workers has resulted. Official estimates put the number of illegal migrants at around 41,000, but social agencies estimate it to be more like 200,000, mainly from the Philippines, Malaysia, Thailand, and Indonesia (Baum 1993).

In Hong Kong's fast-growing economy, labour shortages are exacerbated by an exodus of entrepreneurs and skilled workers leaving in anticipation of the colony's return to China in 1997 (Skeldon 1991). According to Stahl *et al.* (1993), the labour shortage was around 170,000 workers in 1990. Most applications for legal entry are turned down, and consequently there has been a sizeable increase in illegal migration. The Hong Kong Immigration Department estimates that illegal migration from China alone has reached a total of 614,000 persons (Wu and Inglis 1992). Another major stream of immigrants is refugees from Vietnam, with a net figure of 50,000 boat people entering the colony between 1975 to 1990. In recent years, migration from other South-East Asian countries has also increased (*South China Morning Post*, 10 July 1993).

Singapore has a long history of relying on migrant workers, and the 1990 census enumerated some 321,700 foreigners residing in the country, of which more than half were temporary workers. This island nation has a highly-structured system of levies that apply to firms that import workers, as well as to households that hire foreign maids; quotas also limit the number of foreign workers in specific economic sectors (Pang 1992; Stahl *et al.* 1993). Partly because of these regulations, Singapore has experienced chronic labour shortages and a substantial influx of illegal migrants, mainly from neighbouring Malaysia but also from the Philippines, Sri Lanka, and Thailand. According to Prasai (1993), Singapore houses between 200,000 and 300,000 undocumented workers, mostly young males working in unskilled jobs obtained through recruiters and family contacts.

Finally, Malaysia, the newest NIC, has experienced substantial outflows of migrants as well as large influxes of workers from elsewhere in Asia, much as Spain and Italy did during their period of transition from labour-exporting to labour-importing regimes. The largest single flow of illegal migrants in Asia is from Indonesia to Malaysia (Hugo 1991). This movement can be divided into two parts: one major flow is to peninsular Malaysia and the other is to Sabah in East Malaysia. Estimates vary, but the former is generally put at 200,000–300,000 and the latter at 120,000–140,000 (Habir 1984).

Although it may be the newest international migration system in the world today, the Asia Pacific region appears to be following the path of evolution set by its predecessors in North America and Europe. The achievement of rapid economic growth and high levels of development in core nations has led to an abundance of capital and technology combined with a scarcity of labour, which is met through a combination of legal immigration, the entry of 'temporary workers' and 'trainees', and growing illegal migration. Like destination countries in Europe and the Gulf, immigrant-receiving countries in Asia and the

Pacific seem unable to accept the fact that they have become countries of immigration (with the exception of Australia), and they are attempting to implement restrictive immigration policies even as the demand for migrant workers grows.

Research in Asia and the Pacific

As in the European and Gulf migration systems, the literature on international migration in the Asia Pacific region is limited, and the number of studies relevant to the task of evaluating theory is quite small. The neglect of international migration as a topic of investigation by researchers in the region reflects several circumstances. The first is the relative recency of immigration in most countries, which means that there are few demographers, economists, sociologists, and geographers with the training and experience necessary to study international migration. Only Australia has a strong tradition of immigration research, yet even here the record of theoretically-relevant research is rather weak.

Second, data on international migration are of poor quality in virtually all countries. It is not possible, for example, to determine the size and composition of population flows into and out of most receiving countries, let alone address issues pertaining to causes and consequences. Few population censuses in Asia include questions on place of birth or period of entry, and border statistics are invariably poorly collected and typically processed in haphazard and limited ways. In addition, there are no migration-related equivalents to the World Fertility Survey or the Demographic and Health Survey to fill the gap left by inadequate censuses and incomplete population registers.

A third difficulty is that much of the immigration in Asia is clandestine and thus difficult to measure (Hugo 1995a). Although several journals have recently emerged to support the publication of research and data on international migration (notably *Asian Migrant* and *Asia-Pacific Migration Journal*), the information is still largely inaccessible, often lying buried in government reports and student dissertations. A recent issue of the *Asia-Pacific Migration Journal* (5(1), 1996) did attempt to move the field forward, however, by comprehensively reviewing available sources of data on international migration.

A final problem is that much of the literature on international migration is predominantly descriptive and atheoretical, providing little opportunity for hypothesis testing or theoretical generalization. As Goss and Lindquist (1995: 317) point out, 'as a result of the developmentalist orientation of the field, researchers have been more occupied with evaluating the consequences of international labour migration on national economies, communities and households than with identifying the processes that lead individuals to pursue employment overseas.'

In spite of the limited base of empirical and theoretical knowledge about international migration in Asia, many governments in the region are nonetheless turning to international migration as a tool in national development efforts, either as receivers or senders of labour. As a result, programmes and policies are being implemented in a knowledge vacuum. As a first step toward rectifying this situation, we survey what is known about the forces initiating and perpetuating international migration in the Asia Pacific system. We conclude by specifying an agenda for research needed to address the leading conceptual questions and theoretical concerns uncovered in our review.

The Initiation of International Migration

Neoclassical Economics

Although relatively few studies have been conducted in Asia and the Pacific explicitly to test hypotheses derived from neoclassical economics, this theoretical model has nonetheless dominated thinking in the region. Neoclassical economics, of course, explains international migration as a function of cross-national differences in expected wages (income or wages times the rate of employment).

Abella (1995*b*: 132) argues that widening differentials in per capita income within Asia account for the temporal and spatial structure of population movements in the Asia Pacific region. To make his case, he computes the ratio of per capita income in various Asian nations to per capita income in Japan from 1975 to 1991. Whereas the ratio for Singapore and Hong Kong fluctuated between 45 per cent and 60 per cent with no clear trend, in Taiwan it rose steadily from 21 per cent to 31 per cent, while in South Korea it increased from 13 per cent to 24 per cent. Malaysia held fairly steady with a ratio of about 18 per cent until 1991, when it experienced a decline. In contrast, relative income fell steadily in Thailand, the Philippines, Indonesia, and China. By 1991, these nations displayed per capita incomes that were only 6 per cent, 3 per cent, 2 per cent, and 1 per cent of those prevailing in Japan, respectively.

Countries in Asia and the Pacific thus appear to be bifurcating into high- and low-wage blocks: Japan and the NICs, on one side, and the other nations of Asia on the other, with flows of migrants increasingly connecting the two camps. Within certain occupations, income differentials can be vast. Minghuan (1996: 11), for example, reports that Chinese cooks working in the Netherlands earned incomes ranging from 60 to 140 times those in available their home communities. Since incomes in Japan were then about 1.6 times those in the Netherlands, this implies that a Chinese cook working in Japan would earn wages ranging from 96 to 224 times those at home.

One of the largest labour migrations in the Asia Pacific system is from Indonesia, which has a 40 per cent underemployment rate and falling wages, to

Malaysia, a country with strong economic growth, relatively high wages, and a general shortage of labour. Hugo (1993*b*) shows that the ratio of wages in pairs of Indonesian origin and Malaysian destination areas ranges from 3 to 10 times, indicating very large wage differentials.

A distinctive feature of international migration in the Asia Pacific region is that some nations are simultaneously importers and exporters of labour. According to Abella (1992*b*), this pattern mainly characterizes countries located in the middle of the income ladder rather than at the extremes. He cites the example of Taiwan, which simultaneously imports workers from the Philippines where wages are 94 per cent lower, and supplies them to Japan, where wages are five times higher.

A similar situation holds in Malaysia, the system's newest receiving country, which employs more than a million workers from low-wage nations such as Indonesia and Bangladesh, but also sends large numbers of migrant workers to Singapore, Taiwan, and Japan, where wages are higher. Vasquez (1992) indicates that South Koreans no longer seek foreign employment in most countries of Asia, with the sole exception of Japan, the only country in Asia where wage rates are still higher than in Korea.

Based on their review of research, Smart *et al.* (1986) conclude that most international migrants in Asia are motivated by the prospect of earning higher wages overseas, as predicted by neoclassical theory. According to Abella (1988), as long as potential foreign earnings exceed local wages (after subtracting the costs of movement and job placement), workers are likely to respond to higher foreign wage rates by engaging in labour migration to one of the region's core migrant-receiving countries.

Although income and wage differentials are widely accepted as a principal underlying cause of international migration in the Asia Pacific system, there have been relatively few systematic empirical tests of neoclassical hypotheses and propositions. Owing to a paucity of reliable data in most countries, we uncovered no time-series analysis that correlated changes in the volume of international migration to shifts in the value of expected wages, as various investigators in North America have done.

One of the few attempts explicitly to test the Todaro model is that of Gonzalez (1993), who used data from the 1988 National Demographic Survey of the Philippines. This stratified random sample of 19,897 households yielded 1,761 households containing one or more people who had migrated overseas in the last five years, mostly on a temporary basis. A regression analysis showed that the rate of emigration to different countries was positively related to the size of the income differential compared with the Philippines and negatively related to the costs of transportation and the costs of locating a job.

Considerable scholarly attention has focused on the 'migration transition' in Asia: the rapid shift of several NIC's from the importation to the exportation of labor. Indeed, an entire issue of the *Asia-Pacific Migration Journal* (3(1), 1994) was devoted to this turning point, and it concluded that the initiation of labour migration was related to demographic as well as economic factors. Countries such as South Korea, Taiwan, Hong Kong, Singapore, and Japan experienced rapid declines in fertility during the 1960s and reached below-replacement levels during the 1970s. As a result, during the 1990s the number of young people entering the workforce began to decline, causing severe labour shortages just when unprecedented rates of economic growth were creating a high demand for labour across a range of skill levels.

Fields (1994: 25–6) presents a theoretical interpretation of the migration transition that is generally consistent with neoclassical precepts. According to him, export-led growth caused labour demand to increase sharply in newly industrializing countries. The rightward shift of the demand curve for labour brought improvements in the job market, first increasing employment opportunities and then raising wages. Given well-integrated labour markets within most NICs, these improvements rapidly spread to all sectors. As wages and employment conditions improved, workers who formerly emigrated were no longer willing to do so and they either returned home or stayed put, thus terminating significant out-migration.

As labour markets tightened, firms sought to mitigate wage increases in three ways: by importing labour, legally or otherwise; by shifting to labour-saving technologies; and/or by relocating production facilities overseas. Despite the latter two efforts, wages continued to rise, yielding a growing incentive for labour migration within Asia and the Pacific, completing the migration transition, and giving rise to new labour-importing societies.

In some poor Asian countries whose economies are rapidly growing, limited supplies of educated and technically trained workers have also led to the migration of human capital—skilled labour—in a manner predicted by neoclassical theory. Rapid industrial growth in Indonesia, for example, created a demand for specialists in engineering, management, finance, and other professions that could not be met locally, yielding rising returns to human capital (higher salaries for educated workers) that attracted skilled migrants from Australia, the Philippines, Europe, and India, despite a 40 per cent underemployment rate among Indonesian natives (Hugo 1993a, 1993b). Many of these skilled immigrants entered on visitor visas and then began working, so that official statistics grossly underestimate the scale of this movement. A notable feature of the Asia Pacific system is thus the movement of skilled workers—human capital—from 'North to South' (Hugo 1994a).

As already mentioned, data limitations generally preclude the sort of empirical analyses necessary to test neoclassical theory directly. In most nations, undocumented migration is of such a scale that estimating the true size of yearly inflows and outflows is problematic. In addition, national-level measures such as per capita income often bear little relation to the income differentials actually perceived by migrants at points of origin and destination. Because migrants are drawn selectively from particular subregions and they go selectively to specific economic sectors in specific geographic regions, wage differences estimated on the basis of national averages provide very crude indicators of the actual size of wage gaps motivating migrants.

Despite these problems, Stahl (1995) argues that neoclassical theory, as modified by Todaro, elucidates the causes of international migration in the Asia Pacific system. He suggests that common criticisms of the neoclassical model are misplaced. For example, he takes specific issue with the view that the highest emigration rates should always occur among the poorest populations and countries, which obviously is not the case for Asia (ibid. 217). He points out that neoclassical theory allows for the possibility of different migrants having different costs of migration and, hence, different chances of finding employment, yielding different expected wages and, thus, different probabilities of international movement.

Stahl (1995) also takes issue with those who argue that neoclassical theory necessarily predicts that international migration should decrease when the earnings differential between two countries shrinks, which also does not hold in the Asian case. If the probability of finding employment at the place of destination is rising over time, he argues, a decrease in income differentials is consistent with continuing labour migration. Unfortunately, the data to test these propositions do not exist, and most analysts only consider nominal wages in their illustrative examples.

A recurring feature of economic life in Asian labour-exporting nations is currency devaluation. In order to increase the competitiveness of their goods on international markets and to lure foreign investment, developing country governments at times undertake deliberate currency devaluations, as Indonesia did between 1985 and 1992. Godfrey (1996: 137) points out, however, that such a policy encourages emigration in two ways: on the supply side, it increases the real value of overseas wages; on the demand side it reduces the foreign currency equivalent of the price of labour, enabling overseas employers to pay less than would be necessary to attract similar workers from other countries.

To buttress his argument, Godfrey (1996) presents data on real hourly wages for manufacturing workers in various countries of Asia and the Pacific from 1986 to 1992. He shows that Indonesian monetary policy had the effect of lowering hourly wages in manufacturing from a level 16 per cent of those in Singapore in 1986 to a level just 10 per cent only five years later. Over the same period, Indonesian wages fell relative to those in Australia, Japan, Hong Kong, Taiwan, and Korea. Even assuming that migrants are paid less than natives, as is typical, these widening gaps suggest that, owing to currency devaluation, emigration became increasingly attractive to poor Indonesian workers over the course of the 1980s.

Neoclassical modelling has been used less to study the causes of international migration than to explore the consequences of that migration for communities and nations. Several studies have examined the issue from the perspective of capital-rich, labour-importing nations; these generally focus on the relative advantages and disadvantages of capital investment versus labour importation (Markusen 1983; Bhagwati and Srinivasan 1983; Wong 1983; Abella and Mori 1996). Most analyses, however, have concentrated on countries of origin.

Prominent among the latter studies is the work of Knerr (1989, 1990, 1993), who argues that 'maximising the economic benefits from labour migration for the source country requires the application of quantitative methods based on macro-models which can be used for assessing its impact and stimulating alternative policy strategies' (Knerr 1992: 120). She demonstrates how four such approaches can be used for this purpose by examining the effects of international labour migration in South Asian countries. These include partial sectoral analysis by regression computations, cost-benefit analysis, social accounting matrices, and computable general equilibrium models. Unfortunately, the lack of appropriate data once again restricts the applicability of these methods in most labour-exporting countries of Asia.

While the formal testing of neoclassical models remains limited in Asia and the Pacific, the accumulated weight of empirical evidence generally supports neoclassical theory's fundamental proposition that movement into and out of countries of the Asia Pacific system is tied to wage differentials (see Abella 1995b; Battistella 1995; Hugo 1995b; Liu 1995; Martin *et al.* 1995a; Okunishi 1995; Park 1995; Pillai 1995; Skeldon 1995; Soon-Beng and Chew 1995; Sussangkarn 1995; Tsay 1995). To date, however, most studies have been descriptive and not analytic. Rather than relating wage rates and migration rates directly to one another in an empirically convincing fashion, investigators have tended to show only that gaps in income exist between specific areas that send and receive international migrants, and then make the inferential leap that these gaps must have caused the observed movement.

At the same time, it is clear that wage differentials alone do not fully explain trends and patterns of international migration in the Asia Pacific region. The views of Stahl (1995) notwithstanding, several aspects of the system remain anomalous. First, as in other migration systems, it is not the poorest nations that supply the most migrants. Even after taking account of variations in the costs of migration and the probability of employment there is no monotonic relationship between the size of wage differentials and the volume of international migration. Second, within sending nations it is not the poorest regions or population subgroups that supply the largest numbers of out-migrants, but those that are developing most rapidly. Finally, as discussed in more detail below, empirical evidence across many nations demonstrates that wage differentials are a necessary condition but not a sufficient condition for international migration. Although neoclassical theory may be supported in the Asian case, it does not provide a complete explanation of the decision to migrate between countries.

The New Economics of Migration

In contrast to the neoclassical model, the new economics of labour migration does not posit complete and well-functioning markets, with movement being explained solely on the basis of geographic disequilibria in one particular market: that for labour. On the contrary, it argues that international migration stems from failures in markets that threaten the material well-being of families and create barriers to economic advancement, giving them strong incentives to self-insure against risk by sending one or more members abroad for work, and to self-finance their production or consumption needs by sending someone abroad to accumulate capital through foreign work. Higher wages in developed countries make international migration efficacious as a strategy for minimizing risk and overcoming capital constraints (Stark 1991); but they do not cause it *per se*.

As with neoclassical theory, the fundamental elements of the new economic model have yet to be formally tested in the Asia Pacific system, owing to a lack of suitable data and a reluctance of investigators in the region to gather it. Nevertheless, research is generally consistent with a basic precept of the new economics: that migration is a household- rather than an individual-level decision.

Throughout Asia, the family remains the basic unit of production responsible for allocating labour resources over a range of tasks to achieve satisfactory income support. Since individual family members have different capacities, characteristics, and skills, households organize a division of labour to make the best possible use of their human capital resources. In rural areas, this strategy typically involves allocating members to off-farm employment as well as to on-farm tasks. Although most off-farm jobs are located near by, increasingly the allocation of labour has occurred across district, State, and even international boundaries (Colfer 1985; Eelens and Schampers 1986; Fawcett and Arnold 1987; Lauby and Stark 1987; Jacobs and Papma 1992).

Adopting the household as the appropriate unit of analysis does not mean that families necessarily discuss options democratically and reach a consensus decision. Indeed, the decisions very often are authoritarian and patriarchal in nature, and as a general rule it is the kinship system that determines which family member will migrate on the basis of age, birth order, and gender, as well as individual skills and attributes (Rodenburg 1991). In some situations, families adopt a deliberate strategy of keeping older children away from school to work on the family farm while sending younger children to acquire additional education in preparation for eventual labour migration (Connell *et al.* 1976: 46).

The kin group is more likely to make decisions for some family members than others, and not surprisingly, a key line of division is gender. In the Philippines, for example, Torres (1992: 31) concludes that young males typically make autonomous migration decisions, whereas females move and work to comply with family wishes: 'information on job opportunities in Metro

Manila for girls is filtered through the social group . . . vested with normative authority to decide for the girls. Filial piety, or respect for elders, is another strong Filipino value. Young women, therefore, would be expected to respect decisions from their kin group, including those pertaining to accepting work in Manila.'

Despite being restrained by patriarchal kinship structures, women are none-theless active participants in household decision-making who frequently con-test and strongly shape migration outcomes. They are not mere 'associational' followers of male migrants (Hugo 1992). Even when they do not migrate, kinship structures can provide women with a measure of social control over male relatives. According to Rodenburg (1991): 'for a wife, this network is also important in another way since, to a certain extent, it means social control of her husband's activities. In case her husband should have an affair she may soon find out.'

Strategies of family risk diversification, or some versions of them, have operated in Asian societies for a long time. What has changed is the geo-graphic area over which the labour is allocated. Whereas mobility historically was confined to areas near the home community, since the 1970s Asian labour markets have undergone a rapid geographic expansion, and during the 1980s they became transnational. Indeed, for certain professions, they are truly global, with managers, professionals, academics, and others moving frequently between nations as they acquire experience, contacts, and seniority (Salt 1987b).

According to Caces *et al.* (1985), many households in migrant-sending re-gions of the Philippines include a 'shadow' component consisting of absent family members, often sons and daughters, who are working overseas but nonetheless continue to contribute to household income and are considered to be very much part of the family. The success of household strategies involving the geographic dispersal of family labour hinges on the existence of a kinship system that emphasizes intergenerational links, cultivates loyalty to parents, and channels flows of wealth and income upward through the kinship structure (Caldwell 1976).

Whereas neoclassical economics predicts a one-time move to a region of higher wages, the new economics posits successive periods of temporary for-eign labour to achieve specific goals such as risk minimization or capital accumulation. Circularity, of course, reinforces social obligations embedded in Asian kinship structures and ensures continued family control over migrant behaviour, and more significantly, over migrant income. Migrant remittances have been found to attenuate over time as migrants settle abroad (Massey *et al.* 1987), while patriarchal authority tends to diminish across time and space (Hondagneu-Sotelo 1994; Goldring 1996b). Frequent episodes of return mi-gration not only fulfil economic goals consistent with the new economies of migration; they also serve important social functions by reinforcing and main-taining obligations to the family.

Although Smart *et al.* (1986) found that most migrants in Asia moved to earn higher wages, as predicted by neoclassical economics, foreign labour was also widely used as a vehicle for accumulating capital, a goal more consistent with the new economics of migration. In Asian labour-sending countries such as the Philippines (McArthur 1979; Griffiths 1989), Sri Lanka (Spaan 1988; Eelens *et al.* 1991) and Indonesia (Hugo 1993*a*, 1995*b*, 1996*a*), rural communities are far from isolated, economically autonomous entities. Rather they are closely connected to national and international markets and rely heavily on migrant earnings to support local investment and consumption (Caces *et al.* 1985; Amjad 1989; Stahl and Habib 1991; Arnold 1992).

Remittances have become crucial to the economies of several Asian nations. Official data generally understate the size of remittance flows because they do not capture money and goods brought home by migrants or sent home with friends using 'batching' methods. The importance of unofficial channels in transmitting remittances, and the extent to which official sources underestimate the flow, is illustrated by the fact that in 1990, when the Philippine National Bank extended service to Italy, the Netherlands, Germany, and Spain, official per capita labour income from Europe more than doubled (Russell 1991: 20).

Despite data limitations, however, it is clear that remittances from migrants working in core nations of the Asia Pacific system are large and growing. In the Philippines, foreign exchange earned by migrants working abroad grew from around $US700 million in 1984 to $3.3 billion in 1994, an increase of 470 per cent in just ten years (Hugo 1996*b*). Remittances grew by 32 per cent between 1993 and 1994 alone, and equalled one-third of the country's total merchandise exports in the latter year.

The volume of migrant remittances has also grown exponentially in Thailand and Indonesia. In the former country, the 1995 inflow of $US166 million from migrants working abroad represents a doubling of the sum over the mid-1980s; and in the latter case, an estimated inflow of $US356 million in 1995 was more than ten times that of the early 1980s (Hugo 1996*b*; the *Sunday Post*, 27 August 1995; *Far Eastern Economic Review*, 16 May 1996).

As the Asia Pacific system emerged and solidified, the sources of migrant remittances have changed, a trend well exemplified in the Philippines. According to the *Manila Chronicle* (5 April 1995), the Gulf region has declined as a source of migrant remittances, going from $US173 million in 1993 to $US130 million in 1994. In contrast, remittances from within Asia and the Pacific grew from $US75.4 million in 1990 to $US381 million in 1994, increasing Asia's share of the inflow from 6 per cent to 13 per cent of the total. Of course, the largest source of remittances to the Philippines is still the USA, accounting for 57 per cent of the total in 1994.

Thus, even though wage differentials may provide one incentive for international migration, they do not appear to be the only impetus promoting international movement in Asia and the Pacific. Rather than being limited to individuals migrating to maximize future income, international flows are also made up of family members using foreign labour as a means of self-insuring household income against risk and self-financing household production and consumption. Strong family networks and well-defined norms of filial obligation provide circumstantial evidence for the importance of risk-diversification as a motive for movement, and the growth of remittances suggests migration's importance as a strategy of capital accumulation.

The new economics of migration and the neoclassical model thus complement each other in explaining international migration in the Asia Pacific region. One variant on the new economic model has been developed especially for the Pacific by Bertram and Watters (Bertram and Watters 1984, 1985, 1986; Bertram 1986; Watters 1987). Their conceptual scheme links migration, remittances, aid, and bureaucracy together in the so-called MIRAB model, which sees labour surpluses in the Pacific as supported by remittances and foreign aid, while national civil service programmes provide 'employment beyond what is functionally necessary and thus serve as a mechanism for income redistribution and the maintenance of an economic flow' (Hayes 1992: 297). According to the MIRAB model,

the motivation to emigrate arises out of a condition of labour surplus but the decision to migrate . . . is made by the kinship system rather than the individual. The kinship system ('transnational corporations of kin') is treated as an analogue to the multinational corporation which allocates its labour and capital in the most remunerative international markets. (ibid. 299)

Segmented Labour Market Theory

In contrast to neoclassical theory and the new economics of migration, which view migration as originating in deliberate actions taken by families and individuals, segmented labour market theory sees immigration as demand-driven and structural. Specifically, inherent tendencies within advanced industrial economies yield a primary sector of well-paying, stable jobs for natives and a secondary sector of unstable, poorly paid jobs that natives reject. Since employers can't change the jobs, they change the workers by recruiting immigrants (Piore 1979).

Segmented labour market theory is clearly relevant to generation of international migration in Asia and the Pacific, although once again formal tests are few. The literature is nonetheless quite consistent with its leading proposition that immigration is demand-driven (see Crissman 1967; Hugo 1993b; Mori 1994). Abella and Mori (1996), for example, demonstrate that sustained economic growth in Japan, Korea, and Taiwan—when combined with ageing populations, slow rates of labor force growth, and falling rates of labour force participation among the young—led to massive shortages of labour at the entry and unskilled levels which led, in turn, to labour migration. According to Martin *et al.* (1995a: 117), 'nations found themselves short of labour in particular sectors after domestic reservoirs of flexible labour were exhausted and they permitted or tolerated the entry of foreign workers.'

The biggest shortfalls in labour occurred in the class of so-called '3D' jobs: those that are dirty, dangerous, and difficult; these closely fit the profile of secondary labour market positions adumbrated by Piore (1979). As predicted by his theory, alternative mechanisms for coping with the growing labour shortage—namely, mechanization and the export of production—could not solve the structural problem, as the vacancies were concentrated 'in small scale enterprises which also face the greatest difficulty investing in automation or in offshore production in response to tight labour market conditions at home' (Abella and Mori 1996: 35).

Not only was there a shortage of native workers willing to take up secondary-sector employment, but rising educational levels in Japan, Korea, and Taiwan raised job aspirations among the young to the point where most young people would rather be unemployed and wait for a suitable white-collar job than stoop to work in sectors such as agriculture or construction (Abella and Mori 1996). The rejection of 3D jobs is common not only in the advanced economies of East Asia; it is also increasingly common in Malaysia, which hosts more than a million foreign workers who make up more than 10 per cent of the national workforce.

Even during the economic downturn of 1987, when rising levels of unemployment led to the release of large numbers of workers in Singapore and cities throughout Malaysia, natives refused to accept poorly paid, 'dirty' jobs that were available in plantations, agriculture, and construction. As a result, the demand for illegal Indonesian workers continued unabated despite the downturn (Hugo 1993*b*).

Although the gap in wages between manufacturing and services has narrowed in South Korea in recent years, the differential between large and small firms has widened because of the liberalization of policy towards trade unions, which affected larger firms more than smaller ones (as the former had more unionized workers—see Park 1993). Whereas in 1980 the smallest Korean firms (10–20 employees) had average wages that were 93 per cent of those in the largest enterprises (500+ employees), by 1990 the percentage stood at only 74 per cent. Likewise, whereas workers in firms with 30–99 employees had wages that averaged 99 per cent of those in the largest firms in 1980, the ratio had declined to 77 per cent by 1990 (Park 1993).

In spite of the ongoing shortage of entry-level workers, therefore, Korea's labour market grew more segmented during the 1980s and the gap in wages between its primary and secondary sectors widened, contradicting neoclassical predictions, which would predict rising wages owing to an excess of demand over supply. The steady growth in vacancies among what Böhning (1994) calls 'undesired jobs' eventually produced a substantial influx of illegal immigrants into South Korea as the 1980s drew to a close.

The Korean government responded by passing a new law—the Immigration

Law Reform of 1990—which allowed for additional legal immigration but also codified segmentation into the legal structure of the labour market. According to Mori (1994: 621), the 'differing treatment of categories of foreign workers in immigration control practice effectively results in a significant difference in their working conditions. Some are entitled to engage in qualified jobs in comparable or even more favourable conditions than nationals, some are able to work legally as unskilled workers, and some are permitted to work for designated periods of time. Others are forced to work illegally.'

A core hypothesis of segmented labour market theory is that international migration, being demand-driven, is initiated through formal recruitment mechanisms. Consistent with this prediction, Singapore, Hong Kong, Taiwan, South Korea, Japan, Malaysia, and Thailand have all established formal contract labour programmes to facilitate the entry, deployment, and control of workers from labour-surplus countries. According to Knerr (1993: 625), foreign labour recruitment has become an important economic policy parameter in capital-rich countries throughout the region.

Contract-labour migration, which traces its origins to the 'contract coolie' systems of colonial times (Hugo 1980, 1981), has become a dominant form of movement within the Asia Pacific region that distinguishes it from the contemporary flows in North America and Western Europe, where labour recruitment has effectively ended (Martin *et al.* 1995*b*). The implementation of contract-labour migration offers a striking parallel, however, to labour recruitment mechanisms used in the Middle East, an analogy that is clearest in the case of Singapore (Low 1995), where the government recently 'announced that it considers foreign workers an instrument of economic policy-making. Foreign workers are to be imported when needed, charged significant fees that increase government revenue, and sent home when they were not needed' (Martin *et al.* 1995*a*: 117). The strictness of the policy was demonstrated in 1987 when several hundred thousand foreign workers were summarily deported as Singapore experienced a rare period of economic deterioration.

Segmentation generally occurs among migrant workers on the basis of legal status, occupation, and firm size. It also occurs on the basis of country of origin, often in a manner reminiscent of colonial practices that formally segregated Europeans and indigenous groups from one another residentially, legally, and economically, often with the addition of an imported 'middleman' group to act as a social and political buffer (Hugo 1981). In some cases, migrants are also differentiated with respect to English language ability, education, and past migration experience.

Whatever their characteristics, however, illegal migrants are invariably locked into the secondary labour market, which provides them with few opportunities for mobility and few returns to skills or experience. Facing this sort of segmentation abroad, Indonesians with skills and education have tended to migrate not internationally but internally, usually to the capital city of Jakarta, where the returns to education, skill, and experience are greater. In India, however, there is more internal competition for jobs among the well educated and a greater diffusion of English language skills, yielding a stronger tendency for the educated to emigrate, especially if their qualifications can be recognized abroad. Much of this high-end movement, however, goes outside the Asia Pacific System to North America or Europe.

A significant and growing flow in Asia and the Pacific involves the permanent movement of Asians to Australia, a traditional country of immigration (Hugo 1995c). For some Asian groups, there is strong evidence for an ongoing process of labour market segmentation in Australian destination areas (Lever-Tracey 1981; Lever-Tracey and Quinlan 1988). Migrants from China, for example, are generally channelled into a narrow range of occupations at specific locations.

Three decades ago Crissman (1967) analysed what he referred to as the 'segmentary structure of urban overseas Chinese communities'. According to Pieke (1997: 9) the Chinese 'rarely seek cooperation and integration with strangers (members of the indigenous population or overseas Chinese from other areas). New immigrants enter a ready-made social environment: employment, friends, relatives, recreational patterns, way of life, and career pattern are to a large extent predetermined.'

This pattern of ethnic segmentation is consistent with hypotheses advanced by Portes and Bach (1985), who modified dual labour market theory by adding a third sector: the ethnic enclave. This sector provides relatively high returns to education and experience that are closer to those prevailing in the primary sector (at least for men). There is some evidence of the development of ethnic enclaves among Asians in Australia (Hugo 1991), where new arrivals are willing to trade low wages upon arrival for a greater chance of economic advancement later on.

The formation of ethnic enclaves is not only occurring in Australia, but in other destination countries in Asia and the Pacific. In the Malaysian capital of Kuala Lumpur, for example, Indonesian immigrants, many of them illegal, have formed enclaves that seem to operate in conformity with the patterns described by Portes and others. Again, however, there are no formal tests of the enclave hypothesis in Asia comparable to those undertaken in the USA.

Our survey thus reveals a clear pattern of labour market segmentation within the Asia Pacific migration system, in which immigrants play a leading role in the ongoing process of structural change. Immigration appears to be demand-led and supported by formal contract recruitment mechanisms; and in many cases segmentation occurs along the lines predicted by Piore (1979)— with a bifurcation of employment into primary and secondary sectors— although at times it is more complex and includes a third sector: the ethnic enclave posited by Portes and colleagues. Segmented labour market theory thus contributes to our understanding of international migration in the Asia Pacific region.

World Systems Theory

World systems theory argues that international migration stems from the globalization of the market economy (Portes and Walton 1981; Sassen 1988). As capitalism extends outward from global cities located in core capitalist nations, non-capitalist patterns of social and economic organization are disrupted and transformed. In the process, large numbers of people are displaced from traditional livelihoods, creating a mobilized population prone to migrate. Although many of these displaced people relocate internally to burgeoning cities, others follow ideological, material, and political links abroad, where new forms of social and economic organization associated with post-industrialism create a strong demand for their labour (Harvey 1990).

We know of no quantitative study that links the process of capital penetration to out-migration in the manner of Rickets (1987) or other scholars of the North American system. As with the other theoretical paradigms, there is little more than circumstantial evidence to connect patterns of international migration in the Asia Pacific System to processes of capital penetration, and to the formation of ideological and material links connecting regions of labour surplus to global cities in labour-importing countries (Connell 1992).

Shrestha (1988), documents how the penetration of capitalist economic relations into rural Nepal deprived subsistence farmers of their land and shows how, in the absence of alternative local opportunities, they were forced to migrate. A similar pattern is observed in other parts of Asia, where social and economic changes wrought by the Green Revolution led to the consolidation of landholding, the commercialization of agriculture, and the substitution of capital for labour in agrarian production (Hugo 1985).

The penetration of markets into peripheral areas of Asia and the Pacific has been accompanied by significant structural economic change, and the proportion of domestic output linked to agriculture has declined dramatically throughout the region since 1980. From 1980 to 1995, for example, the share of GDP attributable to agriculture fell from 26 per cent to 19 per cent in China, from 42 per cent to 34 per cent in Vietnam, from 37 per cent to 28 per cent in India, and from 31 per cent to 24 per cent in Pakistan (Asian Development Bank 1996).

All the above countries are sending societies in the Asia Pacific system, suggesting that the shift away from agriculture towards an industrial, service-based economy exerts pressure on inhabitants to seek work elsewhere. In the more established economies that receive migrants from these areas, the transition from an agrarian economy is nearly complete. In 1995 only 7 per cent of Korea's GDP was attributable to agriculture, compared with figures of 3 per cent in Taiwan, 14 per cent in Malaysia, 16 per cent in Indonesia, and 11 per cent in Thailand.

Links established during the colonial era by the British, French, Dutch, Portuguese, and American colonists continue to structure migration flows in

the region. During the last century, for example, European colonial administrators deliberately encouraged the movement of Chinese and Indian migrants
throughout the region to create buffers between the rulers and the ruled. As a
result, populations of Chinese and Indian expatriates now provide a natural
social infrastructure that supports the contemporary movement of people,
goods, information, and capital throughout South-East Asia.

Another hypothesis of world systems theory is that core receiving nations
contain 'global cities' that attract a disproportionate share of all immigrants.
Research by Friedman (1986) suggests that each of the receiving nations in the
Asia Pacific system houses a global city. In his empirical analysis of the world's
urban hierarchy, he identified Tokyo and Sydney as a primary global cities,
each of which clearly serves as its nation's principal magnet for international
migrants. Among the emerging industrial nations of the region, Friedmann
(1986) identifies Singapore, Hong Kong, Taipei, and Seoul as secondary global
cities, yielding one such city for each of the nodes in Figure 6.1, except
Malaysia, which emerged as a receiving society after the time of Friedmann's
analysis (analysis of more recent data might have identified Kuala Lampur as
a global city, perhaps along with Bangkok and Jakarta).

Sassen (1988) argues that there are three processes within developed societies that serve to generate immigrant streams: the shifting of production from
core to peripheral areas, the emergence of a global city and its integration into
world markets, and a political realignment that permits foreign companies to
become established and operate in domestic markets. Sassen (1991, 1995)
shows that the first two conditions clearly apply to Japan and that they have
been crucial in promoting the growth of large-scale immigration, much of it
illegal, from other parts of Asia. The third element is emerging more slowly,
largely in response to political pressure from the USA.

Over the last two decades, Japan has pursued a conscious strategy of shifting
labour-intensive industrial activities to low-wage nations in Asia, in the process forging strong ideological, material, and political linkages to potential
sending countries (Sassen 1991). The temporary movement of Japanese technicians, managers, and business people into low-wage nations has been accompanied by a more permanent flow of less skilled people in the opposite
direction. As a result, some 150,000 persons now enter Japan each year as
'company trainees', joined by an even larger number of undocumented migrants (Morita 1992; Spencer 1992; Morita and Sassen 1994).

One final hypothesis emanating from the world systems perspective is that
international migration follows ideological links that are formed between poor
and wealthy countries in the process of market penetration. Thus, the
globalization of the capitalist economy is accompanied by a globalization of
capitalist consumer culture that itself encourages international movement.
According to post-modern theorists, the circulation of people, goods, and
ideas creates a transnational culture that blends values, behaviours, and atti-

tudes core and peripheral societies to create a new, increasingly autonomous social space that transcends national boundaries (Rouse 1989, 1990, 1991, 1992; Georges 1990; Goldring 1992, 1996a, 1996b).

Many observers have commented on the expansion of consumerism in communities in Asia (Adi 1996), and one of the increasing features of migrant communities, in particular, is the satellite dish that links them to global television, with its associated cultural, economic, and social impacts (Hugo 1996a). At the same time, the rising movement of tourists, students, and business travellers also influences international labour migration. Student migration serves as a frequent precursor to permanent settlement and has a long history in the Asian region (Adams 1969; Oh 1973; Pernia 1976; Kritz and Caces 1989; Beng 1990; Dawkins *et al.* 1991; Chang 1992; Sullivan and Gunasekaran 1992); but the effects of the exponential increases in international travel wrought by the falling real costs of air travel have been little studied. In Australia, 34 per cent of recent legal settlers from Asia visited the country before emigrating (Hugo 1992). There are also strong links in Australia between immigration and tourism (National Population Council 1991; Dwyer *et al.* 1993) and between immigration and student travel for education (Dawkins *et al.* 1991).

Gender Perspectives

A salient feature of the Asia Pacific system in recent years has been the increasing scale and significance of female migration (United Nations 1994, 1995; *Asia and Pacific Migration Journal* 5(1) 1996). In several flows within the Asia Pacific region, women outnumber men (Hugo 1995c; Lim and Oishi 1996). Particularly salient is the growing movement of domestic workers out of the Philippines, Indonesia, and Sri Lanka into Japan, Taiwan, and Korea (Asia and Pacific Development Centre 1987; Heyzer *et al.* 1994). The involvement of migrant women in the Asian sex trade is also associated with female migration (Vatikiotis 1995; Brockett 1996), and a final factor is the marriage migration of Asian women to men in developed countries through various mail order schemes (Cahill 1990).

Rapid growth in the participation of women within the Asia Pacific migration system can be explained to some extent by the theoretical perspectives under review here; but some observers suggest that established theoretical formulations—notably neoclassical economics—fail to identify and address important determinants of women's participation in Asian migration, namely patriarchal gender ideologies, life-cycle factors, and class position (Chant and Radcliffe 1992; Lee 1996; Truong 1996). A criticism of economic models in general is that they reduce migrants to homogeneous units of labour, whereas in reality human behaviour is highly structured by gender, age, kinship, ethnicity, and class (Cadwallader 1992; Goss and Lindquist 1995).

The Perpetuation of International Migration

Social Capital Theory: Migrant Networks

Social capital theory argues that migrant networks—interpersonal ties that connect migrants, former migrants, and non-migrants in origin and destination areas—offer a valuable source of capital that acts to lower the costs and risks of international migration, enhance the prospects and rewards of foreign labour, and thus tip the scales decisively in favour of international movement (see Choldin 1973; MacDonald and MacDonald 1974; Boyd 1989; Massey 1990*b*; Gurak and Caces 1992).

The effect of migrant networks in raising rates and probabilities of international migration has been demonstrated convincingly throughout Asia and the Pacific by many different analysts using a variety of data and methodologies. In all of the major sending countries of the Asia Pacific system, networks have been shown to be significant in perpetuating migration once a small number of pioneers has become established at the destination. Such is the case for the Philippines (De Jong *et al.* 1983; Caces *et al.* 1985; Smart *et al.* 1986; Fawcett and Arnold 1987; Fawcett 1989; Lindquist 1993; Goss and Lindquist 1995), Indonesia (Kasto and Sukamdi 1986; Hugo 1993*b*, 1995*b*; Spaan 1994; Adi 1996), Sri Lanka (Spaan 1988; Eelens *et al.* 1991; Mahawewa 1995), China (Thuno 1996), and Thailand (Singhanetra-Renard 1992; Warmsingh 1997).

In general, the existence of a stock of migrants in a potential destination area is the most important predictor of whether a particular community will send migrants to that area in the future, although as with other theories, there is a dearth of studies that formally test this proposition. Nevertheless, the empirical evidence is overwhelming that networks established by earlier generations of migrants act as conduits to channel later generations to the same destinations in an atmosphere of relative security.

In Asia, previous generations of movers not only supply valuable information and encouragement; they often pay for, arrange, and ease the passage. When a migrant arrives at the point of destination, the receiving end of the network offers valuable assistance in the adjustment process, especially in gaining access to housing and employment. Networks greatly reduce the risks associated with migration and many movers in Asia operate in an environment of near-total certainty.

The role of kin- and friendship-based networks in facilitating population movements with the Asia Pacific region can scarcely be exaggerated. While other factors may be required to initiate movement, once pioneer migrants become established at a point of destination, additional movement there proceeds rapidly as they facilitate additional migration by friends and family through legal and illegal channels. Pioneer migrants provide an anchor for interpersonal networks, which then serve to attract larger numbers of migrants to the same location. Undocumented migration, in particular, is risky and problematic without a migrant network to facilitate illicit entry, passage, and employment.

Networks not only link friends and family members across a range of foreign destinations; they often include employers as well. Frequently a patron–client relation of mutual dependence develops that guarantees migrants access to work while providing employers with assured access to a steady supply of labour. Over time, networks come to embrace not only employers, but as explained in the next section, others who facilitate international movement for profit: recruiters, travel agents, transport operators, foremen, contractors, smugglers. In Asia, particularly, migrant networks are not purely 'social' entities based on family and friendship connections.

Networks are not static structures, but are fluid and changing. In a study of migration from Northern Thailand, for example, Singhanetra-Renard (1992: 196) found that networks evolved in three distinct phases. Migration initially occurred under the auspices of a patron–client relationship between employers and employee that was gradually transformed to include obligations beyond the simple remuneration of hours of work. In the second phase, intermediaries became involved in recruitment and job placement, and the network relationships became more commercial, although still primarily legal. In the third and final phase, recruitment agents come to dominate the flow and promote both legal and illegal migration through their own social connections to employers in destination areas.

Family-based social networks, once established, also operate to facilitate the movement of people who before their formation would not have been permitted to migrate, owing to constraints imposed by kinship and gender ideology. Torres (1992: 66) maintains that networks are crucial for Filipino families seeking to deploy educated single daughters to work overseas, as these 'moves are encouraged by both the demands of the labour market, as well as by cultural expectations from the social network.' Young women are encouraged by families to leave not only because they face limited job prospects at home, but because their foreign labour will generate additional household income. Female migrants are expected to remit a sizeable portion of their earnings to support families at home.

In discussing the significance of migrant networks in China, Pieke (1997) stresses that migrants are drawn from a relatively small number of villages that become economically, socially, and psychologically integrated with destination areas abroad, and progressively more isolated from the society and economy of the home country:

[C]hain migration is tied to a representation of reality, including chain migration itself, that focuses migrants in the home community exclusively on an overseas career. Home communities often specialise in emigration. All or most able-bodied men and women emigrate leaving behind villages populated by children and old people.

Thus, migration chains of varying strength appear to link communities in sending and receiving areas throughout Asia and the Pacific, and the existence and development of these chains is a major causal influence on the scale, composition, and spatial patterning of migration within the Asia Pacific system. Although most of the evidence adduced to date takes the form of case studies and descriptive reports rather than analytic studies, network theory nonetheless helps to explain why neighbouring communities with apparently similar social and economic profiles often display very different levels and patterns of migration. Throughout Asia, communities with established migrant networks tend to experience substantial out-migration while those without such linkages are characterized by low levels of mobility.

Social Capital Theory: Migrant Institutions

Over time, social capital in Asia has displayed a tendency to become more accessible and abundant not just through the expansion of traditional family–friend and patron–client linkages, but also through the growth and elaboration of institutional connections. Rather than being limited mainly to interpersonal ties manipulated by individual family members and friends, social capital within Asia and the Pacific also emanates from a variety of institutional linkages that exist apart from the migrants themselves and are manipulated by third parties, primarily for profit.

Labour migration with the Asia Pacific system (and to the Middle East) is perpetuated by commercial and bureaucratic relations carried out through various institutional intermediaries. Migrant institutions are relatively permanent social structures that result from the regularization of social interaction explicitly for the purposes of overseas employment and which regulate and control access to overseas employment through institutional roles. Recruiters, agents, smugglers, contractors, state bureaucracies, and other actors constitute nodes within larger business organizations that connect individual communities to a range of jobs and destinations in the Asia Pacific region (Lindquist 1993). Studies that have examined the 'immigration industry' in Asia document how important these actors can be in persuading potential migrants to move, and in supporting their overseas travel and labour market insertion (Hugo and Singhanetra-Renard 1987; Spaan 1994; Goss and Lindquist 1995). Much of the movement within the Asia Pacific system is facilitated, if not initiated, by these intermediaries, particularly in the case of clandestine migration. It is difficult to think of a major contemporary flow from Asia in which the immigration industry does not play a pivotal role, with the exception of refugees.

In Indonesia, immigration agents variously known as *calo, taikong, tauke,* and *mandor* are highly organized and crucial to the promotion of mass migration into Malaysia, both legal and illegal. Habir (1984: 167) describes the roles played by these middlemen, beginning with recruitment, continuing through transportation, and concluding with the provision of documents, housing, and employment. In this case, it is the agents—not the migrants—who have extensive networks on both sides of the border.

Spaan (1994) offers a detailed description of the complex role that mediators play in promoting the illegal migration of East Javanese into Malaysia, and Figure 6.2 draws upon his work to provide a schematic outline of the resulting social infrastructure. As the figure shows, migrants are passed from one intermediary to another through a chain of well-established links

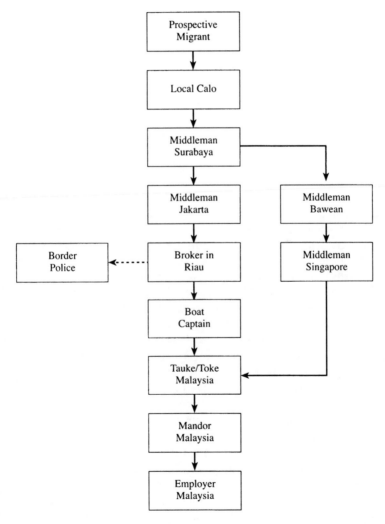

Fig. 6.2 Example of an institutional network linking prospective illegal labour migrants in East Java to employers in Malaysia (modified from Spaan 1994)

extending from origin communities to destination employers. Each intermediary along the chain receives a small payment for services provided, in classic 'involutionary' fashion (see Hugo 1975).

The institutional network is safe and trusted because it begins in the home village with a known *calo*, who is directly answerable to townspeople and kin members if failure or exploitation occurs somewhere in the system. These clandestine networks are often more trustworthy, reliable, and quicker than official recruitment programmes sponsored by the government because the latter cannot offer the same kind of personalized local accountability, and because they usually entail costly delays to obtain correct documentation and bureaucratic permissions.

Another example of how intermediaries operate to promote emigration occurs in the movement of Filipino entertainers to Japan. Torres (1992: 57) reports that a 'complex network of underground travel agents, talent promoters and job brokers are known to expedite the illegal entry of entertainers into Japan.' Many female 'entertainers' are little more than exploited sex workers.

Despite its importance in Asia and elsewhere, the immigration industry is frequently overlooked as a source of social capital, or it is mentioned only in passing by investigators. This neglect partly reflects a reliance on methodologies that focus on migrants, their families, and their communities at the expense of recruiters, agents, contractors, and other migration entrepreneurs. In addition, the empirical distinction between networks and institutions is often confused, as experienced migrants return to establish their own recruitment organizations, labour-contracting firms, or migration-financing schemes and begin using their networks for profit. This shift from migrant networks to migrant institutions has been observed in Thailand (Warmsingh 1997), Indonesia (Hugo 1993*b*; Spaan 1994), and the Philippines (Caces *et al.* 1985; Liu *et al.* 1991; Lindquist 1993; Goss and Lindquist 1995). It is also more difficult to get information from intermediaries because they are reluctant to provide information they see as proprietary, and because many of their business operations are outside the law. According to some observers, the high level of profitability associated with the smuggling of people has led to a 'new slave trade' whereby workers are effectively indentured to entrepreneurs or criminal organizations. Crime syndicates formerly involved in the drug trade have found it profitable and more secure to undertake the smuggling of migrants rather than narcotics.

The roots of such exploitative institutional networks extend back to the slave trade, which flourished in pre-colonial Asia, as well to the 'contract coolie' system of the colonial era. During the late nineteenth and early twentieth centuries, in particular, a variety of surreptitious institutions promoted Chinese migration throughout South-East Asia. A complex network of shipping companies, agents, brokers, innkeepers, and carriers supported massive emigration from China over more than a century (Hicks 1993; Shozo 1995).

This movement continues today by way of human traffickers known as *shetou*, or 'snakeheads' (Thuno 1996: 12; Pieke 1997: 6).

Some of the most important migrant institutions in Asia were not established by private syndicates or profit-seeking entrepreneurs, but by sending-country governments seeking to export labour in order to acquire foreign exchange, reduce unemployment, or building the skills of their workers (Hugo 1995*b*). In sending nations as diverse as the Philippines, Indonesia, Sri Lanka, Bangladesh, India, Pakistan, China, and Vietnam, governments have established special bureaucracies, policies, and procedures to encourage and facilitate the emigration of labour. The national economic plans of the Philippines (Battistella 1995) and Indonesia (Hugo 1995*b*) explicitly incorporate labour migration as a policy tool and go so far as to set specific remittance targets.

The direct involvement of governments in the promotion of international migration is another feature of the Asia Pacific system that sets it apart from migration systems in North America or Western Europe. Pieke (1997: 3) argues that 'chain migration—coupled with the push of poverty in the Chinese countryside and the pull of prosperity [overseas]—is but part of the story of post-war Chinese migration, *political factors* have often been equally if not more important in promoting or inhibiting the migrant flow' (emphasis added). To illustrate his point, he refers to the effective closure of China from the 1950s through the mid-1970s, which prevented prospective emigrants from joining friends and relatives abroad. He also points out that the decolonization of South-East Asia led to massive outflows of overseas Chinese, and that visa restrictions in countries of destination had a major influence on the composition and structure of Chinese expatriate communities.

Unlike internal migration, governments feel they can exert a substantial degree of control over international migration, although the growing volume of illegal migration suggests that control does have its limits (Hugo 1995*a*). Institutional support by government takes a variety of forms. Most poor countries in Asia have established special labour-export agencies within their national bureaucracies to regulate flows, control recruitment, train potential migrants, explore new labour markets, and encourage wealthy nations to employ their workers, although the precise mix of policies varies from setting to setting (see Shah and Arnold 1986; Abella 1992*b*).

Several countries have established special financial programmes to attract remittances: offering tax breaks, establishing banking facilities at destinations, subsidizing interests rates on deposits remitted home, or requiring the remittance of a fixed share of weekly earnings, into government-controlled accounts (Shah and Arnold 1986; Athukorala 1993). Some nations have sought bilateral labour agreements with destination countries, whereas others provide special migrant support services at places of destination. In some cases, countries also provide assistance to migrants seeking to readjust to the home community after a period of labour abroad (Athukorala 1990). Finally, several nations have put in place special programmes to attract back home emigrants who have achieved high levels of skill or wealth overseas (Shah and Arnold 1986; Athukorala 1993). In China, even some provinces have established their own labour-export companies to encourage and facilitate international migration (Qian 1996).

In sum, the institutionalization of migration both by private entrepreneurs and sending-country governments is an important feature of international migration in the Asia Pacific system, setting it apart from the North American and Western European systems, where networks are mainly (although not exclusively) interpersonal and controlled by the migrants themselves. Within Asia, the 'immigration industry' and various 'immigration bureaucracies' have assumed greater importance in promoting movement not only within the Asia Pacific system, but to the Gulf system as well.

Cumulative Causation

Cumulative causation refers to the tendency for international migration to perpetuate itself over time, regardless of the conditions that originally caused it. At the individual level, those who have migrated in the past are quite likely to migrate again in the future, as their foreign work experience increases their value to overseas employers and the knowledge and experience gleaned on earlier trips reduces the costs and risks of subsequent movement. This line of reasoning is consistent with data from the Philippines, which clearly shows that the probability of emigration is strongly increased by having prior migrant experience (Root and De Jong 1991).

At the aggregate level, migrant networks also operate to cause migration cumulatively because each act of migration creates additional social infrastructure to promote more movement. Whenever anyone migrates, all those to whom the migrant is related by kinship or friendship acquire a tie that can be manipulated to improve the odds of undertaking a successful international trip. Although strong quantitative findings are lacking, such a process is consistent with case studies and descriptive reports emanating from the Philippines (Caces *et al.* 1985; Smart *et al.* 1986; Lindquist 1993), Indonesia (Kasto and Sukamdi 1986; Hugo 1993b, 1995b; Spaan 1994; Adi 1996), Sri Lanka (Spaan 1988; Eelens *et al.* 1991; Mahawewa 1995), China (Thuno 1996), and Thailand (Singhanetra-Renard 1992; Warmsingh 1997).

Another process of cumulative causation involves the establishment of norms within a community (Hugo 1981). Once a pattern of behaviour becomes widespread it can assume normative status so that it becomes *expected* behaviour. In hierarchically structured societies, such as many in Asia, norms are especially important in shaping the behaviour of residents. In the case of foreign labour, migration can become so common that it becomes a *rite de passage* for young men, who feel they must migrate to be considered mature and worthy adults. Although cultural elements are not readily quantifiable, there is ample field evidence documenting the emergence of a 'culture of international migration' in parts of Indonesia (1981, 1996*b*; Colfer 1985), Thailand (Warmsingh 1997), and China (Minghuan 1996: 13; Pieke 1997).

A fourth mechanism of cumulative causation has been hypothesized to occur through community income distributions. According to the new economics, a household participates in migration not only to improve its absolute income, but also to its increase income relative to others in the community. During the initial phases of migration, remittances from migrants skew the income distribution upward and increase the relative deprivation of those at the bottom of the distribution, which induces them to migrate and begin remitting, which skews the distribution even more, yielding a process of cumulative causation (Stark and Taylor 1989, 1991*a*, 1991*b*).

Detailed studies of remittances from overseas migrants and their effect on Asian income distributions have been limited. A few village-based studies have addressed this issue and lend it some descriptive support in China (Minghuan 1996: 8) and Thailand (Warmsingh 1997). A case study in rural Pakistan found that while remittances from internal migration have an equalizing effect on rural income distribution, international remittances have a unequalizing one (Adams 1996). Similarly, remittances in the Philippines had an adverse effect on the income distribution because migrants tended to come from better-educated and better-off households (Rodriguez and Horton 1996).

Conclusion

As in North America and Western Europe, our review of research in Asia and the Pacific yields support for all theoretical models. Once again, each has something to offer in constructing a comprehensive explanation for trends and patterns of migration across the nations of Asia and the Pacific. However, although available studies appear to link international migration to wage differentials, market failures, structurally induced demand, and the globalization of markets, they do not reveal which of these forces is more powerful in generating the flows. Similarly, although there is considerable support for the predictions of social capital theory and the cumulative causation of migration, we uncovered no quantitative assessments of the relative power of these forces in perpetuating international movement.

What is clearly needed in the Asia Pacific region is better data, more analysis, and a stronger connection with theory. Compared to migration systems in Europe, North America, and even the Gulf, data on immigration and emigration are quite limited in terms of both quality and quantity for sending as well as receiving nations in the Asia Pacific system. Investigators in the region need to be more active in gathering data and creating datasets than they have to date. Little progress will be made relying on official statistics.

At the same time, researchers need to move beyond case studies and descriptive reports to undertake more sophisticated quantitative analyses using statistical techniques that offer some measure of control and which enable more precise measurement of the strength of theoretical effects. Whatever the sophistication of future analyses, moreover, they should strive for a more direct testing of theoretical propositions and hypotheses, and undertake more direct comparisons between competing models. The disarticulation between empirical research and theory throughout Asia and the Pacific is remarkable, especially in the case of Australia, with its long history of immigration and well-developed traditions of research and data collection. Rather than studying the causes of international migration, Australian research has focused more on the domestic consequences.

Our review uncovered several distinctive features of the Asia Pacific migration system that sets it apart from others in the world today. The first is the relative importance and prevalence of institutions, as opposed to interpersonal networks, in perpetuating (and even initiating) international movement. Intermediate actors associated with the 'immigration industry' and migration-promoting bureaucracies play a much greater role shaping migration within the Asia Pacific system (and the Gulf system) compared with the North American and European systems. While institutional connections are certainly not absent in North America and Europe, they loom much larger in initiating and perpetuating migration throughout Asia.

A second notable feature of international migration in the Asia Pacific region is the relatively direct and forceful role played by governments in shaping flows both within the system and to core destinations in other systems. In receiving countries of all contemporary international migration systems, restrictive immigration and labour policies are critical in determining the size and composition of foreign populations; but throughout Asia and the Pacific, governments have taken an unusually large and active role in promoting, managing, and initiating the export of labour for their own macroeconomic benefit. Authorities in some countries have gone so far as to build labour emigration (and a resulting flow of remittances) into their national or provincial planning targets.

Another facet of international migration in the Asia Pacific region that distinguishes it from other systems is its relative newness, and the consequent fact that several nations within it are simultaneously importers and exporters of labour. In some cases, nations export unskilled workers while importing those with special skills (human capital). This situation is probably a temporary state of affairs that will only characterize NICs for a brief period of transition, as was the case in Spain, Italy, and Portugal. But the newness of the system, and the fact that several nations within it are still making the transition from exporting to importing labour, underscore its inchoate and changeable structure.

Finally, the last notable fact about the system now consolidating within Asia and the Pacific is the tremendous size of its principal sending nations. China's population of 1.2 billion is the world's largest, followed by India's 950 million. Indonesia has 201 million inhabitants and Pakistan another 134 million. Other prominent source countries—Thailand, Bangladesh, Malaysia, and the Philippines—have populations that range from 20 to 100 million. Clearly, there is considerable scope for continuing migration within the system as the various forces we have uncovered operate on these giants, and what happens to them will have profound implications not only for population movements within Asia and the Pacific, but throughout the world.

7 International Migration in South America

In the last of our empirical assessments of migration theory, we consider research on international migration in South America, excluding Mexico, Central America, and the Caribbean, which were already covered in our discussion of the North American system. As in earlier chapters, we seek to compare theoretical predictions with empirical data, to evaluate existing conceptual models, and to foster a closer integration among the various conceptual frameworks. Once again we begin by describing patterns of migration in the region, focusing in particular on the structure and organization of the Argentine subsystem.

International Migration in South America

International migration in South America has been the subject of numerous overviews (see Kritz and Gurak 1979; Diaz Briquets 1983; Lattes 1985; Balán 1988; Pellegrino 1989; Lattes and Recchini de Lattes 1991; Adelman 1995; Finch 1995), yielding a literature that may be grouped into three categories: historical studies of transatlantic migration and its effects on South American societies; studies of contemporary international migration and its relation to internal population movements; and studies of contemporary emigration to developed nations such as USA.

The first category considers the process of European (and in a few cases Asian) immigration, which peaked in the years between 1880 and 1930 (see Bunge and García Mata 1931; Díaz-Alejandro 1970; Morner 1985; Cohen 1995: 203–25). Only a handful of nations—notably Argentina, Brazil, and Uruguay—evolved patterns of industrialization that relied on the large-scale incorporation of immigrant labour. During the late nineteenth and early twentieth centuries, these three countries formed the core of a well-defined international migration system that received massive inflows of migrants from Europe, principally from Italy, Spain, and Portugal (Ferenczi 1929; Germani 1966a).

According to Lattes (1983, 1985), from 1800 to 1970 some 13.8 million immigrants entered Latin America, with roughly three-quarters settling in Brazil or Argentina. Nearly 60 per cent came from Southern Europe, 15 per cent from elsewhere in Europe, and 11 per cent were from Asia. Mass immigration played a central role in the industrial development of cities such as Buenos Aires, São Paulo, and Montevideo, and immigrants and their children ultimately came to dominate all classes in these large metropolitan areas and to play key roles in the structural transformation of their respective societies (see Germani 1966*a*; Oddone 1966; Balán 1974; Beozzo Bassanezi 1995; Celton 1995).

The last waves of European emigration occurred just after the Second World War, and thereafter the number of persons born in Europe began to decline steadily in most countries. The mass immigration of Europeans into the Americas was repeated only once: in Venezuela during the 1950s, when oil revenues financed a wave of industrialization and infrastructure development that led to a high demand for labour. In the course of this decade, some 335,000 persons were added to Venezuela's foreign-born population, 70 per cent from Europe, again mostly from Italy, Spain, and Portugal.

Latin American and Caribbean countries historically have had relatively good data on international migration compiled as part of the IMILA project (Investigación de Migración Internacional en América Latina) of the UN Latin American Demographic Center (CELADE) in Santiago, which routinely tabulated information on the foreign born enumerated in each round of censuses. Owing to financial constraints, however, data from the 1990 round of censuses have not yet been compiled. Nonetheless, the 1970 and 1980 rounds, reported in Table 7.1, show the cumulative effects of mortality and return migration among European immigrants. In Argentina, Brazil, and Chile the number of foreign born fell during the 1970s in both relative and absolute terms, quite sharply in the case of Argentina, which sustained a net loss of 336,000 foreigners.

Historically, much of the population movement between South American countries was confined to border regions. Frontiers imposed in the process of decolonization divided people who formerly shared the same administrative and political region, and artificially split many cultural and ethnic groups. The imposition of national boundaries in the early nineteenth century thus created international migrants out of people who had formerly just been local movers.

These cross-border movements retained a strong rural-to-rural character during the nineteenth and early twentieth centuries, reflecting the incursion of agriculture into frontier regions, the seasonal migration of harvest workers, and systematic movements for resettlement in agrarian regions vacated by earlier migrants. Rural circulation continues today in many regions of South America, forming a complex web of seasonal migration often linked to more permanent kinds of population mobility.

Migration from rural to urban areas became increasingly dominant in South America after 1950, yielding high and rising rates of urbanization throughout the region (United Nations 1980). In two notable cases, this rural–urban movement crossed international borders, transforming the people involved from internal to international migrants. Specifically, during the 1970s immigrants of rural origin joined those of urban origin to transform the composition and structure of international migration into Argentina and Venezuela.

Table 7.1   International migration during the 1970s in selected South American countries ('000s)

	Total foreign born			Percentage foreign born		
	c. 1970	*c.* 1980	Change	*c.* 1970	*c.* 1980	Change
Argentina	2,193.3	1,857.7	−335.6	9.4	6.6	−2.8
Brazil	1,229.1	1,110.9	−118.2	1.3	0.9	−0.4
Chile	88.9	84.3	−24.6	1.0	0.7	−0.3
Paraguay	79.7	169.1	89.4	3.4	5.6	2.2
Peru	67.2	66.9	−0.3	0.5	0.4	−0.1
Uruguay	131.8	131.8	0.0	4.7	4.5	−0.2
Venezuela	582.6	1,074.6	492.0	5.4	7.4	2.0

	Born in Latin America			Percentage of foreigners born in Latin America		
	c. 1970	*c.* 1980	Change	*c.* 1970	*c.* 1980	Change
Argentina	579.1	747.1	168.0	26.4	40.2	13.8
Brazil	70.9	107.7	36.8	5.8	9.7	3.9
Chile	30.1	38.6	7.5	33.9	45.8	11.9
Paraguay	63.8	149.9	86.1	80.1	88.6	8.5
Peru	23.2	24.2	1.0	34.6	36.2	2.2
Uruguay	36.8	32.0	−4.8	27.9	24.3	−5.6
Venezuela	215.4	643.5	428.1	37.0	59.9	22.9

Source: IMILA Database, Centro Latinoamericano de Demografía, Santiago.

As Table 7.1 reports, Argentina experienced a net gain of 168,000 foreign-born Latin Americans during the 1970s, even as it sustained a net loss of 504,000 Europeans of foreign birth through emigration or death. In contrast, Venezuela did not sustain an absolute decline in the number of foreigners; instead, the 1970's oil boom financed a second wave of industrial growth and development that encouraged mass immigration. Unlike the case of the 1950s, however, Venezuela's labour needs in the 1970s were met from sources within Latin America, as 87 per cent of the net increase of 492,000 immigrants came from this region (see Table 7.1).

Nearly half of the immigrants to Venezuela came from just one country, Colombia (Van Roy 1984; Pellegrino 1989), which also served as the principal source for undocumented migrants (Sassen 1979; Gómez Jiménez and Díaz Mesa 1983; Pellegrino 1984; Bidegain 1987; Murillo Castaño 1988). According to Diaz-Briquets and Frederick (1984), during the period 1964–73 illegal migrants outnumbered legal immigrants by a margin of more than two to one, and 88 per cent of all Colombian emigrants in Latin America resided in Venezuela.

Although Colombian migrants had long entered Venezuela seasonally to perform harvest labour, during the 1960s and 1970s they shifted increasingly to urban destinations such as Caracas and other cities experiencing rapid industrial growth. The post-1973 economic boom in Venezuela also coincided with the advent of military dictatorships throughout the Southern Cone, producing a significant movement of political refugees that for a time made Venezuela, along with Mexico, Latin America's leading receiver of the region's emigrés.

In both Argentina and Venezuela, the ongoing loss of older European immigrants during the 1970s, combined with the large influx of new arrivals from elsewhere in Latin America, transformed the composition of the foreign-born population. In Argentina, the percentage of Latin Americans among the foreign born jumped from 26 per cent in 1970 to 40 per cent in 1980, and in Venezuela it went from 37 per cent to 60 per cent (see Table 7.1). During the decade of the 1970s, in other words, immigration in South America was progressively Americanized, a trend that actually began during the 1960s.

With the collapse of oil prices in the early 1980s, Venezuela's migration boom went bust and immigration slowed. Compared with a net in-migration of 316,000 foreigners during the 1970s, Venezuela experienced a net *outflow* of 107,000 foreigners between 1980 and 1984 (Pellegrino 1989). By 1990, only Argentina remained as an important magnet for immigration into South America; and despite its historical status as a country of immigration, after 1950 Brazil received few immigrants from either Europe or Latin America (see Table 7.1).

Strong job growth in Argentine cities, particularly in metropolitan Buenos Aires, combined with low domestic fertility, yielded a strong demand for immigrant labour during the 1950s, 1960s, and 1970s (Marshall 1980*a*, 1984; Marshall and Orlansky 1983), a demand that apparently continued through the 1980s despite difficult conditions in the Argentine economy (Maguid 1990; Montoya and Torres 1992; Maguid and Bankirer 1995). According to the best available estimates, net immigration into Argentina ran at 385,000 during the 1940s and 232,000 during the 1950s (Lattes 1983); it rose to 385,000 during the 1960s (Marshall 1981) and then fell slightly to 320,000 during the 1970s (Balán 1992). The foreign-born population increased from a little over one million at the turn of the century to reach 2.6 million in 1960, and then began to diminish as a result of the death and emigration of ageing European immigrants.

Table 7.2 shows changes in the size of the foreign-born population between 1970 and 1990. Whereas the number of people born in countries bordering Argentina increased steadily throughout the period, the number of persons born elsewhere fell sharply, especially those from Europe, yielding an overall decline in the size of the foreign-born population over the period, which

Table 7.2   Change in size of foreign born population of Argentina, 1970–1990

Country and region	Population ('000)			Change	
	1970	1980	1991	1970–80	1980–91
Bordering countries					
Bolivia	92	118	144	26	26
Brazil	45	43	33	−2	−10
Chile	133	216	244	83	28
Paraguay	212	263	250	51	−13
Uruguay	51	114	133	63	19
TOTAL bordering	533	754	804	221	50
Other countries					
Italy	637	488	328	−149	−160
Spain	515	374	225	−141	−149
Others	525	287	258	−238	−29
TOTAL other	1,677	1,149	811	−528	−338
TOTAL foreign born	2,210	1,903	1,615	−307	−288

Source: República Argentina (1991).

reached just 1.6 million in 1991. Between 1970 and 1980 the number of Italians fell by 149,000 persons, and by 1991 it had dropped by another 160,000. The number of Spanish likewise fell by 141,000 persons during the 1970s and 149,000 persons during the 1980s. In contrast, among immigrants from bordering nations only the number of Brazilians fell steadily across both decades. The number of persons born in Bolivia, Chile, and Uruguay increased during the 1970s and 1980s, and the number of Paraguayans rose in the 1970s before falling slightly during the 1980s.

Changing numbers of foreigners poorly indicate the contemporary structure of transnational population flows, given significant return migration and mortality among ageing foreign populations. In some cases, a substantial number of immigrants may be offset by a large number of deaths or sizeable return flows, yielding a misleading portrait of the current system structure. Like other historical countries of immigration, such as Canada and the USA, Argentina maintains an independent statistics system that annually records the number of persons admitted for legal permanent residence, yielding a statistical series such as that used to define the structure of the North American system (see Table 3.1). Table 7.2 draws on these statistics to consider patterns of international migration into Argentina during the 1980s (República Argentina 1994). These figures capture the gross inflow of legal immigrants during the 1980s, and are not affected by mortality or emigration.

Table 7.3   Gross legal permanent immigration into
Argentina, 1980–1990

Country and region	Number	Percent
Latin America		
Bolivia	54,168	13.5
Brazil	6,717	1.7
Chile	132,516	33.0
Paraguay	60,226	15.0
Peru	6,778	1.7
Uruguay	76,907	19.1
Other	6,528	1.6
Other regions		
USA	6,387	1.6
Europe	22,765	5.7
Asia	27,920	6.9
Africa/Oceania	589	0.1
Unknown	406	0.1
TOTAL	401,907	100.0

Source: República Argentina (1994).

According to these data, nearly 402,000 new immigrants arrived in Argentina from 1980 to 1990. The vast majority of these immigrants (80 per cent) came from just four countries, all sharing a common border with Argentina: Chile (33 per cent), Uruguay (19 per cent), Paraguay (15 per cent), and Bolivia (14 per cent). The same countries also appear to be the primary sources for illegal migration. Of the undocumented migrants who legalized under two amnesties offered by the Argentine government in 1974 and 1984, 35 per cent were from Chile, 33 per cent from Paraguay, 13 per cent from Uruguay, and 14 per cent from Bolivia (Sassone 1987; Balán 1992).

Although emigrants from Paraguay, Bolivia, and Chile were originally rural in both origin and destination (being composed to a significant degree of seasonal harvest workers), over time the flows became increasingly urban-oriented. Emigration to Argentina from Uruguay, in contrast, has for many years been predominantly urban in both origin and destination, and has included well-educated groups as well as labourers and their families (Pellegrino 1989). Immigrants to Argentina have increasingly settled in and around metropolitan Buenos Aires, which in 1980 was home to 80 per cent of all Uruguayans, 62 per cent of all Paraguayans, and 46 per cent of all Bolivians (ibid.). Although the military regime that came to power in 1976 attempted to limit immigration from neighbouring countries, it achieved limited success, despite several repatriation campaigns.

Thus, Argentina presently sits at the core of a small regional migration subsystem within the Southern Cone of South America (Lombardi and Altesor 1987). The structure of this regional subsystem is shown graphically in Figure 7.1. Argentina is connected to its immediate neighbours through modest migration flows and strong economic ties recently formalized in the MERCOSUR agreement, which established a free-trade zone that includes Argentina, Paraguay, Brazil, and Uruguay. The Argentine subsystem differs from the four global migration systems described in earlier chapters in three ways: the scale of the movement is much smaller, it only has one core country, and little of the movement into Argentina is transcontinental.

While Argentina has continued to attract working-class and agrarian immigrants from neighbouring countries in recent decades, it also served as a source of skilled emigration to more developed countries overseas, particularly the USA. This movement began in the 1960s but grew considerably after 1975 when professionals, scientists, and skilled workers left in growing numbers because of political and economic turmoil. Although the USA historically has been the most important destination for skilled emigrants, several European nations also received significant shares of the flow, along with Venezuela, Mexico, and Costa Rica. Bartoncello *et al.* (1986) put the stock of surviving

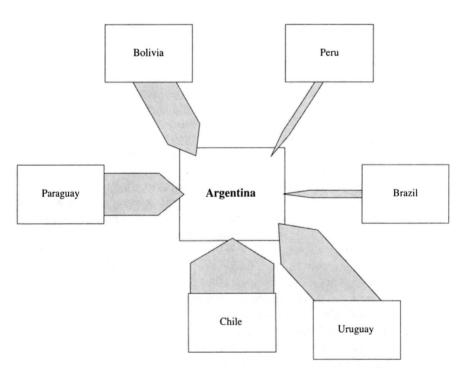

Fig. 7.1   International migration in the Argentinian system, 1980–1990

Argentine emigrants from the 1955–84 period at between 490,000 and 610,000 in the mid-1980s.

After the military coup in 1973, Chile also experienced a significant out-migration of qualified workers, not only to Argentina but also to Venezuela, Brazil, the USA, Europe, and even Australia (Cozzi 1988; Hugo 1994*b*). Before this time, Chilean emigration was composed mainly of agrarian workers who left seasonally for harvest work in neighbouring zones of Argentina. Emigration from Uruguay also rose sharply after the military came to power there in 1973. Uruguayans of Italian and Spanish descent increasingly return to Europe to exercise historical claims on Italian or Spanish citizenship (a growing phenomenon in Argentina as well). Fortuna, *et al.* (1989) estimate that from 1963 to 1985, 12 per cent of Uruguay's population left the country.

Despite much speculation, to date few studies have systematically examined the effects of the economic crisis of the 1980s—widely known as 'the lost decade'—on international migration. Austerity measures and policies of structural readjustment not only increased the number and percentage of people living in poverty; they also shrank employment options and incomes for the middle class. Emigration also occurred among skilled blue-collar workers, especially after the mid-1970s when the failure of Import Substitution Industrialization as a development model ushered in a period of industrial decline. According to statistics compiled by the US Immigration and Naturalization Service (1991), immigration from South America to the USA more than doubled during the 1980s, going from about 40,000 in 1980 to 86,000 in 1990.

Before the onset of the debt crisis in 1982, Latin Americans had come to see education as virtually an automatic guarantee of social and economic mobility, an expectation that was increasingly frustrated as the crisis deepened. The mismatch between the expectations of the middle class and the practical rewards available from the political economy grew acute around the same time that global capitalism was internationalizing labour markets, lifestyles, and patterns of consumption. The combination of falling incomes, frustrated ambitions, and the restructuring of many Latin American economies yielded strong pressures for emigration among the educated, urban, and middle-class sectors of many countries.

In Brazil, the economic crisis of the 1980s generated that country's first sizeable emigration of skilled workers. Recent studies by Goza (1994) and López Patarra and Baeninger (1995) reveal a sharp increase in Brazilian emigration to North America. Goza sampled Brazilian communities in the USA and Canada and found that 56 per cent of Brazilians in the former were missed by the 1990 US census, whereas 44 per cent of Canada's Brazilians were overlooked by its 1991 census. About 80 per cent of the US sample was illegal, consisting of people who had either entered the country surreptitiously through Mexico using a 'coyote', or who had violated the terms of their visa by staying too long and taking a job. In Canada, most illegal immigrants entered with a tourist visa and then overstayed or worked.

López Patarra and Baeninger (1995) estimate that net emigration from Brazil was about 500,000 during 1990–5, mostly to the USA but also to Italy, Portugal, and Japan. The emigration of Japanese Latin Americans back to Japan is particularly interesting. These temporary workers included 120,000 of Brazil's estimated 700,000 population of Japanese origin, along with 18,000 from Peru (out of 80,000), 8,500 from Argentina (out of 30,000), 1,500 from Bolivia (out of 6,000), and 700 from Paraguay (out of 7,000—see Japanese Ministry of Labour 1993).

The South American Research Literature

The task of evaluating theory is considerably more difficult in South America than in North America, Western Europe, or Asia and the Pacific, for a variety of reasons. As in all systems except North America, most empirical work on migration in South America was not designed to test the theories reviewed here. Either the studies were descriptive (as in the reports prepared by CELADE) or they were conducted under the influence of the historical-structural approach (principally dependency theory), which dominated Latin America through the 1970s (see Furtado 1965, 1970; Frank 1967; Cardoso and Faletto 1969). Alternative models such as social capital theory, the new economics of migration, and the theory of cumulative causation emerged mainly in the 1980s, after the Latin American debt crisis had stalled research and data collection throughout the region.

Second, sources of data on South American migration are generally inadequate to the task of theory testing. The IMILA database compiles information on foreign-born persons enumerated in national censuses throughout the region, and when tabulated by place of birth these data provide reliable information on stocks and characteristics of migrants in different countries. Comparisons between censuses also yield a very rough indicator of the volume of international migration by decade. Very few countries publish direct statistics on immigrant entry or departure, and the data that do exist are generally incomplete and of poor quality.

In general, such data are not up to the task of evaluating theory. Whereas many theoretical models offer hypotheses that are best tested at the individual or household level, IMILA and other regional databases only provide aggregate-level information. Few specialized surveys have been conducted among immigrants or emigrants in South America, and relatively few anthropologists have carried out field studies of migrant-sending or receiving communities. Owing to financial constraints, moreover, CELADE has yet to compile a full set of statistics on the foreign born *circa* 1990, yielding a dearth of information on international migration during the critical decade of the 1980s.

The last reason that theory evaluation is difficult in South America centres around the unusual degree of political, social, and economic instability the region has experienced. Since 1970, military governments have come and gone, coups have succeeded and failed, leftist insurgencies have arisen and faded, inflation has raged and subsided, and the debt crisis exploded, moderated, and then returned once again. By the early 1990s, most South American nations had shifted from Import Substitution Industrialization to Export Industrialization as a strategy for economic development, although this transition occurred at different times in different countries for different reasons.

These events, along with their accompanying social upheavals, are necessarily difficult to model and predict, yet they often create migration streams that lead, a posteriori, to the formation of new networks that enable additional migration more firmly grounded in rational economic decisions. As Lim (1993) has noted, political, social, and cultural changes often stimulate migration in ways that are not reducible to variables such as wage differentials and employment rates. Although it may be difficult to distill general conclusions from the diversity of economic, demographic, and historic circumstances in South America, the region nonetheless merits close attention as one of the oldest immigrant-receiving regions in the world, and an important source for international migrants today.

Theory and Research in South America

During the 1950s and 1960s, researchers working in the functionalist tradition visualized societies in terms of a series of dualistic contrasts (traditional versus modern, agrarian versus industrial) and saw migration as a means of transition between two opposing ways of life: rural and urban. Studies analysed the level and intensity of rural-to-urban migration, the characteristics and motivations of these internal migrants, and the processes by which they were assimilated into urban society. Economists such as Lewis (1954), Fei and Ranis (1961), and Todaro (1969) theorized migration to be a rational process balancing the supply of rural workers with the demand for workers in urban areas (see Chapters 8 and 9). Given these preconceptions, academic research prior to 1970 focused almost exclusively on internal population movements (a review of studies from this period may be found in Simmons *et al.* 1977).

During the 1970s, Latin American theorists rejected functionalism and embraced a structural perspective. Rather than viewing societies in terms of a series of dualistic contrasts, historical-structural researchers divided the world into core and peripheral regions and saw migration not as a rational response to wage differentials, but as an inevitable consequence of the unequal distribution of economic and political power among nations of the world (Furtado 1965, 1969). Structural interpretations ultimately came to dominate the work of CLACSO (the Consejo Latinoamericano de Ciencias Sociales), which sponsored numerous studies of internal and international migration. This institution was responsible for considerable theoretical and methodological debate, and for the formation of diverse connections between researchers throughout South America.

Migration research sponsored by CLACSO focused on two general themes: the reproduction of labour and urbanization through internal population movements. A central concern was the specific historical conditions under which migration occurred and its relationship to the broader structure of the national and international political economy (Singer 1975). Historical-structural theory offered an explicit critique of the functionalist approach then prevailing in sociology and economics. According to one CLACSO researcher, functionalist rationality 'fled before a more heterogeneous, macroanalytic, and structural vision' of society (Lattes 1982).

Researchers working in the historical-structural tradition sought to identify specific macro-level processes that promoted migration, urbanization, and other large-scale social movements. With respect to internal migration, they focused on agrarian structures and the changes they sustained following the entry of capitalist forms of production (a concern shared with world systems theory today). Although research done under this framework focused mainly on internal migration and urbanization, in some cases researchers extended their analyses to movements between neighbouring countries, connecting structural factors at places of origin and destination using data on the number of foreign born. This work has been criticized for its lack of empirical rigor, however, and for using aggregate data in a way that obscures the motivations and actions of individuals (Mora y Araujo 1982; Raczynski 1983).

Partly in response to these criticisms, later research focused on micro-level processes and identified the household as the relevant unit of analysis. Once again researchers concerned themselves with internal migration and seasonal circulation within border regions. Arizpe (1978) argued for the rationality of rural peasant households and demonstrated their strategic use of migration to acquire additional income, a pattern also documented among migrants in urban areas by Lomnitz (1976). García, *et al.* (1983) examined the articulation between families and labour markets in Mexico and Brazil. Their development of a new approach centring on 'family survival strategies' improved migration research by making the family or household the unit of analysis and the theoretical locus of migration decision-making.

These micro-level studies were not intended to supplant broader structural interpretations of migration, but to complement them by revealing how macro-level structures shaped the micro-level actions of families and individuals. Although conducted under a very different theoretical tradition, the studies of Lomnitz, Arizpe, and García *et al.* concur with basic precepts of the new economics of labour migration. In both schemes, migration is viewed as a family strategy undertaken to accumulate capital and protect family welfare by diversifying sources of income. A seminar conducted in Quito, Ecuador in 1984 on temporary migration provides several good examples of studies oriented to investigating internal and cross-border migration as household (or at times even community) strategies (see PISPAL 1986).

International migration has received less attention in South America in recent years, partly owing to a scarcity of data and a lack of funding for research, but also because rising poverty and unemployment led social scientists to focus on those issues instead. In addition, the structuralist model is no longer the dominant theory in academia and conceptual approaches to the study of migration have grown more eclectic over the past decade. World systems theory may be considered to be the intellectual inheritor of the historical-structural tradition, updated to the new international context of expanded trade, the end of import substitution industrialization, the neoliberal revolution, and the globalization of the market economy. Although world systems theorists have dealt with these issues generally in Latin America, however, they have not yet developed systematic tests of the consequences of market penetration and economic globalization.

Nonetheless, there is a growing awareness throughout the region that new patterns of mobility have emerged as urban populations have deconcentrated, intermediate cities have grown, and economies have shifted to new, more flexible patterns of capital accumulation (Harvey 1991; Simmons 1993), trends foreshadowed in the work of Lattes (1983). Latin American researchers have met several times to devise projects, evaluate methodologies, and share data about these new mobility processes. These conferences include 'New Patterns of Migration and their Contribution to the Process of Urbanization', which met in Bogotá in 1992; 'New Modes of International Migration, Border Movements, and Processes of Integration', held in Montevideo in 1993 (see Pellegrino 1995); 'The Territorial Mobility of Populations and Human Development', in the city of Bariloche, Argentina in 1994; and two Seminars on International Migration held at the University of Campinas, Brazil, in 1995 and 1996 (López Patarra 1995, 1996).

Studies of Receiving Countries

Although our review focuses primarily on international migration during the 1980s, in order to provide a fuller interpretive context we briefly review studies of European migration to South America during the early twentieth century. Several studies have documented the role played by immigrants in Argentina's transition from a rural agrarian society to an urban industrial economy (Germani 1966b; Díaz-Alejandro 1970). According to Bunge and García Mata (1931), half of all immigrants to Argentina between 1857 and 1926 were from Italy and another third were from Spain. Many authors, notably Germani (1966a), have documented the social and cultural effects that Italians and Spaniards had on Argentine society. Others have studied chain migration and its cumulative causation of European population movements into Argentina

(Baily 1985; Devoto 1988). Network theory also has been applied to explain patterns and processes of social mobility in receiving countries (see Bjerg and Otero 1995).

Studies undertaken to identify the factors responsible for instigating migration are more scarce. Sori's (1985) research suggests that four underlying forces were instrumental in promoting Italian emigration to the New World earlier this century: demographic pressure, economic trends, unemployment, and differentiation in economic development between Italian rural regions. He argued that seasonal emigration emerged as a family strategy to ensure household survival. More recently, several studies have analysed the causes of migration using quantitative models that permit an assessment of how economic conditions in certain European and Latin American nations contributed to the flow of immigrants between them.

Taylor (1994), for example, estimated a set of time-series models to predict gross and net migration into Argentina from Italy and Spain during the periods 1884–1913 and 1919–39 (excluding war years when international travel was disrupted). In keeping with neoclassical theory, his explanatory model included the wage differential between Argentina and each sending country. He also included a proxy for Argentine economic activity (providing a rough test of segmented labour market theory, which sees immigration as demand-led), as well as indices of employment in Italy and Spain (allowing tests of world systems theory, which sees international migration as a product of development itself). The analysis also controls for the number of migrants from Italy and Spain who arrived during the prior year, allowing an assessment of network effects predicted under social capital theory.

All theories receive some support from Taylor's analysis. As postulated by neoclassical theory, annual fluctuations in the rate of migration to Argentina from Italy and Spain are significantly related to yearly variations in the size of the international wage gap, lagged by one year: an increase in the real value of Argentine wages relative to those in Italy or Spain was generally followed by an expansion of immigration from those countries in the following year.

Despite this basic consistency with neoclassical theory, however, wages were neither the strongest, nor the only, predictor of immigration into Argentina. Compared with wage rates, Argentine economic activity exerted a far stronger influence on immigration rates, suggesting a demand-led phenomenon more in keeping with segmented labour market theory. Indicators of period-specific employment strongly predict the rate of immigration from both Italy and Spain, and lagged employment predicts Spanish immigration. In contrast to the predictions of neoclassical theory, moreover, greater economic activity in Italy *increased*, rather than decreased, the rate of emigration to Argentina, an effect that is generally consistent with world systems theory. In all models, the lagged indicator of prior migration was statistically significant, indicating the 'family and friends' effect predicted by social capital theory.

Hatton and Williamson (1994*b*) estimated a slightly different time-series model to predict gross rates of immigration from Spain to the Americas during 1883–1913 using changes in Brazilian economic activity and shifts in Argentine wages as predictors. They found that Spanish emigration was strongly related to changes in Brazilian economic activity, with emigration rising in response to an increase in New World growth. To a lesser extent, emigration was also responsive to economic conditions in Spain, declining during periods of rising activity at home in a manner consistent with neoclassical assumptions. As in Taylor's study, Hatton and Williamson found that immigration was positively associated with the size of the wage differential (supporting neoclassical theory) and with prior arrivals of migrants (supporting social capital theory).

Balán (1974) examined the role played by immigration in the capitalist development of Brazil and its relation to the formation of an open labour market. He compared Brazil with the Argentine and Mexican cases to identify the specific effects of capital penetration and to 'locate within the history of labor market formation in Brazil the migratory currents of the last century, analyzing these forms as they reflect the relation between population and changing social structure' (Balán 1974: 66). Balán's research constitutes an example of the historical-structural approach, seeking to interpret the formation of the Brazilian labour market relative to other countries whose demographic and economic histories could be considered prototypes for the structure of Latin American society.

Carrón (1976, 1979) analysed migration from neighbouring countries into Argentina during two different time-periods to identify the specific traits of each migration stream and to discern the role that immigration played in Argentine economic development at two different stages. He found that before 1950, immigration accompanied economic expansion and migrants occupied the same occupational positions as internal migrants. After this date, however, competitive pressure prompted a segmentation of the labour market. Rather than being associated with economic growth and expansion, international migrants concentrated in the most depressed sectors— agriculture and construction—that were shunned by natives, who gravitated towards more dynamic sectors such as commerce and services. Compared with Argentinians, immigrants from Paraguay occupied the lowest occupational rungs while those from Uruguay were employed in similar categories.

Carrón's analysis thus provides evidence of a clear process of labour market segmentation. The use of immigrant workers apparently allowed Argentinian employers in certain sectors to avoid costly improvements in working conditions and wages, confirming Piore's (1979) view of immigration as a response to demand resulting from market segmentation. Marshall (1979, 1980*a*) reached a similar conclusion after comparing immigration in Argentina to immigration in post-war Europe:

Foreign workers increased the supply of labor in greater Buenos Aires. This increase has been concentrated within a narrow range: mainly in manual jobs, particularly in construction, domestic service and some manufacturing activities. While the foreign workers do not compete for jobs with the non-migrant population of Buenos Aires, their distribution in the labor market does parallel that of recent internal migrants. Even given this similarity, the position of foreign workers is distinctly different from that of native workers. Both foreign and recent internal migrants occupy the bottom of the occupational structure, with the former being even more concentrated in manual jobs, mostly in the unstable, lowing-paying and less skilled positions. (Marshall 1979: 500)

Sana (1996) uses data from 1993 and 1995 demographic surveys conducted in Argentinian urban areas to confirm that this pattern of labour market segmentation has continued to the present. Immigrants are still concentrated in domestic service and construction industries (see also Maguid 1990, 1995), and given their isolation in relatively weak sectors of the economy, they bear the brunt of recessions, experiencing a higher rate of unemployment and a more pronounced decline in wages than either natives or internal migrants (Maguid and Bankirer 1995).

Consistent with theories of cumulative causation, Marshall (1979: 501) sees immigration as being 'part of a reinforcing cycle which encourages migration and which further stimulates these sectors' reliance on labor intensive strategies.' In later work, Marshall (1984) amplified this theme by considering immigration after the economic turmoil and hyperinflation of the early 1980s. She sought to account for the persistence of immigration from surrounding countries during a time when economic growth was low, labour demand was weak, and unemployment was high.

Her analysis revealed that the principal causes of migration into Argentina during the 1980s shifted from the demand to the supply side. Push factors in countries of origin provided the initial impulse for movement while self-feeding migration processes created an ongoing demand for immigrants, permitting the survival of labour-intensive sectors in Argentina without active recruitment, thereby perpetuating flows of immigrants despite high rates of Argentinian unemployment. Marshall's work thus supports the hypothesis of cumulative causation.

Balán (1985, 1992) summarizes the evolution of international migration in the Southern Cone by identifying its characteristics and relating them to demographic and economic processes in each of the source countries. He focuses on the role played by Argentina, and particularly metropolitan Buenos Areas, in the creation of a regional labour market. By the mid-1980s, he concludes, the Southern Cone had emerged as a distinct international migration subsystem with Buenos Aires at its core, sustained by relatively open migration policies and transnational agreements for economic cooperation (MERCOSUR), and increasingly reinforced by the operation of autonomous, self-perpetuating social networks.

Studies of Venezuelan immigration are less well defined theoretically than those conducted in Argentina, perhaps because they are thought to describe an 'atypical' situation where immigration and economic growth stem from an 'external' source (an oil boom) that resists prediction. Another feature of the Venezuelan case is that immigration occurred simultaneously with a high rate of natural increase among natives (unlike in Western Europe, North America, or the Asian NICs), which provided employers with a viable alternative source of labour.

Research on Venezuelan immigration is quite diverse: some studies examine its demographic effects (Picouet 1976); others consider its influence on social structure (Kritz 1975); and still others examine its role in the labour supply (Sassen 1979). Some investigators have sought to measure and characterize clandestine migration (Pellegrino 1984; Van Roy 1984; Torrealba 1987, 1988), and some have undertaken policy evaluations (Chen and Urquijo 1982) or have considered the long-run historical implications of immigration (Pellegrino 1989). As in Argentina, economic reversals during the early 1980s led some investigators to evaluate the effects of the crisis (Torrealba 1987, 1988; Bidegain and Freitez 1989).

Sassen (1979) underscores the complexity of migration into Venezuela compared with other oil-producing countries in the Middle East. In contrast to nations such as Kuwait and Saudi Arabia, the recruitment of immigrant labour has a longer history in Venezuela and occurs in a cultural context that historically has accepted and at times even encouraged long-term settlement.

The occupational status and wages of immigrants to Venezuela during the 1970s suggest they entered the labour force at an unusually opportune moment. The massive increase in oil revenues financed a sharp expansion of professional employment that offered well-paid positions in engineering, management, administration, research, and teaching (Pellegrino 1989). Although wages were lower for unskilled migrants, these workers were also attracted by the strength of the Venezuelan currency against the US dollar, which yielded wages with a high real value at home.

Under these circumstances, sending a family member to work in Venezuela and repatriating remittances became a viable economic strategy widely adopted by families at all levels of South American society (Pellegrino 1989). The drop in world oil prices bought a sharp reversal of Venezuela's economic fortunes after 1983, however, and the subsequent currency devaluation lowered real wages and brought widespread return migration in its wake (Urrea 1989). The natural experiment afforded by the end of the oil boom in Venezuela thus confirms a leading hypothesis of neoclassical theory: when wages fall, in-migration drops and out-migration increases. Compared to a net in-migration of 316,000 foreigners between 1971 and 1979, Venezuela experienced a net out-migration of 107,000 foreigners between 1980 and 1984 (Pellegrino 1989).

The crisis also appears to have changed the socio-economic profile of

Colombian immigrants to Venezuela: compared with Colombian migrants surveyed there in 1981, those interviewed in 1986 had higher average educations, higher mean earnings, and a higher concentration in self-employment, suggesting the movement of skilled immigrants into informal work as the crisis deepened (Bidegain and Freitez 1989), possibly indicating a more pronounced segmentation of the labour force.

Studies in Origin Countries

A variety of studies have considered international migration from the viewpoint of the country of origin: some analyse macrostructural factors to discover the underlying determinants of migration, often complemented with a profile of emigrants in receiving countries; some examine particular subgroups of migrants, such as undocumented migrants or seasonal agrarian workers; and a few evaluate the effect of international migration on households and local communities. The effect of remittances and return migration have been little studied, however, and are limited to a few cases; and studies of urban communities are generally scarce. Even though networks are frequently mentioned as a factor of continuity in movements, few works actually identify social networks empirically or describe the mechanisms through which they operate.

In most cases, empirical information is limited to data culled from censuses of receiving countries, allowing investigators to consider the effects of emigration by describing who left. In some cases it has been possible to profile households that send members overseas using surveys conducted in sending countries, which often include questions about offspring or siblings residing abroad. These data can also be used to estimate the volume and characteristics of emigrants (see Hill 1981; Somoza 1981).

Colombia and Uruguay have probably generated the largest number of studies of emigration. At least until the 1980s, the former country had the largest absolute number of emigrants, while the latter had the largest number relative to population size (followed closely by Paraguay). The emigration streams from Colombia and Uruguay are diverse with respect to destinations, although in both cases they are directed predominantly to neighbouring countries. The two other leading countries of emigration in South America— Paraguay and Bolivia—send migrants almost exclusively to Argentina.

Uruguay and Colombia have political and economic histories that are substantially different from those of Bolivia and Paraguay, being marked by significant industrialization and an early concentration of population in urban centres. The other countries are still heavily rural and rural–urban migration continues to be important, with part of the out-migration being directed towards urban centres in Argentina.

Uruguay began its process of demographic transition early in this century, yielding a rate of natural increase and level of urbanization that are presently comparable to those in developed nations. In addition, compared with other countries in Latin America, illiteracy is very low and schooling levels are high, with substantial shares of the population finishing not only high school, but university. Compared with Uruguay, Colombia experienced its demographic transition rather late: urbanization did not accelerate until the 1950s and fertility did not begin to fall until the 1970s.

Across these four countries, emigration originated in different processes at different stages of economic development; but two elements stand out as common factors in all cases: the existence of significant political violence and social conflict within the sending society, and a rapidly expanding economy in a neighbouring State (Argentina for Bolivia, Paraguay, and Uruguay; and Venezuela for Colombia). The pairing of internal upheavals with neighbouring opportunity yields a powerful formula for international movement.

Studies carried out in Colombia have linked emigration to high rates of population growth and the displacement of workers from traditional agricultural pursuits in rural areas. Working within the structuralist tradition, Urrea (1989) identified two contrary processes that interacted to mutually determine the accumulation of capital and the reproduction of labour. He analysed families at the micro-level, describing how they were incorporated into the labour market through processes of occupational attainment and spatial mobility. García Castro (1979) adopted the concept of the reproduction of labour and used it to analyse the peculiarities of female migration, modes of insertion into labour markets, and articulations of the latter with households. She introduces cultural elements to her hypotheses, seeing the migration of women as a mechanism of flight and a process of breaking ties to nuclear families of origin.

Mármora (1982) relates the processes of rural disintegration and industrial development to processes of internal and international migration in Colombia. Initially rural emigration originated in regions near the Venezuelan border, but later a larger emigration from Colombian cities stemmed from cyclical fluctuations in the industrial economy. Consistent with the historical-structural approach, he connected rates of emigration to stages of economic development in Colombia. According to Mármora, the operative cause of this emigration shifted over time. In the 1960s, high unemployment was the principal factor behind the expulsion of labour from Colombian cities, whereas during the 1970s it was a decline in the real value of wages that was principally responsible. Both effects, of course, are consistent with neoclassical economics.

Gómez Jiménez and Díaz Mesa (1983) interpret migration under the general framework of the accumulation of capital and formulas for the appropriation of surplus labour that ultimately rely upon international flows of labour. Fieldwork conducted in sending and receiving areas in Venezuela reveal the mechanisms by which surplus labour is extracted from poor Colombians who work in the cutting of sugarcane.

Colombia's National Employment Service (known by its Spanish acronym of SENALDE, part of the Ministry of Labour and Social Security) implemented a labour migration programme that included a research component that supported various investigations. Labour markets and wage differentials along border zones were analysed in detail by Velosa (1979), who surveyed migrants deported from Venezuela to discern their labour histories and motivations for movement. Consistent with the new economics of migration, she found that migration to Venezuela arose through a strategic decision to move temporarily for purposes of capital acquisition and risk diversification.

According to Velosa (1979), migrants were not motivated to leave Colombia because of a lack of employment, but because high wages in Venezuela offered the best possibility of accumulating capital in the form of savings and of sending remittances to family members at home in order to diversify income sources. Given the short-term, seasonal nature of most of the moves, migrants—both men and women—generally travelled alone, were unmarried, and were under the age of 30. Their accumulated savings were generally higher than their expected wages in Colombia and were channelled primarily to family maintenance, followed by the purchase and construction of housing (see Murillo Castaño 1981; Murillo Castaño and Silva 1984).

After reviewing the results of this round of SENALDE-sponsored research, Murillo Castaño (1988) concluded that emigration was often the key event that allowed returnees to establish business activities and become self-employed, even though most savings were spent in other ways. Thus, migration to Venezuela was conceived and executed as a strategy of short-term mobility (as expected under the new economics) rather than permanent settlement (as expected under neoclassical theory) and was undertaken specifically to overcome market failures (a lack of access to capital and credit) and thereby accumulate funds for investment (the capitalization of a small business) or large-scale consumption (the construction or purchase of a home).

In contrast to the detail provided on migrant savings, the SENALDE data did not enable investigators to estimate the magnitude or use of remittances. Limited evidence suggests that remittances had a negligible effect on informal sector activities, and that they were used primarily to diversify or supplement household income. In urban areas at least, remittances permitted families to satisfy their basic needs (for medical care, health, and nutrition), whereas savings were used for the establishment informal activities and the generation of self-employment (Murillo Castaño 1988).

Bleier (1988) studied the effects of the Venezuelan recession on five Columbian cities characterized by significant rates of out-migration. She found relatively little return migration, and most of what she observed was concentrated among recent migrants who had not yet achieved a stable occupational situation in Venezuela. She also found that return migration had little effect on rates of Columbian unemployment, but that its effect on household living standards and levels of consumption was often pronounced.

The case of Uruguayan emigration is atypical in two ways: its large size (relative to total population) and its occurrence at a relatively advanced stage of socio-economic development. Between 1963 and 1985, 12 per cent of the Uruguayan population emigrated abroad. The rate of out-movement was especially intense between 1971 and 1976 and it occurred in a population that had already shifted to low levels of fertility and mortality and high levels of urbanization.

Most studies of Uruguayan emigration seek to identify the structural determinants of emigration, focusing particularly on the political crisis of the late 1960s and 1970s. De Sierra (1976) and Wonsewer and Teja (1982) offer macroeconomic interpretations, whereas others attempt to situate emigration more broadly in the context of an emerging regional labour market embracing urban areas in Argentina and Brazil as well as Montevideo (De Sierra *et al.* 1975; Petrucelli 1979; Petrucelli and De Sierra 1979; Lombardi and Altesor 1987).

Most researchers assign a central role to economic stagnation, high unemployment, and the decline in real wages that overtook Uruguay at the close of the 1960s and persisted well into the 1970s. De Sierra (1978) concludes that emigration did not reduce unemployment and that its main effect was to preclude an even more severe drop in wages. Consistent with neoclassical theory, statistical analyses conducted by Wonsewer and Teja (1982) suggest that it was the drop in real wages and not the lack of employment that was most important in explaining Uruguayan emigration. In order to compensate for the decline in real wages, families sent other members into the workforce while individuals increased their hours of work, both of which raised overall employment levels but substantially lowered the quality of life.

Despite the apparent importance of falling wages in explaining emigration from Uruguay, Wonsewer and Teja (1982) point out that the phenomenon is complex, and that its full comprehension requires considering the social-historical context of the movement. The economic crisis not only lowered incomes, it also dashed expectations and hopes, for it was accompanied by the widespread realization that the national model that had sustained Uruguay for more than a century was coming to an end. The nineteenth-century ideology of an open, democratic, participatory society with ample possibilities for social and economic mobility, which had characterized Uruguay for the first half of the century, was increasingly recognized as untenable given the current economic stagnation and political repression.

Filgueira (1989) argued that the deterioration of economic conditions produced a widely shared sense of downward social mobility, which by its collective character generated a significant ideological and cultural shift within Uruguayan society. According to Filgueira, 'the roots of the great international emigration should thus be located in cumulative processes of long duration, that established in vast sectors of the population attitudes and expectations that in the end were increasingly frustrated' (ibid.).

Other analyses emphasize the Southern Cone as a single entity and analyse emigration as part of a regionalization of the labour market brought about by new processes of capital accumulation and industrial concentration (De Sierra *et al.* 1975; Petrucelli and De Sierra 1979; Petrucelli 1979). Lombardi and Altesor (1987) identify an 'urban regional system' in the Southern Cone and demonstrate the progressive decline in the importance of Uruguayan cities within it. They suggest Uruguay's smallness was a principal factor behind its loss of economic and demographic dynamism and ultimately its high rate of emigration.

Aguiar (1982) likewise sees reduction of Uruguay's population as the result of a stable social and economic structure whose principal parameters remained unchanged until the nation was able to complete its process of border consolidation. Emigration and the early drop in fertility constitute the inevitable demographic correlates of limited economic and social growth. Emigration is built into Uruguay's structural position as a small, urbanized country located within in a larger regional economy dominated by Buenos Aires. Wages and employment rates are merely variables of adjustment, accelerating the processes of emigration and demographic contraction. In contrast to most contemporary research and theory, therefore, studies conducted in Uruguay tend to assign population size and growth a central role among the factors promoting emigration.

In Paraguay, population mobility was not expressed in the growth of cities. Rather, rural-to-urban migration was channelled primarily to Argentina, and particularly to Buenos Aires, at least until the 1970s when changes in the Paraguayan economy transformed migratory patterns and the internal distribution of population. The effect of emigration on the socio-economic structure of Paraguay has been studied by Gillespie and Browning (1979), who used labour force and population projections to quantify the function of emigration as an 'escape valve' that adjusted for domestic under-employment and unemployment. They attribute Paraguay's high rate of emigration to the Stroessner dictatorship, which produced economic stagnation that would have generated political resistance had not emigration relieved the pressure and allowed the dictatorship to persist for thirty years.

Along with Carrón (1976) and Rivarola (1977), Gillespie and Browning (1979) also connect Paraguayan emigration to a prevailing agrarian structure of small landholding and *minifundia* production, which discourages capital investment and leads to low levels of productivity. Given ongoing population growth, this stagnation inevitably produces high unemployment rates in the countryside, which lead directly to out-migration. That the rate of internal migration is lower than the rate of international migration demonstrates the limited capacity of Paraguayan urban areas (principally Asunción) to absorb the excess labour. Nearly 30 per cent of Paraguay's potential labour force was lost through emigration between 1960 and 1970 (De Sierra *et al.* 1975; Marshall 1980*b*). A more recent study by Palau and Heikel (1987), who examined the spread of peasant agriculture in the country's Upper Paraná region, suggests that little has changed in the ensuing years.

Bolivia is one South American country where a peasant economy persists as a viable basis for the productive incorporation of rural dwellers. Seasonal migration serves as a mechanism of articulation between the peasant economy and urban labour markets. Research here emphasizes the role of families as informal units of production and reproduction and their connection to different communities. Whiteford (1981), for example, undertook a comparative analysis of two classes of Bolivian emigrants: temporary workers in the sugarcane industry of north-western Argentina, and settlers in the city of Salta who rotated through unstable jobs, alternating periods of work with stays in their places of origin. The analysis considers causal factors operating at several different levels: the macro-level of the political economy, the community level of the local labour market, and the household level of social networks and family strategies.

Dandler and Medeiros (1988) adopt a similar approach. They assign central importance to the Andean family unit and to broader confederations of such families throughout Boilivia. Seasonal activities are structured to ensure the survival of the family unit, which includes not only peasant families at home but also families in the central valley of Cochabamba. Blanes (1986: 113–14) suggests that the strategy of the migrant is 'not to risk the means of reproduction at the place of origin, such as land, community, and family relations', which represent 'an inheritance of "secular security . . .".". Without having assured his reproduction at the place of destination, definitive detachment from the land will not occur.'

Information from surveys implemented by Blanes (1986) and Dandler and Medeiros (1988) in the region of Cochabamba indicates variable durations of residence in Argentina, which extend from a few months to twenty years or more. Migrants generally work in agriculture or other traditional activities before departure, and their point of insertion into the Argentine labour market (usually in Buenos Aires) is usually construction. Rural migrants, upon returning, generally invest their savings in land and in the improvement of dwellings, once again suggesting the use of migration as a means of overcoming market failures and acquiring capital for investment.

This interpretation is reinforced by the Dandler and Medeiros's observation that self-employment increases significantly upon a migrant's return to the home community, compared to the economic activities undertaken prior to the initial departure. In this sense, migrant earnings provide an important source of capital for small business formation, permitting migrants increased independence from nuclear households and facilitating the formation of new family units. According to Dandler and Medeiros (1988: 38), 'migration provides capital that supports households and permits them to develop certain productive activities that do not depend necessarily on wage-earning strategies but rather on self-employment and economic diversification.'

Studies of Emigration to Developed Countries

Studies of emigration to developed countries, usually to the USA, focus primarily on the exodus of skilled human resources during the 1960s and 1970s. They examine the flight not only of the highly educated, but also of skilled workers and the middle classes. Studies of the 'brain drain' had their most important development in Argentina, but other countries with relatively well-developed educational systems and high rates of schooling also figure prominently in the literature: Uruguay, Chile, Colombia, and more recently, Venezuela.

Based on information from the IMILA database, reports have sought to characterize and quantify the loss of skilled workers from Latin America to the USA through 1975 (Torrado 1982) and the loss of professionals and technicians using the 1970 and 1980 round of censuses (Martínez Pizarro 1989; Pellegrino 1993). These works generally report on the characteristics and destinations of skilled emigrants and offer policy proposals for their retention or repatriation, for purposes of employing the experience and expertise they have gained abroad.

Throughout the 1970s, South American studies of the brain drain sought to question the 'internationalist' model, which viewed the emigration of skilled persons as a response to the oversupply of qualified persons in certain professions that functioned as an escape valve promoting national security (Johnson 1967b). In this scheme, the brain drain reflected a series of individual decisions by professionals who left in search of higher salaries and greater professional development.

In his critique of this model, Oteiza (1965) pointed out that international labour markets are not 'free', but are strongly influenced by the laws and policies of developed countries, which usually function explicitly to attract well-educated and technically trained immigrants and discourage the arrival of others, so as to maximize their own reserves of human capital. Oteiza (1971) went on to propose a strategy for empirical analysis that expressed fluctuations in emigration as a function of the distinct economic, political, and educational phases in Argentine history and the conditions of labour demand in the USA. He considers four basic factors: differences in income; differences in logistical support for professional activities; differences in professional recognition and visibility; and a residual differential that measures relative levels of repression and ideological domination in universities and politics.

For Argentina, Sito and Stuhlman (1968) analyse why scientists emigrate, focusing on the discrepancy between high occupational status and limited opportunities for income, and on the relationship between a person's educational level and labour market position. Filgueira (1976) undertook a more detailed analysis of the predisposition of Uruguayan professional graduates to migrate, taking into account factors both inside and outside the country.

Externally he examined international relations issues and the position of different countries in the international system, and internally he focused on the Uruguayan occupational structure.

He found that asynchronous growth between the number of graduates of the educational system and the number of positions in the occupational structure generated what he called 'structural tension'. In general, technically trained personnel emigrated from places of greater to lesser structural tension. Moreover, it is not the degree of economic development that is most relevant in predicting emigration, but the degree of structural tension at different educational levels. As a result, skilled personnel do not always emigrate to the most-developed nations with the highest wages. Filgueira goes on to connect levels of structural tension to the various options available for handling this tension, among them emigration.

In general, the literature examining South American emigrants enumerated in the USA is not as developed as that pertaining to Mexican, Caribbean, or Central American emigrants. During the 1980s, investigators have undertaken some studies of Colombian, and more recently Peruvian and Brazilian migrants, whose volume of entry has increased in recent years. Altamirano (1988) constructed a profile of the US-Peruvian community that included its occupational and locational distribution, and discussed issues related to ethnic and cultural identity. Margolis's (1994) ethnographic study of Brazilian migration into New York included an evaluation by migrants of their US experience and a description of their ongoing contact with their places of origin.

Conclusion

Although the South American research literature does not lend itself readily to a comprehensive evaluation of theories of international migration, it does offer a few rough tests of propositions relevant to the models we have considered. Neoclassical economics receives some support in the studies we reviewed. During the classic era of European immigration to Argentina, short- and long-term fluctuations in the volume of emigration from Italy and Spain were statistically related to short- and long-term changes in the size of the gap between Spanish or Italian and Argentinian wages. Likewise, the rapid expansion of Colombian emigration to Venezuela during the 1970s was linked to a rise in Venezuelan wages and a decline in Colombian wages, a fact clearly demonstrated when a Venezuelan devaluation in the early 1980s brought new entries to a halt and prompted a surge in return migration.

The new economics of migration does not gainsay the influence of wage rates on migration, but sees international movement as motivated by a family's desire to diversify income and acquire capital or credit. Rather than moving permanently, international migrants work abroad temporarily and remit a portion of their earnings home to diversify income sources, and ultimately they return with savings that may be used to finance investment or large consumption expenditures. The widespread adoption of precisely these behaviours has been documented in surveys conducted among deported Colombian migrants, in anthropological fieldwork carried out among Bolivian migrants to Argentina, and among rural in-migrants to burgeoning Latin American cities.

According to segmented labour market theory, international migration stems from a demand for immigrant workers that originates in the bifurcation of mature labour markets into a primary sector of stable, well-paid jobs reserved for natives and a secondary sector of unstable, poorly paid jobs filled by immigrants. The case of Argentina provides ample evidence in support of this view. Immigrants and natives are very clearly concentrated in different sectors of the economy, and historically economic growth in Argentina was the strongest determinant of rates of immigration from Italy and Spain, even compared with relative wages.

Social capital theory explains the perpetuation of international migration through the growth and expansion of migrant networks, and the theory of cumulative causation holds that networks ultimately create a self-perpetuating process that gradually disassociates international movement from its initial causes. This hypothesis again receives support from the South American research literature: the rate of immigration into Argentina from Italy and Spain before 1930 was significantly related to the number of prior arrivals from these countries, yielding a 'family and friends effect', and both Marshall (1979) and Balán (1992) discerned the cumulative effect of social networks in promoting migration into Argentina despite downward shifts in wages and heightened unemployment.

In many ways, the South American literature is most closely connected to world systems theory, the intellectual descendant of the historical-structural approach that dominated Latin American social science through the 1970s and early 1980s. In their critique of neoclassical and modernization theories, researchers working in the historical-structural tradition successfully opened up new lines of thought and inquiry that linked migration to broader international structures and shifted the focus from individuals to households, paving the way for world systems theory and the new economic model.

World systems theory holds that international migration is part and parcel of the process of development itself and necessarily accompanies the spread of capitalist economic relations throughout the world. Consistent with this view, Taylor (1994) found that migration from Italy to Argentina was positively related to Italian economic growth, but aside from this one result, we uncovered few definitive tests of the world systems perspective. Given its close connection to the structural approaches that have dominated Latin American research, it is ironic that this theory receives the least support from the research we have reviewed. Results are not negative, of course, just absent, since a great deal of the work is interpretive rather than analytic.

Considering the heterogeneity of circumstances represented among the countries of South America, the fact that all theories found some measure of support in the accumulated research literature is impressive. As in the other migration systems we have considered, all theoretical models seem to capture a portion of the reality. What the existing body of work cannot do is adjudicate between the models. Owing to a scarcity of data, limitations of methodology, and differences in approach, South American studies offer few opportunities to judge the relative efficacy and importance of explanations advanced by neoclassical economics, the new economics, segmented labour market theory, social capital theory, world systems theory, or the theory of cumulative causation. Nonetheless, the great diversity of South America offers unusual opportunities for comprehensive evaluation, and specification of an integrated theoretical model based on the South American experience represents a pending challenge to our knowledge and ingenuity.

8 International Migration and National Development

As household, regional, and national economies in developing countries become increasingly linked to labour markets in the developed world, policy-makers and researchers have sought to understand the economic effects of international migration on sending regions. The most obvious and visible contribution of migrants to economies of origin is the money they send or bring home to family and friends. Official estimates suggest the potential economic effect of these remittances is large. According to the International Monetary Fund, foreign workers annually remit around $US75 billion back to their countries of origin, a figure that is 50 per cent higher than the total of official development assistance (Russell and Teitelbaum 1992); but even this figure understates the true amount of what Durand (1988) calls 'migradollars', since it does not include clandestine or in-kind transfers, which field studies have shown to be substantial (see Lozano Ascencio 1993; Massey and Parrado 1994).

Although remittances are the most obvious consequence of international migration, they represent only one of its potential economic effects. In addition to influencing national income directly through remittances, international migration may also affect income indirectly through the investments that migrants make in productive activities at home. Recent findings suggest that these indirect effects may be as important as the direct effects in determining the direction and nature of international migration's influence on economic growth. Emigration may also influence economic development through the loss of scarce human capital that is needed to maintain or increase productivity in the sending economy.

A primary issue in the macroeconomics of international migration is the possibility of mobilizing remittances for national economic development. We argue that the effects of international migration on economic development vary from country to country and time to time depending on market conditions, resource endowments, and the ease and cost of foreign exchange. From our review we conclude that an over-reliance on labour export as a strategy for economic development generally produces disappointing results. In countries where labour and/or human capital are in relative surplus, however, policies that facilitate emigration, and which capture a significant share of the resulting remittances for investment, may provide a valuable supplement to, but not a substitute for, a well-designed and carefully implemented national development policy.

Unfortunately, policy-makers often view foreign labour as a panacea rather than a complement to good policy. As a result, prior investigators have often employed unrealistic standards in evaluating the economic consequences of emigration, yielding judgements that we believe are unduly harsh. A typical approach is to describe current economic conditions in a nation and then to compare these against the inflated expectations of government officials and international development planners. A more accurate evaluation would compare current conditions against those that prevailed before migration, or, more subtly, against those that might have prevailed had migration not occurred in the first place.

Weaknesses in design, data, and methodology are compounded by the ideological nature of the debate. Many investigators begin with strong, preconceived ideas about the nature of migration's effects, and when they find a few facts consistent with these preconceptions they conclude that the broader theoretical apparatus from which their expectations were derived must be correct. Little or no effort is devoted to testing underlying theoretical assumptions or evaluating alternative hypotheses against one another.

We take issue with much of this early research and argue that issues of design and data require serious attention, and that most studies conducted to date are so flawed as to be of limited scientific value in assessing the economic effects of emigration. In particular, we believe it is impossible to determine the effects of international migration without having a strong analytic model of migratory behaviour itself, since the selectivity of international movement strongly influences the economic effects likely to be observed.

Background factors and structural conditions that prompt people to emigrate not only influence whether and how much they remit, but how these remittances are spent. Factors both exogenous and endogenous to the migration decision must be incorporated into analytic models in order to evaluate accurately and completely the effect of international migration on economic development. Prior to assessing recent empirical research, therefore, we review macroeconomic theory to identify the various direct and indirect means by which migration influences economic growth.

Macroeconomic Theory

Although the money sent or brought back to sending countries by migrants working abroad is the *raison d'être* of international labour migration (Martin 1991*a*: 33), the theoretical literature in economics has paid surprisingly little attention to migrant remittances in evaluating the effects of emigration. Most theoretical work has focused on the indirect effects of emigration through labour markets rather than on the direct effects through remittances; nor has much attention been paid to the indirect effects through domestic saving and foreign exchange.

Labour Market Effects

On the most fundamental demographic level, of course, international labour migration represents a loss of human resources for migrant-sending countries. If there is surplus labour in the sending country, however, this loss has zero opportunity cost. In the theoretical world developed by Lewis (1954), for example, where migrant-sending areas are characterized by a surplus of workers and a perfectly elastic labour supply, the loss of human resources through migration does not provoke a production decline, nor does it exert upward pressure on wages. The only effect of out-migration is to increase the average product of labour in the non-migrating population, assuming that households at the origin cease to support the out-migrants once they leave and vice versa.

Graphically, this condition is depicted by a marginal product curve for labour in the migrant-sending country that is no longer positive once the entire workforce is employed. In Figure 8.1, any labour force size in excess of L_1 is 'redundant' in the sense that it does not contribute positively to agricultural production. This condition means that an amount of labour equal to $L_T - L_1$ may emigrate without inflicting a production loss on the sending economy. As this labour is withdrawn, the average product of labor—total production divided by the remaining rural workforce—increases until all surplus labour has been lost to emigration (or more precisely, until the marginal product of labour begins to exceed the average product of labour, which occurs at labour force-size L_0: see Ranis and Fei 1961). Beyond this point, the opportunity cost of emigration for the sending economy becomes increasingly large.

The validity of the Lewis surplus labour hypothesis has been challenged

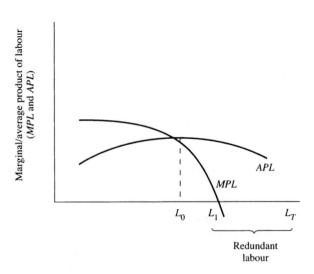

Fig. 8.1   Labour market effects of emigration in a Lewis world

empirically by research showing that, even where surplus-labour conditions prevail most of the year, seasonal bottlenecks may produce a marginal product of labour that is positive (see Gregory 1986, for example). In this circumstance, the opportunity cost of foreign labour migration is not zero, since the loss of workers yields production declines in seasonal industries such as agriculture and construction.

In a perfectly competitive, neoclassical world (without surplus labour or other market imperfections), a worker is paid the marginal value of what he or she produces prior to emigrating. Based on this assumption, early theoreticians argued that emigration should have a neutral effect on the economic welfare of non-migrants: any decrease in local production attributable to the loss of labour through emigration should equal the wages that workers received prior to emigrating (Grubel and Scott 1966). Although local production may decline by an amount equal to the marginal product of the migrant who has departed, the size of the economic pie available to those who do not migrate is exactly the same as before.

This finding does not hold at high, non-marginal levels of out-migration, however, because the loss of emigrant labour reduces the productivity of complementary inputs such as land and capital, and hence, lowers income payments to owners of these assets. Graphically, emigration results in an inward shift in the labour supply curve (from LS_0 to LS_1 in Figure 8.2a), which increases wages (from w_0 to w_1) for those who stay behind. At the same time, however, it reduces the marginal productivity of capital, as shown by the inward shift of the marginal product of capital curve from MPK_0 to MPK_1 in Figure 8.2b.

The latter shift causes a decrease in the returns to capital, or a drop in the marginal profit rate, from r_0 to r_1. The net effect on the economic welfare of non-migrants depends on the size of the wage gains to local labour compared to the loss of profit accruing to owners of land and capital. MacDougal (1960) and Kemp (1964) both concluded that the former will generally be insufficient to offset lower profits, and that emigration will consequently produce a deadweight welfare loss, other things equal.

Again, this conclusion does not hold when a labour surplus exists in the migrant-sending area. In a Lewis (1954) world, emigration neither raises the wages of those left behind nor decreases the productivity of complementary inputs such as land or capital. In the absence of a labour surplus, however, the loss of labour through emigration results, *ceteris paribus*, in a production loss to the sending region and a shift in the functional distribution of income in favour of wages.

Both Johnson (1967a) and Berry and Soligo (1969) argue that the effect of out-migration on economic welfare in sending nations depends on how emigration affects the domestic capital stock—that is, on how much capital migrants take with them. If migrants own capital that they take abroad, then emigration will have a negative effect on the local capital stock.

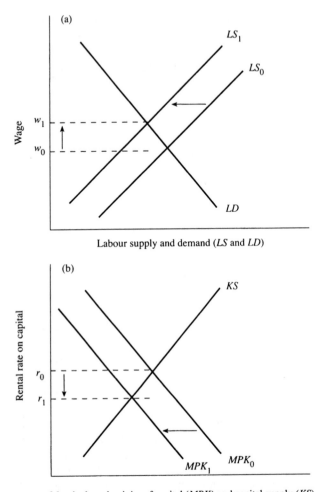

Fig. 8.2 Non-marginal migration in a neoclassical world

A loss of capital through migration has two implications. First, the capital supply curve in Figure 8.2*b* shifts leftward, driving up the local rental rate on capital and raising marginal profits. Second, the loss of capital through emigration reduces the productivity of complementary labour inputs. This effect could be illustrated by an inward shift of the labour demand curve in Figure 8.2*a*, which would reduce the wages of those who stay behind. Berry and Soligo (1969) show that, under neoclassical assumptions, the international migration of labour lowers the total income of non-migrants unless (*a*) emigrants own a disproportionately *large* share of capital and (*b*) they leave this capital behind when they emigrate. If these conditions hold, emigration in-

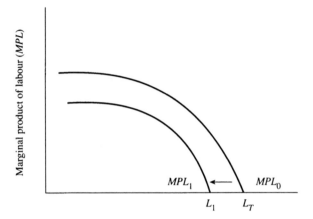

Fig. 8.3 Effect of lost capital in a Lewis world

creases the capital/labour ratio for those who do not emigrate, thereby raising labour productivity and wages.

Even in the Lewis world depicted in Figure 8.1, however, if the 'redundant' workers who emigrate remove capital that would otherwise enter the sending-country production function, then the marginal product of labour decreases for those left behind, as depicted in Figure 8.3. The consequent reduction of marginal product reduces the size of the workforce at which labour becomes redundant, possibly setting the stage for a new round of emigration. It also drives down the average product available for non-migrants.

The most obvious instance in which Barry and Soligo's (1969) conditions (*a*) and (*b*) do not hold is the emigration of human capital, i.e. people with education, skills, entrepreneurial spirit, and a willingness to take risks. By definition, human capital is attached to the migrant and necessarily leaves when he or she does. If international migrants are positively selected with respect to human capital characteristics, therefore, migration will be associated with a 'brain drain' from the sending country whose effects are similar to those of capital flight, lowering the productivity, and hence the wages, of complementary labour in migrant-sending areas.

Thus, two clear lessons emerge from early theoretical research on international migration. First, the effects of labour emigration depend critically on how it affects the capital/labour ratio among non-migrants. Second, the distributional effects of emigration are likely to be unequal across socio-economic groups. Rivera-Batiz (1982), in a seminal piece, explored the theoretical implications of emigration for capital-rich and labour-rich individuals. He showed that if migrants take capital with them (including human capital), then the real income of capital-rich individuals unambiguously increases, but the effect on labour-rich individuals is unclear.

Wong (1983) employed generalized economic models to lend additional theoretical support to the argument that emigration is globally beneficial to those who do not migrate, provided it results in an overall increase in the capital/labour ratio within the migrant-sending economy. Subsequent theoretical studies by Quibria (1988) and Davies and Wooton (1992) also suggest that emigration increases general economic welfare and reduces income inequality in migrant-sending countries.

The Influence of Remittances

In the theoretical world imagined by Lewis (1954) and Ranis and Fei (1961), where migrant remittances to their households of origin implicitly are ruled out, developing country governments have an interest in promoting out-migration only to the extent that the marginal product of the migrating labour is less than the country's average product of labour. In this case, emigration carries no opportunity costs and the average product of workers who remain is increased.

In reality, however, developing-country governments conceive of emigration not in terms of the lost-labour effects just described, but as a potential source of savings and foreign exchange, as well as a safety valve for easing unemployment or exporting troublemakers who question the political status quo. Even if LDCs lose labour that could have produced a positive product at home, they gain income in the form of migrant remittances and repatriated savings or other less tangible benefits. If the opportunity cost of the lost labour is positive but low, as in most LDCs, then the earnings sent home by migrants are likely to exceed the income migrants would have generated if they had stayed at home.

Djajic (1986), in an extension of the neoclassical research cited earlier, concludes that non-migrants benefit from emigration, even if they do not receive any of the remittances themselves, provided that the magnitude of migrants' remittances exceeds a critical threshold roughly equal to the value of the production they would have produced had they stayed.

Migrant remittances, like other types of income transferred from abroad, contribute to the migrant-sending economy in at least two ways: first, they increase national income directly if the preceding conditions hold; and second, they raise national income indirectly by providing foreign exchange and savings.

Even if migrant remittances do not exceed the value of local production lost to emigration (as when migrants spend a large part of their foreign earnings on consumption or keep them in savings accounts abroad), it may still be in a developing country's interest to sponsor emigration if the shadow value of foreign exchange is high—that is, if a lack of foreign exchange is constraining income growth at home. In this case, international migration may be the best way for a country to fill its foreign-exchange gap, especially if other sources of foreign exchange are not available.

In addition to easing foreign exchange constraints, international migration may increase national savings. If a significant share of the foreign earnings are saved in sending-country banks, or if migrant remittances yield a net income gain within households where savings rates are positive, the export of labour will provide a way for poor countries to augment savings. Migrant remittances thus perform the same function as foreign investment and international development assistance in a two-gap model (Chenery 1979), providing scarce foreign exchange as well as additional savings for national development.

Macroeconomic Evidence

From the above theoretical review, it is clear that a complete assessment of the relationship between international migration and economic development must consider both the direct and indirect effects of labour emigration. The direct effect is the contribution of remittances to national income; indirect effects include the shift in production stemming from the withdrawal of labour, the effect remittances have in easing foreign exchange constraints, and the effect of remittances on domestic savings and investment.

In order to assess the relationship between international migration and economic development, therefore, we need four pieces of information: (i) the magnitude of migrant remittances; (ii) the value or economic effect of foreign exchange provided by remittances; (iii) the selectivity of international migration; and (iv) the effect of remittances on domestic savings and investment and the impact of these savings and investment on economic growth.

The Magnitude of Remittances

Beginning with the work of Swamy (1981), investigators have sought to quantify the flow of remittances sent by expatriate workers back to their friends and relatives at home (see Russell 1986, 1992; Keely and Tran 1989). Measuring remittances is difficult because migrants often enter developed countries outside of official channels and repatriate their earnings through informal means. Money may be returned in the form of goods purchased abroad or in the form of cash savings brought back by migrants or visiting family members, what Lozano Ascencio (1993) calls 'pocket transfers'.

Table 8.1 presents estimates of migrant remittances developed by Russell and Teitelbaum (1992) from official banking statistics (which do not report data for one important migrant-sending nation, Vietnam). Since they are based on funds transferred through formal channels and do not include in-kind or pocket transfers, they should be regarded as conservative. In Mexico,

Table 8.1   Absolute and relative size of international migrant remittances to principal sending nations in 1989

Region and country	(1) Total remittances ($m.)	(2)	(3)	(4)	(5)
		Remittances as a percentage of:			
		GDP	Exports	Imports	Balance of payments
Americas					
Colombia	467	1.2	7.7	10.3	31.7
El Salvador	207	3.5	32.6	21.6	−58.1
Jamaica	214	5.5	21.1	13.7	−38.3
Mexico	2,277	1.1	10.0	9.7	−353.0
Asia					
Bangladesh	771	3.8	59.1	23.4	−38.6
India	2,750	1.0	23.1	15.6	−45.0
S. Korea	624	0.3	1.0	1.1	13.6
Pakistan	1,897	4.8	38.7	25.8	−73.4
Europe					
Greece	1,387	2.6	23.1	10.4	−18.8
Portugal	3,706	8.3	29.1	20.7	−76.2
Spain	1,861	0.5	4.3	2.7	−7.6
Turkey	3,040	3.9	26.1	19.2	−72.4
Yugoslavia	6,290	8.0	46.4	46.6	10,844.8
Middle East					
Jordan	623	14.0	56.2	33.3	−80.6
Syria	355	3.1	12.6	19.5	29.8
Yemen	410	5.4	67.6	31.9	−60.6
North Africa					
Algeria	306	0.6	4.0	4.6	26.3
Egypt	3,532	10.6	94.1	30.9	−59.5
Morocco	1,454	6.5	43.9	29.1	−86.6
Sudan	297	2.5	54.7	28.3	−58.6
Tunisia	488	4.8	16.6	11.8	−40.4

Note: Data for El Salvador are for 1988.
Source: Russell and Teitelbaum (1992).

however, where extensive research has been carried out using both official and unofficial sources, the estimates agree rather closely. Studies using a variety of methodologies for different years yield a range of estimates from $2 to $3 billion migradollars annually, and an average around $2.2 billion per year in the late 1980s (see Massey and Parrado 1994). The latter figure is quite close to Russell and Teitelbaum's (1992) estimate of $2.3 billion in 1989.

As column (1) of the table indicates, remittances are very large in absolute terms, ranging from a low of $207 million in El Salvador to a high of $6.3 billion in the former Yugoslavia. Absolute numbers are difficult to interpret, however, because national economies differ so widely in size. When remittances are expressed as a percentage of GDP (column (2)), two nations stand out with notably high fractions: Jordan at 14 per cent and Egypt at 11 per cent. Five other countries have ratios in the 5–10 per cent range (Jamaica, Portugal, Yugoslavia, Yemen, and Morocco); and two others (Pakistan and Tunisia) are just under the 5 per cent threshold, with percentages of 4.8 per cent each. For these countries, in which remittances constitute one-twentieth to one-tenth of total domestic economic activity, the export of labour must be regarded as a vital segment of the national economy, and migradollars therefore constitute a large and potentially important source of funds for development.

Remittances play a critical role as a source of foreign exchange in LDCs, as suggested by the third column of the table, which expresses remittances as a percentage of total merchandise exports. In eleven countries, remittances constitute more than one-quarter of export revenues, and in one case, Egypt, the ratio is 94 per cent, meaning that migrant remittances nearly equal the revenue earned from all other merchandise exports combined. The other ten countries with export percentages above 25 per cent are El Salvador, Bangladesh, Pakistan, Portugal, Turkey, Yugoslavia, Jordan, Yemen, Morocco, and Sudan.

One country is characterized by a remarkably low ratio of remittances to export earnings. In South Korea the figure is just 1 per cent; but other evidence indicates that remittances played a larger role in Korea's development at an earlier date. By 1989, Korea had built a vibrant export economy with a high GDP. During the late 1960s and early 1970s, however, the Korean economy was still in take-off stage and the ratio of remittances to exports averaged about 20 per cent (Hyun 1989). Kim (1983) calculates that remittances accounted for between 3 per cent and 7 per cent of Korea's GNP growth between 1976 and 1981, and Ro and Seo (1988) put the figure as high as 32 per cent as late as 1982. Thus, remittances did provide a crucial source of investment capital and foreign exchange for South Korea at an earlier stage in its development.

Another clue regarding the economic importance of migradollars comes from the ratio of remittances to merchandise imports, shown in column (4) of Table 8.1. As these figures show, remittances also represent a crucial source of hard currency that enables many poor countries to purchase foreign manufactured goods they would otherwise have to forgo (see Rist 1978; Amjad 1989; Stahl and Habib 1991; Arnold 1992). In seven of the countries listed, remittances are sufficient to offset at least a quarter of the cost of merchandise imports (Pakistan, Yugoslavia, Jordan, Yemen, Egypt, Morocco, and Sudan); and in all countries save three (Korea, Spain, and Algeria) remittances make up at least 10 per cent of imports.

In several labour-exporting countries of South-East Asia, the value and importance of migrant remittances have risen dramatically in recent years. In the Philippines, for example, remittances by Filipinos working abroad grew by 528 per cent between 1980 and 1992, when they reached more than $2.2 billion and constituted 5 per cent of that country's total GDP (World Bank 1994). Whereas in 1980, migrant remittances constituted only 7 per cent of merchandise exports in the Philippines, by 1992 the figure had reached 23 per cent; and whereas remittances ran at 5 per cent of imports in 1980 they represented 14 per cent in 1992. In some small Pacific nations, migrant remittances are larger than all merchandise exports or imports combined.

It is thus clear that remittances play an extremely important role in financing the imports of many developing countries. The last column in Table 8.1 indicates the extent to which remittances help to offset the negative terms of trade that characterize so many developing nations; it shows remittances as a percentage of the balance of payments. Of the twenty-one countries displayed in the table, sixteen had trade deficits in 1989, and in nearly all these cases, remittances covered a sizeable portion of the gap. The lowest percentage occurred in the most developed of the sending nations, Spain, which could count on other sources of capital to finance its deficit. The next lowest percentage was in Greece, another relatively developed country where remittances constituted 19 per cent of the negative balance of payments.

In the remaining fourteen countries, the *lowest* percentage observed was 38 per cent (in Jamaica and Bangladesh). The ratio of remittances to deficit extended upwards through percentages in the 40s in India and Tunisia, the 50s in El Salvador, Egypt, and Sudan, and percentages over 60 in Pakistan, Portugal, Turkey, Jordan, Yemen, and Morocco. In Mexico, international migrants provided remittances sufficient to cover the 1989 balance of payments deficit three-and-a-half times over. Indeed, estimated migrant earnings of $2.3 billion made labour the country's third largest export after oil and tourism (Lozano Ascencio 1993).

Remittances as Foreign Exchange

Many developing countries are characterized by a chronic shortage of foreign exchange caused by their need to purchase capital goods and energy on world markets, essential ingredients for industrial development and growth. The degree to which the resulting negative balance of payments constitutes a constraint on economic growth and development depends on a country's ability to finance the gap through other sources. For those countries that experienced a trade deficit in 1989, Table 8.2 compares the size of remittances (column (1)) to total reserves and direct foreign investment (columns (2) and (3)).

For most developing countries with a chronic trade deficit, migrant earnings constitute the major, and in some cases the only, means of financing the gap.

Table 8.2 Remittances compared to other sources of capital
and foreign exchange

Region and country	(1) Total remittances	(2) Total reserves	(3) Direct foreign investment	(4) per cent Change in exchange rate[a]	(5) Annual inflation rate
Americas					
El Salvador	207	162	17	−62	20.9
Jamaica	214	108	57	−24	13.0
Mexico	2,277	6,329	2,684	−93	57.3
Asia					
Bangladesh	771	502	0	−21	9.6
India	2,750	3,859	0	−27	9.0
Pakistan	1,897	521	154	−29	5.9
Europe					
Greece	1,387	3,224	752	−31	15.8
Portugal	3,706	9,952	1,546	−8	11.8
Spain	1,861	41,467	6,955	34	6.6
Turkey	3,040	4,780	663	−81	40.7
Middle East					
Jordan	623	471	−18	−38	2.3
Yemen	410	279	0	−2	10.2
North Africa					
Egypt	3,532	1,520	1,228	57	17.3
Morocco	1,454	488	167	5	4.8
Sudan	297	16	4	−71	35.8
Tunisia	488	962	74	−17	1.6

[a] Calculated as $(ER_{89} - ER_{84})/ER_{84}$, where ER is US dollars per unit of national currency (e.g. dollars per peso).

Note: Data for El Salvador are for 1988.

Sources: Remittances: Russell and Teitelbaum (1992); other indicators: International Monetary Fund (1994).

In all cases except Mexico and Spain, the value of remittances exceeded the value of total direct foreign investment; and in nine of the sixteen countries remittances exceed total reserves. Only Mexico, India, and the sending countries of Europe had reserves in 1989 sufficient to cover a substantial share of the trade gap. In other developing nations, annual remittances substantially exceeded the sum of reserves plus direct foreign investment, making migradollars the principal source of foreign exchange available to finance trade deficits.

Remittances play a particularly crucial role in overcoming exchange constraints in several nations. Pakistan's $1.9 billion in remittances greatly exceeded its $521 million in reserves and $154 million in direct foreign invest-ment. Yemen had no foreign investment at all and only $279 million in re-serves, compared to $410 million in remittances. Morocco's $1.5 billion in remittances was more than twice the sum of its reserves ($488 million) and foreign investment ($167 million); and the Sudan largely kept itself afloat through remittances totalling $297, compared to reserves of just $16 million and foreign investment of only $4 million.

Columns (4) and (5) of Table 8.2 report inflation rates and exchange-rate trends. Trends in real exchange rates are a gauge of changes in the shadow value of foreign exchange. Exchange rate devaluations are a market indication that the price of foreign exchange is too low relative to the true shadow price. Policy-induced currency devaluations represent an effort to increase a coun-try's supply of foreign exchange, reflecting policy-makers' perceptions that the shadow value of foreign exchange is high. High domestic inflation erodes the value of local relative to foreign currencies in which international migrant remittances are denominated. Countries that experience a high rate of infla-tion and a high exchange rate may be characterized as having a relatively high shadow value of foreign exchange.

Most of the countries in the table have relatively high annual inflation rates: twelve of the sixteen nations have domestic inflation rates in excess of 9 per cent per year, a rate sufficient to cause the value of a currency to fall by one-half every eight years. Most, including some of the most remittance-dependent countries, also display deteriorating exchange rates. This deterioration occurs despite the positive effect that inflows of foreign remittances have on the value of local currencies (other things being equal). Although impressionistic, these data strongly suggest the severe nature of foreign exchange constraints faced by most migrant-sending countries.

Taken together, the data presented in Tables 8.1 and 8.2 indicate that migrant remittances constitute a large and important source of capital for developing countries. Migradollars play an extremely important role in easing savings and exchange constraints, and they represent a crucial means by which developing countries are able to finance their trade deficits. Although remit-tances, by themselves, may not guarantee the achievement of self-sustaining economic growth, the export of labour carries considerable potential as a strategy of capital acquisition and as a means of overcoming exchange barriers to economic development.

Selectivity of Emigration

Whether or not the development potential of remittances is fully realized depends on a variety of other factors, one of which is the selectivity of interna-tional migration. Here the research record begins to grow somewhat murky. Although a few studies have examined the issue of migrant selectivity, they have not addressed the specific issue of how much capital is owned by migrants or how much capital—human and financial—migrants take with them when they leave. The few studies that have been conducted on the selectivity of international migrants have focused largely on human capital characteristics.

Research from several nations suggests that international migrants tend to be selected from the middle to upper-middle ranges of the socio-economic hierarchy, at least initially. Such a pattern has been documented in Mexico (Portes 1979; Taylor 1987; Massey *et al.* 1994); the Dominican Republic (Ugalde *et al.* 1979; Georges 1990; Grasmuck and Pessar 1991; Portes and Guarnizo 1991); Jamaica (Anderson 1982; Marshall 1982); El Salvador (Funkhouser 1992); Turkey (Paine 1974; Oguzkan 1975, 1976; Neuloh 1976; Ebiri 1985); Egypt (Adams 1989); Yugoslavia (Baucic 1972); India (Madhavan 1985); Korea (Yoon 1991); and the Philippines (Tan and Canias 1989).

Birks and Sinclair (1980: 144) examined occupational distributions of emigrants from a variety of Middle Eastern countries working in Kuwait. They found that emigrants from capital-poor Arab countries were drawn primarily from the technical, skilled, and semi-skilled sectors of society. They only identified two countries where immigrants were predominantly unskilled: India and Yemen. Those coming from Palestine, Egypt, Jordan, Lebanon, Syria, Iraq, Pakistan, and Iran tended to hold Kuwaiti jobs that required secondary or post-secondary training.

Adams (1991) obtained somewhat different results from his surveys of three Egyptian sending communities. Although he found that international migrants were self-selected on the basis of higher education, he also noted higher rates of out-migration among landless agricultural workers, who tended to be less skilled. Birks and Sinclair (1980: 141) report that Tunisian migrants to Libya were predominantly unskilled, although those emigrating to France were skilled, white-collar, or highly skilled.

In his review of international labour migration from six Asian countries, Demery (1986) found that emigrants tended to be better educated than origin populations and were largely concentrated in skilled blue-collar occupations. Although several authors report that emigrants from Thailand are generally agricultural workers, they tend to come from more affluent and educated households (Peerathep 1982; Kanok and Uitrakul 1985; Sumalee 1986). Based on this evidence, Demery (1986: 33) concludes 'that migrants from Asia can by no means be considered as unskilled and surplus to domestic requirements', although this may not be true of all countries in the region.

Recent analyses of US census data by Borjas (1991, 1994) reveal that average schooling levels for immigrants from Asia and Africa are substantially above those of their countries of origin. Whereas immigrants from Egypt averaged nearly two years of university training, for example, mean schooling in the country itself did not exceed the primary level; and whereas immigrants from China averaged nearly thirteen years of schooling, the average at home was a little over eight years.

A similar pattern generally holds for Latin American immigrants to the USA if one excludes Mexico. Argentinian immigrants to the USA report an average of more than thirteen years of schooling, compared with less than nine years at home; and for Brazil the differential is even greater—more than fifteen years of education for immigrants but less than nine at home. Average education in Guatemala is only around three years, whereas Guatemalan immigrants have some nine years of schooling. Only in Mexico does the average education of immigrants approach that of the country as a whole: roughly 6.5 years of schooling among immigrants compared to an average of around 6.1 years in Mexico itself (Borjas 1991).

These averages conceal extremes, however, and often obscure the loss of very highly educated people to emigration. Even though the number of highly skilled individuals may be small relative to total emigration or to the number of skilled people in the receiving country, it is frequently large relative to the skilled population in the sending country. In this event, the loss of human capital may retard scientific and technological development and yield an effect similar to that of capital flight, lowering the productivity, and hence the wages, of complementary workers. The flight of human capital also tends to widen inequalities between North and South by augmenting the concentration of skill and expertise in developed countries.

The tendency for individuals to allocate their time to labour markets in which returns to their human capital are highest suggests that selectivity will vary across sending areas with different human capital endowments and different access to foreign labour markets. In rural Mexico, which has extensive networks that lead to low-skilled US jobs, but where the economic returns to schooling in these jobs are low or nil, the selectivity of international migration strongly favours low-skilled persons. Barriers to legal entry make it difficult for migrants with intermediate levels of schooling to reap high returns in the US labour market.

Despite the predominance of low-skill migrants, there appears to be a significant brain drain at the upper end of Mexico's skill distribution. This outcome is encouraged by US immigration law, which selects migrants on the basis of skills when issuing employment-related visas. As a result, even though most Mexicans, particularly those who enter the USA illegally, have low levels of human capital, international migration absorbs a relatively large share of Mexico's educated workforce. In 1994, 843 legal Mexican immigrants reported professional-technical occupations and 428 described themselves as executives or managers; another 15,290 entered as temporary workers in skilled occupational categories, and 14,773 Mexicans were admitted as students (US Immigration and Naturalization Service 1996). Although these people constitute a relatively small share of the total flow of Mexicans into the USA, they represent a significant fraction of Mexico's educated workforce.

In other countries, which do not share a long and porous border with a developed country and do not have extensive networks leading into low-skilled jobs, international movement is more costly, thereby precluding much emigration from the low end of the skill distribution and leaving a predominance of brain-drain migrants at the top. The emigration of human capital is far more visible and much more of a policy concern elsewhere in Latin America than in Mexico.

US census data generally reveal a continuum of skills for emigrants from Latin America. Average schooling is lowest for Mexican immigrants, higher among those from Central America, and highest among those from the Southern Cone. According to Borjas's (1991) analysis of 1980 census data, the difference between the average education of recent immigrants and the countrywide mean was 0.4 years for Mexico, 2.7 years for the Dominican Republic, 6.1 years for Guatemala, and 6.8 for Brazil, and the average schooling of immigrants progressed from 6.5 years among Mexicans, to 8.9 years among Dominicans, to 9.0 years among Guatemalans, to 15.4 years among Brazilians.

The brain drain often begins within universities of developed countries. A recent report by the Institute for International Education (1995) found, for example, that the number of foreign students in the USA rose from 145,000 in 1970 to 407,000 in 1990, and exceeded 450,000 in 1994. According to the National Science Foundation (1987), roughly one-half of all foreign students interviewed in the USA did not intend to return home after completing their studies, and the percentage is significantly higher in some fields, such as engineering and the physical sciences. According to the US Immigration and Naturalization Service (1996), nearly 30,000 students 'adjusted status' to become permanent residents of the USA in 1994, and 90 per cent of these were from the developing world.

In general, then, international migrants appear to be positively selected with respect to human capital characteristics such as education, occupational status, skill, and, presumably, unobserved traits such as risk-taking and creativity. We do not, however, know the extent to which international migrants possess financial capital, or the degree to which they take such capital with them when they leave, variables critical in determining how emigration affects sending countries (see Johnson 1967a; Berry and Soligo 1969). Although recent indirect evidence suggests that people migrate precisely to gain access to capital (see Taylor 1992), in general we have little or no direct evidence on the financial resources possessed and/or transported by emigrants when they leave to work abroad.

We also lack information on how skill and education affect the propensity to remit. If highly skilled migrants are more likely to establish permanent ties abroad and less likely to remit funds home, or to remit smaller amounts, then sending countries experience a double deprivation: as well as losing valuable human capital, they do not receive a return flow of capital to compensate for the loss. Durand *et al.* (1996) found that the likelihood of remitting declined significantly as education rose among Mexican migrants to the USA, suggesting such a double loss. The amount sent, however, rose with education among those who did remit.

Few efforts have been made to estimate the economic value of the human capital lost through emigration from less to more developed countries. One exception is a study conducted by the United Nations (1975), which sought to quantify the amount of human capital lost by developing countries through emigration during the period 1961–72. It calculated the imputed value of lost human capital to be around $50 billion ($121 billion in 1990 dollars). To put this number into perspective, total official development assistance by the three major recipients of international migrants over the same period (Canada, USA, and Britain) totalled only $46 billion ($112 billion in 1990 dollars).

The difficulty with such imputations is that the value of expertise and skills varies substantially between sending and receiving nations. Differences in value stem from the relative abundance of complementary capital in developed countries (such as advanced infrastructure), as well as economies of scale that result from having a critical mass of expertise in particular geographic areas—what might be characterized as the 'Silicon Valley effect'.

Recent technological advances, however, such as the internet, cellular phones, and satellite-based communications, make it possible to coordinate scientific research and productive activities over large geographic distances, and thus hold substantial promise for alleviating future 'Silicon Valley effects' on emigration. The recent boom in the software industry of Bangalore, India, is one such example. Technology, however, can offer an alternative to emigration only for those countries that invest in education and become incorporated into the global infrastructure of technology and communications.

Other things being equal, a shortage of highly skilled workers in less developed countries should create a scarcity premium for schooling, keeping highly educated people at home. But schooling typically generates the highest returns when combined with other forms of capital that are relatively more abundant in developed countries. A classic example is the Ph.D. scientist who requires state-of-the art laboratory facilities to carry out his or her research. Since the demand for highly skilled workers, and human capital markets generally, are more developed in the North than the South, a brain drain often results. The immigration policies of most developed countries encourage this flight by selectively easing restrictions on entry for the most highly skilled foreigners.

Thus, developing countries face a difficult migration-and-development dilemma with respect to human capital. On the one hand, the accumulation of complementary capital required to make highly skilled individuals more productive at home is a prerequisite for competing in international labour markets to retain scarce, high-end human capital. Increasing productivity, including that of highly skilled people, is a fundamental goal of development. On the other hand, in the short run, lucrative opportunities for skilled people abroad make the opportunity cost of working at home extraordinarily high.

Most countries lack the will and/or ability to invest in costly programmes aimed at keeping highly skilled workers at home and creating a critical mass of skills vital to development in the long run.

To be sure, the economic returns through remittances by highly educated emigrants are often greater than those that would have accrued had the migrants remained home and worked (see Hugo 1996c). Nonetheless, the end result for many countries is a brain-drain syndrome, in which poor developing countries subsidize wealthier developed nations by investing public resources to create human capital that subsequently migrates abroad. To the extent that emigration selects positively on human capital, public investment in education may have the unintended effect of encouraging emigration, and if high-end migration is not offset by the return of remittances, it will constitute a deadweight loss to the developing country. Thus, creating better conditions to utilize and ensure a high economic return to human capital at home is a prerequisite to reducing the loss of human capital through emigration.

Remittances and Investment

We found relatively little information on how international migration affects domestic savings and investment. Ideally, a systematic empirical analysis would use cross-national data to estimate the effect of the rate and pattern of emigration on savings, investment, and income growth in sending countries. Unfortunately in our exhaustive survey of the literature we found no such study. The only evidence available on this important topic comes from aggregate case studies of individual sending nations, and for the most part they yield very pessimistic conclusions about migration's role in promoting productive investment.

Southern Europe

Probably the best documented case is that of Turkey, which between 1961 and 1987 exported some 814,000 workers to Europe, mostly to the Federal Republic of Germany, which received 81 per cent of the total outflow from that nation (Martin 1991a: 22–3). This labour migration, together with the associated movement of spouses, children, and other dependants, had by 1988 produced a population of 2.1 million Turks in Europe, 1.5 million of whom lived in Germany (ibid. 28).

This massive movement was encouraged by Turkish authorities as part of an explicit strategy of migration-led development. During the early 1960s:

[E]xporting workers on a temporarily recruited basis became an increasingly attractive policy to the government, especially when it discovered the inflow of savings and remittances to which labour export led. The outflow of migrant workers was primarily determined by host country demand and so was subject to large fluctuations. But despite the high risk attached to the adoption of mass labour export policy, the achievement of Turkey's development plans was made increasingly dependent on labour export. (Paine 1974: 36)

The research literature associated with this migratory movement is singularly negative about the effects of emigration on investment and economic growth. The first comprehensive study of Turkish emigration was carried out by Paine (1974), who conducted a detailed analysis of survey data gathered from returning guestworkers. Based on her exhaustive analysis of responses, she concluded that:

[S]avings and remittances out of earnings abroad have been mainly utilized not for agricultural or industrial investment but for consumption expenditure. . . . Despite the government's hopes, there have . . . been few examples of returned workers setting up their own productive enterprises. . . . Indeed insofar as ex-migrants have attempted to establish businesses, they have tended to be in the service sector, though rural migrants have tended to set themselves up as small farmers. Few returned workers have learnt new skills abroad . . . and those who have done so have not tended to use them on return. . . . In other words, emigration has not provided substantial capital formation and has tended to reduce the supply of trained manpower for new industrial projects. (Paine 1974: 147)

Paine's study was followed by another comprehensive assessment conducted by a binational team of Dutch and Turkish researchers who specifically evaluated the ability of workers' companies and village development cooperatives to channel foreign earnings into development (see Abadan-Unat *et al.*: 1975; and Penninx and Van Renselaar 1978). The former ventures were launched by idealistic migrants in Europe and the latter were founded initially by migrants, but later taken over and controlled by the central government.

The investigators found that neither the workers' companies nor the village cooperatives had much success in promoting savings or investment among migrants. Neither venture was able to overcome the disincentives stemming from Turkey's broader macroeconomic policies, which favoured urban dwellers at the expense of small-town producers, kept agricultural prices low, imposed controls on the international transfer of goods and capital, and generally displayed a heavy, bureaucratic hand in managing economic affairs (see Martin 1991a). As Abadan-Unat *et al.* (1975: 137) concluded, 'failure to establish institutional facilities to accommodate migrants' savings [and] the present shortage of sources of financial and technical planning advice for investors, must be laid at the feet of the government. Waste of capital has been the unfortunate consequence.'

In those relatively few cases where investments were made in productive enterprises by returning Turkish guestworkers, the results were singularly unpromising. Writing four years after the completion of the study, Penninx (1982: 812) concluded that:

[the] direct positive effects for development in rural areas and also in the sector of small and middle scale enterprises in urban areas are marginal. The fortune of a huge

capital flow from abroad becomes available in small change in the hands of many and seems to be absorbed according to rules of the existing economic system, thereby creating new or strengthening existing demand, but not changing the system significantly.

Keyder and Aksu-Koc (1988) report that by 1981, 70 per cent of the workers' companies had closed with losses, causing many migrants to lose their hard-earned savings entirely and forcing them back into foreign wage labour.

Surveys conducted among Turkish guestworkers consistently show that repatriated foreign earnings are spent primarily on consumption (Paine 1974; Gokdere 1978; Keyder and Aksu-Koc 1988; Martin 1991a). When foreign earnings are not spent in this way, they tend to be invested in real estate (Keles 1976, 1985) or in small enterprises that create few jobs and generate little income (Penninx and Van Renselaar 1978; Gitmez 1983; Keyder and Aksu-Koc 1988; Martin 1991a). When Turkish migrants do return to establish businesses, moreover, they tend to settle in more developed towns and cities instead of their rural villages of origin (Gitmez 1983), thereby exacerbating Turkey's pattern of uneven economic growth and regional inequality (Keles 1985; Keyder and Aksu-Koc 1988).

Despite the relatively large quantity of capital that has flowed into Turkey over the years as a result of international migration, the country has not grown faster than other non-migrant sending countries in the region (Gitmez 1991); and unlike these countries, Turkey has become dependent on remittances to finance its imports and quite vulnerable to shifts in the immigration policies of receiving nations, particularly Germany (Paine 1974; Straubhaar 1992).

Summing up two decades of research on migration and development in Turkey, Martin (1991b: 39) concluded that 'remittances and development are . . . another example of good intentions gone awry. Remittances do make individual migrants and their families better off, but they are rarely the spark which creates enough economic activity to make emigration unnecessary.' Only Kolan (1975) reached a more optimistic conclusion. From his survey of macroeconomic indicators he concluded that emigration did promote capital accumulation and GNP growth within Turkey, but that employment and labour productivity were unaffected.

Country studies carried out elsewhere in Southern Europe, although small in number, yield similarly pessimistic conclusions about the effects of emigration on economic development. In Greece, returning migrants settled in urban rather than rural areas, leaving the latter without a labour force capable of attracting industry (Gitmez 1991). Greek remittances were expended largely on housing, leading to inflated real estate values that made property less accessible to non-migrant households (Papademetriou and Emke-Poupoloupos 1991). In the former Yugoslavia, studies conducted by Baucic (1972), Morokvasic (1984), and Kjurciev (1987), found that remittances were channelled into home construction and consumer durables rather than investment. To Baucic, therefore, international migration was 'an adverse factor in the country's economic and social development' (1972: 43).

In Spain and Portugal, a systematic evaluation carried out by Gregory and Pérez (1985) revealed some benefits at the national level, with the billions of dollars in remittances helping to promote the expansion of Spain's internal market; but they also found deleterious effects on specific sending regions: 'while migration has resulted in the physical improvement of thousands of communities, it has done little to change the basic economic or social structures that were responsible for migration. The modes of production have continued with only slight variations decade after decade without creating significantly more employment' (ibid. 258–9).

The Middle East and Africa

According to a dated but still the most comprehensive review of migration and development in the Arab region,

[I]t appears that opportunities for investment in other than housing stock and transport are limited in the areas from which many of the migrants come, and they seem disinclined to invest large sums in agriculture. . . . Countries receiving remittances appear to lack both an effective short-term strategy and long-term policies in respect of migrants' earnings. (Birks and Sinclair 1980: 105)

In Oman, Birks and Sinclair (1980) found that remittances were directed towards the establishment of small irrigated gardens; but these plots were not farmed efficiently or profitably and were unable to offset the decline in agricultural output caused by a withdrawal of emigrant labour. In Yemen, Fergany (1982) found that:

although improvements in the level of material consumption have been made possible through workers' remittances, this has not been the result of developing the commodity-producing sectors of Yemen's economy. On the contrary, agriculture, the main economic activity, deteriorated and a strong industrial base was not built. The country's meagre exports actually suffered a significant decline during the 1970s. (ibid. 778)

In his analysis of Yemen, Swanson (1979) points out that the lack of development was not for want of trying by emigrants: 'while some of this cash inflow is dissipated in conspicuous consumption, there is a clear desire on the part of the migrant to translate at least part of his wealth into productive enterprises.' He goes on to state that 'the desire to translate wealth into capital coupled with a dearth of investment opportunities intervenes in the relation between higher wages and land so that land prices are inflated and consolidation fails to occur as predicted' (ibid. 89–90).

As with other countries, Lazaar (1987) found that remittances sent to Morocco were spent primarily on housing. In Algeria remittances played 'a significant but critical role in the . . . economy as a whole' but their effect 'on consumption is far more significant than on investments' (Adler 1985: 279). A survey of Egyptian emigrants likewise revealed that emigrants displayed a strong tendency to channel foreign earnings into consumption, although their marginal propensity to consume was no higher than that of the non-migrant population—they just had more money (Fergany 1986). In a follow-up study, Fergany (1988) found that foreign remittances also tended to promote income inequality in sending regions.

Relatively few studies have examined international migration and development in sub-Saharan Africa. Based on scattered evidence, Adepoju (1991) argued that out-migration led to uneven development resulting in large, fluctuating wage differentials that only served to encourage more migration. He maintained that local development suffered as a result of the loss of better-skilled and more-educated workers. Cobbe (1982) reported that remittances to Lesotho were spent primarily on consumer durables and housing, and Choucri (1985) estimates that two-thirds of remittances to the Sudan go to consumption. Lucas (1987), using a more rigorous econometric approach, found that African countries sending workers to South Africa experienced a short-run decline in agricultural production as a result of lost labour. In the long run, however, investment from remittances led to higher crop productivity and the accumulation of cattle among migrant households.

Asia and the Pacific

The Asian research literature is generally more upbeat in its assessment of the relationship between migration and development. Pakistan is a case in point. According to Gilani (1988: 215), 'labour emigration from Pakistan has brought net benefits to its economy', and the Economic and Social Commission for Asia and the Pacific (ESCAP 1987) found that remittances significantly boosted Pakistani economic growth by increasing domestic savings and providing scarce foreign exchange. The added growth came at a price, however: Kazi (1989) found that the surge in demand caused by migrant remittances, when combined with supply constraints in certain sectors, led to higher prices and inflation.

As in Southern Europe, Africa, and the Middle East, Pakistani emigrants tend to channel their foreign earnings into consumption rather than production. According to Burki (1991), 62 per cent of savings repatriated by Pakistani migrants are spent in this fashion, with about 15 per cent going into real estate alone. He found that poor households tend to spend for family maintenance, but wealthier households tend to invest in land and housing, thereby contributing to inflation in property values. Amjad (1986) and Gilani (1981) reported similar findings.

Probably the most sophisticated analysis of emigration's economic effects in Pakistan was conducted by Burney (1989). He estimated a series of regression models to demonstrate that the marginal propensity to use remittances for consumption was quite high, about 85 cents for each dollar remitted. The added demand created by remittances, however, was responsible for 14 per cent of the growth in Pakistani GNP during 1982–3. Remittances also improved Pakistan's balance of payments position, but did not appear to have any effect on savings or fixed private investment, yielding little increment on the country's capital stock. The only sector to show an increase in private investment was housing.

Given India's immense size, Nayyar (1989) found relatively small effects of emigration on its economy: during the mid-1980s remittances were equivalent to just 1.5 per cent of GDP, 2 per cent of consumer demand, 6 per cent of domestic savings, and 7 per cent of gross domestic capital formation. Madhavan (1985) found that remittances accounted for 8.3 per cent of total household savings during 1980–1. An in-depth regional analysis, however, revealed that specific sending States, such as Kerala, reaped few economic benefits from labour emigration, owing mainly to the absence of linkages between migrants and the wider economy (Nair 1989). The only industries to show positive effects were housing and real estate, and wage inflation was observed in the construction trades.

A survey of emigrants from the Philippines revealed that after buying basic necessities and paying off debts, migrant households tended to use remittances primarily for housing, education, and land, in that order (Go and Postrado 1986). Despite this tendency, however, Smart *et al.* (1986) found that while

> pay levels are high relative to the Philippines, savings and asset accumulation does (*sic*) not appear to be sufficient to set workers up as independent entrepreneurs and at the same time permit maintenance of a higher family standard of living. In fact, Middle East employment risks a vicious circle whereby workers return home on a seemingly permanent basis but, because savings are soon consumed, find that they have to return overseas in order to meet life-style expectations. (ibid. 123)

Nonetheless, it is clear that these expenditures have substantial second- and third-round multiplier effects in the areas to which migrants return. In the Philippines, the *Manila Chronicle* (18 July 1995) reported that some 8 million jobs are supported by remittance income, and Tiglao (1996) reports that remittances are a major reason for the turnaround in the growth rate of the Philippines' GDP after the end of the Marcos regime in 1985, constituting more than a quarter of the total capital inflow during both the Aquino (1986–91) and Ramos (1992–5) administrations.

Similar effects have been reported on other Pacific islands by Brown and Foster (1995); and studies by Bertram (1986) and Watters (1987) have documented the degree to which island nations and their bureaucracies have become reliant on remittances for their continued survival (see Bertram and Watters 1984, 1985, 1986). Strong regional effects of migration on development have been documented for parts of Indonesia. For example, in West Nusa Tenggara, one of the nation's poorest provinces, 10,000 migrant workers in Malaysia send back 120 billion Rupiah each year, a sum substantially greater than the total provincial government budget of 80.4 billion Rupiah (*Indonesian Observer*, 18 March 1995).

Surveys of migrants from Thailand confirm the by-now familiar pattern of spending remittances for consumption rather than investment (see Peerathep 1982; Kanok and Uitrakul 1985; Sumalee 1986). Tingsabadh (1989), for example, found that Thai workers in the Gulf States spend a relatively large share of their earnings on housing: one-third of all remittance income went to housing, followed by 21 per cent going to the repayment of debts, 18 per cent to consumer goods, 6 per cent to farm investment, and 5 per cent to vehicles. The surge in demand for home construction was an important stimulus to the Thai economy, accounting for 20 per cent of all housing expenditures in 1981 (ibid. 329).

Over time, the role of remittances in Thai farm investment appears to have grown, and several studies report international migration to be an important component of skill formation in Thailand (Stahl 1986; Tingsabadh 1989). Summing up the situation in Thailand and other South-East Asian countries, Stahl (1986: 93) concludes that 'labor export, although certainly giving rise to some social and economic costs, undoubtedly yields a net material benefit. Contract labour migration has probably promoted the growth of employment and, at least in the case of Thailand, has promoted skill formation.'

The more positive assessment of emigration's role in promoting development within Asia stems from three factors. First, compared to assessments done in Southern Europe, Africa, and the Middle East, studies in Asia have endeavoured to measure and assess the indirect effects of remittances rather than focusing solely on their direct effects. Second, many Asian countries—notably Korea, Thailand, and Indonesia—have implemented macroeconomic policies favourable to market development, yielding economic contexts more conducive to productive investment, and they have incorporated labour migration directly into their macroeconomic planning. Finally, several Asian governments have implemented specific policies to encourage the repatriation of foreign earnings and capture remittances for development purposes (Athukorala 1993).

The Republic of Korea, for example, instituted a requirement that migrants remit 80 per cent of their earnings through the state bank, while the Philippines required migrants to repatriate 50–70 per cent of their earnings in this fashion (Shah and Arnold 1986). Sri Lanka, Bangladesh, Pakistan, and India have each established foreign currency accounts in state banks (denominated in US dollars or pounds sterling) that pay above-market interest rates and convert into local currencies at premium rates (Shah and Arnold 1986).

Latin America

Perhaps the most pessimistic conclusions regarding migration and development are drawn from research conducted in the Americas. Based on their review of the evidence, for example, Brana-Shute and Brana-Shute (1982: 281) concluded that 'the overall picture tends to be disappointing, if one looks for capital accumulation and application that finances national development.' Likewise, Rubenstein (1982: 260) writes that 'remittances, and perhaps the entire migratory system as presently constituted, are detrimental to the long-term prospects for economic improvement in the regions' societies.' According to Pessar (1991: 208), 'there is little evidence that migration and remittances spur agricultural production and productivity'; rather, 'migrants cut back on their commercial and subsistence farming activities as they become more reliant on remittances for consumption needs.' Diaz-Briquets (1991: 190), however, asserts that the negative effects follow partly from the characteristics of the sending nation: 'in the least populous countries, where internal markets are small and the number of potential customers limited, emigration . . . has a detrimental impact.'

The foregoing pessimistic conclusions are generally not backed up with quantitative analyses based on large-scale surveys or national statistics. With a few exceptions, there has been a notable lack of interest in assessing the connection between international migration and macroeconomic indicators, and virtually no attention has been paid to estimating the complex indirect effects of emigration, even for important sending nations such as Mexico (Gregory 1986) and Colombia (Murillo Castana 1988).

A surprising amount of work has been carried out on El Salvador, however. Funkhouser (1992) analysed national survey data from that nation and determined that remittances played an extremely important role in maintaining household incomes during the economic and political chaos of the 1980s. Using a different survey, López and Seligson (1990) confirmed this finding. They found that remittances largely sustained the capacity of Salvadorean households to purchase imported goods and had a small, positive influence on domestic consumption. Montes and García (1988) found that, among families with members working in the USA in 1987, remittances comprised 61 per cent of total household income; and a survey undertaken by the United Nations Economic Commission for Latin America and the Caribbean (CEPAL) put the figure at 42 per cent in 1990 (CEPAL 1993).

Parallel surveys carried out by CEPAL in Guatemala and Nicaragua obtained figures of 54 per cent and 25 per cent, respectively. In all three countries, remittances were used overwhelmingly for consumption, with more than 80 per cent going to food in each place (CEPAL 1993). The share of remittances devoted to investment and savings was only 5.7 per cent in El Salvador, 9.4 per cent in Guatemala, and 8 per cent in Nicaragua. When asked why they did not invest their remittances more productively, most respondents answered that they were unable to do so given the pressing demands they faced. Only 15 per cent of Salvadorean households said they were really uninterested in making investments, although the figure was 42 per cent in Guatemala and 30 per cent in Nicaragua (CEPAL 1993).

In El Salvador, remittances from the USA probably prevented an absolute decline in national income during the years of turmoil. López and Seligson (1990) estimated that without remittances, the country's GDP would have fallen by 1 per cent in real terms, rather than sustaining growth of 0.6 per cent during 1986. At the same time, they found that the marginal propensity of remittance-receiving households to save or invest was small, confirming the results of the earlier CEPAL study. Even though the propensity to invest was much greater among business owners, the investments they made had little capacity to create profits or generate additional employment.

The Caribbean

Several national surveys and case studies have been carried out in the Caribbean islands. A survey of migrant sugarcane cutters interviewed in Florida and reported by Wood (1982) and McCoy (1985) found that 'rather than serving as a source of investment capital, the wages earned harvesting Florida cane are primarily devoted to the maintenance and reproduction of the worker and his household' (Wood 1982: 303–4). Wood and McCoy (1985: 251) found 'no evidence that seasonal stateside employment expands agricultural output, or enhances the productive capacity of small farmers in the Caribbean.' Likewise, Griffith (1986: 36) reported that 'seasonal migration to the USA from Jamaica does not result in migrants achieving agricultural production and marketing advantages over non-migrants.'

Case studies of migration and development from small Caribbean islands suggest that remittances are channelled primarily into the purchase of land and the construction, repair, or furnishing of homes, a pattern that appears to hold in Carriacou (Smith 1962) the Bahamas (Otterbein 1966), Saba (Crane 1971), Tortola (Dirks 1972), St Lucia (Midgett 1975), and Nevis (Frucht 1968). In Montserrat, Philpott (1968, 1973) found that remittances go primarily to family support, but with substantial shares devoted to the purchase of land and the payment of migration costs for other family members.

Given this pattern of remittance expenditure, several investigators report that land prices have inflated and agricultural production has fallen on islands characterized by high levels of out-migration (Philpott 1973; Rubenstein 1983). Thomas Hope (1985, 1986) additionally reports that many local communities have been flooded with imported consumer goods. In the Dominican Republic, however, the flow of remittances between New York City and the island have been instrumental in the formation, capitalization, and growth of migrant-owned businesses at both locations (Portes and Guarnizo 1991).

Remittances in comparative perspective

In general, the picture that emerges from national case studies of international migration and development—especially those done in Southern Europe, the Middle East, Latin America, and the Caribbean—is that remittances alleviate the exchange constraints faced by developing countries, bolster domestic savings and consumption, and raise the living standards of migrant-sending households, but have few positive long-term effects on economic growth and development for the sending nations themselves. Not only does migration fail to increase production and investment, according to these studies, but often it has negative consequences in the form of inflation, inequality, and, in some cases, declines in agricultural production.

Although he characterized the relationship between international migration and development as 'uncertain', Papademetriou's (1991: 261) final assessment was more pessimistic:

[T]he major conclusion of my analysis is that, as a rule, most labor sending countries or regions are unable either to derive the full complement of economic benefits which are thought to come from the temporary/circular emigration process, or to contain the social and political/economic costs which are an ever present byproduct of this emigration process.

Only Asian case studies depart from the prevailing pessimism regarding migration and development. Not only do they find that emigration has a positive influence on foreign exchange and family standards of living; they also find, through an analysis of emigration's indirect effects, that remittances yield significant gains in GDP, production, employment, and investment. Several observers of the Asian scene are quite critical of the literature's general inattention to these indirect influences, both in Asia and especially in other regions (see Shah and Arnold 1986; Stahl 1986; Stahl and Habib 1991).

Economy-Wide Effects

In general, pessimistic conclusions emanating from country case studies are poorly supported by hard empirical evidence. Models designed to estimate emigration's indirect effects are conspicuously absent, as are rigorous analyses of how migrant selectivity influences income growth. In order to ascertain the full effect of remittances in migrant-sending countries, however, one needs to measure more than just the quantity of remittances and how they are spent; one also needs to determine the *net* gain that they represent (net of income that migrants would have earned by working at home); their multiplier effects within the migrant-exporting economy; their contribution to local savings; and their effect in easing foreign-exchange constraints.

Estimates of these indirect effects can only be derived using economy-wide modelling techniques, which trace how remittances influence income and production as they work their way through the migrant-sending economy. Unfortunately, with a few exceptions, such models have not made their way into the migration-and-development literature, at least at the macro-level. As noted above, a few studies in Asia have used Computable General Equilibrium Models to quantify emigration's effects on sending economies. In addition,

Adelman and Taylor (1990) have developed a Social Accounting Matrix (SAM) model for one major sending nation, Mexico.

Table 8.3 presents these SAM income multipliers for international migrant remittances. They not only capture the direct effect of migrant remittances on the households that receive them, but also the indirect effects that result from expenditures by these households. If households that receive remittances spend their income on goods and services produced within the Mexican economy, then remittances generate positive, second-round effects on production, which generate more income, and so on. The table reports the total multiplier effect of remittances on production and incomes in Mexico.

According to Adelman and Taylor (1990), for every dollar sent or brought into Mexico by migrants working abroad (virtually all in the USA), GNP increases by somewhere between $2.69 and $3.17, depending on which household group receives these remittances. Remittances produce the largest income multiplier when they flow into rural households, whose consumption and

Table 8.3 Estimated effects on production of a $1 change in migrant remittances sent by members of selected socio-economic groups

	Socio-economic Group				Average dollar remitted
	Small farmer	Rural worker	Urban worker	Urban marginal	
By economic sector					
Basic grains	0.1402	0.1102	0.0445	0.0843	0.08
Livestock	0.1760	0.1749	0.1208	0.1638	0.14
Other agriculture	0.1520	0.1465	0.1024	0.1381	0.12
Petroleum	0.0519	0.0538	0.0433	0.0469	0.05
Fertilizer	0.0063	0.0058	0.0038	0.0053	0.00
Agricultural processing	0.5721	0.5861	0.4028	0.5418	0.48
Industry	0.8506	0.8456	0.6844	0.7495	0.76
Services	0.9338	1.0672	0.8895	0.9163	0.94
Commerce	0.6912	0.7270	0.5625	0.6429	0.63
By socio-economic group					
Small farm	1.1837	0.1587	0.0915	0.1485	0.38
Rural workers	0.0728	1.0694	0.0521	0.0773	0.29
Agribusiness	0.1045	0.1014	0.0696	0.0948	0.09
Urban workers	0.6224	0.6687	1.5387	0.5855	1.11
Urban capitalists	0.6623	0.7171	0.5760	0.6284	0.62
Merchant capitalists	0.3182	0.3346	0.2589	0.2959	0.29
Urban marginal	0.1187	0.1274	0.1013	1.1119	0.11
Gross domestic product	3.0826	3.1773	2.6881	2.9423	2.90

Source: Adelman and Taylor (1990).

expenditure patterns favour goods produced domestically with relatively labour-intensive production technologies and few imported inputs. When migrant remittances go to urban households, more of the money leaks out of the country in the form of import demand.

The effect of remittances on domestic production activities is summarized in the upper panel of the table. Higher incomes for remittance-receiving households increase the demand for both agricultural and urban goods and services. To satisfy this demand, producers in Mexico increase their output, purchasing intermediate inputs from one another and employing additional labour and capital. This, in turn, increases the incomes of households that supply these factors to domestic production activities. As a result, remittances not only raise incomes in households that receive them, they also boost incomes in non-migrant households.

The lower panel shows multipliers by socio-economic group and reveals that the effect of remittances on incomes is always greatest for the household group that receives the remittances, because this group benefits both directly and indirectly. Nevertheless, the indirect effects of remittances on non-remittance-receiving households is substantial. For example, urban worker and capitalist household incomes increase by $.60 to $.70 for every $1 of remittances to rural households.

The last column of the table presents income multipliers for a $1 increase in remittances when this $1 is distributed across household groups in the proportion observed in Mexico in the mid-1980s. That is, it reports the multiplier effect of an average dollar of international migrant remittances. These numbers are an average of the numbers in the other four columns weighted by the socio-economic group's share of total remittances. The income multiplier effect of the average international migrant remittance is about $2.90, and the production effects are as high as $.94 (in services).

These estimates also reveal that migrant remittances have an equalizing effect on the distribution of income among socio-economic groups in Mexico. In the first instance, they favour poor rural and urban families. In the second instance, they create second-round income linkages that also favour the poor. As a result, $1 in remittances translates into a $.29 to $.38 increase in small-farmer and rural-worker incomes and a $1.11 increase in the income of urban-worker households, despite the fact that most remittances do not flow into the latter group.

In other words, *many of the benefits of remittances accrue to households other than the ones that receive them.* This effect occurs because income linkages between migrant and non-migrant households transfer the benefits away from the remittance-receiving household. When a rural household uses remittances to purchase a good manufactured in the urban sector, the second-round income multiplier effects of remittances move to the urban sector. Part of these effects may eventually make their way back to the rural sector, such as when an urban household that gets income from producing the good spends part of this income on food. Nevertheless, in order to see the full effect of remittances on the migrant-sending economy, one has to look beyond the household that receives the remittances, and indeed beyond the socio-economic sector or region in which that household is located.

A few studies have estimated national computable general equilibrium (CGE) models to analyse the full range economic effects of remittances in Asian sending nations. In South Korea, Kim (1983, 1986) found that between 3 per cent and 7 per cent of 1976–81 GNP growth was attributable, directly or indirectly, to migrant remittances. Ro and Seo (1988) set the figure at a remarkable 33 per cent in 1982. Likewise, Hyun (1984) reported that a 10 per cent increase in remittances brought a 0.32 per cent increase in private consumption, a 0.53 per cent increase in fixed investment, a 0.22 per cent increase in GDP, and a 0.13 per cent increase in prices.

Based on his CGE analysis of Bangladesh, Habib (1985) estimated that the money remitted by Bangladeshi overseas workers in 1983 gave rise to an additional final demand of $351 million, which, in turn, generated 567,000 jobs. Ali (1981) and Mahmud (1989) found that while remittances to Bangladesh were targeted primarily to current consumption, a significant share went to non-traded goods such as land, housing, and education. After estimating employment multipliers, Stahl and Habib (1991) found that each migrant created an average of three jobs through remittances.

Rodrigo and Jaytissa (1989) found positive but rather small effects of migrant remittances in their CGE analysis of Sri Lanka. When they estimated the first-round effects of remittances on production they found the additional output comprised between 0.60 per cent and 0.65 per cent of GDP, a small but statistically significant effect. Korale (1986: 234) concluded that in Sri Lanka 'the advantages [of labour emigration] at this point seem to far outweigh the negative consequences of migration.'

The Macroeconomics of Migration and Development Reconsidered

Although the country case studies summarized above highlight the importance of contextual variables in shaping both the determinants of migration and the impacts of migration on development, most suffer from a lack of theoretical and statistical rigour and have not brought state-of-the-art methodological tools to bear on the migration-and-development question. The generally negative findings of these studies also appear to be influenced by the high hopes which governments once pinned on labour exports as a centrepiece of national development, particularly in Turkey where government officials viewed guestworker programmes as a means of creating a dynamic and self-sustaining development process at home (see Paine 1974; Abadan-Unat *et al.* 1975; Penninx and Van Renselaar 1978).

It is remarkable that such high development expectations could be attached to a single export, human or inanimate. Given these lofty expectations, it is difficult to imagine how any emigrant-worker programme could be deemed a success. In retrospect, these hopes clearly were unrealistic (Gitmez 1991; Martin 1991). Production activities that were stimulated by migrant remittances often depended on a continuation of remittances—and thus, of international migration—to keep them going, and the continuing dependence of economies on migrant earnings is often cited as evidence that migration does not promote development.

This view is unduly harsh. Just as a highly developed North American suburb would be thrown into recession without its commuter workers, labour-exporting countries inevitably are entangled in a web of global economic interdependence involving flows of both capital and labour. The income multipliers presented above suggest that income sent home by foreign migrants has an effect on the migrant-sending nation that is similar to the effect of commuters' pay cheques on suburban downtowns. The effect of the former, however, is much larger than a typical American 'downtown multiplier'.

The experience of labour-exporting countries in the past two decades reveals that making labour exports the centrepiece of a national development strategy is probably a mistake. Many of the conditions that promote emigration, such as low incomes and low productivity in migrant-sending regions, also limit the profitably of potential investments. Poor macroeconomic policies—those that yield high inflation and economic uncertainty—encourage families to invest their remittances in real property such as land and housing, rather than in production activities that create new employment. A recent analysis by Durand *et al.* (1996) found that a high rate of inflation strongly raised the odds that Mexican migrants spent their remittances and savings on housing, while a high rate of interest strongly lowered the odds that they put their money into productive investments.

Restrictive industrial policies also make it difficult or impossible for migrants to create small businesses (Ilahi 1993). Poor infrastructure—roads, communications, irrigation, education, and other public services—make the returns to local investment too low and uncertain for migrant households to take the step of tying their life savings up with local production activities.

In short, labour exports are not a substitute for sound macroeconomic policies and well-designed development strategies at home. None of the pessimistic country case studies cited above refers to countries that are models of sound macroeconomic management or growth-oriented development policy. Nevertheless, in a labour-abundant country, labour exports—like other export—may be a useful complement to a sound development strategy.

A downside risk, however, is that emigration, being a selective process, may stimulate the loss of scarce human capital needed for development. If the loss of highly skilled workers creates bottlenecks in production and lowers the productivity of complementary workers, then international migration could undermine economic growth, particularly when the loss of human capital is not offset by significant remittances. Only if international migration involves the movement of abundant labour rather than scarce human capital is there much potential for development. By providing income, foreign exchange, and domestic savings, and by creating significant income multipliers, migrant remittances can stimulate local demand for goods and services while helping to overcome the local constraints on meeting this demand.

The extent to which local production is able to expand to meet the demand stimulated by remittances depends critically on the degree to which government policies create an economic environment that is conducive to local investment. If, on the one hand, remittances are large but the local supply response is low, income from migrants will generate inflationary pressures and fuel the demand for imports, bringing about the conditions decried by many observers. If, on the other hand, economic policies and public investment encourage local production activities, supply may expand and meet the increasing demand for goods and services created by remittances, and remittances will therefore yield large income and employment multipliers.

9 International Migration and Community Development

In the last chapter we reviewed the accumulated research on international migration and economic development at the national level. We found that once the various direct and indirect effects are taken fully into account, international migration carries considerable potential for national economic development, but that this potential is often unrealized in practice. All too frequently, countries pin their hopes on labour export while ignoring more basic economic problems.

The crux of the dilemma is that conditions promoting emigration (low income and low productivity) generally discourage investment, while macroeconomic policies pursued in many developing countries yield high rates of inflation and economic uncertainty that encourage investment in real property rather than productive activities. The same conditions also promote the loss of scarce human capital needed for economic growth through the emigration of educated, highly trained professionals, in addition to the loss of surplus workers, creating serious bottlenecks to development. In the absence of sound policies to promote stable economic growth, therefore, emigration by itself cannot lead to national economic development.

At the community level, prior investigators have generally concluded that emigration undermines the prospects for local economic growth. International migration is widely thought to reinforce a pattern of dependent community development, whereby higher living standards are achieved through the inflow of money from abroad rather than the expansion of economic activity at home. The end result is a way of life that cannot be sustained through local labour, yielding a host of negative side effects, including income inequality, inflation, lost production, and higher unemployment.

Most studies reporting these consequences, however, are based on theoretical frameworks and empirical designs incapable of measuring the full range of indirect effects that emigration has on sending communities. Much of the evidence is anecdotal, and even when quantitative data are offered, they are limited in scope. Few studies have marshalled the kind of empirical information or statistical analyses needed to establish a clear link between international migration and presumed ills such as income inequality and inflation, and even fewer have employed designs capable of studying the indirect effects of emigration on local economies through consumer demand or investment. To design a good study of emigration's effects on community development, one needs a clear theoretical model of how migration influences the economy of a sending region.

Microeconomic Theory: Classical and Neoclassical Views

The starting point in theorizing the relationship between migration and community development is the household itself. Individual migrants originate in households, and most of the effects of emigration on sending areas are expressed through domestic units of one sort or another, magnified or dampened by household economic actions. The first-round effects of international migration on economic development are, therefore, concentrated in the household itself.

Until recently, economic research did not focus on the development effects of international migration *per se*, but on internal migration as a vehicle to mobilize surplus rural labour to support the development of a modern industrial sector (see Lewis 1954; Ranis and Fei 1961), or as a mechanism to equilibrate rural and urban labour markets across sectors (see Jorgenson 1967). Although this research lacked an explicit international or developmental focus, its findings implied certain effects of migration on sending areas which, although limited by the standards of today's theories, nevertheless provide a starting point for understanding migration–development interactions at the community level.

The Lewis model, formalized by Ranis and Fei (1961), was discussed in earlier chapters. Given its assumption of surplus labour, the opportunity cost of out-migration in terms of production at the place of origin is nil: surplus labour can be syphoned off from the rural labour pool, where its marginal product is near zero, and channelled into an expanding modern, urban sector, where its marginal product is positive. The assumption of zero marginal productivity for labour in the rural sector means that the agricultural production needed to sustain a growing urban workforce does not decline as a result of rural–urban migration.

Zero marginal productivity of rural workers also implies that the supply of labour to the modern sector is highly, if not perfectly, elastic. As a result, the modern sector expands and increases its demand for labour without exerting any upward pressure on urban wages. This condition theoretically ensures a large and growing profit share in the modern sector, which may then be invested in new modern-sector activities. These classical assumptions hold until the labour surplus in migrant-supplying sectors disappears, at which point the opportunity cost of out-migration (the marginal product of labour) becomes positive. Once the marginal product of labour in the rural sector equals that in the modern sector (adjusted for the cost of relocating workers from the rural to the urban sector), the analysis becomes neoclassical.

If one substitutes 'sending country' for 'rural sector' and 'destination country' for 'modern sector' in the foregoing discussion, the Lewis model is easily recast to fit the case of international migration. In this context, the neoclassical model predicts that migration will persist until rising wages in the migrant-sending country equal declining wages in migrant-receiving country, minus the costs, monetary and psychological, of migrating across borders (see Todaro and Maruszko 1987). In this view, labour migration will have certain microeconomic effects in sending areas, but they will be limited to labour-supply effects in the short run, and to changes in technologies and production mixes in response to rising labour costs in the long run.

At the place of origin, international migration shifts the labour-supply curve to the left, which increases local wages in a neoclassical world devoid of labour surpluses. Higher wages, in turn, induce labor-saving technological change, or, in the long run, a shift towards the production of less labour-intensive goods. This change is depicted in Figure 9.1 by a shift to the left in labour demand in migrant-sending areas. The interaction of direct (labour-supply) and indirect (labour-demand) effects determines the overall effect of international migration on production, wages, and profits in migrant-sending areas.

If the migration of workers is accompanied by the transnational movement of capital, as envisioned in some of the macro-level models, then an additional shift to the left in labour demand (to D_2) will result. The greater the indirect, negative effects of migration on labour demand, the smaller the benefits of out-migration for workers who remain behind, and the more likely these benefits will be negative. The neoclassical migration model essentially views the migrant as being cut off from the sending region once migration occurs: it does not provide a rationale for remitting.

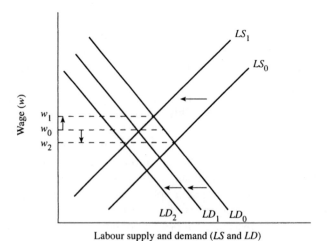

Fig. 9.1 Effects of migration and labour-saving technological change on sending area labour market area

The pioneering work of Todaro (1969) and Harris and Todaro (1970) offered a theoretical explanation for the persistence of rural out-migration in the face of high rates of unemployment at places of destination. Although originally expressed in terms of rural–urban migration, the expected income hypothesis is equally relevant to international migration and leads to policy prescriptions that seek to regulate migration by intervening in labour markets at home or abroad, or by influencing the costs of movement (see Todaro and Maruszko 1987).

One implication of Todaro's work is that raising expected incomes in rural areas through the creation of rural employment is an effective means of reducing rural out-migration; the creation of rural jobs may also be an effective way of reducing unemployment in the urban sector, even more effective than job creation in the urban sector itself. The Todaro model thus provides a theoretical rationale for government-sponsored rural development programmes. The implications of migration for rural development, however, are relatively limited in the Todaro model, as in its predecessors.

For more than a decade, this accepted theoretical wisdom did not agree with empirical research on the effects of migration in sending areas. In practice, empirical research on migration and development moved far ahead of theory. This state of affairs was unfortunate because data collection and analysis were left without a strong theoretical guide. As a result, migration research foundered, dedicating itself primarily to reinventing, retesting, and exploring in increasing depth the implications of the Todaro theoretical wheel. Most rural economic surveys did not include a migration component, either because they regarded migrant remittances as insignificant, or because they assumed that migration was separable from (i.e. did not affect) household production activities.

Meanwhile, inspired by their observation of large and increasing flows of migrant earnings into rural areas, empirically inclined researchers began to carry out surveys to quantify remittances and their uses. A number of village counterparts to national migration-and-development studies appeared in anthropology, demography, economics, geography, and sociology during the 1970s. This empirical research consisted primarily of remittance-use surveys and qualitative impressions about how villages were reshaped by migration. Often influenced by dependency theory (Frank 1967; Kearney 1986), and lacking a theoretical rationale anticipating complex migration-development interactions, village studies usually produced negative findings that mirrored those of the country studies summarized in our earlier article.

Microeconomic Evidence: Community Remittance-Use Studies

Remittance-use studies focus on how migrant remittances and savings are actually spent, or on comparisons of expenditures between households with and without foreign income. The data are partial in the sense that they do not address the more data- and computationally-demanding question of how the appearance of a new or potential source of support, namely remittances, changes net household income. They offer some preliminary insights into the effects of remittances on development, but because they are partial they are also potentially misleading. This failure is due in no small way to the relative underdevelopment of migration theory until the 1980s, which effectively ruled out most of the interesting and important migration–development interactions.

Like the national-level surveys we reviewed before, small-scale regional surveys and fieldwork carried out in specific villages indicate that the bulk of remittances are spent on consumption. Study after study conducted throughout the world confirms that money earned through foreign labour is targeted overwhelmingly to housing, the purchase of other real property, and family maintenance, leaving little money available for productive investment. This, at least, is the consensus view of scholars who have examined the issue to this point.

Rempel and Lobdell (1978), reporting on a survey of fifty remittance-use studies for the International Labour Office, concluded that 'most of the money remitted is used for increased consumption, education, and better housing.' Lipton (1980) likewise concluded that investment is a low-priority use of remittances in migrant-sending villages and that 'everyday [consumption] needs often absorb 90 per cent or more of a village's remittances.' One study cited in Chandavarkar (1980: 39) concluded that remittances are 'frittered away in personal consumption, social ceremonies, real estate, and price-escalating trading.'

Most of the studies reviewed by the foregoing authors focused on internal migrants, however, who tend to remit smaller portions of their incomes than international migrants. Nonetheless, scattered studies of international migrant-sending communities in Africa and the Middle East generally support these pessimistic conclusions. Village surveys administered in Egypt (Adams 1991a, 1991b; Amin and Awny 1985), Turkey (Kaysar 1972; Abadan-Unat et al. 1975; Toepfer 1985), and Yemen (Swanson 1979a, 1979b) all show that international remittances are spent on consumption rather than production; and similar findings emerge from sub-Saharan Africa (see Bohning 1981; Adepoju 1988; Russell et al. 1990). For example, Condé et al. (1983) found that 89 per cent of remittances sent by Sahelian migrants to France were spent on basic necessities such as food, clothing, toiletries, and the payment of taxes; and Abdulla Ali (1981) found that housing was a primary spending target among emigrants from villages in Sudan.

Comparable patterns of remittance use are reported in continents as diverse as Europe and Asia. Rhoades (1978, 1979) estimated that 65 per cent of remittances to the Spanish town of Alcudia went to housing, luxury goods, or some other form of consumption; and in the Western Samoan town of Saasi, Shankman (1976: 63) reported that 'most remittances were not used for capital investment.... Rather, they went into *security* investments, such as houses, small-scale luxury consumption, and redistribution within the Samoan status system, including church donations.' The same story is repeated in Thailand (Mills 1993), India (Helweg 1983), and the Philippines, where McArthur (1979: 93) notes that 'nothing stands out more against the relative poverty of most Ilocos region towns and barrios than the brightly painted "luxury" houses of the pensionados (returned migrants)', which are filled with 'stereo sets, electric refrigerators, televisions, vans, and gas stoves, etc'.

Similar patterns of spending are observed in the Americas. Dandler and Medeiros (1988) studied households in the Bolivian town of Cochabamba and found that 81 per cent of those receiving remittances from Argentina used the money for housing or daily living expenses. In their review of community studies from the Caribbean, Brana-Shute and Brana-Shute (1982: 280) concluded that 'because neither the magnitude nor the actual uses of remittances have been the primary object of study, it is very difficult to assess the impact remittances have had on the region', but judging from qualitative impressions and reports, spending on consumer goods, real estate, and housing appears to use up most of the funds remitted by emigrants from St Vincent (Rubenstein 1976, 1979, 1982), Grenada (Hill 1977), Nevis (Frucht 1968), and Monteserrat (Philpott 1973).

More precise quantitative data were gathered on remittances sent to the Dominican Republic. In their review of findings from seven communities, Ferrán and Pessar (1991) concluded that 'remittances appear to have encouraged migrant farming households to reduce or abandon agricultural activity altogether.' In the Dominican towns of Los Pinos and El Guano, Georges (1990) reports that remittances went primarily to paying the expenses of daily living, and that the rest were targeted to housing, the repayment of loans, and luxury consumption. In the community of Santiago, Grasmuck and Pessar (1991) found that remittances enabled migrants to elevate their standard of living through the purchase of housing and consumer goods.

Mexico provides the richest and most extensive collection of field studies of international migration and remittance use. A survey of thirty-seven community studies by Durand and Massey (1992: 25) found that they 'are remarkably unanimous in condemning international migration as a palliative that improves the material well-being of particular families without leading to sustained economic growth within migrant communities.' As a result, ethnographers generally refer to Mexican emigration in starkly negative terms. Reichert (1981) calls Mexico–USA migration an 'illness' or 'syndrome' that undermines local development; Weist (1979) calls it an 'addiction'; and Stuart and Kearney (1981) characterize it as a 'dangerous dependence'.

These conclusions are typically based on the finding that US earnings are spent primarily on 'non-productive' ends: basic needs, home remodelling or construction, and the purchase of consumer goods. In the town of Huecorio, Michoacán, Dinerman (1982) found that 67 per cent of remittances were spent on one of these ends. González and Escobar (1990) report a figure of 93 per cent among migrants from Jalostitlán, Jalisco; and Cornelius (1990) found that 92 per cent of remittances and 66 per cent of savings were spent on consumption in three towns that he surveyed. In their study of four Mexican communities, Massey *et al.* (1987) found that between 68 per cent and 86 per cent of US savings were spent on consumption. Although they do not cite specific figures, similar patterns are reported by Shadow (1979), Wiest (1979, 1984), Reichert (1981), Stuart and Kearney (1981), Mines and DeJanvry (1982), and Fernández (1988).

Village studies from around the world thus replicate the remittance-use patterns discovered in national surveys: foreign earnings are spent primarily on food, clothing, consumer goods, and housing, a fact that has led village-level researchers to conclude that international migration stifles development and promotes dependency (see Swanson 1979*b*; Bohning 1981; Rubenstein 1983; Kearney 1986; Diaz-Briquets 1991; Papademetriou and Martin 1991). During a recent visit by one of the authors to the International Labour Office in Geneva, in fact, an official remarked: 'Migration and development— nobody believes that anymore.'

Despite this harsh judgement, the pessimism prevailing among most field researchers may be unwarranted. Virtually all of the village studies cited above report *some* productive spending, which at times can reach significant levels. In their review of studies carried out in Mexico, for example, Durand and Massey (1992) found that the relative share of migradollars spent on production, although always under 50 per cent, fluctuated considerably from place to place and often reached substantial levels. Remittances enabled many communities to overcome capital constraints to finance public works projects such as parks, churches, schools, electrification, road construction, and sewers (Reichert 1981; Massey *et al.* 1987; Goldring 1990).

Other studies report that remittances have been critical to the capitalization of migrant-owned businesses. Escobar and Martinez, for example, found that 31 per cent of migrants surveyed in Guadalajara used US savings to set up a business. Massey *et al.* (1987), in their survey of the same city, put the figure at 21 per cent; and in a survey of businesses located in three rural Mexican communities, Cornelius (1990) found that 61 per cent were founded with US earnings.

Under the right circumstances, then, a significant percentage of migrant remittances and savings may be devoted to productive enterprises. Durand and Massey (1992: 27) thus took issue with the pessimistic conclusions emanating from earlier work:

Rather than concluding that migration inevitably leads to dependency and a lack of development, it is more appropriate to ask why productive investment occurs in some communities and not in others. In general, a perusal of . . . communities suggests that the highest levels of business formation and investment occur in urban communities, rural communities with access to urban markets, or rural communities with favorable agricultural conditions.

A close examination of community studies from other sending regions reaffirms this conclusion and reveals that a non-trivial and sometimes large portion of migrant remittances may be channelled into productive investment. Griffiths (1979), for example, cites overseas earnings as being instrumental in raising agricultural productivity in a Philippine village, where remittances provided both a source of capital for cash-crop production and a means of acquiring land and ending exploitation by wealthy landlords. Significant productive investment has also been reported in remittance-use studies done in Africa (see Russell *et al.* 1990), including Ghana (Caldwell 1969; Hill 1970), Sudan (Galaleldin 1979; Al-Ghul 1982; Choucri 1985; Young 1987), Lesotho (Mueller, in Palmer 1985), Zambia (Jackman 1973; Chilivumbo 1985), Kenya (Bradshaw 1988; Gould 1988; Hill 1970), Swaziland (Palmer 1985), Malawi (Boeder 1973), Mozambique (Russell 1984), and the Sahel (Findley 1989).

Nonetheless, two obstacles to the effective promotion of development through emigration emerge from a careful reading of the research literature. First, poor public services and infrastructure seriously limit the potential for contributions to local production. Most migrant-sending communities are rural villages distant from natural markets and lacking basic infrastructure such as paved roads, electricity, running water, sewage, and telephones. Many are characterized by poor-quality land, a fragmented tenure system and unequal land distribution. It is unrealistic to expect migration to promote development where complementary infrastructure, services, and ecological conditions are so unfavourable (see Grindle 1988; Durand and Massey 1992). As Georges (1990: 170) put it, people migrate 'because of the lack of meaningful development in the first place. In the absence of policies designed to channel migrants' savings into productive investment, it is naïve to expect migrants to behave very differently.'

The second obstacle is closely related to the first: a lack of well-functioning factor markets (notably, rural credit markets). The absence of such markets means that migrants and their families end up serving as both the procurers of migrant savings and the intermediaries between migration and development. To expect migrants to be proficient at turning savings into production is unrealistic. Migration is likely to have a larger effect on development where local institutions exist to gather savings by migrant households and make them available to local producers—that is, where migrants do not have to play simultaneous roles as workers, savers, investors, and producers.

These limitations have been noted by other researchers. Van Dijk (1978: 9), for example, states that migrants are 'not indisputably the most appropriate agents for contending . . . with underdevelopment', and notes 'how negligibly the social and economic *structure* of under-developed regions [in Turkey, Tunisia and Morocco] has been affected by two decades of international labour migration.' He blames this outcome on the lack of complementary government investment rather than the deficiencies of the migrants themselves.

Likewise, Stahl and Habib (1991: 177), in their review of emigration from four South and South-East Asian countries, note that:

[I]f certain conditions exist, for example, that a country's economic structure is relatively diverse, that it has an adequate supply of labor, and that there is a financial system capable of mopping up small amounts of savings from a wide variety of sources and channeling them to businesses willing and able to respond to a rising demand for their output, then remittances will promote economic growth as should any other external stimulus to the economy. In the absence of these conditions, neither remittances nor any other stimulus will be of much value to . . . development.

One important reason for the pessimism that characterizes most community studies is the lack of a good theoretical yardstick to measure the effects of migration on economic growth. Village studies universally confuse consumption with the non-productive use of remittances, ignoring the extensive and potentially large economic linkages that remittances create in local economies. They also tend to confound remittance use with the effect of remittances on family expenditures; and many studies employ a rather limited definition of 'productive investments', restricting them to investments in equipment while ignoring productive spending on livestock, schooling, housing, and land.

Finally, as in many country case studies, village-level analyses use remarkably narrow criteria to determine whether or not migration has, in fact, promoted development. Frequently they require migration to set in motion a self-sustaining process of economic development that would be unaffected if remittances were suddenly cut off. At no level of analysis—national, regional, town, household, or individual—is such a severe criterion for development appropriate, even in relatively wealthy, developed countries.

A fundamental problem is that complex interactions between migration and development lie outside the purview of remittance-use studies. Findings from remittance-use studies, whether optimistic or pessimistic, simply do not constitute a test for the full range of effects that remittances have on economic behaviour within families and communities. Testing for such influences requires assessing how remittances influence the propensity of families to invest, not a description of how the remittances were spent. Understanding the complex relationship between migration and development requires new theories about the multiple ways that remittances interact with and influence the economic status of households and communities.

The New Economics of Labour Migration

Stark (1978) injected new theoretical life into research on international migration and development by viewing migration in the context of household economic relationships, and by placing the household in the context of the imperfect credit and risk markets that characterize migrant-sending areas in the developing world. Subsequent theoretical and empirical research has elucidated and tested new hypotheses about migration and development that are implicit in, or that emerge from, this view. The new economics of labour migration marks a fundamental shift in the way that the connection between migration and development is conceptualized and modelled.

Earlier research generally decoupled the determinants of migration from the effects of migration on sending areas; but in the new economics, migration is hypothesized to originate in the desire to overcome market failures that constrain local production. This theoretical viewpoint implies that migration positively influences production in sending areas, as remittances and implicit-risk contracts within families enable households to overcome market failures. This perspective yields propositions about the interrelation of migration and development that go well beyond the purview of neoclassical economics, and these views have inspired better-designed surveys to test for the complex and often indirect means by which migration influences economic growth.

The fundamental view of the new economics of labour migration is presented in Stark (1980), who expounds migration's role as an intermediate investment that facilitates the transition from familial to commercial production. It performs this role by providing rural households with capital and a means to reduce risk by diversifying income sources. Lacking access to credit and income insurance outside the household, households self-finance new production methods and self-insure against perceived risks to household income by investing in the migration of one or more family members.

Stark and Katz (1986) formalized the argument that rural–urban migration, a labour-market phenomenon, is caused by imperfections in capital markets. Stark and Lucas (1988) offer theoretical and empirical evidence from Botswana to show that remittances are part of a self-enforcing contractual arrangement between families and migrants, shifting the focus of migration theory away from individual independence (as in the Todaro model) to mutual interdependence (as the Stark formulation).

Stark and Levhari (1982) use a graphical presentation to argue that migration is a means to spread risk, rather than being a manifestation of risk-taking behaviour on the part of migrants. Stark's research with Rosenzweig (1989) and Lucas (1985) provide econometric evidence, using household data from rural India and Botswana, that families insure themselves against risk by placing members in labour markets outside their village, where incomes are not positively correlated with local farm incomes. These 'migration and development' hypotheses are equally applicable, if not more so, to the context of international migration.

In the new economics of labour migration, emigration can have several distinct effects on income within migrant households. First, as in the old economics of migration, there is a lost-labour effect: the household sacrifices the marginal product of the departed migrant in the local labour market. Once the migrant is established at his or her destination and begins sending home money, however, these remittances have a range of direct and indirect effects on household income.

The money remitted after paying migration costs and covering the lost marginal product of the departed migrant (minus subsistence costs at home) contributes directly to household income. By relieving financial constraints on household production activities and providing a means to insure against income risks, however, migration also produces a host of indirect effects. The importance of these indirect effects depends on the extent to which risk and lack of capital constrain local production in the absence of migration. If families do not face binding liquidity and risk constraints, then the indirect effects of migration on household income will be minimal and the family will have less incentive to engage in migration by sending members abroad. If credit and risk constraints are binding, however, families' incentives to send migrants abroad to gain access to liquidity and income security will be stronger, and the subsequent indirect effects on family incomes may be quite large (Taylor and Wyatt, 1996). The size and direction of the net effects on household income, however, are indeterminant a priori.

In order to test the Stark formulation, Lucas (1987) uses aggregate time-series data on migration to the Union of South Africa from five African sending nations. His econometric analysis finds that, initially, the lost-labour effects of emigration are large: output in migrant-sending households falls as labour is withdrawn from farm production. In the long run, however, productivity increases for two reasons. First, migrant remittances are invested in production at home, loosening financial constraints on productivity-enhancing ventures and yielding a higher output. Second, migration diversifies the sources of income and encourages risk-averse households to undertake unproven, but potentially productive, investments.

Consistent with these predictions, Adams (1991b) finds that rural Egyptian households containing foreign migrants have a higher marginal propensity to invest than do their non-migrant counterparts. Migration thus has a positive effect on investment that is independent of its contribution to total household income. Policy biases against agriculture, however, discourage agricultural investments in favour of land purchases, yielding the remittance-use pattern frequently observed in community studies.

Taylor (1992) estimated the marginal effect of migrant remittances on farm income and asset accumulation using data from households interviewed at two points in time in rural Mexico. Initially (in 1982), the marginal effect of remittances on household income was less than unity—that is, a $1 increase in remittances produced less than a $1 increase in total income within remittance-receiving households—an effect that is consistent with the hypothesis that the marginal product of migrant labour is positive prior to migration.

In a later period (1988), however, the marginal impact of remittances on total income was greater than unity: a $1 increase in remittances brought a

$1.85 increase in total household income. This finding suggests that remittances loosen constraints on local production, once migrants become established abroad. In the Mexican case, Taylor (1992) also found that remittances promoted the accumulation of livestock over time and increased the rate of return to livestock assets (through complementary investments). Moreover, subsequent research using these data showed that the marginal income effect of remittances was greatest in the most liquidity-constrained households (Taylor and Wyatt, forthcoming).

These studies, while offering micro-level econometric evidence in support of the new economics of labour migration, also suggest that the relationship between migration and development is not invariant over time or across settings. Over time there appears to be a pattern first of negative and then of positive effects of migration on non-remittance income in sending households. Across settings, the extent of the positive effect depends on the profitably of investments in new production activities, which in turn depend on other local conditions.

In Taylor's rural Mexican communities, livestock production proved to be a viable income-generating activity because pasture land was available, transportation links were relatively well developed, and marketing facilities were accessible. Once households were able to overcome the constraint of having limited resources to invest in livestock herds, the potential for economic growth and development was quite large. In other communities, however, profitable investment opportunities in cattle-raising were limited by environmental conditions, market constraints, and government policies that structured the terms of trade against agricultural production.

Thus, government policies represent a vital link between migration and development. Compared with the neoclassical model posited by Todaro and others (or the dependency model of Frank and others), the new economics of labour migration developed by Stark and his successors leads to a radically different set of policy prescriptions to reduce emigration. Rather than intervening directly in labour markets, governments that wish to reduce out-migration should attempt to correct failures in local capital and risk markets, thereby offering households credit and insurance alternatives to migration. In the new economic model, failures in credit and risk markets, not a low equilibrium wage in the migrant-sending labour market, are the fundamental cause of international migration.

Microeconomy-wide Evidence

Providing migrant households with liquidity and income security that will enable them to invest in new technologies and production activities is an indirect, first-round effect of emigration. It is indirect in the sense that it occurs in addition to the contribution that remittances make to household incomes. It is a first-round effect because it concerns only those households that have migrants; it is one of migration's initial effects on incomes in migrant-sending areas.

Remittances, like other injections of income from outside an economy, also generate second-round effects, as expenditures by migrant-sending households stimulate economic activities in other households. If local (usually informal) credit markets exist, remittances may also generate growth linkages by providing liquidity, as when migrant households make loans to non-migrant households. Economy-wide modelling techniques are required to explore the direct and indirect effects of such exogenous shocks, taking into account the complex income and investment linkages that typically exist among households in a community. The first model able to estimate income and investment multipliers for a migrant-sending community was that developed by Adelman, *et al.* (1988) for a rural Mexican village.

These investigators found that $1 of international migrant remittances generated $1.78 in additional village income, or 78 cents worth of second-round effects. The additional income was created by expenditures from remittance-receiving households, which generated demand for locally produced goods and services, bolstering the incomes of others in the village. They also found that remittances created new rural–urban growth linkages by increasing the demand for manufactured goods produced in Mexican cities. They also stimulated investments in physical capital and schooling (by $0.25 and $0.13 per dollar of remittances, respectively) among both migrant and non-migrant households.

The Adelman *et al.* model is an income multiplier model that does not take into account local wage and price effects reflecting competition between migration and local activities over scarce family resources. A new generation of village models, using computable general-equilibrium (CGE) methods (Taylor and Adelman 1996), probably offers a more realistic (and sanguine) view of migration–development interactions.

The short-run income effects (income elasticities) of internal migrant remittances, estimated from CGE models of communities in Mexico, Java, and Kenya, are reported in Table 9.1. These estimates take into account the income linkages among households and also price effects, but they ignore the long-run effects that remittances may have on income by stimulating productive investments in migrant-sending communities. As can be seen, a 1 per cent change in international migrant remittances yields a 0.3 per cent change in total income in the Mexican village, a 0.4 per cent change in income in the Kenyan community, and a smaller (0.03) percentage income change in the Javanese village. The shares of international migrant remittances in total household income for the three communities were 0.19, 0.11, and 0.10, respectively. A comparison of income elasticities with remittance shares reveals that the general equilibrium effects of migration and remittances on income from

Table 9.1 Short-run percentage effects of a 1 per cent change in international migrant remittances on total household incomes (remittance elasticities of income) in selected village-wide models

| | Village study site | | |
	Mexico	Kenya	Java
By socio-economic group			
Subsistence farmer	0.20	0.69	−0.02
Medium Landholder	0.44	n/a	−0.02
Large Landholder	0.17	0.33	0.12
Non-farm worker	n/a	0.47	n/a
TOTAL	0.30	0.43	0.03
Income share of international migrant remittances	0.19	0.11	0.10

Source: Taylor (1996).

local production are positive in the Mexican and Kenyan case but negative in the Javanese case.

When the data are broken down by socio-economic group, the Mexican and Kenyan data suggest that subsistence, medium-holder and (in the Kenyan case) non-farm households benefit the most in percentage terms from international migrant remittances. The findings are different for Java, however. Here, the village economy is highly commercialized, labour is relatively scarce, and most of the benefits from international migration flow to large-holder households. In this village, the higher wages that result from the loss of labour to international migration reduce local employment opportunities and adversely affect both subsistence and medium-holder incomes.

In all three villages, migration competes with local production for scarce family resources, and in the short run provides some evidence of a 'migrant syndrome' in which community production reorganizes itself around migration. These findings, however, incorporate only the short-term effects of migration through remittances and lost labour, not the long-term effects of migration on financial and risk constraints faced by community households. Because of this omission, the income elasticities shown in the table represent lower-bound estimates of how migration and remittances influence community incomes.

In the long run, remittance-induced investments may magnify the positive effects of migration on community income. The positive investment effects of migration can be estimated using a two-period community CGE model, in which migration in period 1 stimulates investment that, in turn, increases productive capital available in period 2. Income elasticities from period-2

Table 9.2   Long-run[a] percentage effects of a 1 per cent change in international migrant remittances on total household incomes (remittance elasticities of income) in selected village-wide models

	Village study site		
	Mexico	Kenya	Java
By socio-economic group			
Subsistence farmers	0.22	0.95	0.00
Medium Landholder	0.47	n/a	−0.01
Large holder	0.20	0.62	0.12
Non-farm workers	n/a	0.73	n/a
TOTAL	0.33	0.71	0.04

[a]Taking into account the effects of remittances on income-generating investments in a 2-period model.
Source: Taylor (1996).

CGE models for the Mexican, Kenyan, and Javan communities are presented in Table 9.2. The long-run investment effects of migrant remittances raise the income elasticity by 10 per cent (from 0.30 to 0.33) in Mexico, by one-third (from 0.03 to 0.04) in Java, and by nearly two-thirds (from 0.43 to 0.71) in Kenya. They also dampen or reverse the negative effect of migration on local production in most cases (Taylor 1996). Both the household and regional effects of migration depend, however, on how remittances, and the losses and gains of human resources through out-migration, are distributed across households, on the existence of non-tradable consumer and investment goods in the migrant-sending economy, and on production constraints in different households (Taylor 1995, 1996).

In general, migration is likely to have the largest positive effect on household income and economic production when the losses of human resources from out-migration are small; when the benefits of migration accrue disproportionately to households that face the greatest initial constraints to local production; and when households that receive remittances have expenditure patterns that produce the largest local income multipliers.

Migration and Inequality

A number of researchers have examined the distributional effects of migrant remittances by comparing income distributions with and without remittances (Oberai and Singh 1980; Knowles and Anker 1981) or by using income-source decompositions of inequality measures (Stark *et al.* 1986, 1988; Adams 1989,

1991*a*; Adams and Alderman 1992). These studies offer conflicting findings about the effect of remittances on income distribution.

Stark *et al.* (1986) provide a theoretical explanation for these conflicting findings. They argue that migration, like the adoption of a new production technology, initially entails high costs and risks. The costs and risks are likely to be especially high in the case of international migration. Given this fact, pioneer migrants tend to come from households at the upper-middle or top of the sending-area's income distribution (see Portes 1979; Portes and Rumbaut 1990), and the income sent home in the form of remittances is therefore likely to widen income inequalities.

This initial unequalizing effect of remittances is dampened or reversed over time as access to migrant labour markets becomes diffused across sending-area households through the growth and elaboration of migrant networks (see Massey *et al.* 1994). Thus, Stark *et al.* (1988) found that migrant remittances had an unequalizing effect on the income distribution in a Mexican village that recently had begun to send migrants to the USA, but an equalizing effect on another village that had a long history of participating in Mexico-to-USA migration.

Taylor (1992) extended this analysis by taking into account the indirect effects of international migration on income and asset accumulation over time. He provides longitudinal evidence in support of the Stark *et al.* hypothesis. Lost-labour effects tend to dampen the unequalizing effects of remittances in the short run, but the positive indirect effects of migration on household income in poorer families (achieved by loosening capital and risk constraints on local production) make migration more of an income equalizer in the long run.

Over time, the indirect effects of migration on both income and inequality become increasingly important. If the Stark *et al.* hypothesis is correct, then we would expect poorer households to have the largest capital and risk constraints on investments in local income-generating activities, and therefore, the largest incentives to place migrants abroad as 'financial intermediaries' to facilitate the tasks of risk management and capital acquisition, other things being equal. Initially, however, barriers to international migration in the form of high costs, poor information, and uncertainty discourage poor households from sending their family members to labour abroad.

Stark *et al.* (1988) find evidence of such barriers in the Mexican case. As these barriers to international migration fall with the expansion of migrant networks, however, the benefits of international migration flow increasingly to the households that are most capital- and risk-constrained (i.e. lower-income households). If these households invest in local income-generating activities, then indirect income effects should reinforce the increasingly favourable direct impacts of remittances on sending-area income distributions.

This expectation is consistent with Taylor's (1992) and Taylor and Wyatt's (forthcoming) findings. The importance of income inequalities in stimulating emigration also has been documented (Stark and Taylor 1989, 1991). Although hypotheses about migration, development, and income inequality to date have been developed and tested for rural migrant-sending areas, they are just as applicable to urban areas, which have increasingly become the staging ground for international migration (Cornelius 1992).

Selectivity of International Migration

The indirect effects of emigration on income in migrant-sending communities underscore the importance of understanding the selective nature of international migration. As mentioned earlier, social science research on the determinants of migration using household-level data generally find that human capital variables (education, past migration experience) are positively related to the likelihood of out-migration (see Yap 1977). This finding suggests that migrants take (human) capital with them when they migrate, possibly with detrimental effects on the productivity of workers left behind.

Recent research suggests two qualifications to this conclusion, however. First, while schooling is positively related to the likelihood of internal migration, it is not always positively related to the odds of international migration. Studies of migrants and non-migrants in rural Mexico reveal that education is positively related to rural-to-urban migration but not to international migration (Taylor 1986; Massey 1987; Massey and García España 1987; Stark and Taylor 1991; Massey *et al.* 1996; Massey and Espinosa 1997). This result occurs because the economic returns to schooling are high for migrants within Mexico, but low in both the village and among illegal migrants to the USA (Taylor 1987). No matter how much education they have received in Mexico, without documents migrants are confined to the same poorly paid jobs in the USA.

Second, extensive research by Massey and colleagues (Massey *et al.* 1987, 1994) reveals that, although socio-economic differences between migrants and non-migrants are significant initially, these differences narrow as networks of family contacts at migrant destinations expand and the psychological and economic costs and risks of migration are progressively reduced. This finding is similar to the finding in the technology adoption literature that differences in farm size and other socio-economic variables become less significant over time in explaining adoption behaviour. Migration may be viewed as the adoption of a new 'labour-market technology', which becomes accessible to an increasingly broad segment of individuals and households over time. Econometric findings reported by Taylor (1987) do not support the hypothesis that rural Mexicans who migrate to the USA would be more productive working in the local economy than those who stay behind. However, they do have significantly better 'migration capital', or contacts and past experience at migrant destinations, than non-migrants (see also Massey and Espinosa 1997).

These findings suggest that if international migration selects individuals, positively or negatively, on the basis of human capital variables, it does so less and less over time. If this is the case, then the extent to which studies discover lost-labour effects of international migration may depend entirely on the stage of the migration process at which they are carried out.

Individual migrants and their households may experience a remittance-and-development life-cycle, as well. Initially, remittances may be low or negative (that is, migrants may receive net income assistance from their households of origin until they secure a foothold in the destination economy). This stage may be followed by a period of relatively high remittances, motivated by considerations that have been explored in some detail by Lucas and Stark (1985) and Durand *et al.* (1996). Finally, if migrants decide to settle in the host country or save to establish a household of their own, remittances may fall off (as documented by Massey *et al.* 1987). Perhaps the migrant will begin to play the role of income insurer instead of income supporter for the household of origin, remitting only when unexpected needs arise. In other words, migrant family members may retain an insurance function even if they have ceased remitting regularly to support the household on a day-to-day basis, because they always can be called upon to provide support in an emergency. The shift in remitting strategies may be possible because earlier remittances have enabled the household to invest in a sustainable local income base, or because other family members (for example, younger siblings) take over the migrant's income-supplementing role.

The impact of migration and remittances on local incomes also may change over time. If credit and risk constraints on local production motivate families to send migrants abroad to overcome these constraints, as Stark (1982) has argued, then as migration enables families to invest in income-producing assets, the conditions that originally motivated migration change. As constraints on local production activities diminish, so too will migration's indirect effects on household income; and if migration drains labour and human capital out of the local labour market, it may exacerbate human-resource constraints on local income growth, including the production–leisure trade-off in migrant households. In return, however, the productivity of non-migrants may increase, as econometric findings by Lucas (1987) and Taylor (1992) suggest.

On the other hand, if migrants return home intermittently or, after a time, permanently, and if migrants' experience and skills obtained abroad make them more productive at home, international migration may contribute to human capital accumulation in migrant-sending societies. It also may have a favourable effect on the human-resource base if it enables households to invest in schooling. The impact of migration on local income depends on both the liquidity and insurance that migration offers households and the efficiency with which family resources are put to use to create local income.

Although the sending-country governments' enthusiasm about the potential of guestworker programmes to contribute to worker skills through return migration has generally fizzled, there is some microeconomic evidence that migration promotes schooling investment, and that return migrants are more productive than individuals who lack international work experience (controlling for the self-selection of migrants, of course—see Stark and Taylor 1991).

Migration and Community Development Reconsidered

Our review has clearly established that interactions between migration and community development are multifaceted and complex. Here and in the prior chapter, we showed how migration can influence the economic status of nations, communities, and households through a variety of direct and indirect channels. For most of the past two decades, however, theory has been inadequate to the task of identifying and understanding the multiple means by which international migration influences economic development.

Partly as a result of this theoretical underdevelopment, the data gathered to assess the relationship between migration and community development have been seriously deficient. Whereas international migration influences economic conditions in migrant-sending communities and households through complicated channels whose importance and effects vary across time, the data that have been collected have focused only on the most direct influences at single points in time, and very often the information gathered has been quite impressionistic and filtered through one or another ideological lens.

Because neither theory nor data have been up to the task of evaluating migration's effects on economic development, and have largely asked and answered the wrong questions, we believe the prevailing view is unduly pessimistic and harsh. Whereas the consensus view emanating from intensive community ethnographies (at least from those done in the European, North American, and South American systems) is that migration undermines the prospects for local economic development and yields a state of stagnation and dependency, these assessments typically fail to appreciate the more complex, indirect ways that migration influences the sending community's economy, and they do not account for the constraints on local development produced by ill-founded government policies.

When more advanced econometric methods are used at the community level to model and then measure the direct and indirect effects of migration on development, a very different and much more optimistic picture emerges. By incorporating recent theoretical advances, surveying newer and better data, and controlling for structural impediments to growth, our review of the extensive literature that has grown up around the issue of migration and community development yields several conclusions that stand in sharp contrast to the pessimistic tone of earlier work.

First, although the loss of labour through international migration may indirectly lower household incomes, suggesting that the marginal productivity of emigrant labour is positive, other indirect effects of emigration may be even more important. Remittances from international labour migration loosen financial and risk constraints on local production and thereby play an important role promoting economic growth and development. The balance of negative lost-labour effects and positive remittance effects also tends to change over time, being negative initially but becoming positive as investment within migrant households yields new sources of income.

Second, income and employment multipliers from remittances are quite high, and many of the indirect benefits do not accrue to migrant households themselves, but to others who provide them with goods and services that would not be consumed in the absence of international migration. This finding stands in stark contrast to the negative conclusions of village case studies that tend to emphasize lost-labour effects and to judge the effects of migration against rather lofty and unrealistic expectations. These studies show that migrant remittances are rarely invested in productive activities, but they take a very narrow view of what constitutes 'productive' and ignore the indirect, second-round effects on household incomes and employment. Few researchers have attempted to estimate remittance multipliers, but those who have generally find strong positive effects of migration on employment, income, and production.

Third, labour exports are neither a panacea nor a substitute for sound development policy. As best, they, like other exports, can be a useful component of community development strategies in labour-abundant countries where the opportunity cost of exporting workers abroad is relatively low and the potential gain from remittances is quite high. If foreign exchange and savings are not available from other sources, it may make sense for governments in developing countries to invest in providing a labour-export pool with skills for which there is a high return abroad, and then creating arrangements and incentives for migrants to repatriate their earnings in the form of remittances and savings.

Fourth, and most important, schemes to harness international migrant remittances for local development are destined to fail if governments do not create an economic environment that is conducive to investment in productive activities at home. Land, housing, and other speculative investments, for which migrant families have been much criticized, are a rational response to the uncertain, inflationary environments created by misguided macroeconomic policies and sectoral policies that discriminate against small-scale production within the reach of migrant families. These policies discourage productive investments not only by migrants but also by non-migrants, including people who benefit by selling real assets to migrant families at inflated prices.

In light of these considerations, one of the best ways for a country to promote community development through migration is to get its economic house in order, and to finance public works and infrastructure that will ensure a high return to investments made by migrants in their home communities. Without these changes, the establishment of village cooperatives, workers' companies, special banks, or other local schemes designed to channel foreign earnings into productive enterprises are likely to fail, and diatribes by academics and policy-makers against migrants for their profligate and unproductive ways are likely to persist.

10 Conclusions for the Next Century

The foregoing chapters have laid the groundwork for a larger and more important task: building a conceptually accurate and empirically valid theoretical model to explain the emergence of international migration worldwide in the late twentieth century. Prior to the Second World War, world migration flows were dominated by Europeans. Mass emigration began in the British Isles with the Industrial Revolution and moved south and east across the Continent as industrialism spread. The vast majority of emigrants went to one of five frontier societies that were themselves in the throes of rapid economic development: the USA, Canada, Argentina, Brazil, or Australia. The massive out-migration of Europeans ended during the Great Depression of the 1930s, and a revival of significant international movement was largely precluded during the 1940s by the hostilities of the Second World War.

New origin and destination countries emerged after 1950 to yield entirely new international migration systems. Canada and the USA formed the core of a new North American system that attracted migrants not from Europe, but from Asia, Latin America, and the Caribbean. Europe, meanwhile, gradually shifted from the exportation to the importation of labour, a transformation that began in Britain and Germany shortly after 1950 and ended in Spain, Italy, and Portugal during the mid-1970s, yielding a well-defined system structure that by the 1990s connected Western Europe to source countries in Eastern Europe, the Middle East, Africa, and Asia.

The rapid accumulation of capital in oil-exporting countries of the Middle East after 1973 led to a massive investment in infrastructure that required the importation of labour on a grand scale. With a few years, the Gulf States had joined the ranks of immigrant-receiving nations to form the core of an international migration system that steadily expanded its geographic reach away from sources in the Middle East towards the Indian subcontinent, East Asia, and South-East Asia. By the 1990s most migrants into the Gulf region were from Asia rather than the Middle East.

During the 1980s, Japan and the newly industrialized countries of Singapore, Taiwan, Hong Kong, South Korea, and Malaysia underwent a rapid shift from the exportation to the importation of labour, pulling in workers from poorer countries throughout Asia and the Pacific. In Australia, long a country of immigration, the number of immigrants did not change so much as their origins, which shifted decisively from Europe to Asia and the Pacific. By the 1990s, the outlines of a new, multipolar migration system with four receiving nodes had assumed nascent form in Asia and the Pacific, as Australia, Japan, the East

Asian NICs (Hong Kong, Taiwan, and South Korea) and the South-East Asian NICs (Singapore and Malaysia) imported a large and growing number of immigrants and migrant workers in various legal categories.

In South America, Brazil ceased being a country of immigration during the 1970s and began to export people to North America. After experiencing large-scale immigration financed by oil revenues during the 1950s and 1970s, Venezuela's oil bust of the 1980s brought a halt to its immigration boom. As of the early 1990s, only one nation on the South American continent—Argentina—had experienced a consistent history of in-migration throughout the post-war era. Rather than coming from Southern Europe, the principal source region for Argentinian immigrants before 1950, the new immigrants came overwhelmingly from the neighbouring states of Paraguay, Chile, Bolivia, and Uruguay, yielding a compact regional subsystem.

In this book we have sought to understand the forces responsible for the emergence of these migration systems in the latter half of the twentieth century by undertaking a comprehensive survey of migration theory and research. We began by evaluating theories formulated in several disciplines to explain the *initiation* of international migration—neoclassical economics, the new economics of labour migration, segmented labour market theory, and world systems theory—and then surveyed models put forth to account for the *perpetuation* of migration across space and time—social capital theory and the theory of cumulative causation.

Our review uncovered few propositions in these models that were inherently contradictory. On purely deductive grounds, the various theories were neither logically inconsistent nor mutually exclusive; all could be true simultaneously and none could be dismissed a priori. Given their logical compatibility, the only way to distinguish between them became empirical: which theoretical propositions were most consistent with the accumulated evidence, and which seemed to be most efficacious in accounting for trends and patterns of international migration throughout the world?

To answer these questions we undertook a systematic evaluation of empirical research on international migration into North America, Western Europe, the Gulf States, the four nodes of the Asia Pacific region, and South America. We began by characterizing each system empirically using data from the 1980s, and then surveyed available studies methodically to evaluate propositions associated with each theory. Following this system-by-system evaluation, we considered the issue of migration and development in two additional chapters: one reviewing studies at the national level, and the other surveying research done at the community level. Together, these seven chapters yield an extensive bibliography and a comprehensive base of knowledge that leaves us in a good position to generalize about the forces that are responsible for initiating and perpetuating international migration throughout the world today.

Why International Migration? A Theoretical Synthesis

Our review of research from around the world suggests that international migration originates in the social, economic, and political transformations that accompany the penetration of capitalist markets into non-market or pre-market societies (as hypothesized under world systems theory). In the context of a globalizing economy, the entry of markets and capital-intensive production technologies into peripheral regions disrupts existing social and economic arrangements and brings about a widespread displacement of people from customary livelihoods, creating a mobile population of workers who actively search for new ways of achieving economic sustenance. Studies consistently show that international migrants do not come from poor, isolated places that are disconnected from world markets, but from regions and nations that are undergoing rapid change and development as a result of their incorporation into global trade, information, and production networks. In the short run, international migration does not stem from a lack of economic development, but from development itself.

One means by which people displaced from traditional livelihoods seek to assure their economic well-being is by selling their services on emerging national and international labour markets (neoclassical economics). Because wages are generally higher in urban than in rural areas, much of this process of labour commodification is expressed in the form of rural-to-urban migration. This movement occurs even when the probability of obtaining an urban job is low, because when multiplied by high urban wages the low employment probabilities yield expected incomes above those prevailing in rural areas, where wages and employment are both low. According to the neoclassical model, if the difference between incomes expected in urban and rural sectors exceeds the costs of movement between them, as is typical, people migrate to cities to reap higher lifetime earnings.

Wages are even higher, of course, in developed countries overseas, and the larger size of these international wage differentials inevitably prompts some people displaced in the course of economic development to offer their services on international labour markets by moving abroad for work. Whenever researchers have examined the empirical connection between wages in receiving nations and emigration from sending nations, they have found a significant positive correlation.

Despite the reliability of this association, however, international wage differentials are not the only factor motivating people to migrate, or even the most important. Our review of empirical evidence suggests that people displaced in the course of economic growth do not move simply to reap higher lifetime earnings by relocating permanently to a foreign setting (although some clearly do). Rather, households struggling to cope with the jarring transformations of early economic development also use international migration as a means of overcoming market failures that threaten their material well-being (the new economics of labour migration).

In most developing countries, labour markets—both rural and urban—are volatile, characterized by wide oscillations and structural limitations that render them unable to absorb streams of workers being displaced from pre-capitalist or non-capitalist sectors. Since national insurance markets are rudimentary and government unemployment insurance programmes are limited or non-existent, households cannot adequately protect themselves from risks to their well-being stemming from under-employment or unemployment. Thus, the lack of access to unemployment insurance creates an incentive for families to self-insure by sending one or more members overseas for work. By allocating members to different labour markets in multiple geographic regions—rural, urban, and foreign—a household can diversify its labour portfolio and reduce risks to income, as long as conditions in the various labour markets are weakly or negatively correlated.

Household members who remain behind to participate in the ongoing structural transformation of agriculture, meanwhile, generally lack access to insurance markets for crops and futures. As households shift from subsistence to commercial farming, they are forced to adopt new production methods that make use of untested technologies, unfamiliar crops, and untried inputs. As they plunge into the unknown world of capitalist production, the lack of insurance or futures markets leaves them vulnerable to economic disaster should these new methods fail, providing yet another incentive for families to self-insure against risk through international migration. Should crops fail or commodity prices fall precipitously, households with at least one worker employed overseas will not be left without a means of subsistence.

Another failure common to developing countries occurs in capital and consumer credit markets. Families seeking to engage in new forms of agriculture or looking to establish new business enterprises need capital to purchase inputs and begin production. The shift to a market economy also creates new consumer demands for expensive items such as housing, cars, and appliances. The financing of both production and consumption requires cash, but the weak and poorly developed banking industries characteristic of most developing nations cannot meet the demands for loans and credit, giving households one final motivation for international labour migration. By sending a family member temporarily abroad for work, a household can accumulate savings and overcome failures in capital and consumer credit markets by self-financing production or consumption.

Whereas the rational actor posited by neoclassical economics takes advantage of geographic disequilibria in labour markets to move abroad *permanently* to achieve higher lifetime earnings, the rational actor assumed by the new economics of labour migration seeks to cope with failures in insurance, futures, capital, and credit markets by moving overseas *temporarily* to repatriate earnings in the form of regular remittances or lump-sum transfers. In this way they control risk by diversifying sources of income and they self-finance production or consumption by acquiring alternative sources of capital.

Direct empirical contrasts between neoclassical economics and the new economics of labour migration are scarce and confined largely to the North American system (indeed they primarily concern Mexico–USA migration); but wherever they have been carried out, propositions associated with the new economics have proven to be more powerful and efficacious in explaining the migration behaviour of individuals and households. In practice, wage differentials often do not produce international movement, and migration often ceases before wage differentials have disappeared, outcomes that are difficult (though not impossible) to explain under neoclassical assumptions, but which are readily accommodated under the new economics of labour migration. In addition, the massive flows of remittances catalogued around the world (and the uses to which they are put) are anomalous under neoclassical theory, but specifically predicted by the new economics.

In sum, a preponderance of evidence from around the world suggests that wage differentials, the favoured explanatory factor of neoclassical economics, account for some of the historical and temporal variation in international migration, but that failures in capital, credit, futures, and insurance markets, key factors hypothesized by the new economics of labour migration, constitute more powerful causes. In purely theoretical terms, wage differentials are neither necessary nor sufficient for international migration to occur. Even with equal wages across labour markets, people may have an incentive to migrate if other markets are inefficient or poorly developed. In practical terms, however, wage differentials function as a necessary, though still not sufficient, condition for international migration to occur. In general, large-scale international movement is rarely observed in the absence of a wage gap; but the existence of a wage differential still does not guarantee international movement, nor does its absence preclude it.

While the early phases of economic development in poor nations may create a mobile population seeking to earn more money, self-insure against risk, or self-finance production or consumption, post-industrial patterns of economic growth in wealthy nations yield a bifurcation of labour markets. Whereas jobs in the primary sector provide steady work and high pay for native workers, those in the secondary sector offer low pay, little stability, and few opportunities for advancement, repelling natives and generating a structural demand for immigrant workers (segmented labour market theory). The process of labour market bifurcation is most acute in global cities, where a concentration of managerial, administrative, and technical expertise leads to a concentration of wealth and a strong ancillary demand for low-wage services (world systems theory). Unable to attract native workers, employers turn to immigrants and often initiate immigrant flows directly through formal recruitment (segmented labour market theory).

Although instrumental in initiating immigration, recruitment becomes less important over time because the same processes of economic globalization that create mobile populations in developing regions, and which generate a demand for their services in global cities, also create links of transportation, communication, as well as politics and culture, to make the international movement of people possible, even likely (world systems theory). Immigration is promoted by foreign policies and military actions that core capitalist nations undertake to maintain international security, protect foreign investments, and guarantee access to raw materials; these foreign entanglements create links and obligations that generate ancillary flows of refugees, asylees, and military dependants.

Eventually, labour recruitment becomes superfluous, for once begun, immigration displays a strong tendency to continue through the growth and elaboration of migrant networks (social capital theory). The concentration of immigrants in certain destination areas creates a 'family and friends' effect that channels immigrants to the same places and facilitates their arrival and incorporation. If enough migrants arrive under the right conditions, an enclave economy may form, which further augments the demand for immigrant workers (segmented labour market theory).

The spread of migratory behaviour within sending communities sets off ancillary structural changes, shifting distributions of income and land and modifying local cultures in ways that promote additional international movement. Over time, the process of network expansion becomes self-perpetuating because each act of migration creates social infrastructure capable of promoting additional movement (the theory of cumulative causation). As receiving countries implement restrictive policies to counter rising tides of immigrants, they create a lucrative niche into which enterprising agents, contractors, and other middlemen move to create migration-supporting institutions that also serve to connect areas of labour supply and demand for purposes of profit, providing migrants with another resource capable of supporting and sustaining international movement (social capital theory).

During the initial phases of emigration from any sending country, the effects of capitalist penetration, market failure, social networks, and cumulative causation dominate in explaining the flows, but as the level of out-migration reaches high levels and the costs and risks of international movement drop, movement is increasingly determined by international wage differentials (neoclassical economics) and labour demand (segmented labour market theory). As economic growth in sending regions occurs, international wage gaps gradually diminish and well-functioning markets for capital, credit, insurance, and futures come into existence, progressively lowering the incentives for emigration. If these trends continue, the country ultimately becomes integrated into the international economy as a developed, capitalist society, whereupon it undergoes a migration transition: net out-migration progressively ceases and the nation itself becomes an importer of labour.

Migration Theory Reconsidered

As the foregoing synthesis indicates, all theories play some role in accounting for international migration in the contemporary world, although different models predominate at different phases of the migration process, and different explanations carry different weights in different regions depending on the local circumstances of history, politics, and geography. Our review nonetheless suggests the outlines of what an integrated theory of international migration should look like.

It is clear that any satisfactory theoretical account of international migration must contain four basic elements: a treatment of the structural forces that promote emigration from developing countries; a characterization of the structural forces that attract immigrants into developed nations; a consideration of the motivations, goals, and aspirations of the people who respond to these structural forces by becoming international migrants; and a treatment of the social and economic structures that arise to connect areas of out- and in-migration. Any theoretical explanation that embraces just one of these elements will necessarily be incomplete and misleading, and will provide a faulty basis for understanding international migration and developing policies to accommodate it.

Because each theory specified to date focuses on just one or two of these four elements, all are necessary to build a comprehensive, integrated understanding of international migration in the late twentieth century. The leading theoretical treatment of the forces that promote emigration from developing countries is world systems theory. Together, world systems theory, segmented labour market theory, and neoclassical macroeconomics offer explanations for why developed countries attract immigrants. Social capital theory and world systems theory explain how structural links emerge to connect areas of origin and destination. Neoclassical microeconomics and the new economics of labour migration deal with selectivity and the motivations of the people who become international migrants; and the theory of cumulative causation describes how international migration promotes changes in personal motivations and origin, destination, and intervening structures to give immigration a self-perpetuating, dynamic character.

In this seemingly complete theoretical account of the forces that produce and shape international migration, however, two topics have been neglected: population and the State. No critical synthesis of migration theories would be complete without considering the interaction between population growth and international migration; and even though governments may not be able to control fully the powerful forces surrounding international migration fully, state policies clearly have an influence in determining the size and composition of immigration.

International Migration and Population Growth

A demographic-push view of international migration has infused much of the historical literature on immigration. An extensive body of empirical research confirms that an increase in the number of births yields an increase in the rate of emigration fifteen to twenty years later, as the number of labour-force entrants increases by an amount corresponding to the earlier increase in births (see Easterlin 1961; Thomas 1973; Hatton and Williamson 1994a, 1994c). Given this association, population growth is widely regarded as a principal 'cause' of emigration from Europe during the late nineteenth and early twentieth centuries. David Kennedy, for example, argues that Europe's nineteenth-century population boom—in which the continent's population more than doubled—was 'the indispensable precondition for Europe to export people on the scale that it did' (Kennedy 1996: 56).

Kennedy ascribes a similar importance to population growth in contemporary emigration from Latin American and Asian countries, arguing that 'most of the countries now sending large numbers of immigrants to the USA are undergoing the same convulsive demographic and economic disruptions that made migrants out of so many nineteenth-century Europeans: population growth and the relatively early stages of their own industrial revolutions' (Kennedy 1996: 64).

A demographic approach to explaining economically motivated international migration focuses on the migration potential created by gaps between labour-force growth and job creation in countries of origin. The larger the gap, other things being equal, the greater the migration potential. Reynolds (1992), for example, argues that, Mexico's current population growth (and, by extrapolation, its later labour-force growth), combined with the relatively capital-intensive nature of its manufacturing sector, implies that its economy has to grow at the unlikely rate of 7 per cent per year to absorb all new potential entrants into its labour markets.

At the same time, Reynolds estimates that, in order to sustain a 3 per cent rate of economic growth per year, the USA will need between 5 and 15 million more workers than can be supplied from domestic sources, given prevailing rates and patterns of childbearing. The inescapable conclusion, from a strictly demographic viewpoint, is that 'Mexico and the USA need each other.' Espenshade (1989) reached similar conclusions for the Caribbean basin after projecting labour supply and demand throughout the region.

In Asia and the Pacific, patterns of international migration have not only been shaped by structural economic transformations in the region, but by the course of the fertility transition as well. Countries such as South Korea, Taiwan, Hong Kong, Singapore, and Japan experienced a very rapid decline in fertility during the 1970s, reaching rates of childbearing that were below replacement levels by the end of the decade. Accordingly, the size of cohorts entering the labour force in these rapidly developing nations declined each year during the 1990s. The combination of a demographically constricting labour supply and unprecedentedly high economic growth rates created a severe labour shortage and high levels of demand for workers across a range of skill levels. Although this *interaction* of demographic and economic factors in creating a gap between low-wage, labour-surplus countries (such as the Philippines) and high-wage, labour-scarce nations (such as Taiwan) has been little explored, it is no doubt of fundamental importance in understanding the burgeoning of labour migration in the Asia Pacific system.

International migration thus becomes the vital demographic link joining origin and destination economies. Although this demographic perspective is useful in obtaining a 'first-cut' approximation of future potential international migration pressure, however, several caveats are necessary. First, a projected imbalance between labour supply and demand represents a demographic-economic accounting scheme rather than an actual theory of migration. Future labour-force growth is fed by past natural increase, of course; but even if future employment shortfalls are known, it remains a matter of theory to explain how this 'migration potential' manifests itself as actual movement between countries.

In the case explored by Reynolds (1992), for example, no one really knows what a projected shortfall in Mexican employment will mean for Mexico–USA migration ten years down the road. Economic conditions in the USA, circumstances in the North American market, the state of the global economy, Mexican economic performance, US immigration policies, and the expansion of migrant networks are just a few of the factors that could affect how projected demographic pressures are translated into actual movement between the two countries.

Second, correctly projecting future migration potential is far from a trivial exercise. Even though the size of the working-age population can be reliably estimated fifteen years into the future—given that members of this population are already born and mortality trends are fairly predictable—future employment gaps depend on more than population projections: they also depend crucially on labour-force participation rates displayed by various subgroups—men and women, young and old—as well as on future labour demand, all of which are currently unknown and notoriously difficult to predict.

Migration potential is not simply a function of past demographic growth and a set of exogenous economic variables; rather it is a product of complex interactions between population growth, labour-supply decisions, and structural features of migrant-sending and receiving economies. The task of projection is further complicated by the fact that economic development entails profound structural changes in patterns of social, economic, and political organization. Predicting future employment is thus challenging, to say the least.

The prevailing wisdom that migration and trade are substitutes offers a clear case in point. The free trade agreements negotiated or planned in different world regions—NAFTA, MERCOSUR, the EC, the GCC, and APEC—rest on the assumption that freer trade will encourage employment growth in migrant-sending countries, thereby reducing international migration pressures and, in the words of former Mexican president Carlos Salinas de Gortari, enable poor countries to 'export goods and not people'. If free trade agreements dramatically expand labour-intensive manufacturing for export, however, they may substantially alter the employment parameters used to estimate future migration potential.

These considerations hint at a broad conclusion regarding the role of demographic factors in explaining international migration: although they are an essential complement to theories of international migration and key variables to be controlled in testing them, by themselves they are atheoretical and cannot explain or reliably predict international migration. Rapid population growth does not necessarily yield high rates of emigration, nor do low rates inevitably produce low out-migration. To the extent that high past fertility rates produce large current or future cohorts, they will influence the *scale* of the migration that ultimately results from the operation of other social and economic forces described by the theories considered here.

A neoclassical economist using an expected-income model, for example, might argue that demographic variables already are incorporated into the theory. Labour-force growth, *ceteris paribus*, reduces wages (or increases unemployment) in the short run, tipping the scales towards more migration and encouraging a shift to more labour-intensive economic growth in the long run. In this sense, a purely demographic model of migration potential might be regarded as a sort of 'reduced-form' model in which key population–development interactions are not made explicit.

In regressing total out-migration on lagged population growth, therefore, estimated regression coefficients will contain a complex mix of direct and indirect effects, including the influence of demographic growth on the structure of migrant-sending economies. Because variables besides those that are demographic also influence migration outcomes, however, such a simple population–migration equation—the sort usually estimated—is severely underspecified and biased. Although the effects of population growth on international migration are undoubtedly important, caution should be exercised when explicitly incorporating demographic variables into migration models.

Once a researcher has controlled for the effects of other social and economic determinants of migration, the nature of the population's direct effects are not obvious. In neoclassical terms, for example, once the effect of past natural increase on individuals' expected earnings in their home country is removed, what is the rationale for hypothesizing an independent effect of population growth on international migration? We do not rule out such an effect; we only suggest that careful thought must be given to the indirect as well as direct effects of population growth, and to the rationale for modelling the latter.

Another complication arises because researchers modelling internal and international migration almost always treat population growth as exogenous, ignoring the possible feedback effects of migration on fertility. Migration, especially to distant labour markets, entails contact with new societies, almost always with fertility levels significantly below those of migrant-sending areas, and in the case of international labour migration, it often entails separation of spouses for long periods of time. As a result, international migration can, at times, reduce the fertility rate of sending areas (see Massey and Mullan (1984) for an empirical demonstration).

As individuals' migration experience and networks expand, moreover, the opportunity costs of birth and childraising invariably increase. Such an outcome is especially likely when migration opportunities increase for women; but even if husbands migrate alone, women may adopt new economic roles at home, taking over tasks previously performed by males (see Georges 1990; Grasmuck and Pessar 1991; Hongagneu-Sotelo 1992; Kanaiaupuni 1995; Goldring 1996b). If migration by one or more family members increases family incomes in migrant-sending areas, and the perceived value of family time changes as a result of income effects, the family's budget constraint is also reduced (Lindstrom 1995). Although the combined influences of these migration-induced changes in a household fertility model are not entirely clear, we expect them to discourage the rate of childbearing, due to the time-intensity of childraising (see Becker 1981).

In developing-country settings, where children may be parents' most important asset, access to relatively high-paying international migration may also affect the 'investment demand' for children. There is some evidence that higher expected wages for children as young adults encourage fertility (see Rosenzweig and Evenson's (1977) study of fertility and wages in rural India). By extension, if access to migrant labour markets increases parents' future economic returns from having children, raising them, and sending them off to work as migrants, this may increase desired fertility (Stark 1984b). As with the effect of higher interest rates on savings, however, the sign of this migration-asset effect on fertility is ambiguous.

The point of this discussion is not that the effects of demographic variables on international migration are unimportant or unknowable. On the contrary, they are probably very important and are, in principle, estimable. Our purpose is simply to make clear that the effects of demographic factors on international migration are not as simple or unambiguous as often assumed, and that population growth by itself does not constitute a theoretical explanation for international migration. Determining how demographic factors influence emigration requires the a priori specification of a theoretical model capable of identifying which direct, indirect, and feedback effects need to be estimated.

Bringing the State Back In: Migration Policy

Among the theories we have reviewed, surprisingly little attention has been devoted to nation States, their governments, or their policies. Segmented labour market theory considered the State relevant only insofar as it acted on behalf of employers to establish labour-recruitment programmes. World systems theory treated the State primarily as a handmaiden to capitalist interests, working on their behalf to project military and political power to secure the expansion of markets, the acquisition of raw materials, and the guarantee of free trade. Social capital theory mentioned the State only insofar as its use of family reunification criteria in immigrant admissions reinforced the operation of migrant networks. The remaining theoretical paradigms—neoclassical economics, the new economics of labour migration, and the theory of cumulative causation—did not deal directly with the State at all.

In general, therefore, contemporary theories of international migration do not consider the State to be a significant independent actor capable of shaping international migration for its own purposes, or for the purposes of the politicians and bureaucrats who administer it. To the extent that the State is discussed at all, moreover, attention has focused primarily on immigrant-receiving nations; little has been said about the interests and behaviour of governments or politicians in regions of origin. Thus, the role of the State in initiating and promoting (or stopping and preventing) international migration is remarkably under-theorized and little studied.

Although scholars have surveyed national immigration policies (see Kubat 1979; Dib 1988; Cornelius *et al.* 1994; Papdemetriou 1996), conducted case studies of specific state agencies (Calavita 1992), and compiled legislative histories of immigration law in specific countries (Hutchinson 1981), with the recent exception of Meyers (1994), they have not attempted to theorize the behaviour of governments or the actions of politicians themselves. Hypotheses concerning the interests, role, and behaviour of the State constitute a missing link in theories of international migration.

Receiving societies

The lack of theoretical attention paid to the behaviour of political actors in migrant-receiving States is surprising given the salience of immigration as a political issue in developed countries today. When it comes to policy, however, the efforts of immigration scholars have been practical rather than theoretical, focusing on the degree to which specific programmes and procedures might succeed in 'controlling' immigration. Typically the analyst begins with a pre-conceived theoretical paradigm and from its basic premises, which are assumed to be true, derives practical policies to regulate immigrant flows (see Todaro and Maruszko 1987).

For our purposes, immigration control is defined as the ability of a State to import migrants when it wants, where it wants, with the qualities it desires, in numbers it specifies, under conditions it defines, and for durations it chooses. Since 1945, governments in immigrant-receiving States around the world have tried various policy schemes to achieve these desiderata, all with a notable lack of success. When an immigration stream first begins, of course, policy-makers think they are in control: relatively small numbers of immigrants enter; they do so with the acquiescence or support of the State; they go to where jobs are vacant or the government sends them; they have qualities that are desired or at least tolerated by policy-makers and the public (a willingness to work at unpleasant jobs or a nationality that qualifies them as refugees or asylees); they generally occupy a legal status recognized by the State (guestworker, refugee, asylee, trainee); and to citizens and policy makers they appear 'temporary', entering for specific periods to earn set incomes in circumscribed jobs.

In time, however, this impression of control held by policy-makers and the public proves illusory, as immigrants with undesired qualities end up entering in large numbers through unauthorized channels for longer periods of time. Although scholars and officials may conceptualize immigrants as belonging to discrete legal categories or fitting into well-ordered behavioural typologies, what is often overlooked is the fluidity of people across categories and how quickly they adjust their behaviour in response to changes in laws, policies, and circumstances.

These shifts in immigrant behaviour often provoke a hostile reaction among native voters, putting public officials in a difficult position that requires them to take some action to bring immigration back under 'control'. In essence, immigration is unproblematic as long as 'control' means initiating immigration to satisfy a perceived short-term demand for labour, or permitting the entry of refugees to satisfy limited political objectives. It is only when 'control' comes to mean restricting or stopping a well-established immigrant flow that difficulties arise. Time and time again policy-makers in developed countries have found that immigration is much easier to start than to stop, and that it cannot simply be turned on and off like a tap.

Few of the causal processes we have identified as underlying mass immigration are easily controllable using the policy levers normally available to public officials. Receiving-country governments can do little about the penetration of markets into developing regions of the world, or about the progressive incorporation of peripheral areas into global trade, information, and production networks anchored in world cities. Likewise, reducing a demand for unskilled labour that stems from the structural segmentation of the labour market would require a wholesale re-engineering of society that most political leaders find unpalatable. Finally, state policies cannot prevent social networks and other transnational structures from arising to support international migration; all they can do is desist from encouraging them, but even this has proved difficult in practice.

State efforts at immigration control typically conceptualize international movement in relatively simple neoclassical terms. By patrolling the border, castigating employers who hire unauthorized workers, barring immigrants from social programmes, and limiting the rights of the foreign born to housing, health care, schooling, and employment, public officials seek to drive up the costs and lower the benefits of international migration, in hopes of reducing the incentives for entry.

Such repressive policies, however, do not address the broader structural causes of international migration, and they focus on income maximization to the exclusion of other motives for international movement such as risk diversification and capital acquisition. Given a disparity between the structural forces and diverse motives driving immigration and the narrow means employed to regulate it, two common policy trends have emerged in nations throughout the developed world: the *convergence* in the policy instruments chosen for immigration control and a widening *gap* between the goals of these instruments and actual immigration outcomes (Cornelius *et al.* 1994).

Faced with mounting public pressure to 'control' immigration, but with the root causes of international migration lying largely beyond their reach, elected leaders and bureaucrats increasingly have turned to *symbolic* policy instruments to create an *appearance* of control (Calavita 1992; Cornelius *et al.* 1994; Andreas 1998). Police actions at the border, the internal harassment of aliens, the purging of immigrants from public service rolls, and the implementation of restrictions on the civil liberties of foreigners are not very effective in stopping immigrants; but these measures serve important political purposes: they are visible, concrete, punitive, and enable otherwise feckless public officials to appear decisive, tough, and actively engaged in combating the rising tide of immigration.

Although officials and the general public may believe that repressive enforcement will reduce the volume of unwanted immigration (see Espenshade and Calhoun 1993; Espenshade and Hempstead 1996), recent evidence from the USA suggests that, in reality, they do not deter new migrants from coming or experienced migrants from re-entering (see Donato *et al.* 1992b; Massey and Espinosa 1997). They have a stronger effect on the *composition* of international migration, pushing immigrants towards a clandestine existence that leaves them economically exploitable and socially vulnerable (Donato *et al.* 1992a; Donato and Massey 1993). The failure of States to recognize the complex, multi-causal nature of contemporary international migration thus yields the worst of all possible worlds: continuing immigration from abroad combined with lower wages, poorer working conditions, increased crime, more disease, and greater social marginalization at home.

In many receiving societies, repressive enforcement policies also fail for another reason: the rise of rights-based liberalism. According to Cornelius *et al.* (1994: 9), the gradual extension of rights to ethnic minorities and foreigners over a period of several decades, from the 1960s through the 1980s, is one of the most salient aspects of political development in the advanced industrial democracies. Although the history of rights-based policies is played out differently in different nations, the net effect is similar: increased civil rights for immigrants, an outcome that significantly undermines the capacity of democratic States to control immigration. As they also note (1994: 10), 'it is the confluence of *markets* (the push-pull factors describe above) and *rights* that explains much of the contemporary difficulty of immigration control in Europe and the USA' (emphasis in original).

In sum, repressive policies seeking to regulate immigration by influencing the costs and benefits of immigration seem likely to fail, a conclusion that certainly holds for industrial democracies in North America, Europe, and the Pacific, but which also applies to a surprising degree in the centralized, autocratic monarchies of the Persian Gulf. As long as the world's powerful, capital-rich economies are incorporated within global trade, information, and production networks, they will tend to receive international migrants. In both theoretical and practical terms it has proved difficult to lower barriers to the movement of capital, information, and goods while at the same time raising barriers to the movement of workers. Immigration is simply the labour component of globalizing factor markets.

Rather that trying to stop international migration through repressive means, a more successful (and realistic) approach might be to consider immigration a natural outgrowth of a country's insertion into the global economy and to encourage its desirable features while working to mitigate its negative consequences. Repressive enforcement actions would be reserved for immigrants from nations otherwise unconnected to the receiving country by virtue of trade or investment relations. For immigrants coming from nations connected via well-established flows of capital, information, goods, and culture, policy-makers would work to achieve outcomes that serve the interests of the receiving society rather than simply trying to suppress the flow: i.e. promoting shorter stays, limited settlement, and a high likelihood of return migration; protecting internal wages and labour standards; and encouraging economic development in sending regions.

To the extent that repressive immigration policies are successful, they generally have the perverse effect of transforming circular flows into more permanent and settled communities. When the governments of Western Europe suspended labour recruitment in 1973, for example, and barred the re-entry of guestworkers, migrants who normally would have returned home chose to stay on and sent for their family dependants to join them. As a result, Europe's foreign population grew and its composition shifted decisively from sojourners to settlers and from workers to dependants (Martin and Miller 1980). In the USA, the implementation of repressive enforcement policies in the late 1980s reduced the odds of return migration among Mexican immigrants (Massey and Espinosa 1997).

Rather than trying to suppress a natural flow and inviting counter-productive outcomes, an alternative is to accept immigration as inevitable and to design programmes to enhance immigrants' connections to the sending society and to maximize their propensity for return migration. These goals could be accomplished in a variety of ways. One is to make temporary work visas freely available, so that migrants can reasonably expect to migrate again should their economic circumstances warrant, thus lowering the incentives to stay on in the receiving country for fear of not being able to return. A portion of immigrants' wages might be held back and only paid to a foreign bank account upon return to the sending country. Interest rates might be subsidized in foreign accounts to provide a return above the market, thus luring back migrants and their money. Finally, since migrants are often motivated by lack of access to insurance and capital, destination countries might enter into cooperative agreements with sending nations to establish public programmes and private businesses to meet these needs.

With state resources freed up from unproductive attempts to suppress immigration, receiving countries could increase internal inspections of work sites in sectors that employing large concentrations of immigrants, not to round up and deport illegal aliens but to assure employers' compliance with minimum wage laws, social insurance legislation, occupational safety and health regulations, tax codes, and mandated fair labour standards. This enforcement strategy has two advantages for the receiving society: it lowers the demand for immigrant workers by preventing employers from using them to avoid expensive labour regulations, and it prevents the formation of an underground, clandestine economy that puts downward pressure on the economic and social well-being of natives and immigrants alike.

Finally, since much international migration is brought about by the displacement of people from traditional livelihoods and an absence of well-developed markets for insurance, capital, and consumer credit, an indispensable part of any enlightened immigration policy should be the creation of transnational programmes to enhance markets and promote economic growth and development in sending regions. Some of the initiatives already proposed to encourage return migration simultaneously achieve these goals: namely, the creation of social insurance programmes and development banks accessible to former migrants. Funds for these enterprises might be raised through a special tax levied on migrant workers and their employers. Developed nations might also work more broadly to finance development programmes and promote balanced economic growth within the nation as a whole.

Sending societies

Ultimately, of course, responsibility for economic growth and development lies with officials and entrepreneurs in migrant-sending nations, and while receiving societies can encourage policies to reduce the structural pressures for emigration and lower the incentives for international movement, they cannot directly implement them. Thus, sending nations also have an important role to play in formulating and implementing policies with respect to international migration.

Based on the failure of emigration to satisfy unrealistic and rather inflated expectations of officials and researchers in Mexico, Turkey, and elsewhere, the prevailing view of migration's influence on economic development has been rather pessimistic. Officials in multilateral organizations and national governments generally view emigration as promoting national and local dependency rather than autonomous economic growth. In the words of the ILO official we quoted in Chapter 8, 'migration and development—nobody believes that anymore.'

More recent research and the experience of several Asian nations call this pessimistic view into serious question. Migradollars repatriated by emigrants working abroad ease the savings and exchange constraints faced by most developing nations and represent an important way of financing chronic trade deficits. Investments made by migrants and their families directly increase productivity in sending nations, and their spending has strong multiplier effects that raise national income and production indirectly. Although international migration, by itself, cannot guarantee achieving self-sustaining economic growth, it carries considerable potential as a source of development capital and as a means of overcoming bottlenecks to production.

At the same time, however, over-reliance on labour export as a strategy for economic development has historically yielded disappointing results. Ultimately there is no substitute for a well-designed and carefully implemented development policy, which includes several key features. The first is macroeconomic: the avoidance of monetary and fiscal policies that generate high rates of inflation and economic uncertainty, conditions which encourage families to invest in real property rather than in production and encourage migration as a means of controlling risk. States should also avoid agrarian policies that subsidize urban consumers at the expense of rural producers because these generate disincentives for rural dwellers to invest in agriculture. Third, States should invest in basic infrastructure to increase the feasibility, profitability, and productivity of private investments by migrants and non-migrants alike. Poor infrastructure—roads, airports, railroads, electrical power, telecommunications, irrigation, and education—make the returns to local investment too low and uncertain for migrant households to take the step of tying their life savings up with local production activities.

Finally, although the emigration of underemployed workers may enhance the prospects for economic development by lowering domestic unemployment rates, reducing exchange deficits, spurring investment, reducing political demands on the State, and increasing spending and income, sending countries must be vigilant to avoid the loss of human capital essential for national economic growth. If the loss of highly skilled workers creates bottlenecks in production and lowers the productivity of complementary workers, then international migration necessarily undermines economic development. Only if international migration involves the movement of abundant labour rather than scarce human capital is the potential for economic advancement likely to be realized. Whenever necessary, therefore, labour-exporting societies should implement programmes to retain educated, highly productive workers through special incentives, possibly channelling a portion of the migradollars generated by labour migration into salary subsidies, infrastructure, and other perquisites of employment in critical economic sectors.

The Road Ahead

The advent of massive international migration worldwide in the late twentieth century offers many formidable challenges. For theoreticians, a principal challenge is to model the behaviour of nation States and political actors, filling a void in the general theory of international migration we have constructed here (see Myers 1994). In the industrial era, when theories about immigration were first developed, nation States were relatively minor players in defining the process of international migration, as borders were open and movement for the most part was unrestricted. States sought to impose numerical limitations on immigration only in the 1920s, just as the industrial era of migration was drawing to a close (it effectively ended with the onset of the Great Depression in 1929).

Before 1930, receiving States imposed few qualitative or quantitative restrictions on international movement and governments were not very involved in determining the volume or character of immigration. Under these circumstances, the behaviour of States and the politicians who controlled them could be safely ignored. In the latter half of the twentieth century, however, all developed countries imposed numerically restrictive immigration policies. Although these policies do not prevent international movement or eliminate unauthorized migration, they do select immigrants—qualitatively and quantitatively, intentionally as well as inadvertently—and thus influence both the volume and composition of contemporary international flows.

Our theoretical understanding of international migration will necessarily be incomplete until theories of state behaviour have been advanced, tested, and incorporated into the general body of theoretical knowledge. As our reviews suggest, we are on the verge of developing a good theoretical understanding of the structural forces that promote emigration from developing nations and immigration into developed areas of the world, as well as the transnational social and economic structures that support this movement and the motivations of migrants in responding to these structural dynamics. What we lack is an adequate theory to account for the motivations, interests, and behaviour of the political actors who employ state power to intervene in this process, and how these interventions determine immigrant outcomes at the individual and aggregate levels.

For empirical researchers perhaps the greatest challenge is to design studies that are more closely connected to theory. In reviewing empirical literature from around the world, the most striking feature is the degree to which current research is unconnected not just to a particular theory, but to any theory at all. If our knowledge of international migration is to advance, researchers working in all systems must make greater efforts to familiarize themselves with the principal contemporary theories of international migration, and formulate research designs capable of testing their leading propositions. What is especially needed at this point are studies that simultaneously test the propositions of several theories at once, so that the relative efficacy of different explanations can be directly compared and contrasted. Given the current state of knowledge, it is less important whether or not a theory is 'true' than how well it compares with others in explaining international migration. Only a handful of studies anywhere test more than two theories at once, let alone examine the six theoretical paradigms we have reviewed here; and at this point in time, the research literature is far too restricted geographically to serve as a sound basis for generalization. Too many of the rigorous theoretical tests conducted so far have been based on samples of Mexican rural areas. Rural- and urban-origin emigrants may differ in important ways that are not yet well understood, and the case of Mexico–USA migration is unique by any criterion.

Finally, perhaps the most profound challenge of all will be faced by citizens and policy-makers in migrant sending and receiving countries. Inhabitants of the latter will have to move beyond the state of denial that so often has characterized their approach to immigration policy to date. They must develop policies that recognize the inevitability of labour flows within a globalized economy characterized by well-established regional networks of trade, production, investment, and communications. Attempts to suppress population flows that are a natural consequence of a nation's insertion into these economic networks will not be successful, but they will present grave threats to individual rights, civil liberties, and human dignity.

In sending societies, citizens and policy-makers face different but equally vexing issues. Rather than passively acquiescing to emigration and simply waiting for remittances to materialize, our review makes clear that developing countries must actively plan to derive benefits from what is potentially an important engine of economic growth. Unless concrete steps are taken to attract migradollars and channel them into productive ends, to capture remittances for purposes of foreign exchange, and to forestall the loss of human capital, development outcomes are likely to be disappointing.

Finally, the globalization of capital and labour markets and the internationalization of production pose strong challenges to the very concept of the nation State and the idea of national sovereignty itself, requiring political leaders and citizens in both sending and receiving nations to abandon nineteenth-century conceptions of territory and citizenship and to expand them to embrace the transnational spaces that are currently being formed throughout the world as a result of massive immigration. These changes are especially daunting because they will have to occur at a time when the forces of globalization are also producing downward pressure on wages and incomes.

These are formidable challenges indeed, but they will have to be met, for international migration will surely continue. Barring an international catastrophe of unprecedented proportions, immigration will most likely expand and grow, for none of the causal forces responsible for immigration show any sign of moderating. The market economy is expanding to ever farther reaches of the globe, labour markets in developed countries are growing more rather than less segmented, transnational migration and trade networks are expanding, and the power of the nation State is faltering in the face of this transnational onslaught. The twenty-first century will be one of globalism, and international migration undoubtedly will figure prominently within it.

References

Abad-Unat, Nermin (1995), 'Turkish migration to Europe', in Robin Cohen (ed.), *The Cambridge Survey of World Migration*, Cambridge University Press, Cambridge: 274–8.

Abadan-Unat, Nermin, Rusen Kelles, Rinus Penninx, Herman Van Renselaar, Leo Van Velzen, and Leyla Yenisey (1975), *Migration and Development: A Study of the Effects of International Labor Migration on Bogazliyan District*, Ajans-Turk Press, Ankara.

Abella, Manolo I. (1984), 'Labour migration from South and South-East Asia: some policy issues' *International Labour Review*, 123: 491–506.

——(1988), 'Emigration and return migration policies: sending country perspectives'. Paper presented to the Seminar on International Migration Systems, Processes and Policies, International Union for the Scientific Study of Population, Liège.

——(1992), 'Contemporary labour migration from Asia: policies and perspectives of sending countries', in Mary M. Kritz, Lin Lean Lim, and Hania Zlotnik (eds.), *International Systems: A Global Approach*, Clarendon Press, Oxford: 263–78.

——(1992b), 'International migration and development', in Graziano Battistella and A. Paganoni (eds.), *Philippine Labor Migration: Impact and Policy*, Scalabrini Migration Center, Quezon City: 35–62.

——(1995a), 'Asian migrant and contract workers in the Middle East', in Robin Cohen (ed.), *The Cambridge Survey of World Migration*, Cambridge University Press, Cambridge: 418–23.

——(1995b), 'Asian labour migration: past, present and future', *ASEAN Economic Bulletin*, 12: 125–138.

——and H. Mori (1996), 'Structural change and labour migration in East Asia', in D. O'Connor and L. Farsakh (eds.), *Development Strategy, Employment and Migration: Country Experiences*, OECD Paris: 35–62.

Abdulla Ali, Ali (1984), *Arab Labor in the Arab Republic of Yemen: A Socioeconomic Study of Sudanese between 1979–1981*, Council on Economic and Social Research, Khartoum.

Ackerman, Sune (1976), 'Theories and methods of migration research', in Harald Runblom and Hans Norman (eds.), *From Sweden to America*, University of Minnesota Press, Minneapolis: 19–75.

Adams, Richard H. (1989), 'Worker remittances and inequality in rural Egypt', *Economic Development and Cultural Change*, 38: 45–71.

——(1991a), 'The economic uses and impact of international remittances in rural Egypt', *Economic Development and Cultural Change*, 39: 695–722.

——(1991b), *The Effects of International Remittances on Poverty, Inequality, and Development in Rural Egypt*, International Food Policy Research Institute, Washington, DC.

——(1993), 'The economic and demographic determinants of international migration in rural Egypt', *Journal of Development Studies*, 30: 146–67.

——(1996), 'Remittances, inequality, and asset accumulation: the case of rural Pakistan', in D. O'Connor and L. Farsakh (eds.), *Development Strategy, Employment and Migration: Country Experiences*, OECD, Paris: 149–70.

——and H. Alderman (1992), 'Sources of inequality in rural Pakistan: a decomposition analysis', *Oxford Bulletin of Economics and Statistics*, 54: 591–608.

Adams, Walter (1969), *The Brain Drain*, Macmillan, New York.

Addleton, J. (1991), 'The impact of the Gulf War on migration and remittances in Asia and the Middle East', *International Migration*, 29: 509–28.

Adelman, Irma, and J. Edward Taylor (1990), 'Is structural adjustment with a human face possible? the case of Mexico', *Journal of Development Studies*, 26: 387–407.

——J. Edward Taylor, and Stephen Vogel (1988), 'Life in a Mexican village: a SAM perspective', *Journal of Development Studies*, 25: 5–24.

Adelman, Jeremy (1995), 'European migration to Argentina, 1880–1930', in Robin Cohen (ed.), *The Cambridge Survey of World Migration*, Cambridge University Press, Cambridge: 208–15.

Adepoju, Aderanti (1988), 'International migration in Africa south of the Sahara', in Reginald T. Appleyard (ed.), *International Migration Today, I: Trends and Prospects*, University of Western Australia for the UN Education, Scientific, and Cultural Organization, Perth: 17–88.

——(1991*a*), 'Binational communities and labor circulation in sub-Saharan Africa', in Demetrios G. Papademetriou and Philip Martin (eds.), *The Unsettled Relationship: Labor Migration and Economic Development*, Greenwood Press, New York: 45–64.

——(1991*b*), 'South-north migration: the African experience', *International Migration*, 29: 205–21.

Adi, R. (1996), 'The impact of international labour migration in Indonesia', Unpublished Ph.D. thesis, Department of Geography, University of Adelaide, Australia.

Adler, Stephen (1985), 'Emigration and development in Algeria: doubts and dilemmas', in Rosemarie Rogers (ed.), *Guests Come to Stay: The Effects of European Labor Migration on Sending and Receiving Countries*, Westview Press, Boulder, Colo.: 263–84.

Aguiar, C. A. (1980), 'La emigración de recursos humanos calificados y el adjuste en el mercado de empleo del Uruguay', Working Paper, International Labour Office, Geneva.

Alarcón, Rafael (1992), 'Norteñización: self-perpetuating migration from a Mexican town', in Jorge Bustamante, Clark Reynolds, and Raul Hinojosa (eds.), *US-Mexico Relations: Labor Market Interdependence*, Stanford University Press, Stanford, Calif.: 302–18.

Al-Ghul, and Allah Al-Sharif (1982), *Mulahathat an al-Higrat al-Kharagiyya* (Observation on External Migration), Council on Economic and Social Research, Khartoum.

Ali, Sayed A. (1981), *Labor Migration from Bangladesh to the Middle East*, World Bank, Washington, DC.

Al-Moosa, Abdulrasool, and Keith McLachlan (1985), *Immigrant Labour in Kuwait*, Croom-Helm, London.

Al-Qudsi, Sulayman S., and Nasra M. Shah (1991), 'The relative economic progress of male foreign workers in Kuwait', *International Migration Review*, 25: 141–66.

Altman, Ida (1995), 'Spanish migration to the Americas' in Robin Cohen (ed.), *The Cambridge Survey of World Migration*, Cambridge University Press, Cambridge: 28–32.

Altamirano, T. (1988), 'Inmigrantes Peruanos en los Estados Unidos de Norteamérica', Unpublished Paper, Pontífica Universidad Católica del Perú, Facultad de Ciencias Sociales.

Amemiya, T. (1985), *Advanced Econometrics*, Harvard University Press, Cambridge, Mass.

Amin, Galal, and Elizabeth Awny (1985), *International Migration of Egyptian Labour: A Review of the State of the Art*, International Development Research Centre, Ottawa.

Amin, Samir (1974), *Accumulation on a World Scale: A Critique of the Theory of Underdevelopment*, Monthly Review Press, New York.

——(1976), *Unequal Development: An Essay on the Social Formations of Peripheral Capitalism*, Monthly Review Press, New York.

Amjad, Rashid (1986), 'Impact of worker's remittances from the Middle East on Pakistan's economy: some selected issues', *Pakistan Development Review*, 25: 621–34.

——(1989), 'Economic impact of migration to the Middle East on the major labour sending countries-an overview', in Rashid Amjad (ed.), *To the Gulf and Back: Studies on the Economic Impact of Asian Labour Migration*, International Labour Office, Geneva: 1–27.

Anderson, Patricia Y. (1982), 'Migration and development in Jamaica', in William F. Stinner, Klaus de Albuquerque, and Roy S. Bryce-Laporte (eds.), *Return Migration and Remittances: Developing a Caribbean Perspective*, Smithsonian Institution, Washington, DC: 117–39.

Andreas, Peter (1998), 'Changing border games: US immigration in the post-NAFTA era', *Political Science Quarterly*, forthcoming.

Anwar, Muhammad (1995), 'New Commonwealth migration to the UK', in Robin Cohen (ed.), *The Cambridge Survey of World Migration*, Cambridge University Press, Cambridge: 271–3.

Appleyard, Reginald T. (1988), 'International migration in Asia and the Pacific', in Reginald T. Appleyard (ed.), *International Migration Today, I: Trends and Prospects*, University of Western Australia for the UN Education, Scientific, and Cultural Organization, Perth: 89–167.

Arab Population Conference (1993), *Hijrat El Amala El Arabia*, Arab Population Conference, Amman.

Arango, Joaquín (1985), 'Las leyes de las migraciones de E. G. Ravenstein, cien años después', *Revista Española de Investigaciones Sociológicas*, 32: 7–26.

Ardittis, Solon (1990), 'Labour migration and the single European market: a synthetic and prospective note', *International Sociology*, 5: 461–74.

Arizpe, Lourdes (1978), 'La migración por revelos y la reproducción social del campesinado', in *Poblaciones en Movimiento*, UN Educational, Social, and Cultural Organization, Paris: 205–29.

Arnold, Fred (1992), 'The contribution of remittances to economic and social development', in Mary M. Kritz, Lin Lean Lim, and Hania Zlotnik (eds.), *International Systems: A Global Approach*, Clarendon Press, Oxford: 205–20.

——Benjamin V. Cariño, James T. Fawcett, and Insook Han Park (1989), 'Estimating the immigration multiplier: an analysis of recent Korean and Filipino immigration to the United States', *International Migration Review*, 23: 813–38.

——Rand Nasra M. Shah (1984), 'Asian labor migration to the Middle East', *International Migration Review*, 18: 294–318.

Arroyo, Jesús (1989), *El Abandono Rural*, Editorial Universidad de Guadalajara, Guadalajara.

——Adrian de León, and Basilia Valenzuela (1990), 'Patterns of migration and regional development in the state of Jalisco, Mexico', in Sergio Díaz-Briquets and Sidney Weintraub (eds.), *Regional and Sectoral Development in Mexico as Alternatives to Migration*. Westview Press, Boulder, Colo.: 49–90.

Asia and Pacific Development Centre (1989), *Trade in Domestic Helpers: Causes, Mechanisms and Consequences*, Asian and Pacific Development Centre, Kuala Lumpur, Malaysia.

Athukorala, Premachandra (1990), 'International contract migration and the reintegration of return migrants: the experience of Sri Lanka', *International Migration Review*, 24: 323–46.

——(1993), 'Improving the contribution of migrant remittances to development: the experience of Asian labour-exporting countries', *International Migration*, 31: 103–24.

Australian Bureau of Statistics (1995), *Australia Year Book 1995*, Australian Bureau of Statistics, Canberra.

Awonohara, S. (1986), 'Open the door some more?', *Far Eastern Economic Review*, 4 Sept., pp. 23–5.

Azzam, H., and D. Sahib (1980), *The Women Left Behind: A Study of the Wives of Lebanese Migrant Workers in the Oil-Rich Countries of the Region*, Working Paper 3, International Labour Office, Regional Office for Arab States, Beirut.

Baddou, T. (1983), 'L'emigration ou la persistance d'une illusion: elements pour une analyse des problèmes de la réinsertion-formation au Maroc', in *Maghrébins en France: Emigré ou Immigré*, Centre National de la Recherche Scientifique, Paris: 442–50.

Bade, K. (1993), 'Re-migration to their fathers' land? Ethnic Germans from the east in the Federal Republic of Germany', *The Refugee Participation Network*, 14: 1–27.

Bailey, Samuel (1985), 'La cadena migratoria de los Italianos a la Argentina', in F. Devoto and G. Rosoli (eds.), *La Inmigración Italiana en la Argentina*, Editorial Bilbos, Buenos Aires: 45–61.

Balán, Jorge (1974), 'Migraciones y desarrollo capitalista en el Brazil: ensayo de interpretacion histórico-comparativo', *Migración y Desarrollo*, 3: 65–102.

——(1985), 'Las migraciones internacionales en el Cono Sur', Working Paper, Hemispheric Migration Project, Intergovernmental Committee on Migration and Georgetown University, Washington, DC.

——(1988), 'International migration in Latin America: trends and consequences', in Reginald Appleyard (ed.), *International Migration Today, I: Trends and Prospects*, University of Western Australia for the UN Educational, Scientific, and Cultural Organization, Perth: 210–63.

——(1992), 'The role of migration policies and social networks in the development of a migration system in the Southern Cone', in Mary M. Kritz, Lin Lean Lim, and Hania Zlotnik (eds.), *International Systems: A Global Approach*, Clarendon Press, Oxford: 115–32.

Baldwin-Edwards, M. (1991), 'Immigration after 1991', *Policy and Politics*, 19: 199–211.

Baletic, Zvonimir (1982), 'International migration in modern economic development: with special reference to Yugoslavia', *International Migration Review*, 16: 736–56.

Baran, Paul A. (1957), *The Political Economy of Growth*, University of California Press, Berkeley and Los Angeles.

—— (1973), 'On the political economy of backwardness', in K. Wilber (ed.), *The Political Economy of Development and Underdevelopment*, Random House, New York: 82–93.

Barrett, George (1993), 'Migrant tide threatens a flood', *The Age*, 7 July pp. 1–10.

Barsotti, O., and L. Lecchini (1990), 'L'Immigration des pays du tiers-monde en Italie', *Revue Européenne des Migrations Internationales*, 5: 45–56.

Bartoncello, Rodolfo, Alfredo E. Lattes, César Moyano, and Susana Schkolnik (1986), *Argentinos en el Exterior*, Centro de Estudios de Población, Buenos Aires.

Battistella, Graziano (1995), 'Philippine overseas labour: from export to management', *ASEAN Economic Bulletin*, 12: 257–274.

Baucic, Ivo (1972), *The Effects of Emigration from Yugoslavia and the Problems of Returning Emigrant Workers*, Martinus Nijhoff, The Hague.

Baum, J. (1993), 'Human wave', *Far Eastern Economic Review*, 5 Aug.

Bean, Frank D., Harley L. Browning, and W. Parker Frisbie (1984), 'The sociodemographic characteristics of immigrant status groups: implications for studying undocumented migrants', *International Migration Review*, 18: 672–91.

—— Thomas J. Espenshade, Michael J. White, and Robert F. Dymowski (1990), 'Post-IRCA changes in the volume and composition of undocumented migration to the United States: an assessment based on apprehensions data', in Frank D. Bean, Barry Edmonston, and Jeffrey S. Passel (eds.), *Undocumented Migration to the United States: IRCA and the Experience of the 1980s*, Urban Institute Press, Washington, DC: 111–58.

Beauge, G. (1986), 'La Kafala: un système de gestion transitoire de la main-d'oeuvre et du capital dans les pays du Golfe', *Revue Européenne des Migrations Internationales*, 1: 109–21.

Becker, Gary S. (1981). *A Treatise on the Family*, Harvard University Press, Cambridge, Mass.

Bedford, Richard (1992), 'International Migration in the South Pacific Region,' in Mary M. Kritz, Lin Lean Lim, and Hania Zlotnik (eds.), *International Migration: A Global Approach*, Clarendon Press, Oxford: 41–62.

Belous, Richard S., and Jonathan Lemco (1995), *NAFTA as a Model of Development: The Benefits of Merging High- and Low-Wage Areas*, State University of New York Press, Albany, NY.

Bencherifa, A., A. Berriane, and M. Refass (1992), *Etude des Mouvements Migratoires du Maroc vers la Communauté Européenne*, Editoriale Passau, Rabat, Morocco.

Beng, C. S. (1990), 'Brain drain in Singapore: issues and prospects', *Singapore Economic Review*. 35: 55–77.

Bennett, Brian C. (1979), 'Migration and rural community viability in central Dalmatia (Croatia), Yugoslavia', *Papers in Anthropology*, 20: 75–84.

Benton, G. (1979), *Two Revolutions: Political and Economic Development in Saudi Arabia under the Saud Family*, Exeter University, Exeter.

Beozzo Bassanezi, M. S. (1995), 'Imigraçoes internaçionais no Brasil: um panorama histórico', in Neide López Patara (ed.), *Emigracio e Imigraçao Internaçionas no Brasil Contemporáneo*, Universidade Estadual de Campinas, Campinas, Brazil.

Berrier, Robert J. (1985), 'The French textile industry: a segmented labor market', in Rosmarie Rogers (ed.), *Guests Come to Stay: The Effects of European Labor Migration on Sending and Receiving Countries*, Westview Press, Boulder, Colo.: 51–69.

Berry, R. A., and R. Soligo (1969), 'Some welfare aspects of international migration', *Journal of Political Economy*, 77: 778–94.

Bertram, G. (1986), 'Sustainable development in Pacific micro-economies', *World Development*, 14: 809–22.

——and R. F. Watters (1984), *New Zealand and its small island neighbours*. Institute of Policy Studies, Victoria University, Wellington.

————(1985), 'The MIRAB economy in South Pacific microstates', *Pacific Viewpoint*, 26: 489–519.

————(1986), 'The MIRAB process: earlier analyses in context', *Pacific Viewpoint*, 27: 47–59.

Bhagwati, J. N., and T. N. Srinivasan (1983), 'On the choice between capital and labour mobility', *Journal of International Economics*, 14: 209–21.

Bibb, Robert, and William Form (1977), 'The effects of industrial, occupational, and sex stratification on wages in blue-collar labor markets', *Social Forces*, 55: 974–6.

Bidegain, G. (1987), 'Democracia, migración y retorno: los Argentinos, Chilenos, y Uruguayos en Venezuela', *International Migration*, 25: 299–324.

——and L. Freitez (1989), *Los Colombianos en Venezuela: mito y realidad*, Centro de Estudios de Pastoral y Asistencia Migratoria, Caracas.

Birks, J. S., and A. Sinclair (1980), *International Migration and Development in the Arab Region*, International Labour Office, Geneva.

————(1992), *GCC Market Report 1992*. Mountjoy Research Centre, Durham, UK.

——Ian J. Seccombe, and C. A. Sinclair (1986), 'Migrant workers in the Arab Gulf: the impact of declining oil revenues', *International Migration Review*, 20: 799–814.

————(1988), 'Labour migration in the Arab Gulf states: patterns, trends, and prospects', *International Migration*, 26: 253–66.

Bjerg, María, and Hernán Otero (1995), *Inmigración y Redes Sociales en la Argentina Moderna*, Centro de Estudios Migratorios, Instituto de Estudios Histórico Sociales, Tandil, Argentina.

Black, Jan K. (1986), *The Dominican Republic: Politics and Development in an Unsovereign State*, Allen & Unwin, Boston.

Blanco Fernández de Valderrama, Cristina (1993), 'The new hosts: the case of Spain', *International Migration Review*, 27: 169–81.

Blanes, J. (1986), 'Movilidad espacial en Bolivia: reflexiones sobre su carácter temporal', in Programa de Investigaciones Sociales sobre Población en América Latina (PISPAL), *Se Fue a Volver: Seminario sobre Migraciones Temporales en América Latina*, El Colegio de México, Mexico: 139–80.

Bleier, Elisabeth Ungar (1988), 'Impact of the Venezuelan recession on return migration to Colombia: the case of the principal urban sending areas', in Patricia R. Pessar (ed.), *When Borders Don't Divide: Labor Migration and Refugee Movements in the Americas*, Center for Migration Studies, Staten Island, NY: 73–95.

Blejer, Mario I., Harry G. Johnson, and Arturo C. Prozecanski (1978), 'An analysis of the economic determinants of legal and illegal Mexican migration to the United States', *Research in Population Economics*, 1: 217–31.

Bloom, David E., and Morley Gunderson (1991), 'An analysis of the earnings of Canadian immigrants', in John M. Abowd and Richard B. Freeman (eds.), *Immigration, Trade, and the Labor Market*, University of Chicago Press, Chicago: 321–42.

Bodega, Isabel, Juan A. Cebrian, Teresa Franchini, Gloria Lora-Tamayo, and Asuncion Martin-Lou (1995), 'Recent migrations from Morocco to Spain', *International Migration Review*, 29: 800–19.

Boeder, R. (1973), 'The effects of labour emigration on rural life in Malawi', *Rural African*, 20: 1–25.

Böhning, Wolf R. (1970), 'The differential strength of demand and wage factors in intra-European labour mobility: with special reference to Germany, 1957–1968', *International Migration*, 8: 193–202.

——(1972), *The Migration of Workers in the United Kingdom and the European Community*, Oxford University Press, Oxford.

——(1981), *Black Migration to South Africa: A Selection of Policy-Oriented Research*, International Labour Office, Geneva.

——(1984), *Studies in International Labour Migration*, St Martin's Press, New York.

——(1994), 'Undesired jobs and what one can do to fill them: the case of the Republic of Korea', Paper presented at the Korea Small Business Institute Seminar, Seoul, 11–14 April.

Borjas, George J. (1982), 'The earnings of male Hispanic immigrants in the United States', *Industrial and Labor Relations Review*, 35: 343–53.

——(1985), 'Assimilation, changes in cohort quality and the earnings of immigrants', *Journal of Labor Economics*, 4: 463–89.

——(1987), 'Self-selection and the earnings of immigrants', *American Economic Review*, 77: 532–53.

——(1989), 'Economic theory and international migration', *International Migration Review*, 23: 457–85.

——(1990), *Friends or Strangers: The Impact of Immigrants on the US Economy*, Basic Books, New York.

——(1991), 'Immigration and self-selection', in John M. Abowd and Richard B. Freeman (eds.), *Immigration, Trade, and the Labor Market*, University of Chicago Press, Chicago: 29–76.

——(1994), 'The economics of immigration', *Journal of Economic Literature*, 32: 667–717.

Bourdieu, Pierre (1986), 'The forms of capital', in John G. Richardson (ed.), *Handbook of Theory and Research for the Sociology of Education*, Greenwood Press, New York: 241–58.

——and Loic Wacquant (1992), *An Invitation to Reflexive Sociology*, University of Chicago Press, Chicago.

Bouvier, Leon F., and Robert W. Garnder (1986), *Immigration to the US: The Unfinished Story*, Population Reference Bureau, Washington, DC.

Boyd, Monica (1989), 'Family and personal networks in international migration: recent developments and new agendas', *International Migration Review*, 23: 638–70.

Bradshaw, York W. (1988), 'Urbanization, personal income, and physical quality of life: the case of Kenya', *Studies in Comparative International Development*, 13: 15–40.

Brana-Shute, Rosemary, and Gary Brana-Shute (1982), 'The magnitude and impact of remittances in the Eastern Caribbean: a research note', in William F. Stinner, Klaus de Albuquerque, and Roy S. Bryce-Laporte (eds.), *Return Migration and Remittances: Developing a Caribbean Perspective*, Smithsonian Institution, Washington, DC: 267–91.

Braudel, Fernand (1981), *The Structures of Everyday Life: Civilization and Capitalism 15th–18th Century, 1*, Harper & Row, New York.

——(1982), *The Wheels of Commerce: Civilization and Capitalism 15th–18th Century, 2*, Harper & Row, New York.

Bray, David (1984), 'Economic development: the middle class and international migration in the Dominican Republic', *International Migration Review*, 18: 217–36.

Brennan, Ellen M. (1984), 'Irregular migration: policy responses in Africa and Asia', *International Migration Review*, 18: 409–25.

Brettell, Caroline (1979), 'Emigrar para voltar: a Portuguese ideology of return migration', *Papers in Anthropology*, 20: 21–38.

Brimelow, Peter (1995), *Enough is Enough: Common Sense About Immigration*, Random House, New York.

Brockett, L. (1996), 'Thai sex workers in Sydney: a study of labour and migration', Unpublished MA thesis, Dept. of Geography, University of Adelaide, Australia.

Brown, R. P. C., and J. Foster (1995), 'Some common fallacies about migrants' remittances from the South Pacific: lessons from Tongan and Western Samoan research', *Pacific Viewpoint*, 36: 29–45.

Buchele, Robert (1976), 'Jobs and Workers: A Labor Market Segmentation Perspective of the Work Experience of Young Men', Unpublished Ph.D. diss., Dept. of Economics, Harvard University, Cambridge, Mass.

Bulow, Jeremy I., and Lawrence H. Summers (1986), 'A theory of dual labor markets with application to industrial policy, discrimination, and Keynesian unemployment', *Journal of Labor Economics*, 4: 376–414.

Bun, Chan Kwok (1995), 'The Vietnamese boat people in Hong Kong', in Robin Cohen (ed.), *The Cambridge Survey of World Migration*, Cambridge University Press, Cambridge: 380–5.

Bunge, A. E., and C. García Mata (1931), 'Argentina', in Imre Ferenczi and W. F. Wilcox (eds.), *International Migrations, 2*, National Bureau of Economic Research, New York: 143–60.

Bureau of Immigration Research (1991), *Australian Immigration: Consolidated Statistics, 16*, Bureau of Immigration Research, Canberra.

——(1992), *Immigration Update*, Bureau of Immigration Research, Canberra.

Burki, Shahid Javed (1991), 'Migration from Pakistan to the Middle East', in Demetrios G. Papademetriou and Philip L. Martin (eds.), *The Unsettled Relationship: Labor Migration and Economic Development*, Greenwood Press, New York: 139–62.

Burney, Nadeem (1989), 'A macro-economic analysis of the impact of workers' remittances on Pakistan's economy', in Rashid Amjad (ed.), *To the Gulf and Back: Studies on the Economic Impact of Asian Labour Migration*, International Labour Office, Geneva: 197–222.

Caces, Fe, Fred Arnold, and James T. Fawcett (1985), 'Shadow households and competing auspices: migration behavior in the Philippines', *Journal of Development Economics*, 17: 5–25.

Cadwallader, M. (1992), *Migration and Residential Mobility: Macro and Micro Approaches*, University of Wisconsin Press, Madison. .

Cahill, D. (1990), *Intermarriages in International Contexts*, Scalabrini Migration Center, Quezon City, Philippines.

Cain, Glenn (1976), 'The Challenge of segmented labor market theories to orthodox theory', *Journal of Economic Literature*, 14: 1215–57.

Calavita, Kitty (1992), *Inside the State: The Bracero Program, Immigration, and the INS*, Routledge, New York.

Caldwell, John C. (1969), *African Rural-Urban Migration: The Movement to Ghana's Towns*, Australian National University Press, Canberra.

—— (1976), 'Toward a restatement of demographic transition theory', *Population and Development Review*, 2: 321–66.

Calvaruso, C. (1987), 'Illegal Migration in Italy', in *The Future of Migration*, OECD, Paris: 306–14.

Cammaert, M. F. (1986), 'The long road from Nador to Brussels', *International Migration*, 24: 635–50.

Camp, Roderick (1993), *Politics in Mexico*, Oxford University Press, New York.

Campani, Giovanna (1989), 'Du tiers-monde à l'Italie: une nouvelle immigration féminine', *Revue Européenne des Migrations Internationales*, 5: 4–29.

—— and Maurizio Catani (1985), 'Les réseaux associatifs Italiens en France et les jeunes', *Revue Européenne des Migrations Internationales*, 1: 143–60.

—— —— and Salvatore Palidda (1987), 'Italian immigrant associations in France', in John Rex, Daniele Joly, and Czarina Wilpert (eds.), *Immigrant Associations in Europe*, Gower, Aldershot: 166–201.

Cardoso, Fernando H., and Enzo Faletto (1969), *Dependencia y Desarrollo en América Latina*, Siglo XXI, Mexico.

—— (1979), *Dependency and Development in Latin America*, University of California Press, Berkeley and Los Angeles.

Cariño, Benjamin V. (1987), 'The Philippine national recording systems on international migration', *International Migration Review*, 21: 1258–64.

Carnoy, M., and R. Rumberger (1980), 'Segmentation in the US labor market: its effects on the mobility and earnings of whites and blacks', *Cambridge Journal of Economics*, 4: 117–32.

Carrón, Juan M. (1976), *Factores Condicionantes de las Migraciones Intra-Regionales en el Cono Sur de América*, Centro Latinoamericano Demográfico, Santiago.

—— (1979), 'Shifting patterns in migration from bordering countries to Argentina: 1914–1970', *International Migration Review*, 13: 475–87.

—— (1980), 'Factores de atracción de la inmigración de orígen limítrofe en la Argentina', *Migraciones Internacionales en las Américas*, 1: 114–31.

—— (1991), 'Migración temporaria de Cochabamba, Bolivia a la Argentina: patrones e impacto en las áreas de envío', in Patricia R. Pessar (ed.), *Fronteras Permeables, Migración Laboral y Movimientos de Refugiados en América*, Planeta, Buenos Aires: 118–32.

Castells, Manuel (1989), *The Informational City: Information Technology, Economic Restructuring and the Urban-Regional Process*, Basil Blackwell, Oxford.

Castles, Stephen (1984), *Here for Good: Western Europe's New Ethnic Minorities*, Longwood, New York.

—— (1986), 'The guest-worker in Western Europe: an obituary', *International Migration Review*, 20: 761–78.

—— (1988), 'Temporary migrant workers-economic and social aspects', Consultant's Report No.1.10 in *Immigration: A Commitment to Australia*, Australian Government Printing Service, Canberra.

—— and Godula Kosack (1973), *Immigrant Workers and Class Structure in Western Europe*, Oxford University Press, London.

—— and Mark J. Miller (1993), *The Age of Migration: International Population Movements in the Modern World*, Guilford Press, New York.

Castillo-Freeman, Alida J., and Richard B. Freeman (1992), 'When the minimum wage really bites: the effect of the US-level minimum wage on Puerto Rico', in George J. Borjas and Richard B. Freeman (eds.), *Immigration and the Work Force: Economic Consequences for the United States and Source Areas*, University of Chicago Press, Chicago: 177–212.

Celton, D. (1995), 'Plus d'un siècle d'immigration internationalle en Argentine', *Revue Européenne des Migrations Internationales*, 11: 145–66.

Centeno, Miguel Angel (1994), *Democracy within Reason: Technocratic Revolution in Mexico*, Pennsylvania State University Press, University Park, Pa.

CEPAL (Comisión Económica para América Latina) (1993), *Remesas y Economía Familiar en El Savador, Guatemala, y Nicaragua*, UN Economic Commission for Latin America, Washington, DC.

Champion, A., and R. King (1993), 'New trends in international migration in Europe', *Geographical Viewpoint*, 21: 45–56.

Chandavarkar, A. B. (1980), 'Use of migrants' remittances in labor-exporting countries', *Finance and Development*, 17: 36–44.

Chaney, Rick (1986), *Regional Emigration and Remittances in Developing Countries: The Portuguese Experience*, Praeger, New York.

Chang, S. L. (1992), 'Causes of brain drain and solutions: the Taiwan experience', *Studies in Comparative International Development*, 2: 27–43.

Chant, S., and Radcliffe, S. A. (1992), 'Migration and development: the importance of gender', in S. Chang (ed.), *Gender and Migration in Developing Countries*, Belhaven Press, London: 1–29.

Chavez, Leo R. (1988), 'Settlers and sojourners: the case of Mexicans in the United States', *Human Organization*, 47: 95–108.

——(1990), 'Coresidence and Resistance: Strategies of survival among undocumented Mexicans and Central Americans in the United States', *Urban Anthropology*, 19: 31–61.

Chayanov, Alexander V (1966), *Theory of Peasant Economy*, Richard D. Irwin, Homewood, Ill.

Chen, Chi Yi, and J. Urquijo (1982), 'Los movimientos migratorios internacionales en Venezuela: políticas y realidades', *Revista Sobre Relaciones Industriales y Laborales*, 6: 10–11.

Chenery, Hollis B. (1979), *Structural Change and Development Policy*, Oxford University Press, Oxford.

Chesnais, Jean-Claude (1991), *Migration from Eastern to Western Europe: Past (1946–1989) and Future (1990–2000)*, Council of Europe, Strasbourg.

Chilivumbo, A. (1985), *Migration and Uneven Rural Development in Africa: The Case of Zambia*, University Press of America, Lanham, Md.

Chiswick, Barry R. (1978), 'The effect of Americanization on the earnings of foreign-born men', *Journal of Political Economy*, 86: 897–921.

——(1979), 'The economic progress of immigrants: some apparently universal patterns', in William Feller (ed.), *Contemporary Economic Problems, 1979*, American Enterprise Institute, Washington, DC: 357–99.

——(1980), 'The earnings of white and coloured male immigrants in Britain', *Economica*, 47: 81–7.

——(1984), 'Illegal aliens in the United States labor market: an analysis of occupational attainment and earnings', *International Migration Review*, 18: 714–32.

——(1988). *Illegal Aliens: Their Employment and Employers*, Upjohn Institute for Employment Research, Kalamazoo, Mich.

——and Paul W. Miller (1988), 'Earnings in Canada: the roles of immigrant generation, French ethnicity, and language', in T. Paul Shultz (ed.), *Research in Population Economics*, 6, JAI Press, Greenwich, Conn.: 183–228.

Choldin, Harvey M. (1973), 'Kinship networks in the migration process', *International Migration Review*, 7: 163–76.

Choucri, Nazli (1978), *Migration Processes among Developing Countries: The Middle East*, MIT Center for International Studies, Cambridge, Mass.

——(1985), 'A study of Sudanese nationals working abroad', Unpublished Paper, MIT Center for International Studies, Cambridge, Mass.

Chozas, J. (1993), 'Migration in Spain: recent developments', Paper presented at the Conference on Migration and International Cooperation, OECD, Paris.

Christiansen, Drew (1996), 'Movement, asylum, borders: Christian perspectives', *International Migration Review*, 30: 7–17.

Clogg, Clifford C., and James W. Schockey (1985), 'The effect of changing demographic composition on recent trends in underemployment', *Demography*, 22: 395–414.

Cobbe, James (1982), 'Emigration and development in Southern Africa: with special reference to South Africa', *International Migration Review*, 16: 837–69.

Cohen, Robin (1995), *The Cambridge Survey of World Migration*, Cambridge University Press, Cambridge.

Coleman, James S. (1988), 'Social capital in the creation of human capital', *American Journal of Sociology*, 94S, S95–S120.

——(1990), *Foundations of Social Theory*, Harvard University Press, Cambridge, Mass.

Colfer, C. J. (1985), 'On circular migration: from the distaff side', in Guy Standing (ed.), *Labour Circulation and the Labour Process*, Croom-Helm, London: 219–51.

Condé, J., P. S. Diagne, N. K. Ouaidou, K. Boye, and A. Kader (1983), *Les Migrations Internationales Sud-Nord: Une Etude de Cas: Les Migrants Maliens, Mauritaniens et Sénégalais de la Vallée de Fleuve Sénégal en France*, OECD, Paris.

Connell, John (1992), 'International manpower flows and foreign investment in Asia', *International Migration Review*, 26: 133–8.

——B. Dasgupta, R. Lashley, and M. Lipton (1976), *Migration from Rural Areas: The Evidence from Village Studies*, Oxford University Press, New Delhi.

Conroy, Michael E. (1980), 'Socio-economic incentives for migration from Mexico to the United States: cross-regional profiles, 1969–78', Paper presented at the Annual Meetings of the Population Association of America, Denver, 11 April.

Cornelius, Wayne (1990), *Labor Migration to the United States: Development Outcomes and Alternatives in Mexican Sending Communities*, US Commission for the Study of International Migration and Cooperative Economic Development, Washington, DC.

——(1992), 'From sojourners to settlers: the changing profile of Mexican labor migration to California in the 1980s, in Jorge Bustamante, Raul Hinojosa, and Clark Reynolds (eds.), *US–Mexico Relations: Labor Market Interdependence*, Stanford University Press, Stanford, Calif.: 155–95.

——Philip L. Martin, and James F. Hollifield (1994), 'Introduction: the ambivalent quest for immigration control', in Wayne A. Cornelius, Philip L. Martin, and James

F. Hollifield (eds.), *Controlling Immigration: A Global Perspective*, Stanford University Press, Stanford, Calif.: 3–41.

Corona, Rodolfo (1993), 'Migración permanente interestatal e internacional, 1950–1990', *Comercio Exterior*, 43: 750–63.

Cozzi, F. (1988), *A Profile of the Chilean-Born Community in Victoria*, DILGEA, Melbourne.

Crissman, L. (1967), 'The segmentary structure of urban overseas Chinese communities', *Man*, 2: 185–204.

Crane, Julie G. (1971), *Educated to Emigrate: The Social Organization of Saba*, Van Gorcum, Assen, Netherlands.

Curtin, Philip D. (1969), *The Atlantic Slave Trade: A Census*, University of Wisconsin Press, Madison.

Cuthbert, Richard W., and Joe B. Sterens (1981), 'The net economic incentive for illegal Mexican migration: a case study', *International Migration Review*, 15: 541–49.

Dandler, Jorge, and Carmen Medeiros (1988), 'Temporary migration from Cochabamba, Bolivia to Argentina: patterns and impact in sending areas', in Patricia R. Pessar (ed.), *When Borders Don't Divide: Labor Migration and Refugee Movements in the Americas*, Center for Migration Studies, Staten Island, NY: 8–41.

Davies, James B., and Ian Wooton (1992), 'Income inequality and international migration', *Economic Journal*, 102: 789–802.

Davila, Alberto, and Rogelio Saenz (1990), 'The effect of maquila employment on the monthly flow of Mexican undocumented immigration to the US, 1978–1982', *International Migration Review*, 24: 96–107.

Davis, Kingsley (1974), 'The migrations of human populations', in *The Human Population*, W. H. Freeman, San Francisco: 53–65.

——(1988), 'Social science approaches to international migration,' in Michael S. Teitelbaum and Jay M. Winter (eds.), *Population and Resources in Western Intellectual Traditions*, Population Council, New York: 245–61.

Dawkins, P., P. Lewis, K. Noris, M. Baker, F. Robertson, N. Groenewold, and A. Hagger (1991), *Flows of Immigrants to South Australia, Tasmania and Western Australia*, Australian Government Publishing Service, Canberra.

DeJong, Gordon F., Ricardo G. Abad, Fred Arnold, Benjamin V. Cariño, James T. Fawcett, and Robert W. Gardner (1983), 'International and internal migration decision making: a value-expectancy based analytical framework of intentions to move from a rural Philippine province', *International Migration Review*, 17: 470–84.

Demery, Lionel (1986), 'Asian labor migration: an empirical assessment', in Fred Arnold and Nasra M. Shah (eds.), *Asian Labor Migration: Pipeline to the Middle East*, Westview Press, Boulder, Colo.: 17–46.

De Sierra, Gerónimo (1976), 'Migrantes Uruguayos hacia la Argentina: tendencias recientes', *Migración y Desarrollo*, 5: 113–27.

——(1978), 'L'émigration massive des travailleurs', *Notes et Etudes Documentaires*, Documentation Francaise, Paris: 4485–6.

——D. Marcotti, and J. Rojas (1975), *Quelques elements d'analyse sur les migrations internationales entre les pays du 'Cono Sur' de l'Amerique Latine (Argentine, Chili, Bolivie, Paraguay, Uruguay)*, Institut D'Etude des Pays en Développement, Université de Louvain, Louvain.

Devoto, F. (1988), 'Las cadenas migratorias Italianas a la Argentina', *Estudios Migratorios*, 8: 25–33.

——and G. Rosoli (1985), *La Inmigración Italiana en la Argentina*, Editorial Bilbos, Buenos Aires.

Díaz-Alejandro, C. F. (1970), *Essays on the Economic History of the Argentine Republic*, Yale University Press, New Haven.

Diaz-Briquets, Sergio (1983), *International Migration within Latin America: An Overview*, Center for Migration Studies, Staten Island, NY.

——(1991), 'The effects of international migration on Latin America', in Demetrios G. Papademetriou and Philip L. Martin (eds.), *The Unsettled Relationship: Labor Migration and Economic Development*, Greenwood Press, New York: 183–200.

——and Melinda J. Frederick (1984), 'Colombian emigration: a research note', *International Migration Review*, 18: 99–110.

Dib, George (1988), 'Laws governing migration in some Arab countries', in Reginald T. Appleyard (ed.), *International Migration Today, I: Trends and Prospects*, University of Western Australia for the United Nations Educational, Scientific, and Cultural Organization, Perth: 168–79.

Dickens, William T., and Kevin Lang (1985), 'A test of dual labor market theory', *American Economic Review*, 75: 792–805.

——(1988), 'The reemergence of segmented labor market theory', *American Economic Review*, 78: 129–34.

Dinerman, Ina R. (1982), *Migrants and Stay-at Homes: A Comparative Study of Rural Migration from Michoacán, México*, Program in United States–Mexican Studies, University of California at San Diego, La Jolla.

Dirks, Robert (1972), 'Networks, groups, and adaptation in an Afro-Caribbean community', *Man* 7: 565–85.

Djajic, Slobodan (1986), 'International migration, remittances and welfare in a dependent economy', *Journal of Development Economics*, 21: 229–34.

Donato, Katharine M. (1991), 'Understanding US immigration: why some countries send women and others men', in Donn R. Gabaccia (ed.), *Seeking Common Ground: Women Immigrants to the United States*, Greenwood Press, New York: 159–84.

——Jorge Durand, and Douglas S. Massey (1992*a*), 'Changing conditions in the US labor market: effects of the Immigration Reform and Control Act of 1986', *Population Research and Policy Review*, 11: 93–115.

————(1992*b*). 'Stemming the tide? Assessing the deterrent effects of the Immigration Reform and Control Act', *Demography*, 29: 139–57.

——and Douglas S. Massey (1993), 'Effect of the Immigration Reform and Control Act on the wages of Mexican migrants', *Social Science Quarterly*, 74: 523–41.

Duke, Lynne (1995), 'The huddled masses are flocking to South Africa', *Washington Post National Weekly Edition*, 21–7 Aug. p. 19.

Dunlevy, James A. (1991), 'On the settlement patterns of recent Caribbean and Latin immigrants to the United States', *Growth and Change*, 22: 54–67.

——(1992), 'The role of nationality-specific characteristics on the settlement patterns of late nineteenth century immigrants', *Explorations in Economic History*, 29: 228–49.

——and Henry A. Gemery (1977), 'The role of migrant stock and lagged migration in the settlement patterns of nineteenth-century immigrants', *Review of Economics and Statistics*, 59: 137–44.

————(1978), 'Economic opportunity and the response of "old" and "new" migrants to the United States', *Journal of Economic History*, 38: 901–17.

Durand, Jorge (1988), 'Los migradólares: cien años de inversión en el medio rural', *Argumentos: Estudios Críticos de la Sociedad*, 5: 7–21.

——and Douglas S. Massey (1992), 'Mexican migration to the United States: a critical review', *Latin American Research Review*, 27: 3–42.

——William Kandel, Emilio A. Parrado, and Douglas S. Massey (1996), 'International migration and development in Mexican communities', *Demography*, 33: 249–64.

Dywer, L., I. Burnley, P. Forsyth, and P. Murphy (1993), *Immigration and Tourism*, Australian Government Publishing Service, Canberra.

Easterlin, Richard A. (1961), 'Influences on European overseas emigration before World War I', *Economic Development and Cultural Change*, 9: 331–51.

Ebiri, Kutlay (1985), 'Impact of labor migration on the Turkish economy', in Rosemarie Rogers (ed.), *Guests Come to Stay: The Effects of European Labor Migration on Sending and Receiving Countries*, Westview Press, Boulder, Colo.: 207–30.

Ecevit, Zafer H. (1981), 'International labor migration in the Middle East and North Africa: trends, effects, and policies', in Mary M. Kritz, Charles B. Keely, and Silvano M. Tomasi (eds.), *Global Trends in Migration: Theory and Research on International Population Movements*, Center for Migration Studies, Staten Island, NY: 133–57.

Economic and Social Commission for Asia and the Pacific (1987), *Migration and Remittances Between the Developing ESCAP Countries and the Middle East: Trends, Issues, and Policies*, Economic and Social Commission for Asia and the Pacific, Bangkok.

Eelens, Frank (1988), 'Early return of Sri Lankan migrants in the Middle East', *International Migration*, 26: 401–16.

——T. Schampers, and J. D. Speckman (1991), *Labour Migration to the Middle East: From Sri Lanka to the Gulf*, Kegan Paul, London.

——and J. D. Speckmann (1990), 'Recruitment of labor migrants for the Middle East: the Sri Lankan Case, *International Migration Review*, 24: 297–322.

El-Mallakh, R. (1982), *Saudi Arabia: Rush to Development*, Croom-Helm, London.

Elnajjar, Hassan (1993), 'Planned emigration: the Palestinian case', *International Migration Review*, 27: 34–50.

Employment and Immigration Canada (1992), *Managing Immigration: An Agenda for the 1990s*, Employment and Immigration Canada, Quebec.

Escobar, Agustin, and María de la O. Martinez (1990), *Small-Scale Industry and International Migration in Guadalajara, Mexico*, US Commission for the Study of International Migration and Cooperative Economic Development, Washington, DC.

Espenshade, Thomas J. (1989), 'Growing imbalances between labor supply and labor demand in the Caribbean basin', in Frank D. Bean, Jurgen Schmandt, and Sidney Weintraub (eds.), *Mexican and Central American Population and US Immigration Policy* Center for Mexican American Studies, University of Texas, Austin, Tex.

——(1990), 'Undocumented migration to the United States: evidence from a repeated trials model', in Frank D. Bean, Barry Edmonston, and Jeffrey S. Passel (eds.), *Undocumented Migration to the United States: IRCA and the Experience of the 1980s*, Urban Institute Press, Washington, DC: 159–82.

——and Maryann Belanger (1997), 'US public perceptions and reactions to Mexican migration', in Frank D Bean, Rodolfo O. de la Garza, Bryan R. Roberts, and Sidney Weintraub (eds.), *At the Crossroads: Mexico and US Immigration Policy*, Rowman & Littlefield, Lanham, Md.: 227–64.

——and Charles A. Calhoun (1993), 'An analysis of public opinion toward undocumented immigration', *Population Research and Policy Review*, 12: 189–224.

——and Katherine Hempstead (1996), 'Contemporary American attitudes toward US immigration', *International Migration Review*, 30: 535–70.

Espinosa, Kristin E., and Douglas S. Massey (1997), 'Undocumented migration and the quantity and quality of social capital', *Social Welt*, forthcoming.

Fakiolas, Rossettos (1995), 'Italy and Greece: from emigrants to immigrants', in Robin Cohen (ed.), *The Cambridge Survey of World Migration*, Cambridge University Press, Cambridge: 313–15.

Farley, Reynolds (1984), *Blacks and Whites: Narrowing the Gap?* Harvard University Press, Cambridge, Mass.

——and Walter R. Allen (1987), *The Color Line and the Quality of Life in America*, Russell Sage Foundation, New York.

Fassmann, Heinz, and Rainer Münz (1992), 'Patterns and trends of international migration in Western Europe', *Population and Development Review*, 18: 457–81.

Fawcett, James T. (1989), 'Networks, linkages, and migration systems', *International Migration Review*, 23: 671–80.

——and Fred Arnold (1987), 'Explaining diversity: Asian and Pacific immigration systems', in James T. Fawcett and Benjamin V. Cariño (eds.), *Pacific Bridges: The New Immigration from Asia and the Pacific Islands*, Center for Migration Studies, Staten Island, NY: 453–73.

Fee, Lian Kwen (1995), 'Migration and the formation of Malaysia and Singapore', in Robin Cohen (ed.), *The Cambridge Survey of World Migration*, Cambridge University Press, Cambridge: 392–6.

Feiler, Gil (1991), 'Migration and recession: Arab labour mobility in the Middle East', *Population and Development Review*, 17: 134–56.

Ferenczi, Imre (1929), *International Migrations, I: Statistics*, National Bureau of Economic Research, New York.

Fergany, Nader (1982), 'The impact of emigration on national development in the Arab region: the case of the Yemen Arab Republic', *International migration Review*, 26: 757–80.

——(1984), 'Al Hijra Illa Naft', Research Center of the Arab League, Cairo.

——(1985), 'On labour migration in Egypt: 1974–1985', Paper presented at the Annual Seminar, UN Demographic Centre, United Nations, Cairo.

——(1988), 'Some aspects of return migration in Egypt', Unpublished paper, UN Demographic Centre, Cairo.

Fernández, Celestino (1988), 'Migración hacia los Estados Unidos: el caso de Santa Inés, Michoacán', in Gustavo López and Sergio Pardo (eds.), *Migración en el Occidente de México*, El Colegio de Michoacán, Zamora: 113–24.

Ferrán, Fernando I., and Patricia R. Pessar (1991), 'Dominican Agriculture and the effect of international migration', in Anthony P. Maingot (ed.), *Small Country Development and International Labor Flows: Experiences in the Caribbean*, Westview Press, Boulder, Colo.: 137–66.

Fields, Gary S. (1994), 'The migration transition in Asia', *Asian and Pacific Migration Journal*, 3: 7–30.

Filgueira, Carlos (1976), 'Predisposición migratoria: la situación de egresados profesionales', *Cuadernos de Trabajo* 5, Centro de Informaciones y Estudios del Uruguay, Montevideo.

——(1989), 'Prólogo', in N. Niedworok, Juan C. Fortuna, and Adela Pellegrino (eds.), *Uruguay y la Emigración de los 70*, Ediciones de la Banda Oriental, Montevideo, pp. i–iv.

Finch, Henry (1995), 'Uruguayan Migration', in Robin Cohen (ed.), *The Cambridge Survey of World Migration*, Cambridge University Press, Cambridge: 203–4.

Findlay, A. M. (1984), 'Migrations de travail dans le Golfe et croissance des quartiers périphériques d'Amman', *Études Méditerranéennes*, 6: 205–24.

——and A. Stewart (1986), 'Migrations des travailleurs qualifiés Britanniques sous contrat au Moyen-Orient', *Revue Européene des Migrations Internationales*, 2: 95–107.

Findley, Sally E. (1987), 'An interactive contextual model of migration in Ilocos Norte, the Philippines', *Demography*, 24: 163–90.

——(1989), 'Choosing between African and French destinations: the role of family and community factors in migration from the Senegal River Valley', Working paper 42, African Studies Center, Boston University, Boston.

Fjellman, Stephen M., and Hugh Gladwin (1985), 'Haitian family patterns of migration to south Florida', *Human Organization*, 44: 301–12.

Fleisher, Belton M. (1965), 'Some economic aspects of Puerto Rican migration to the United States', *Review of Economics and Statistics*, 45: 2245–53.

Fletcher, Peri, and J. Edward Taylor (1992), 'Migration and the transformation of a Mexican village house economy', Paper presented at the Conference on 'New Perspectives on Mexico-US Migration', University of Chicago, Center for Latin American Studies, 23–24 October.

Fortuna, Juan C., N. Niedworok, and A. Pellegrino (1989), *Emigración de Uruguayos, Colonias en el Exterior y Perspectivas de Retorno*, Ediciones de la Banda Oriental, Montevideo.

Frank, Andre Gundre (1969), *Capitalism and Underdevelopment in Latin America*, Monthly Review Press, New York.

Furtado, Celso (1965), *Development and Underdevelopment*, University of California Press, Berkeley and Los Angeles.

——(1970), *Economic Development of Latin America*, Cambridge University Press, Cambridge.

Freeman, G. P., and J. Jupp (1992), *Nations of Immigrants: Australia, the United States, and International Migration*, Oxford University Press, Melbourne.

Frey, William H. (1994), 'The new white flight', *American Demographics*, 16: 40–51.

Friedmann, John (1986), 'The world city hypothesis', *Development and Change*, 17: 69–83.

Frisbie, W. Parker (1975), 'Illegal migration from Mexico to the United States: A longitudinal analysis', *International Migration Review*, 9: 3–13.

Frucht, Richard (1968), 'Emigration, remittances, and social change: aspects of the social field of Nevis, West Indies', *Anthropologica*, 10: 193–208.

Funkhouser, Edward (1992), 'Mass emigration, remittances, and economic adjustment: the case of El Salvador in the 1980s', in George J. Borjas and Richard B. Freeman (eds.), *Immigration and the Workforce: Economic Consequences for the United States and Source Areas*, University of Chicago Press, Chicago: 135–75.

Galaleldin, Muhammed Al-Awad (1979), 'Migration of Sudanese abroad', Council on Economic and Social Research, Khartoum.

Galarza, Ernest (1964), *Merchants of Labor: The Mexican Bracero Story*, McNally & Loftin, Santa Barbara, Calif.

Gallaway, Lowell E., and Richard K. Vedder (1971), 'The increasing urbanization thesis—did "new immigrants" to the United States have a particular fondness for urban life?', *Explorations in Economic History*, 8: 305–19.

Gamio, Manuel (1930), *Mexican Immigration to the United States*, University of Chicago Press, Chicago.

García, Brígida, Humberto Muñoz, and Orlandina de Olieira (1983), *Familia y Mercados de Trabajo: Un Estudio de dos Ciudades Brasileñas*, Universidad Nacional Autónoma de México and Colegio de México, Mexico.

García Castro, M. (1979), *Migración Femenina en Colombia*, Ministerio de Trabajo y Seguirdad Social de Colombia, Bogotá.

García y Griego, Manuel (1987), 'International migration data in Mexico', *International Migration Review*, 21: 1245–57.

Garson, Jean-Pierre (1988), 'Migration and interdependence: the migration system between France and Africa', in Mary M. Kritz, Lin Lean Lim, and Hania Zlotnik (eds.), *International Migration Systems: A Global Approach*, Oxford University Press, London: 80–94.

Gemery, Henry A., and James Horn (1992), 'British and French indentured servant migration to the Caribbean: a comparative study of seventeenth century emigration and labor markets', in *Proceedings of the Conference on the Peopling of the Americas, I*, International Union for the Scientific Study of Population, Liège: 283–300.

Georges, Eugenia (1990), *The Making of a Transnational Community: Migration, Development, and Cultural Change in the Dominican Republic*, Oxford University Press, New York.

Germani, Gino (1966a), 'Mass immigration and modernization in Argentina', *Studies in Comparative International Development*, 2: 165–82.

——(1966b), *Política y Sociedad en una Epoca de Transición: de la Sociedad Tradicional a la Sociedad de Masas*, Editorial Paidós, Buenos Aires.

Giddens, Anthony (1990), 'Structuration theory and sociological analysis', in J. Clark, C. Modgil, and S. Modgil (eds.), *Anthony Giddens: Consensus and Controversy*, Falmer Press, New York: 297–315.

Gilani, Ijaz S. (1981), *Labour Migration from Pakistan to the Middle East and its Impact on the Domestic Economy*, Pakistani Institute of Development Economics, Islamabad.

——(1988), 'Effects of emigration and return on sending countries: the case of Pakistan', in Charles Stahl (ed.), *International Migration Today, 2: Emerging Issues*, University of Western Australia for the UN Educational, Social, and Cultural Organization, Perth: 204–17.

——Fahim Khan, and Munawar Iqbal (1981), *Labor Migration from Pakistan to the Middle East and its Impact on the Domestic Economy: Final Report in Three Parts*, Pakistan Institute of Development Economics, Islamabad.

Gillespie, Francis, and Harley L. Browning (1979), 'The effect of emigration upon socioeconomic structure', *International Migration Review*, 13: 502–18.

Gitmez, Ali S. (1984), 'Geographical and occupational reintegration of returning Turkish workers', in Daniel Kubat (ed.), *The Politics of Return: International Return Migration in Europe*, Center for Migration Studies, Staten Island, NY: 113–21.

——(1991), 'Migration without development: the case of Turkey', in Demetrios G. Papademetriou and Philip L. Martin (eds.), *The Unsettled Relationship: Labor Migration and Economic Development*, Greenwood Press, New York: 115–34.

——and Czarina Wilpert (1987), 'A micro-society or an ethnic community? Social organization and ethnicity amongst Turkish migrants in Berlin', in John Rex, Danièle Joly, and Czarina Wilpert (eds.), *Immigrant Associations in Europe*, Gower, Aldershot: 86–125.

Glaser, William (1978), *The Brain Drain: Emigration and Return*, Pergamon Press, Oxford.

Go, Stella P., and Leticia T. Postrado (1986), 'Filipino overseas contract workers: their families and communities', in Fred Arnold and Nasra M. Shah (eds.), *Asian Labor Migration: Pipeline to the Middle East*, Westview Press, Boulder, Colo.: 125–44.

Godfrey, M. (1996), 'Indonesia: notes on employment, earnings and international migration', in D. O'Connor and L. Farsakh (eds.), *Development Strategy, Employment and Migration: Country Experiences*, OECD, Paris: 127–45.

Gokdere, A. Y. (1978), *Ybanci Ulkelere Isgucu Akimi ve Turk Ekonomisi Uzerindeki Etkileri* (Migration and its Effects on the Turkish Economy), Is Bankasi Yayini, Ankara.

Goldring, Luin (1990), *Development and Migration: A Comparative Analysis of Two Mexican Migrant Circuits*, US Commission for the Study of International Migration and Cooperative Economic Development, Washington, DC.

——(1992), 'La migración México-EUA y la transnacionalización del espacio político y social: perspectivas desde el México rural', *Estudios Sociológicos*, 10: 315–340.

——(1996a), 'Blurring borders: constructing transnational community in the process of Mexico-US Migration', *Research in Community Sociology*, 6: 69–104.

——(1996b), 'Gendered memory: constructions of rurality among Mexican transnational migrants', in E. Melanie DuPuis and Peter Vandergeest (eds.), *Creating the Countryside: The Politics of Rural and Environmental Discourse*, Temple University Press, Philadelphia: 303–29.

Golini, A., G. Gerano, and F. Heins (1991), 'South-north migration with special reference to Europe', *International Migration*, 29: 253–80.

Gómez Jiménez, Alcides, and Luz Marina Díaz Mesa (1983), *La Moderna Esclavitud: Los Indocumentados en Venezuela*, Editorial La Oveja Negra, Bogotá.

Gonzalez, E. T. (1993), 'Do income differentials influence the flow of migrant workers from the Philippines?' Paper presented at the IUSSP General Population Conference, Montreal, 1 Sept.

González, Mercedes, and Agustín Escobar (1990), *The Impact of IRCA on the Migration Patterns of a Community in Los Altos, Jalisco, Mexico*, US Commission for the Study of International Migration and Cooperative Economic Development, Washington, DC.

Goss, Jon D., and Bruce Lindquist (1995), 'Conceptualizing international labor migration: a structuration perspective', *International Migration Review*, 29: 317–51.

Gould, W. T. S. (1988), 'Urban-rural return migration in Western Province, Kenya', African Population Conference, International Union for the Scientific Study of Population, Dakar, Senegal, 7–12 Nov.

Goza, Franklin (1994), 'Brazilian immigration to North America', *International Migration Review*, 28: 136–52.

Grasmuck, Sherri, and Patricia R. Pessar (1991), *Between Two Islands: Dominican International Migration*, University of California Press, Berkeley and Los Angeles.

Grecic, V. (1990), 'The importance of migrant workers' and emigrants' remittances for the Yugoslav economy', *International Migration*, 28: 201–14.

Greenwell, Lisa, Julie DaVanzo, and R. Burdiaga Valdez (1997), 'Social ties, wages, and gender in a study of Salvadorean and Pilipino immigrants in Los Angeles', *Social Science Quarterly*, 78: 559–77.

Greenwood, Michael J. (1981), *Migration and Economic Growth in the United States*, Academic Press, New York.

——(1985), 'Human migration: theory, models, and empirical evidence', *Journal of Regional Science*, 25: 521–44.

——Gary L. Hunt, and John M. McDowell (1987), 'Migration and employment change: empirical evidence on the spatial and temporal dimensions of the linkage', *Journal of Regional Science*, 26: 223–34.

Gregory, David D., and J. Cazorla Pérez (1985), 'Intra-European migration and regional development: Spain and Portugal', in Rosemarie Rogers (ed.), *Guests Come to Stay: The Effects of European Labor Migration on Sending and Receiving Countries*, Westview Press, Boulder, Colo.: 231–62.

Gregory, Peter (1986), *The Myth of Market Failure: Employment and the Labor Market in Mexico*, Johns Hopkins University Press, Baltimore.

Griffith, David C. (1986), 'Social organization obstacles to capital accumulation among returning migrants: the British West Indies Temporary Alien Labor Program', *Human Organization*, 45: 34–42.

Griffiths, Stephen L. (1979), 'Emigration and entrepreneurship in a Philippine peasant village', *Papers in Anthropology*, 20: 127–43.

——(1989), *Emigrants, Entrepreneurs, Evil Spirits: Life in a Philippine Village*, New Day Publishers, Quezon City, Philippines.

Grindle, Merilee S. (1988), *Searching for Rural Development: Labor Migration and Employment in Mexico*, Cornell University Press, Ithaca, NY.

Grubel, H., and A. D. Scott (1966), 'The international flow of human capital', *American Economic Review*, 56: 268–74.

Gurak, Douglas T., and Fe Caces (1992), 'Migration networks and the shaping of migration systems', in Mary Kritz, Lin Lean Lim, and Hania Zlotnick (eds.), *International Migration Systems: A Global Approach*, Clarendon Press, Oxford: 150–76.

Habib, Ansanul (1985), 'Economic Consequences of International Migration for Sending Countries: Review of Evidence from Bangladesh', unpublished Ph.D. thesis, Dept. of Economics, University of Newcastle, Australia.

Habir, M. (1984), 'A migration equation', *Far Eastern Economic Review*, 26 April: 166–8.

Hagan, Jacqueline Maria (1994), *Deciding to be Legal: A Maya Community in Houston*, Temple University Press, Philadelphia.

——and Susan Gonzalez Baker (1993), 'Implementing the US legalization program: the influence of immigrant communities and local agencies on immigration policy reform', *International Migration Review*, 27: 513–36.

Hall, Stuart (1988), 'Migration from the English-speaking Caribbean to the United Kingdom, 1950–80', in Reginald T. Appleyard (ed.), *International Migration Today, I: Trends and Prospects*, University of Western Australia for the UN Educational, Scientific, and Cultural Organization, Perth: 264–310.

Halliday, F. (1984), 'Labour migration in the Arab World', *Middle East Research and Information Project Report*, 123.

Hammar, Tomas (1995), 'Labour migration to Sweden: the Finnish case', in Robin Cohen (ed.), *The Cambridge Survey of World Migration*, Cambridge University Press, Cambridge: 297–301.

Hannan, D. (1970), *Rural Exodus: A Study of the Forces Influencing the Large-Scale Migration of Irish Youth*, Gregory Chapman, London.

Harker, Richard, Cheleen Mahar, and Chris Wilkes (1990), *An Introduction to the Work of Pierre Bourdieu: The Practice of Theory*, Macmillan, London.

Harris, J. R., and Michael P. Todaro (1970), 'Migration, unemployment, and development: a two-sector analysis', *American Economic Review*, 60: 126–42.

Hart, John Mason (1987), *Revolutionary Mexico: The Coming and Process of the Mexican Revolution*, University of California Press, Berkeley and Los Angeles.

Harvey, David (1990), *The Condition of Postmodernity*, Basil Blackwell, Oxford.

Haskey, J. (1991), 'The immigrant populations of the different countries of Europe: their sizes and origins', *Population Trends*, 69: 37–47.

Hatton, Timothy J., and Jeffrey G. Williamson (1992), 'International migration and World Development: A Historical Perspective', *NBER Working Paper Series on Historical Factors in Long Run Growth*, National Bureau of Economic Research, Cambridge, Mass.

————(1994*a*.), 'What drove the mass migrations from Europe in the late nineteenth century?', *Population and Development Review*, 20: 533–60.

————(1994*b*), 'Latecomers to mass emigration: the Latin experience', in Timothy J. Hatton and Jeffrey G. Williamson (eds.), *Migration and the International Labour Market: 1850–1939*, Routledge, London: 55–71.

————(1994*c*), 'International migration 1850–1939: an economic survey', in Timothy J. Hatton and Jeffrey G. Williamson (eds.), *Migration and the International Labour Market: 1850–1939*, Routledge, London: 3–32.

Hayes, G. (1992), 'The use of scientific models in the study of Polynesian migration', *Asian and Pacific Migration Journal*, 1: 278–312.

Heckman, James J., and V. Joseph Hotz (1986), 'An investigation of the labor market earnings of Panamanian males: evaluating the sources of inequality', *Journal of Human Resources*, 21: 507–42.

Heckmann, Friedrich (1985), 'Temporary labor migration or immigration? "Guest Workers" in the Federal Republic of Germany', in Rosemarie Rogers (ed.), *Guests Come to Stay: The Effects of European Labor Migration on Sending and Receiving Countries*, Westview Press, Boulder, Colo.: 69–84.

Hefferman, Michael (1995), 'French colonial migration', in Robin Cohen (ed.), *The Cambridge Survey of World Migration*, Cambridge University Press, Cambridge: 33–8.

Helweg, A. W. (1983), 'Emigrant remittances: their nature and impact on a Punjabi village', *New Community*, 10: 67–84.

Hernández-Cruz, Juan E. (1985), 'Migración de retorno o circulación de obreros Boricuas?', *Revista de Ciencias Sociales*, 24: 81–110.

——(1986), 'Reintigration of circulating families in southwestern Puerto Rico', *International Migration*, 24: 397–410.

Heyzer, N. G., Lycklama Nijeholt, and N. Weerakoon (1994), *The Trade in Domestic Workers: Causes, Mechanisms and Consequences of International Migration, 1*, Asian and Pacific Development Centre, Kuala Lumpur.

Hicks, G. L. (1993), *Overseas Chinese Remittances from Southeast Asia, 1910–1940*, Select Books, Singapore.

Hill, Donald R. (1977), 'The impact of migration on the metropolitan and folk society of Carriacou, Grenada', *Anthropological Papers of the American Museum of Natural History 54, Part 2*, American Museum of Natural History, New York.

Hill, Kenneth (1981), 'A proposal for the use of information on residence of siblings to estimate emigration by age', in Working Group on the Methodology for the Study of International Migration (ed.), *Indirect Procedures for Estimating Emigration*, International Union for the Scientific Study of Population, Liège, 19–34.

Hill, Polly (1970), *Migrant Cocoa Farmers of Southern Ghana: A Study in Rural Capitalism*, Cambridge University Press, London.

Hily, Marie-Antoinette, and Michel Poinard (1987), 'Portuguese associations in France', in John Rex, Danièle Joly, and Czarina Wilpert (eds.), *Immigrant Associations in Europe*, Gower, Aldershot: 126–65.

Ho, Christine G. T. (1993), 'The internationalization of kinship and the feminization of Caribbean migration: the case of Afro-Trinidadian immigrants in Los Angeles', *Human Organization*, 52: 32–40.

Hodson, Randy, and Robert L. Kaufman (1981), 'Circularity in the dual economy: a comment on Tolbert, Horan, and Beck, 1980', *American Journal of Sociology*, 86: 881–7.

———— (1982), 'Economic dualism: a critical review', *American Sociological Review*, 47: 727–40.

Hoffmann-Nowotny, Hans-Joachim (1995), 'Switzerland: a non-immigration immigration country', in Robin Cohen (ed.), *The Cambridge Survey of World Migration*, Cambridge University Press, Cambridge: 302–7.

Holmes, Colin (1995), 'Jewish economic and refugee migrations, 1880–1950', in Robin Cohen (ed.), *The Cambridge Survey of World Migration*, Cambridge University Press, Cambridge: 148–52.

Hondagneu-Sotelo, Pierette (1994a), 'Regulating the unregulated? Domestic workers social networks', *Social Problems*, 41: 50–64.

—— (1994b), *Gendered Transitions: Mexican Experiences of Immigration*, University of California Press, Berkeley and Los Angeles.

—— (1995), 'Beyond the longer they stay (and say they will stay): women and Mexican immigrant settlement', *Qualitative Sociology*, 18: 21–43.

Hope, Elizabeth M. Thomas (1986), 'Transients and settlers: varieties of Caribbean migrants and the socio-economic implications of their return'. *International Migration*, 24: 559–72.

Horan, Patrick M., Charles M. Tolbert II, and E. M. Beck (1981), 'The circle has no close', *American Journal of Sociology*, 86: 887–94.

Houben, A. (1987), *Een Onderzoek Naar de Recrutering van Arbeidsmigranten*, Leiden University Press, Leiden.

Hugo, Graeme J. (1975), 'Population Mobility in West Java, Indonesia', Unpublished Ph.D. thesis, Dept. of Demography, Australian National University, Canberra.

—— (1980), 'Population movements in Indonesia during the colonial period', in J. J. Fox, R. G. Garnaut, T. McCawley, and J. A. C. Mackie (eds.), *Indonesia: Australian Perspectives*, Australian National University, Canberra: 95–135.

—— (1981), 'Village-community ties, village norms, and ethnic and social networks: a review of evidence from the Third World', in Gordon F. DeJong and Robert W. Gardner (eds.), *Migration Decision Making: Multidisciplinary Approaches to Microlevel Studies in Developed and Developing Countries*, Pergamon Press, New York: 186–224.

—— (1985), 'Structural change and labour mobility in rural Java', in Guy Standing (ed.), *Labour Circulation and the Labour Process*, Croom-Helm, London: 46–88.

——(1991), 'Knocking at the door: Asian immigration to Australia', *Asian and Pacific Migration Journal*, 1: 100–44.

——(1992), 'Women on the move: changing patterns of population movement of women in Indonesia', in S. Chant (ed.), *Gender and Migration in Developing Countries*, Belhaven Press, London: 174–96.

——(1993*a*), 'Manpower and employment situation in Indonesia, 1992', Dept. of Manpower, Government of Indonesia, Jakarta.

——(1993*b*), 'Indonesian labour migration to Malaysia: trends and policy implications', *Southeast Asian Journal of Social Science*, 21: 36–70.

——(1994*a*), *The Economic Implications of Emigration from Australia*, Australian Government Publishing Service, Canberra.

——(1994*b*), 'Demographic and spatial aspects of immigration', in Mark Wooden, Robert Holton, Graeme Hugo, and Judith Sloan (eds.), *Australian Immigration: A Survey of the Issues*, Australian Government Publishing Service, Canberra: 30–110.

——(1995*a*), 'Illegal migration in Asia', in Robin Cohen (ed.), *Cambridge Survey of World Migration*, Cambridge University Press, Cambridge: 397–402.

——(1995*b*), 'Labour export from Indonesia: an overview', *ASEAN Economic Bulletin*, 12: 275–98.

——(1995*b*), 'Migration of Asian women to Australia', in *International Migration Policies and the Status of Female Migrants*, United Nations, New York: 192–220.

——(1996*a*), 'Economic impacts of international labour emigration on regional and local development: some evidence from Indonesia', Paper presented at the Annual Meeting of the Population Association of America, New Orleans, 9–11 May.

——(1996*b*), 'Asia on the move: research challenges for population geography', *International Journal of Population Geography*, 2: 95–118.

——(1996*c*), 'Brain drain and student movements', in P. J. Lloyd and L. S. Williams (eds.), *International Trade in the APEC Region*, Oxford University Press, Melbourne: 210–28.

——and Anchalee Singhanetra-Renard (1987), *International Migration of Contract Labour in Asia: Major Issues and Implications*, International Development Research Centre, Ottawa.

Hui, Ong Jin (1995), 'Chinese indentured labour: coolies and colonies', in Robin Cohen (ed.), *The Cambridge Survey of World Migration*, Cambridge University Press, Cambridge: 51–6.

Huntoon, Laura (1995), 'Return migration when savings differ', *Journal of Urban Affairs*, 17: 219–39.

Hutchinson, Edward P. (1981), *Legislative History of American Immigration Policy: 1798–1965*, University of Pennsylvania Press, Philadelphia.

Hyun, Oh-Seok (1984), 'A Macroeconometric Model of Korea: Simulation Experiments with a Large-Scale Model for a Developing Country', unpublished Ph.D. thesis, Dept. of Regional Science, University of Pennsylvania, Philadelphia.

——(1989), 'The impact of overseas migration on national development: the case of the Republic of Korea', in Rashid Amjad (ed.), *To the Gulf and Back: Studies on the Economic Impact of Asian Labour Migration*, International Labour Office, Geneva: 143–66.

Ibrahim, A. (1984), 'Athar El Amala Al Ajnabiah Ala Athaqafa El Arabia', Centre for Arab Unity Studies, Beirut.

Ibrahim, S. E. (1982), *The New Arab Social Order: A Study of the Impact of Oil Wealth*, Westview Press, Boulder, Colo.

——and A. Mahmoud (1983), *Migration of the Arab Labor Force*, Centre for Arab Unity Studies, Beirut.

Ilahi, Nadeem (1993), 'Guestworker Return Migration and Occupational Choice: Evidence from Pakistan', Unpublished Ph.D. thesis, Dept. of Agricultural Economics, University of California, Davis.

Institute for International Education (1995), *Open Doors 1992–1993: Report on International Educational Exchange*, Institute for International Education, New York.

Institution de Estudos para o Desenvolvimento (1983), 'Return, emigration, and regional development in Portugal', Instituto de Estudos para o Desenvolvimento, Lisbon.

Instituto Brasileiro de Geografía e Estatística (1990), *Anuário Estatístico do Brasil*, 1990, Ministério da Economía, Fazenda, e Planejamento, Rio de Janeiro.

Instituto Nacional de Estadística y Censos (1994), *Anuario Estadístico de la República Argentina*, Ministerio de Economía y Obras y Servicios Públicos, Buenos Aires.

International Monetary Fund (1994), *International Financial Statistics Yearbook*, International Monetary Fund, Washington, DC.

Islam, R. (1980), *Export of Manpower from Banladesh to the Middle East: The Impact of Remittance Money on Household Expenditure*, National Foundation for Research on Human Resource Development, Dhaka.

Ismael, J. S. (1986), 'The conditions of Egyptian labor in the Gulf: a profile of Kuwait', *Arab Studies Quarterly*, 8: 390–403.

Jaakkola, Magdalena (1987), 'Informal networks and formal associations of Finnish immigrants in Sweden', in John Rex, Danièle Joly, and Czarina Wilpert (eds.), *Immigrant Associations in Europe*, Gower, Aldershot: 201–18.

Jackman, M. E. (1973), 'Recent population movements in Zambia', Social Research Institute, Lusaka.

Jackson, Philip (1984), 'Migration and social change in Puerto Rico', in C. Clarke, D. Ley, and C. Peach (eds.), *Geography and Ethnic Pluralism*, Allen & Unwin, London: 195–213.

Jacobs, E. J., and Papma, L. (1992), 'The socio-economic position and religious status of Sri Lankan Muslim women migrating to the Gulf', in F. Eelens, T. Schampers, and J. D. Speckmann (eds.), *Labour Migration to the Middle East: From Sri Lanka to the Gulf*, Kegan Paul, London: 199–214.

Japanese Ministry of Labour (1993), *Monthly Labour Statistics and Research Bulletin*, Japanese Ministry of Labour, Tokyo.

Jasso, Guillermina, and Mark R. Rosenzweig (1988), 'Family reunification and the immigration multiplier: US immigration law, origin-country conditions, and the reproduction of immigrants', *Demography*, 23: 291–311.

——(1990), *The New Chosen People: Immigrants in the United States*, Russell Sage, New York.

Jazwinska, Ewa, and Marek Okolski (1996), *Causes and Consequences of Migration in Central and Eastern Europe*, Migration Research Centre, Institute for Social Studies, University of Warsaw. Warsaw.

Jenkins, J. Craig (1977), 'Push/pull in recent Mexican migration to the US', *International Migration Review*, 11: 178–89.

Johnson, H. G. (1967*a*), 'Some economic aspects of the brain drain', *Pakistani Development Review*, 7: 379–411.

—— (1967*b*), 'Un modelo internacionalista', in Walter Adams (ed.), *El Drenaje de Talento*, Editorial Paidós, Buenos Aires: 121–83.

Joly, Danièle (1987), 'Associations amongst the Pakistani population in Britain', in John Rex, Danièle Joly, and Czarina Wilpert (eds.), *Immigrant Associations in Europe*, Gower, Aldershot: 62–85.

—— (1995), 'Whose protection? European harmonization on asylum policy', in Robin Cohen (ed.), *The Cambridge Survey of World Migration*, Cambridge University Press, Cambridge: 496–501.

Jones, Richard C. (1989), 'Causes of Salvadoran migration to the United States', *Geographical Review*, 79: 183–94.

—— (1992), 'US Migration: an alternative mobility ladder for rural central Mexico', *Social Science Quarterly*, 73: 496–510.

Jorgenson, D. W. (1967), 'Testing alternative theories of the development of a dual economy', in Irma Adelman and E. Thorbecke (eds.), *The Theory and Design of Economic Development*, Johns Hopkins University Press, Baltimore: 45–60.

Josephides, Sasha (1987), 'Associations amongst the Greek Cypriot population in Britain', in John Rex, Danièle Joly, and Czarina Wilpert (eds.), *Immigrant Associations in Europe*, Gower, Aldershot: 420–62.

Kamiar, M. S., and H. F. Ismail (1992), 'Family ties and economic stability concerns of migrant labour families in Jordan', *International Migration*, 29: 561–72.

Kanaiaupuni, Shawn M. (1995), 'The Role of Women in the Social Process of Migration: Household Organizational Strategies among Mexican Families', Unpublished Ph.D. dissertation, Dept. of Sociology, University of Chicago.

Kandil, M., and M. F. Metwally (1990), 'The impact of migrants' remittances on the Egyptian economy', *International Migration*, 28: 159–80.

—— (1992), 'Determinants of the Egyptian labour migration', *International Migration*, 30: 39–56.

Kannappan, Subbiah (1968), 'The brain drain and developing countries', *International Labour Review*, 98: 1–26.

Kanok, Tosurat, and Preecha Uitrakul (1985), *Impact of the Return of Thai Labour Force from the Middle East*, Social Science Association of Thailand, Bangkok.

Kasto, L., and K. Sukamdi (1986), 'Mobilitas Ankatan Kerja Indonesia Ke Timur Tenga (D.I. Yogyakarta)', in *Mobilitas Angkatan Kerja Indonsia Ke Timur Tengah Laporan Akhir, Buki II*, Kerjasama Kanto Menteri Negara Kependudakan Dan Lingkungan Hidup dengan Pusat Penelitian Kependudukan Universitas, Gadja Mada, Yogyakarta: 206–75.

Katz, E., and Oded Stark (1986), 'Labor migration and risk aversion in less developed countries', *Journal of Labor Economics*, 4: 131–49.

Kay, Diana (1995), 'The resettlement of displaced persons in Europe, 1946–1951', in Robin Cohen (ed.), *The Cambridge Survey of World Migration*, Cambridge University Press, Cambridge: 154–8.

Kaysar, Barnard (1972), *Cyclically-Determined Homeward Flows of Migrant Workers*, OECD, Paris.

Kearney, Michael (1986), 'From the invisible hand to visible feet: anthropological studies of migration and development', *Annual Review of Anthropology*, 15: 331–61.

Keely, Charles B. (1979), 'The United States of America', in Daniel Kubat (ed.), *The*

Politics of Migration Policies, Center for Migration Studies, Staten Island, NY: 51–66.

——and Bao Nga Tran (1989), 'Remittances from labor migration: evaluations, performance, and implications', *International Migration Review*, 23: 500–25.

——and B. Saket (1984), 'Jordanian migrant workers in the Arab region: a case study of consequences for labour supplying countries', *Middle East Journal*, 38: 685–98.

Keles, Rusen (1976), 'Investment by Turkish migrants in real estate', in Nermin Abadan-Unat (ed.), *Turkish Workers in Europe: 1960–1975*, E. J. Brill, Leiden: 169–80.

——(1985), 'The effects of external migration on regional development in Turkey', in Ray Hudson and Jim Lewis (eds.), *Uneven Development in Southern Europe: Studies of Accumulation, Class, Migration, and the State*, Methuen, London: 54–75.

Kelly, John J. (1987), 'Improving the comparability of international migration statistics: contributions of the Conference of European Statisticians from 1971 to date', *International Migration Review*, 21: 1017–38.

Kemp, M. C. (1964), *The Pure Theory of International Trade*, Prentice-Hall, Englewood Cliffs, NJ.

Kennedy, David M. (1996), 'Can we still afford to be a nation of immigrants?' *Atlantic Monthly*, 278(5): 52–68.

Keyder, Caglar, and Ayhan Aksu-Koc (1988), *External Labour Migration from Turkey and its Impact: An Evaluation of the Literature*, International Development Research Centre, Ottawa.

Khoshkish, A. (1966), 'Intellectual migration: a sociological approach to brain drain', *Journal of World History*, 10, 178–97.

Kim, Sooyong (1983), 'Economic analysis of Korean manpower migration', *Sogang University Journal of Economics and Business*, 3–16 Sept.

——(1986), 'Labor migration from Korea to the Middle East: its trends and impact on the Korean economy', in Fred Arnold and Nasra M. Shaw (eds.), *Asian Labor Migration: Pipeline to the Middle East*, Westview Press, Boulder, Colo.: 163–76.

Kindleberger, Charles P. (1967), *Europe's Postwar Growth: The Role of Labor Supply*, Oxford University Press, New York.

Kiray, Mubeccel B. (1976), 'The family of the immigrant worker', in Nermin Abadan-Unit (ed.), *Turkish Workers in Europe 1960–1975: A Socio-Economic Reappraisal*, E. J. Brill, Leiden: 210–34.

Kiser, G., and M. Woody (1979), *Mexican Workers in the United States: Historical and Political Perspectives*, University of New Mexico Press, Albuquerque.

Kjurciev, T. Alexander (1987), 'Contribution of workers' remittances to development', in Silvio Borner and Alwyn Taylor (eds.), *Structural Change, Economic Interdependence and World Development*, Macmillan, London: 159–72.

Knerr, Beatrice (1989), 'Labour emigration and its effects on the economies of South Asia', *Internationales Asianforum: International Quarterly for Asia Studies*, 20: 263–93.

——(1990), 'Effects of international labour migration on the economic growth of Bangladesh', in M. Holmström (ed.), *Work for Wages in South Asia*, Oxford University Press, New Delhi: 118–59.

——(1992), 'Methods for assessing the impact of temporary labour emigration', *Pakistan Development Review*, 31: 1207–39.

——(1993), 'International labor migration: economic implications for the population in the source country', in *International Population Conference, Montreal 1993, 1*, International Union for the Scientific Study of Population, Liège: 625–50.

Knowles, James C., and Richard B. Anker (1981), 'Analysis of income transfers in a developing country: the case of Kenya', *Journal of Development Economics*, 8: 205–26.

Kolan, Tufan (1975), 'International labor migration and Turkish economic development', in Ronald E. Krane (ed.), *Manpower Mobility across Cultural Boundaries: Social, Economic, and Legal Aspects, The Case of Turkey and West Germany*. E. J. Brill, Leiden: 138–60.

——(1976), 'An analysis of individual earnings effects due to external migration', in Nermin Abadan-Unit (ed.), *Turkish Workers in Europe 1960–1975: A Socio-Economic Reappraisal*, E. J. Brill, Leiden: 139–54.

Korale, R. B. M. (1986), 'Migration for employment in the Middle East: its demographic and social effects on Sri Lanka', in Fred Arnold and Nasra M. Shah (eds.), *Asian Labor Migration: Pipeline to the Middle East*, Westview Press, Boulder, Colo.: 213–34.

Korte, Hermann (1985), 'Labor migration and the employment of foreigners in the Federal Republic of Germany since 1950', in Rosemarie Rogers (ed.), *Guests Come to Stay: The Effects of European Labor Migration on Sending and Receiving Countries*, Westview Press, Boulder, Colo.: 29–50.

Kossoudji, Sherrie A. (1992), 'Playing cat and mouse at the US-Mexican border', *Demography*, 29: 159–80.

Kraly, Ellen Percy, and K. S. Gnanasekaran (1987), 'Efforts to improve international migration statistics: a historical perspective', *International Migration Review*, 21: 967–95.

——and Robert Warren (1991), 'Long-term immigration to the United States: new approaches to measurement', *International Migration Review*, 25: 60–92.

————(1992), 'Estimates of long-term immigration to the United States: moving US Statistics toward United Nations concepts', *Demography*, 29: 613–26.

Krane, Ronald E. (1979), *International Labor Migration in Europe*, Praeger, New York.

Kritz, Mary M. (1975), 'The impact of international migration on Venezuelan demographic and social structure', *International Migration Review*, 9: 513–14.

——(1992), 'The British and Spanish migration systems in the colonial era: a policy framework', in *Proceedings of the Conference on the Peopling of the Americas, I*, International Union for the Scientific Study of Population, Liège: 263–82.

——and Fe Caces (1989), 'Science and technology transfers and migration flows', Working Paper, Population and Development Program, Cornell University, Ithaca, NY.

——and Douglas T. Gurak (1979), 'International migration trends in Latin America: research and data survey', *International Migration Review*, 13: 407–27.

——Charles B. Keely, and Silvano M. Tomasi (1981), *Global Trends in Migration: Theory and Research on International Population Movements*, Center for Migration Studies, Staten Island, NY.

——Lin Lean Lim, and Hania Zlotnik (1992), *International Migration Systems: A Global Approach*, Clarendon Press, Oxford.

Kubat, Daniel (1979), 'Canada', in Daniel Kubat (ed.), *The Politics of Migration Policies*, Center for Migration Studies, Staten Island, NY: 19–36.

Kudat, Ayse (1975), 'Structural change in the migrant Turkish family', in Ronald E. Krane (ed.), *Manpower Mobility Across Cultural Boundaries: Social, Economic, and Legal Aspects*, E. J. Brill, Leiden: 77–94.

Kuhn, Thomas S. (1962), *The Structure of Scientific Revolutions*, University of Chicago Press, Chicago.

Kuijsten, Anton (1994), 'International migration in Europe: patterns and implications for receiving countries', in Miroslav Macura and David Coleman (eds.), *International Migration: Regional Processes and Responses*, United Nations, New York: 21–40.

Kumcu, M. Ercan (1989), 'The savings behavior of migrant workers: Turkish workers in W. Germany', *Journal of Development Economics*, 30: 273–86.

Kuthiala, S. K. (1986), 'Migrant workers: a passage from India to the Middle East', *International Migration*, 24: 441–60.

Kyle, David Jané (1995), 'The macrohistorical development of New York City s largest undocumented migrant community: transnational migration from the Ecuadoran Andes', Paper presented at the Annual Meeting of the American Sociological Association, Washington, DC, 22 August.

Lamm, Richard D., and Gary Imhoff (1985), *The Immigration Time Bomb: The Fragmenting of America*, Dutton, New York.

Lattes, Alfredo E. (1982), 'Introducción', *Migración y Desarrollo*, 6: 1–2.

——(1983), *Acerca de los Patrones Recientes de Movilidad Territorial de la Población en el Mundo*, Centro de Estudios Políticos, Buenos Aires.

——(1985), 'Migraciones hacia América Latina y el Caribe desde principios del siglo XIX', *Cuaderno del CENEP 35*, Centro de Estudios Políticos, Buenos Aires.

——and Zulma Recchini de Lattes (1991), 'International migration in Latin America: patterns, implications, and policies', Paper presented at the Informal Expert Group Meeting on International Migration, UN Economic Commission for Europe, Geneva, 17 June.

Lauby, Jennifer, and Oded Stark (1988), 'Individual migration as a family strategy: young women in the Philippines', *Population Studies*, 42: 473–86.

Lazaar, Mohamed (1987), 'Conséquences de l'émigration dans les montagnes du Rif Central (Maroc)', *Revue Européenne des Migrations Internationales*, 3: 97–114.

——(1993), 'La migration internationale et la stratégie d'investissement des emigrés', *Revue de Géographie du Maroc*, 15: 167–80.

Lebon, André (1984), 'Les envois de fonds des migrants et leur utilisation', *International Migration*, 22: 281–333.

Lee, Everett S. (1966), 'A theory of migration', *Demography*, 3: 47–57.

Lee, S. M. (1996), 'Issues in research on women, international migration, and labour', *Asian and Pacific Migration Journal*, 5: 5–26.

Lefebvre, Alain (1990), 'International labor migration from two Pakistani villages with different forms of agriculture', *Pakistan Development Review*, 29: 1–20.

Lelievre, Eva (1987), 'Migration définitives vers la France et constitution de la famille', *Revue Européenne des Migrations Internationales*, 3: 35–53.

Lewis, B. D., and E. Thorbecke (1992), 'District-level economic linkages in Kenya: evidence based on a small regional social accounting matrix', *World Development*, 20: 881–97.

Lewis, W. Arthur (1954), 'Economic development with unlimited supplies of labour', *Manchester School of Economic and Social Studies*, 22: 139–91.

Levine, Barry B. (1987), *The Caribbean Exodus*, Praeger, New York.

Levine, Daniel B., Kenneth Hill, and Robert Warren (1985), *Immigration Statistics: A Story of Neglect*, National Academy Press, Washington, DC.

Lever-Tacy, C. (1981), 'Labour market segmentation and diverging migrant incomes', *Australia and New Zealand Journal of Sociology*, 17: 17–21.

—— and M. Quinlan (1988), *A Divided Working Class: Ethnic Segmentation and Industrial Conflict in Australia*, Routledge & Kegan Paul, London.

Levy, Mildred B., and Walter J. Wadycki (1973), 'The influence of family and friends on geographic labor mobility: an intercensal comparison', *Review of Economics and Statistics*, 55: 198–203.

Lim, Lin Lean (1993), 'Growing economic interdependence and its implications for international migration', Paper presented at the Expert Group Meeting on Population Distribution and Migration, UN Population Division and UN Fund for Population Activities, Santa Cruz, Bolivia, 18–22 Jan.

—— and N. Oishi (1996), 'International labour migration of Asian women: distinctive characteristics and policy concerns', *Asian and Pacific Migration Journal*, 5: 85–116.

Lindquist, B. A. (1993), 'Migration networks: a case study from the Philippines', *Asian and Pacific Migration Journal*, 2: 75–104.

Lindstrom, David P. (1995), 'The Relationship between Temporary US Migration and Fertility in a Rural Mexican Township', Unpublished Ph.D. dissertation, Dept. of Sociology, University of Chicago.

—— and Douglas S. Massey (1994), 'Selective emigration, cohort quality, and models of immigrant assimilation', *Social Science Research*, 23: 315–49.

Ling, L. Huan-Ming (1984), 'East Asian migration to the Middle East: causes, consequences, and considerations', *International Migration Review*, 18: 19–36.

Lipton, Michael (1980), 'Migration from rural areas of poor countries: the impact on rural productivity and income distribution', *World Development*, 8: 10–20.

Liu, John M., Paul M. Ong, and Carolyn Rosenstein (1991), 'Dual chain migration: post-1965 Filipino immigration to the United States', *International Migration Review*, 25: 487–513.

Liu, Y. (1995), 'Labour migration of China', *ASEAN Economic Bulletin*, 12: 299–308.

Lockwood, Victoria S. (1990), 'Development and return migration to rural French Polynesia', *International Migration Review*, 24: 347–71.

Logan, John R., Richard D. Alba, and Thomas L. McNulty (1994), 'Ethnic economies in metropolitan regions: Miami and beyond', *Social Forces*, 72: 691–724.

Loiskandl, Helmut (1995), 'Illegal migrant workers in Japan', 'in Robin Cohen (ed.), *The Cambridge Survey of World Migration*, Cambridge University Press, Cambridge: 371–5.

Lombardi, M., and C. Altesor (1987), *Los Cambios de las Ciudades*, Centro de Informaciones y Estudios del Uruguay, Montevideo.

Lomnitz, Larissa (1976), *Como Sobreviven los Marginados*, Editorial Siglo XXI, Mexico.

Looney, R. E. (1990), 'Macroeconomic impacts of worker remittances on Arab world labor exporting countries', *International Migration*, 28: 25–46.

—— (1992), 'Manpower options in a small labor-importing state: the influence of ethnic composition on Kuwait's development', *International Migration*, 30: 175–200.

López, Gustavo (1986), *La Casa Dividida: Un Estudio de Caso Sobre Migración a Estados Unidos en un Pueblo Michoacano*, Editorial el Colegio de Michoacán, Zamora.

——(1988), 'La migración a Estados Unidos en Gómez Farías, Michoacán', in Gustavo López (ed.), *Migración en el Occidente de México*, Editorial el Colegio de Michoacán, Zamora: 125–34.

López, José Roberto, and Mitchell A. Seligson (1990), *Remittances and Small Business Development: The Case of El Salvadorans Residing in the United States*, US Commission for the Study of International Migration and Cooperative Economic Development, Washington, DC.

López Patarra, Neide (1995), *Emigracio e Imigraçao Internaçionas no Brasil Contemporáneo, 1*, Universidade Estadual de Campinas, Campinas, Brazil.

——(1996), *'Emigracio e Imigraçao Internaçionas do Brasil Contemporáneo, 2*, Universidade Estadual de Campinas, Campinas, Brazil.

——and Rosana Baeninger (1995), 'Migraçoes internaçionais recentes: o caso do Brasil (consideraçoes preliminares)', in Adela Pellegrino (ed.), *Migración e Integracion: Nuevas Formas de Movilidad de la Población*, Ediciones Trilce, Montevideo: 130–42.

Loury, Glenn C. (1977), 'A dynamic theory of racial income differences', in Phyllis A. Wallace and Anette M. LaMond (eds.), *Women, Minorities, and Employment Discrimination*, D. C. Heath & Co., Lexington, Mass.: 153–86.

Low, Linda (1995), 'Population movement in the Asia Pacific region: Singapore perspectives', *International Migration Review*, 29: 745–64.

Lowell, B. Lindsay (1987), *Scandinavian Exodus: Demography and Social Development of 19th-Century Rural Communities*, Westview Press, Boulder, Colo.

Lozano Ascencio, Fernando (1993), *Bringing it Back Home: Remittances to Mexico from Migrant Workers in the United States*, Center for US-Mexican Studies, University of California at San Diego, La Jolla.

Lucas, Robert E. B. (1987), 'Emigration to South Africa's mines', *American Economic Review*, 77: 313–30.

——and Oded Stark. (1985), 'Motivations to remit: evidence from Botswana', *Journal of Political Economy*, 93: 901–18.

Lucassen, Jan (1995), 'Emigration to the Dutch colonies and the USA', in Robin Cohen (ed.), *The Cambridge Survey of World Migration*, Cambridge University Press, Cambridge: 21–7.

Lustig, Nora, Barry P. Bosworth, and Robert Z. Lawrence (1992), *Assessing the Impact: North American Free Trade*, Brookings Institution, Washington, DC.

Mabogunje, A. L. (1970), 'A systems approach to a theory of rural-urban migration', *Geographic Analysis*, 2: 1–18.

McArthur, Harold J., jun. (1979), 'The effects of overseas work on return migrants and their home communities: the Philippine case', *Papers in Anthropology*, 20: 85–104.

McCoy, Terry L. (1985), 'The impact of US temporary worker programs on Caribbean development: evidence from H-2 workers in Florida sugar', in William F. Stinner, Klaus de Albuquerque, and Roy S. Bryce-Laporte (eds.), *Return Migration and Remittances: Developing a Caribbean Perspective*, Smithsonian Institution, Washington, DC: 178–207.

McDonald, Ian M., and Robert M. Solow (1985), 'Wages and employment in a segmented labor market', *Quarterly Journal of Economics*, 100: 1115–41.

MacDonald, John S., and Leatrice D. MacDonald (1974), 'Chain migration, ethnic neighborhood formation, and social networks', in Charles Tilly (ed.), *An Urban World*, Little, Brown & Co., Boston: 226–36.

MacDougall, G. D. A. (1960), 'The benefits and costs of private investment from abroad: a theoretical approach', *Economic Record*, 36: 13–35.

Madhavan, M. C. (1985), 'Indian emigrants: numbers, characteristics, and economic impact', *Population and Development Review*, 11: 457–81.

Maguid, Alicia (1990), 'Migrantes limítrofes en la Argentina de los 1980: diferenciales sociodemográficos y ocupacionales a nivel provincial', Naciones Unidas Departmento de Población, Dirección de Políticas Migratorias, Buenos Aires.

——(1995), 'Migrantes limítrofes en la Argentina: su inserción e impacto en el mercado de trabajo', *Estudios del Trabajo*, 10: 66–84.

——and Monica Bankirer (1995), 'Argentina: saldos migratorios internacionales 1970–1990', *Jornadas Argentinas de Estudios de la Poblacion*, 2: 93–102.

Mahawewa, W. R. S. (1995), 'The process of international female migration: the case study of Sri Lanka', Unpublished MA thesis, Dept. of Geography, Flinders University, Adelaide.

Mahmoud, Mahgoub el-Tigani (1983), 'Sudanese emigration to Saudi Arabia', *International Migration*, 21: 500–14.

Mahmud, Wahiduddin (1989), 'The Impact of overseas labour migration on the Bangladesh economy', in Rashid Amjad (ed.), *To the Gulf and Back: Studies on the Economic Impact of Asian Labour Migration*, International Labour Office, Geneva: 55–94.

Maingot, Anthony P. (1991), 'Emigration and development in the English-speaking Caribbean', in Sergio Díaz-Briquets and Sidney Weintraub (eds.), *Determinants of Emigration from Mexico, Central America, and the Caribbean*, Westview Press, Boulder, Colo.: 99–120.

Makinwa-Adebusoye, Paulina (1987*a*), 'The nature and scope of international migration data in Nigeria', *International Migration Review*, 21: 1258–64.

——(1987*b*), 'International migration in tropical Africa: current trends', Paper presented at the Workshop on International Migration Systems and Networks sponsored by the International Union for the Scientific Study of Population, University of Benin, Africa.

Maldonado, Rita (1976), 'Why Puerto Ricans migrated to the United States in 1947–1973', *Monthly Labor Review*, 99(9): 7–18.

Ma Mung, Emmanuel, and Michell Guillon (1986), 'Les commerçants etrangers dans l'agglomération Parisienne', *Revue Européenne des Migrations Internationales*, 2: 105–32.

Margolis, Maxine L. (1994), *Little Brazil: An Ethnography of Brazilian Immigrants in New York City*, Princeton University Press, Princeton, NJ.

Markusen, J. R. (1983), 'Factor movements and commodity trade as complements', *Journal of International Economics*, 14: 341–56.

Mármora, Lelio (1982), 'Las migraciones internacionales laborales en Colombia', Technical Seminar on Labor Migration in the Andean Group, Haiti, and the Dominican Republic, Quito, 10 Feb.

Marshall, Adriana (1979), 'Immigrant workers in the Buenos Aires labor market', *International Migration Review*, 13: 488–501.

——(1980*a*), 'Inmigración, demanda de fuerza de trabajo y estructura ocupacional en el área metropolitana Argentina', *Migración y Desarrollo*, 5: 422–79.

——(1980*b*), 'Tendencias estructurales en la migración internacional de fuerza de trabajo: el Cono Sur de América Latina', in Mary M. Kritz (ed.), *Migraciones*

Internacionales en las Américas, Centro de Estudios de Pastoral y Asistencia Migratoria, Caracas: 133–53.

——(1981), 'Structural trends in international labor migration: the Southern Cone of Latin America', in Mary M. Kritz, Charles B. Keely, and Silvano M. Tomasi (eds.), *Global Trends in Migration: Theory and Research on International Population Movements*, Center for Migration Studies, Staten Island, NY: 234–58.

——(1984), 'Las migraciones de países limítrofes a la Argentina', *Memorias del Congreso Latinoamericano de Población y Desarrollo, 2*, El Colegio de México, Mexico.

——and Dora Orlansky (1983), 'Inmigración de países limítrofes y demanda de mano de obra en la Argentina, 1940–1980', *Desarrollo Económico*, 23(89): 35–57.

Marshall, Dawn I. (1982), 'Migration and development in the Eastern Caribbean', in William F. Stinner, Klaus de Albuquerque, and Roy S. Bryce-Laporte (eds.), *Return Migration and Remittances: Developing a Caribbean Perspective*, Smithsonian Institution: 91–116.

Martin, John B. (1966), *Overtaken by Events: From the Death of Trujillo to the Civil War*, Doubleday, New York.

Martin, Philip L. (1991a), *The Unfinished Story: Turkish Labour Migration to Western Europe*, International Labour Office, Geneva.

——(1991b), 'Labor migration: theory and reality', in Demetrios G. Papademetriou and Philip L. Martin (eds.), *The Unsettled Relationship: Labor Migration and Economic Development*, Greenwood Press, New York: 27–42.

Martin, Philip L., Andrew Mason, and C. L. Tsay (1995a), 'Overview', *ASEAN Economic Bulletin*, 12: 117–24.

————(1995b), *Labour Migration in Asia*, Special Issue of *ASEAN Economic Bulletin*, 12(2).

——and Mark J. Miller (1980), 'Guestworkers: lessons from Western Europe', *Industrial and Labor Relations Review*, 33: 315–30.

——and J. Edward Taylor (1991), 'Immigration reform and farm labor contracting in California', in Michael Fix (ed.), *The Paper Curtain: Employer Sanctions' Implementation, Impact, and Reform*, Urban Institute Press, Washington, DC: 239–61.

————(1996), 'The anatomy of a migration hump', in J. Edward Taylor (ed.), *Development Strategy, employment, and Migration: Insights from Models*, OECD, Development Centre, Paris: 43–62.

Martínez Pizarro, Jorge (1989), 'La migración de mano de obra calificada dentro de América Latina', Unpublished paper, Centro Latinoamericano Demográfico, Santiago.

Massey, Douglas S. (1981), 'New Immigrants to the United States and the Prospects for Assimilation', *Annual Review of Sociology*, 7: 57–85.

——(1985), 'The settlement process among Mexican migrants to the United States: new methods and findings', in Daniel B. Levine, Kenneth Hill, and Robert Warren (eds.), *Immigration Statistics: A Story of Neglect*, National Academy Press, Washington, DC: 255–92.

——(1986), 'The settlement process among Mexican migrants to the United States', *American Sociological Review*, 51: 670–85.

——(1987a), 'Do undocumented migrants earn lower wages than legal immigrants? New evidence from Mexico', *International Migration Review*, 21: 236–74.

——(1987*b*), 'Understanding Mexican migration to the United States', *American Journal of Sociology*, 92: 1372–1403.

——(1987*c*), 'The ethnosurvey in theory and practice', *International Migration Review*, 21: 1498–1522.

——(1988), 'International migration and economic development in comparative perspective', *Population and Development Review*, 14: 383–414.

——(1990*a*), 'The social and economic origins of immigration', *Annals of the American Academy of Political and Social Science*, 510: 60–72.

——(1990*b*), 'Social structure, household strategies, and the cumulative causation of migration', *Population Index*, 56: 3–26.

——(1995), 'The new immigration and the meaning of ethnicity in the United States', *Population and Development Review*, 21: 631–52.

——Rafael Alarcón, Jorge Durand, and Humberto González (1987), *Return to Aztlan: The Social Process of International Migration from Western Mexico*, University of California Press, Berkeley and los Angeles.

——Joaquin Arango, Ali Koucouci, Adela Pelligrino, and J. Edward Taylor (1994), 'An evaluation of international migration theory: the North American case', *Population and Development Review*, 20: 699–752.

——and Felipe García España (1987), 'The social process of international migration', *Science*, 237: 733–38.

——and Kristin E. Espinosa (1997), 'What's driving Mexico-US migration? A theoretical, empirical, and policy analysis', *American Journal of Sociology*, 102: 939–99.

——Luin P. Goldring, and Jorge Durand (1994), 'Continuities in transnational migration: an analysis of 19 Mexican communities', *American Journal of Sociology*, 99: 1492–533.

——and Zai Liang (1989), 'The long-term consequences of a temporary worker program: the US Bracero experience', *Population Research and Policy Review*, 8: 199–226.

——and Brendan P. Mullan (1984), 'A demonstration of the effect of seasonal migration on fertility', *Demography*, 21: 501–19.

——and Emilio A. Parrado (1994), 'Migradollars: the remittances and savings of Mexican migrants to the United States', *Population Research and Policy Review*, 13: 3–30.

——and Audrey Singer (1995), 'New estimates of undocumented migration and the probability of apprehension', *Demography*, 32: 203–13.

Melendez, Edwin (1994), 'Puerto Rican migration and occupational selectivity, 1982–88', *International Migration Review*, 28: 49–67.

Mellor, J. (1976), *The New Economics of Growth*, Cornell University Press, Ithaca, NY.

Meyer, G. (1984), 'Arbeitsemigration un wirtschaftsenwicklung in der Arabischen Republik Jemen untersucht am beispel der beschäftigten in bausektor von Sana', in H. Kopp and G. Schweizer (eds.), *Entwicklungsprozesse in der Arabischen Republik Jemen*, Ludwig Reichart Verlag, Wiesbaden.

Meyers, Eytan (1995), 'The Political Economy of International Immigration Policies', Unpublished Ph.D. dissertation, Dept. of Political Science, University of Chicago, Chicago.

Midgett, Douglas K. (1975), 'West Indian ethnicity in Great Britain', in Helen I. Safa and Brian DuToit (eds.), *Migration and Development: Implications for Ethnic Identity and Political Conflict*, Mouton, The Hague: 57–81.

Miller, Mark J. (1992), 'Evolution of policy modes for regulating international labour migration', in Mary M. Kritz, Lin Lean Lim, and Hania Zlotnik (eds.), *International Migration: A Global Approach*, Clarendon Press, Oxford: 300–14.

——(1995), 'Illegal Migration', in Robin Cohen (ed.), *The Cambridge Survey of World Migration*, Cambridge University Press, Cambridge: 537–40.

Mills, M. E. (1993), 'We Are Not Like Our Mothers: Migration, Modernity and Identity in Northeast Thailand', Ph.D. dissertation, Dept. of Anthropology, University of California, Berkeley.

Mines, Richard (1981), *Developing a Community Tradition of Migration: A Field Study in Rural Zacatecas, Mexico and California Settlement Areas*, Program in United States Mexican Studies, University of California at San Diego, La Jolla.

——(1984), 'Network migration and Mexican rural development: a case study', in Richard C. Jones (ed.), *Patterns of Undocumented Migration: Mexico and the United States*, Rowman & Allanheld, Totowa, NJ: 136–58.

——Beatriz Boccalandro, and Susan Gabbard (1992). *Report on the Americas*, 24: 42–6.

——and Alain DeJanvry (1982), 'Migration to the United States and Mexican rural development: a case study', *American Journal of Agricultural Economics*, 64: 444–54.

Minghuan, L. (1996), 'To get rich quick in Europe: reflections', Paper presented to the Conference on European Chinese and Chinese Domestic Migrants, Oxford University, 3–7 July.

Mingot, Michel (1995), 'Refugees from Cambodia, Laos and Vietnam', in Robin Cohen (ed.), *The Cambridge Survey of World Migration*, Cambridge University Press, Cambridge: 452–7.

Montoya, Silvia, and Alejandro Torres (1992), 'Intgegración de los mercados laborales de Argentina y Brazil', Unpublished paper, Centro de Estudios Internacionales, Ministerio de Relaciones Exteriores y Culto de la Rebública Argentina, Buenos Aires.

Morawska, Ewa (1990), 'The sociology and historiography of immigration', in Virginia Yans-McLaughlin (ed.), *Immigration Reconsidered: History, Sociology, and Politics*, Oxford University Press, New York: 187–240.

Mora y Araujo, Manuel (1982), 'Teoría y datos: comentario sobre el enfoque histórico estructural', in W. Mertens (ed.), *Reflexiones Teóricas Metodológicas Sobre Investigaciones en Población*, El Colegio de México, Mexico: 151–9.

Mori, H. (1994), 'Migrant workers and labour market segmentation in Japan', *Asian and Pacific Migration Journal*, 3: 619–38.

Morita, Kiriro (1992), 'Japan and the problem of foreign workers', Research Institute for the Japanese Economy, Faculty of Economics, University of Tokyo-Hongo, Tokyo.

——and Saskia Sassen (1994), 'The new illegal immigration in Japan 1980–1992', *International Migration Review*, 28: 153–64.

Morner, Magnus (1985), *Adventurers and Proletarians: The Story of Migrants in Latin America*, University of Pittsburgh Press, Pittsburgh.

Morokvasic, Mirjana (1984), 'Strategies of return of Yugoslavs in France and the Federal Republic of Germany', in Daniel Kubat (ed.), *The Politics of Return: International Return Migration in Europe*, Center for Migration Studies, Staten Island, NY: 87–92.

Muñoz, Humberto, Orlandina de Oliveira, and Claudio Stern (1977), *Migración y*

Desigualdad Social en la Ciudad de México, Universidad Nacional Autónoma de México and Colegio de México, Mexico.

Muñoz-Pérez, Francisco, and Antonio Izquierdo Escribano (1989), 'L'Espagne, pays d'immigration', *Population*, 44: 257–90.

Murillo Castaño, Gabriel (1981), 'La migración de trabajadores Colombianos a Venezuela: la relación ingreso-consumo como uno de los factores de expulsión', Unpublished paper, Ministerio de Trabajo y Seguridad Social, Bogotá.

—— (1988), 'Effects of emigration and return on sending countries: the case of Colombia', in Charles Stahl (ed.), *International Migration Today, 2: Emerging Issues*, UN Educational, Social, and Cultural Organization, Paris: 191–203.

—— and Babriel Silva (1984), 'La migración de los trabajadores Colombianos a Venezuela: antecedentes y perspectivas', in *Memorias del Congreso Latinoamericano de Población y Desarrollo, 2*, El Colegio de México, Mexico: 251–62.

Myrdal, Gunnar (1957), *Rich Lands and Poor*, Harper & Row, New York.

Nagi, Mostafa H. (1986*a*), 'Determinants of current trends in labor migration and the future outlook', in Fred Arnold and Nasra M. Shah (eds.), *Asian Labor Migration: Pipeline to the Middle East*, Westview Press, Boulder, Colo.: 47–64.

—— (1986*b*), 'Migration of Asian workers to the Arab Gulf: policy determinants and consequences,' *Journal of South Asian and Middle Eastern Studies*, 9: 19–34.

Nair, P. R. Gopinathan (1989), 'Incidence, impact, and implications of migration to the Middle East from Kerala (India)', in Rashid Amjad (ed.), *To the Gulf and Back: Studies on the Economic Impact of Asian Labour Migration*, International Labour Office, Geneva: 344–64.

National Population Council (1991), *The Working Holiday Maker Program*, Australian Government Publishing Service, Canberra.

National Research Council (1989), *A Common Destiny: Blacks and American Society*, National Academy Press, Washington, DC.

National Science Foundation (1987), *Social Science and Engineering Indicators*, National Science Foundation, Washington, DC.

Nayyar, Deepak (1989), 'International labour migration from India: a macroeconomic analysis', in Rashid Amjad (ed.), *To the Gulf and Back: Studies on the Economic Impact of Asian Labour Migration*, International Labour Office, Geneva: 95–142.

Nelson, Philip (1959), 'Migration, real income, and information', *Journal of Regional Science*, 1: 43–74.

Neuloh, Otto (1976), 'Structural unemployment in Turkey: its relation to migration', in Nermin Abadan-Unat (ed.), *Turkish Workers in Europe: 1960–1975*, E. J. Brill, Leiden: 40–73.

New Zealand Department of Statistics (1990), *New Zealand Official Yearbook 1988–89*, New Zealand Department of Statistics, Wellington.

Noiriel, Gérard (1995), 'Italians and Poles in France, 1880–1945', in Robin Cohen (ed.), *The Cambridge Survey of World Migration*, Cambridge University Press, Cambridge: 142–5.

Oberai, A., and H. K. Singh (1976), 'Migration, remittances and rural development: findings of a case study in the Indian Punjab', *International Labor Review*, 119: 229–41.

Oberg, S., and A. B. Wils (1991), 'East-west migration in Europe', *Popnet*, 22: 1–7.

Oddone, J. A. (1966), *La Formación del Uruguay Moderno: La Inmigración y el*

Desarrollo Económico y Social, Editorial Universitaria de Buenos Aires, Buenos Aires.

O Gráda, Cormac (1986), 'Determinants of Irish emigration: a note', *International Migration Review*, 20: 650–6.

Ogden, Philip E. (1995), 'Labour migration to France', in Robin Cohen (ed.), *The Cambridge Survey of World Migration*, Cambridge University Press, Cambridge: 289–97.

Oguzkan, Turhan (1975), 'The Turkish brain-drain: migration tendencies among doctoral level manpower', in Ronald E. Krane (ed.), *Manpower Mobility Across Cultural Boundaries: Social, Economic, and Legal Aspects, The Case of Turkey and West Germany*, E. J. Brill, Leiden: 205–20.

——(1976), 'The scope and nature of the Turkish brain drain', in Nermin Abadan-Unat (ed.), *Turkish Workers in Europe: 1960–1975*, E. J. Brill, Leiden: 74–103.

Oh, T. K. (1973), 'A new estimate of the student brain drain from Asia', *International Migration Review*, 7: 449–56.

Okolski, Marek, Ana Giza-Poleszezuk, Kristina Iglicka-Okolska, Ewa Jazwinska, Tadeusz Poplawski, and M. Tefelsk (1995), 'Causes and consequences of migration from Central and Eastern Europe: the case of Poland', Report presented at the Third Training Workshop on International Migration Surveys in Central and Eastern Europe, United Nations, Geneva, 11–13 December.

Okunishi, Y. (1995), 'Labour importers: Japan', *ASEAN Economic Bulletin*, 12: 139–62.

Omran, Abdel R., and Farzameh Roudi (1993), *The Middle East Population Puzzle*, Population Reference Bureau, Washington, DC.

Organization for Econonic Cooperation and Development (1992), *Trends in International Migration*, OECD, Paris.

Ortiz, Vilma (1986), Changes in the characteristics of Puerto Rican migrants from 1955–1980', *International Migration Review*, 20: 612–28.

Osterman, Paul (1975), 'An empirical study of labor market segmentation', *Industrial and Labor Relations Review*, 28: 508–23.

Oteiza, E. (1965), 'La emigración de ingenieros Argentinos dentro del contexto de las migraciones internacionales: un caso de brain drain Latinoamericano', *Revista Internacional del Trabajo*, 72: 6–10.

——(1971), 'Emigración de profesionales, técnicos, y obreros calificados Argentinos a los Estados Unidos: análisis de las fluctuaciones, Junio de 1950 a Junio de 1970', *Desarrollo Económic*, 39: 430–53.

Otterbein, Keith F. (1966), *The Andros Islanders: A Study of Family Organization in the Bahamas*, University of Kansas Press, Lawrence.

Paine, Suzanne (1974), *Exporting Workers: the Turkish Case*, Cambridge University Press, Cambridge.

Palau, V. T., and M. Y. Henkel (1987), *Los Campesinos, el Estado, y las Empresas en la Frontera Agrícola*, Programa de Investigaciones Sociales sobre Población en América Latina, Asunción.

Palmer, Colin (1992), 'The human dimensions of the British Company trade to the Americas, 1672–1739: questions of African Phenotype, age, gender, and health', in *Proceedings of the Conference on the Peopling of the Americas, I*, International Union for the Scientific Study of Population, Liège: 161–82.

Palmer, I. (1985), *The Impact of Male Out-Migration on Women in Farming*, Kumarian Press, West Hartford, Conn.

Palmer, R. W. (1974), 'A decade of West Indian migration to the United States, 1962–72: an economic analysis', *Social and Economic Studies*, 23: 571–87.

Pang, E. F. (1992), 'Absorbing temporary foreign workers: the experience of Singapore', *Asian and Pacific Migration Journal*, 1: 495–509.

Papdemetriou, Demetrios G. (1988), 'International migration in North America and Western Europe: trends and consequences', in Reginald Appleyard (ed.), *International Migration Today: Trends and Prospects*, University of Western Australia Press for the UN Economic, Social, and Cultural Organization, Perth: 311–88.

——(1991a), 'Temporary migration to the United States: composition, issues, and policies', Paper presented to the joint East-West Center/Nihon University Conference on International Manpower Flows and Foreign Investment in the Asia Pacific Region, Tokyo, 9–13 Sept.

——(1991b), 'International migration in North America: issues, policies, and implications', Paper presented to the Joint UN Economic Commission for Europe/UN Fund for Population Activities Conference, Geneva, 16–19 July.

——(1991c), 'Migration and development: the unsettled relationship', in Demetrious G. Papademetriou and Philip L. Martin (eds.), *The Unsettled Relationship: Labor Migration and Economic Development*, Greenwood Press, New York: 213–20.

——(1996), *Coming Together or Pulling Apart? The European Union s Struggle with Immigration and Asylum*, Carnegie Endowment for International Peace, Washington, DC.

——and Ira Emke-Poulopoulos (1991), 'Migration and development in Greece: the unfinished story', in Demetrios G. Papademetriou and Philip L. Martin (eds.), *The Unsettled Relationship: Labor Migration and Economic Development*, Greenwood Press, New York: 91–114.

——and Philip L. Martin (1991), 'Labor migration and development: research and policy issues', in Demetrios G. Papademetriou and Philip L. Martin (eds.), *The Unsettled Relationahip: Labor Migration and Economic Development*, Greenwood Press, New York: 3–26.

Park, Thomas K. (1992), 'Moroccan migration and mercantile money', *Human Organization*, 51: 205–13.

Park, Y. B. (1993), *Labor in Korea*, Korea Labor Institute, Seoul.

——(1995), 'Labour importers: Korea', *ASEAN Economic Bulletin*, 12: 163–74.

Passel, Jeffrey S. (1985), 'Undocumented immigrants: how many?', *Proceedings of the Social Statistics Section, Meetings of the American Statistical Association 1985*, American Statistical Association, Washington, DC: 65–72.

——(1995), 'Illegal migration: how large a problem?' Paper presented at the Conference on Latin American Migration: The Foreign Policy Dimension. Meridian International House, Washington, DC, 17 March.

——and Karen A. Woodrow (1987), 'Change in the undocumented alien population in the United States, 1979–83', *International Migration Review*, 21: 1304–23.

Peach, Ceri (1968), *West Indian Migration to Britain: A Social Geography*, Oxford University Press, Oxford.

Peerathep, Roongshivin (1982), *Some Aspects of Socio-Economic Impacts of Thailand's Emigration to the Middle East*, Australia Population Project, Canberra.

Pellegrino, Adela (1984), 'Venezuela: illegal migration from Colombia', *International Migration Review*, 18: 748–67.

——(1989), *Historia de la Inmigración en Venezuela Siglos XIX y XX*, Academia Nacional de Ciencias Económicas, Caracas.

——(1993), 'La movilidad de profesionales y técnicos Latinoamericanos', *Notas de Poblacion*, 12(57): 161–216.

——(1995), *Migración e Integracion: Nuevas Formas de Movilidad de la Población*, Ediciones Trilce, Montevideo.

Penninx, Rinus (1982), 'A critical review of theory and practice: the case of Turkey', *International Migration Review*, 16: 781–818.

——and Herman van Renselaar (1978), *A Fortune in Small Change*, REMPLOD, The Hague.

Pernia, E. M. (1976), 'The question of the brain drain from the Philippines', *International Migration Review*, 10: 63–72.

Pessar, Patricia R. (1991), 'Caribbean emigration and development', in Demetrios G. Papademetriou and Philip L. Martin (eds.), *The Unsettled Relationship: Labor Migration and Economic Development*, Greenwood Press, New York: 201–10.

Petras, Elizabeth M. (1981), 'The global labor market in the modern world-economy', in Mary M. Kritz, Charles B. Keely, and Silvano M. Tomasi (eds.), *Global Trends in Migration: Theory and Research on International Population Movements*, Center for Migration Studies, Staten Island, NY: 44–63.

Petrucelli, José L. (1979), 'Consequences of Uruguayan emigration: a research note', *International Migration Review*, 13: 519–26.

——and Gerónimo De Sierra (1979), 'Processo de las migraciones internacionales de Uruguayos, 1963–1975', Research Report, Programa de Investigaciones Sociales sobre Población en América Latina, Mexico.

Picouet, Michel (1976), 'Effects démographiques des migrations internationales de type conjencturel sur la structure par age et sexe de la population du Venezuela', *Science Humane*, 13: 227–44.

Philpott, Stuart B. (1968), 'Remittances obligations, social networks and choice among Montserratian migrants in Britain', *Man*, 3: 465–76.

——(1973), *West Indian Migration: The Montserrat Case*, Athlone Press, London.

Phuaphongsakorn, Niphon (1982), 'Thai migrant workers in foreign countries: causes, impacts, problems, and politics', Research Report, Thammasat University, Bangkok.

Pieke, F. N. (1997), 'Introduction', G. Beaton and F. N. Pieke (eds.), *The Chinese in Europe*, Macmillan, Basingstoke, forthcoming.

Pillai, P. (1995), 'Malaysia', *ASEAN Economic Bulletin*, 12: 221–36.

Piore, Michael J. (1977), 'Alcune note sul dualismo ne mercato de lavoro', *Revista di Economia e Politica Industriale*, 3: 350–8.

——(1979), *Birds of Passage: Migrant Labor in Industrial Societies*, Cambridge University Press, New York.

PISPAL (Programa de Investigaciones Sociales sobre Población en América Latina), (1986), *Se Fue a Volver: Seminario sobre Migraciones Temporales en América Latina*, El Colegio de México, Mexico.

Pohjola, A. (1991), 'Social networks: help or hindrance to the migrant?', *International Migration*, 24: 435–44.

Poitras, Guy (1980a), *International Migration to the United States from Costa Rica and El Salvador*, Research Report, Border Research Institute, Trinity University San Antonio, Texas.

Pongsapich, A. (1989), 'The case of Asian migrants to the Gulf region', *International Migration*, 27: 171–82.

Portes, Alejandro (1979), 'Illegal immigration and the international system: lessons from recent legal immigrants from Mexico', *Social Problems*, 26: 425–38.

——and Robert L. Bach (1985), *Latin Journey: Cuban and Mexican Immigrants in the United States*, University of California Press, Berkeley and Los Angeles.

——and Jòsef Böröcz (1987), 'Contemporary immigration: theoretical perspectives on its determinants and modes of incorporation', *International Migration Review*, 23: 606–30.

——and Luis E. Guarnizo (1991), *Capitalistas del Trópico: La Inmigración en los Estados Unidos y el Desarrollo de la Pequeña Empresa en la República Dominicana*, Facultad Latinoamericana de Ciencias Sociales, Programa República Dominicana, the Johns Hopkins University, Baltimore.

——and Leif Jensen (1987), 'What's an ethnic enclave? The case for conceptual clarity', *American Sociological Review*, 52: 768–71.

——(1989), 'The enclave and the entrants: patterns of ethnic enterprise in Miami before and after Mariel', *American Sociological Review*, 54: 929–49.

——and Robert D. Manning (1986), 'The immigrant enclave: theory and empirical examples', in Susan Olzak and Joane Nagel (eds.), *Competitive Ethnic Relations*, Academic Press, Orlando, Fla. 47–68.

——and Rubén G. Rumbaut (1990), *Immigrant America: A Portrait*, University of California Press, Berkeley and Los Angeles.

——and Julia Sensenbrenner. (1993), 'Embeddedness and immigration: notes on the social determinants of economic action', *American Journal of Sociology*, 98: 1320–351.

——and Alex Stepick (1993), *City on the Edge: The Transformation of Miami*, University of California Press, Berkeley.

——and John Walton (1981), *Labor, Class, and the International System*, Academic Press, New York.

Power, Jonathan (1979), *Migrant Workers in Western Europe and the United States*, Pergamon press, Oxford.

Prasai, S. B. (1993), 'Asia's labour pains', *Far Eastern Economic Review*, 29 April.

Price, Charles (1979), 'Australia', in Daniel Kubat (ed.), *The Politics of Migration Policy*, Center for Migration Studies, Staten Island, NY: 3–18.

Prothero, R. Mansell (1990), 'Labor recruiting organizations in the developing world: introduction', *International Migration Review*, 24: 221–8.

Pyrozhkov, Serhyi, E. Malinovskaya, and N. Marchenko (1995), 'Causes and consequences of migration from Central and Eastern Europe: the case of Ukraine', Report presented at the Third Training Workshop on International Migration Surveys in Central and Eastern Europe, United Nations, Geneva, 11–13 December.

Qian, W. (1996), 'The features of international migration in China', Paper presented at the Conference on European Chinese and Chinese Domestic Migrants, Oxford University, 3–7 July.

Quibria, M. G. (1988), 'A note on international migration, non-traded goods and economic welfare in the source country', *Journal of Development Economics*, 28: 377–87.

Raczynski, Dagmar (1983), 'La movilidad territorial de la población en América

Latina: perspectivas de análisis y lineamientos de investigación', Paper presented at the Latin American Congress on Population and Development, Mexico.

Ralston, Katherine (1992), 'An Economic Analysis of Factors Affecting Nutritional Status of Households in Rural West Java, Indonesia', Unpublished Ph.D. dissertation, Department of Agricultural and Resource Economics, University of California, Berkeley.

Ramos, Fernando (1992), 'Out-migration and return migration of Puerto Ricans', in George J. Borjas and Richard B. Freeman (eds.), *Immigration and the Work Force: Economic Consequences for the United States and Source Areas*, University of Chicago Press, Chicago: 49–66.

Ranis, Gustav, and J. C. H. Fei (1961), 'A theory of economic development', *American Economic Review*, 51: 533–65.

Ravenstein, E. G. (1885) 'The laws of migration', *Journal of the Royal Statistical Society*, 48: 167–227.

——(1889), 'The laws of migration', *Journal of the Royal Statistical Society*, 52: 241–301.

Reichert, Joshua S. (1979), 'The Migrant Syndrome: An Analysis of US Migration and its Impact on a Rural Mexican Town', Unpublished Ph.D. dissertation, Dept. of Anthropology, Princeton University, Princeton, NJ.

——(1981), 'The migrant syndrome: seasonal US wage labor and rural development in Central Mexico', *Human Organization*, 40: 56–66.

——(1982), 'Social stratification in a Mexican sending community: the effect of migration to the United States', *Social Problems*, 29: 422–33.

——and Douglas S. Massey (1982), 'Guestworker programs: evidence from Europe and the United States and some implications for US Policy', *Population Research and Policy Review*, 1: 1–17.

Reisler, Mark (1976), *By the Sweat of their Brow: Mexican Immigrant Labor in the United States: 1900–1940*, Greenwood Press, New York.

Rempel, Henry, and Richard A. Lobdell (1978), 'The role of urban-to-rural remittances in rural development', *Journal of Development Studies*, 14: 324–41.

República Argentina (1991), Censo Nacional de Argentina, Instituto Nacional de Estadística y Censos, Buenos Aires.

——(1994), *Anuario Estadístico de la República Argentina, 1994*, Instituto Nacional de Estadística y Censos, Buenos Aires.

Reynolds, Clark (1992), 'Will a free trade agreement lead to wage convergence? Implications for Mexico and the United States', in Jorge A. Bustamante, Clark W. Reynolds, and Raul Hinojosa Ojeda (eds.), *US-Mexico Relations: Labor Market Interdependence*, Stanford University Press, Stanford, Calif.

Rhoades, Robert E. (1978), 'Intra-European return migration and rural development: lessons from the Spanish case', *Human Organization*, 37: 136–47.

——(1979), 'From caves to main street: return migration and the transformation of a Spanish village', *Papers in Anthropology*, 20: 57–74.

Rickets, Erol (1987), 'US investment and immigration from the Caribbean', *Social Problems*, 34: 374–87.

Rist, Ray C. (1978), *Guestworkers in Germany: The Prospects for Pluralism*, Praeger, New York.

Rivarola, D. M. (1977), 'Paraguay: estructura agraria y migraciones desde una perspectiva histórica', Paper presented at the Sixth Meeting of the Working

Group on Migration, Commission on Population and Development, Consejo Latinoamericano de Ciencias Sociales, Mexico.

Rivera-Batiz, Francisco L. (1982), 'International migration, non-traded goods and economic welfare in the source country', *Journal of Development Economics*, 11: 81–90.

——(1994), *Puerto Ricans in the United States: A Changing Reality*, The National Puerto Rican Coalition, Washington, DC.

Ro, K. K., and J. K. Seo (1988), 'The economic impact of Korea's out-migration', *Asian Migrant*, 1: 13–15.

Roberts, Kenneth D. (1982), 'Agrarian structure and labor mobility in rural Mexico', *Population and Development Review*, 8: 299–322.

Robinson, W. G. (1984), 'Illegal immigrants in Canada: recent developments', *International Migration Review*, 18: 474–85.

Rodenburg, J. (1991), 'Emancipation or subordination? Consequences of female migration for migrants and their families', Paper presented to the Expert Group Meeting on the Feminization of Internal Migration, United Nations, Mexico City, 14–15 Oct.

Rodríguez, Clara (1988), 'Puerto Ricans and the circular migration thesis', *Journal of Hispanic Policy*, 3: 5–9.

Rodriguez, E. R. and S. Horton (1996), 'International return migration and remittances in the Philippines', in D. O'Connor and L. Farsakh (eds.), *Development Strategy, Employment and Migration: Country Experiences*, OECD, Paris: 171–202.

Rodrigo, Chandra, and R. A. Jaytissa (1989), 'Maximizing benefits from labour migration: Sri Lanka', in Rashid Amjad (ed.), *To the Gulf and Back: Studies on the Economic Impact of Asian Labour Migration*, International Labour Office, Geneva: 255–303.

Rogge, J. R. (1993), 'Refugee migration: changing characteristics and prospects', Paper presented at the Expert Group Meeting on Population Distribution and Migration, Santa Cruz, Bolivia, 18–22 Jan.

Root, Brenda D., and Gordon F. DeJong (1991), 'Family migration in a developing country', *Population Studies*, 45: 221–34.

Rose, Arnold M. (1969), *Migrants in Europe: Problems of Acceptance and Adjustment*, University of Minnesota Press, Minneapolis.

Rosenzweig, Mark R., and R. Evenson (1977), 'Fertility, schooling, and the economic contribution of children in rural India: an econometric analysis', *Econometrica*, 45: 1065–79.

Rouse, Roger C. (1989), 'Mexican Migration to the United States: Family Relations in the Development of a Transnational Migrant Circuit', Unpublished Ph.D. dissertation, Dept. of Anthropology, Stanford University, Stanford, Calif.

——(1990), 'Men in space: power and the appropriation of urban form among Mexican migrants in the United States', Unpublished MS, Dept. of Anthropology, University of Michigan.

——(1991), 'Mexican migration and the social space of postmodernism', *Diaspora*, 1: 8–23.

——(1992), 'Making sense of settlement: class transformation, cultural struggle, and transnationalism among Mexican migrants in the United States', *Annals of the New York Academy of Sciences*, 645: 25–52.

Rubenstein, Hymie (1976), 'Black Adaptive Strategies: Coping with Poverty in an

Eastern Caribbean Village', Ph.D. dissertation, Dept. of Anthropology, University of Toronto, Toronto.

——(1979), 'The return ideology in West Indian migration', *Papers in Anthropology*, 20: 330–7.

——(1982), 'Return migration to the English-speaking Caribbean: review and commentary', in William F. Stinner, Klaus de Albuquerque, and Roy S. Bryce-Laporte (eds.), *Return Migration and Remittances: Developing a Caribbean Perspective*, Smithsonian Institution, Washington, DC: 3–34.

——(1983), 'Remittances and rural underdevelopment in the English-speaking Caribbean', *Human Organization*, 42: 295–306.

Rumbaut, Rubén G. (1991), 'Passages to America: perspectives on the new immigration', in Alan Wolfe (ed.), *America at Century's End*, University of California Press, Berkeley and Los Angeles: 208–44.

——(1992), 'The Americans: Latin American and Caribbean peoples in the United States', in Alfred Stepan (ed.), *Americas: New Interpretive Essays*, Oxford University Press, New York: 275–307.

——(1994), 'Origins and destinies: immigration to the United States since World War II', *Sociological Forum*, 9: 583–622.

Russell, Margo (1984), 'Beyond remittances: the redistribution of cash in Swazi society', *Journal of Modern African Studies*, 22: 595–615.

Russell, Sharon S. (1986), 'Remittances from international migration: a review in perpsective', *World Development*, 14: 687–9.

——(1989), 'Politics and ideology in migration policy formation: the case of Kuwait', *International Migration Review*, 23: 24–47.

——(1991), 'Population and development in the Philippines: an update', Research Report, Asia Country Department II, Population and Human Resources Division, Word Bank, Washington, DC.

——(1992a), 'International migration and political turmoil in the Middle East', *Population and Development Review*, 18: 719–27.

——(1992b), 'Migrant remittances and development', *International Migration*, 30: 267–88.

——(1993), 'Migration between developing counties in the African and Latin American regions and its likely future', Paper presented at the Expert Meeting on Population Distribution and Migration, Organized by the Population Division of the UN Secretariat, Santa Cruz, Bolivia, 18–22 Jan.

——Karen Jacobsen, and William D. Stanley (1990), *International Migration and Development in Sub-Saharan Africa, I, Overview*, World Bank, Washington, DC.

——and Michael S. Teitelbaum (1992), *International Migration and International Trade*, World Bank, Washington, DC.

Salt, John (1976), 'International labour migration: the geographical pattern of demand', in John Salt and Hugh Clout (eds.), *Migration in Post-War Europe: Geographical Essays*, Oxford University Press, Oxford: 80–126.

——(1987a), 'The SOPEMI experience: genesis, aims, and achievements', *International Migration Review*, 21: 1067–73.

——(1987b), 'Contemporary trends in international migration study', *International Migration* 25: 242–65.

——(1992), 'Migration processes among the highly skilled in Europe', *International Migration Review*, 26: 484–505.

Samha, M. (1990), 'The impact of migratory flows on population changes in Jordan: a Middle Eastern case study', *International Migration*, 28: 215–28.

Samuel, T. J., P. M. White, and J. Perreault (1987), 'National recording systems and the measurement of international migration in Canada: an assessment', *International Migration Review*, 21: 1170–211.

Sana, Mariano (1996), 'Migrants, Unemployment, and Earnings in the Buenos Aires Metropolitan Area', Unpublished master's thesis, Graduate Group in Demography, University of Pennsylvania.

Sanders, Jimy, and Victor Nee (1987), 'Limits of ethnic solidarity in the enclave', *American Sociological Review*, 52: 745–67.

Santiago, Carlos E. (1991), 'Wage policies, employment, and Puerto Rican migration', in Edwin Melendez, Clara Rodriguez, and Janis Barry Figueroa (eds.), *Hispanics in the Labor Force: Issues and Policies*, Plenum Press, New York: 225–46.

——(1993), 'The migratory impact of minimum wage legislation: Puerto Rico, 1970–1987', *International Migration Review*, 24: 772–95.

Sassen, Saskia (1979), 'Economic growth and immigration in Venezuela', *International Migration Review*, 13: 455–74.

——(1988), *The Mobility of Labor and Capital: A Study in International Investment and Labour Flow*, Cambridge University Press, Cambridge.

——(1991), *The Global City: New York, London, Tokyo*, Princeton University Press, Princeton, NJ.

——(1993), 'Economic internationalization: the new migration in Japan and the United States', *International Migration*, 31: 73–102.

Sassone, S. M. (1987), 'Migraciones ilegales y amnistías en la Argentina', *Estudios Migratorios Latinoamericanos*, 2(6–7): 249–90.

Schaeffer, Peter V. (1993), 'A definition of migration pressure based on demand theory', *International Migration*, 31: 43–72.

Schmeidl, Susanne (1997), 'Exploring the causes of forced migration: a pooled time-series analysis, 1971–1990', *Social Science Quarterly*, 78: 284–308.

Seccombe, Ian J. (1985), 'International labor migration in the Middle East: a review of literature and research, 1974–84', *International Migration Review*, 19: 335–52.

——(1988), 'International migration in the Middle East: historical trends, contemporary patterns and consequences', in Reginald Appleyard (ed.), *International Migration Today: Trends and Prospects*, University of Western Asutralia Press, for the UN Economic, Social, and Cultural Organization, Perth: 180–209.

——and R. I. Lawless (1985), 'Some new trends in Mediterranean labour migration: the Middle East connection', *International Migration*, 23: 123–48.

————(1986), 'Foreign worker dependence in the Gulf and the international oil companies: 1910–1950', *International Migration Review*, 20: 548–74.

Sell, Ralph R. (1988), 'Egyptian international labor migration and social processes: toward regional integration', *International Migration Review*, 22: 87–108.

Selya, Roger Mark (1992), 'Illegal migration in Taiwan: a preliminary overview', *International Migration Review*, 26: 787–806.

Sell, Ralph R. (1988), 'Egyptian international-labor migration and social processes: toward regional integration', *International Migration Review*, 22: 87–108.

Shadow, Robert D. (1979), 'Differential out-migration: a comparison of internal and international migration from Villa Guerrero, Jalisco (Mexico)', in Fernando Camara and Robert Van Kemper (eds.), *Migration across Frontiers: Mexico and the United*

States, Institute of Mesoamerican Studies, State University of New York, Albany, NY: 67–84.

Shah, Nasra M. (1986), 'Foreign workers in Kuwait: implications for the Kuwaiti labor force', *International Migration Review*, 20: 815–34.

—— (1993), 'Migration between Asian countries and its likely future', Paper presented at the Expert Meeting on Population Distribution and Migration, Organized by the Population Division of the UN Secretariat, Santa Cruz, Bolivia, 18–22 Jan.

—— (1995), 'Structural changes in the receiving country and future labor migration: the case of Kuwait', *International Migration Review*, 29: 1000–23.

—— (1996), 'Social integration of South Asian male workers in Kuwait: the role of networks', Paper presented at the Arab Regional Conference, Cairo, 8–12 Dec.

—— Sulayman S. Al-Qudsi, and Makhdoom A. Shah (1991), 'Asian women workers in Kuwait', *International Migration Review*, 25: 464–87.

—— and Fred Arnold (1986), 'Government policies and programs regulating labor Migration', in Fred Arnold and Nasra M. Shah (eds.), *Asian Labor Migration: Pipeline to the Middle East*, Westview Press, Boulder, Colo.: 65–80.

Shankman, Paul (1976), *Migration and Underdevelopment: The Case of Western Samoa*. Westview Press, Boulder, Colo.

Shaw, R. Paul (1979), 'Migration and employment in the Arab world: construction as a key policy variable', *International Labour Review*, 118: 589–605.

—— (1983), *Mobilizing Human Resources in the Arab World*, Kegan Paul, London.

Sheahan, John (1991), *Conflict and Change in Mexican Economic Strategy: Implications for Mexico and for Latin America*, Center for US-Mexican Studies, University of California at San Diego, La Jolla.

Shozo, F. (1995), *With Sweat and Abacus: Economic Roles of Southeast Asian Chinese on the Eve of World War II*, Select Books, Singapore.

Shrestha, N. (1988), 'A structural perspective on labor migration in underdeveloped countries', *Progress in Human Geography*, 12: 179–207.

Simon, Gildas (1990), 'Les transferts de revenus des travailleurs Maghrébins vers leurs pays d'origine', in Gildas Simon (ed.), *Les Effets des Migrations Internationales Sur les Pays D'Origine: Le Cas du Maghreb*, Centre National de la Recherche Scientifique, Paris: 18–32.

Simmons, Alan B. (1987), 'The United Nations recommendations and data efforts: international migration statistics', *International Migration Review*, 21: 996–1016.

—— (1989), 'World system-linkages and international migration: new directions in theory and method with an application to Canada', in *International Population Conference, New Delhi 1989, 2*, International Union for the Scientific Study of Population, Liège: 159–72.

—— (1993), 'Migration and flexible accumulation', Ponencia presentada en el Taller Nuevas Modalidades y Tendencias de la Migración Internacional Frente a los Procesos de Integración, Programa de Población, Facultad de Ciencias Sociales, Universidad de la Repúblic, Montevideo, 27–9 Oct.

—— Sergio Diaz Briquets, and A. Laquian (1977), *Social Change and Internal Migration: A Review of Research Findings from Africa, Asia, and Latin America*, International Development Research Centre, Ottawa.

—— and Jean Pierre Guengant (1992), 'Caribbean exodus and the world system', in Mary M. Kritz, Lin Lean Lim, and Hania Zlotnik (eds.), *International Systems: A Global Approach*, Clarendon Press, Oxford: 94–114.

Singer, Paul (1971), 'Dinámica de la población y desarrollo', in *El Papel del Crecimiento Demográfico en el Desarrollo Económico*, Editorial Siglo XXI, Mexico: 21–66.

——(1975), *Economía Política de la Urbanización*, Editorial Siglo XXI, Mexico.

Singh, I., L. Squire, and J. Strauss (1986), 'An overview of agricultural household models—the basic model: theory, empirical results, and policy conclusions', in I. Singh, L. Squire, and J. Strauss (eds.), *Agricultural Household Models: Extensions, Applications, and Policy*, Johns Hopkins University Press, Baltimore: 17–47.

Singhanetra-Renard, Anchalee (1992), 'The mobilization of labour migrants in Thailand: personal links and facilitating networks', in Mary M. Kritz, Lin Lean Lim, and Hania Zlotnik (eds.), *International Systems: A Global Approach*, Clarendon Press Oxford: 190–204.

Sipavicience, Audra, R. Ciurlonyte, and V. Kanopiene (1995), *Causes and Consequences of Migration from Central and Eastern Europe: The Case of Ukraine*, Report Presented at the Third Training Workshop on International Migration Surveys in Central and Eastern Europe, United Nations, Geneva, 11–13 Dec.

Sito, N., and L. Stuhlman (1968), *La Emigración de Científicos de la Argentina*, Fundación Bariloche, Bariloche, Argentina.

Sjaastad, Larry A. (1962), 'The costs and returns of human migration', *Journal of Political Economy*, 70S: 80–93.

Skeldon, R. (1991), 'Hong Kong and Singapore as nodes in an international migration system', Paper presented at the International Conference on Migration, Centre for Advanced Studies, National University of Singapore, Singapore.

——(1995), 'Labour migration to Hong Kong', *ASEAN Economic Bulletin*, 12: 201–20.

Smart, John E., Virginia A. Teodosio, and Carol J. Jimenez (1985), 'Filipino workers in the Middle East: social profile and policy implications', *International Migration*, 25: 29–44.

————(1986), 'Skills and earnings: issues in the developmental impact on the Philippines of labor export', in Fred Arnold and Nasra M. Shaw (eds.), *Asian Labor Migration: Pipeline to the Middle East*, Westview Press, Boulder, Colo.: 101–24.

Smith, Michael (1962), *Kinship and Community in Carriacou*, Yale University Press, New Haven.

Smith, Robert C. (1992), 'Los ausentes siempre presentes: the imagining, making, and politics of a transnational community between New York City and Ticuani, Puebla', Paper presented at the Conference of the Latin American Studies Association, Los Angeles, 11–14 Sept.

Solé, Carlota (1995), 'Portugal and Spain: from exporters to importers of labour', in Robin Cohen (ed.), *The Cambridge Survey of World Migration*, Cambridge University Press, Cambridge: 316–20.

Somoza, Jorge L. (1981), 'Indirect estimates of emigration: applications of two procedures using information on precedence of children and siblings', in *Indirect Procedures for Estimating Emigration*, Working Group on the Methodology for the Study of International Migration (ed.), International Union for the Scientific Study of Population, Liège: 25–60.

Soon-Beng, C., and R. Chew (1995), 'Immigration and foreign labour in Singapore', *ASEAN Economic Bulletin*, 12: 191–200.

SOPEMI (Systeme d'Observation Permanente des Migrations Internationales) (1992), *Trends in International Migration*, OECD, Paris.

Sori, Ercole (1985), 'Las causas económicas de la emigración Italiana', in F. Devoto and G. Rosoli (eds.), *La Inmigración Italiana en la Argentina*, Editorial Bilbos, Buenos Aires: 15–42.

Spaan, Ernst (1988), 'Labour migration from Sri Lanka to the Middle East', *ICA Publication No. 83*, Leiden: ICA.

——(1994), 'Taikongs and calos: the role of middlemen and brokers in Javanese international migration', *International Migration Review*, 28: 93–113.

Spencer, Steven A. (1992), 'Illegal migrant laborers in Japan', *International Migration Review*, 26: 754–86.

Stahl, Charles W. (1986), 'Southeast Asian labor in the Middle East', in Fred Arnold and Nasra M. Shah (eds.), *Asian Labor Migration: Pipeline to the Middle East*, Westview Press, Boulder, Colo.: 81–100.

——(1992), 'Asian international labour migration: trends, issues, and prospects', Paper presented to the Sixth National Conference of the Australian Population Association, Sydney, 29 Sept.

——(1995), 'Theories of international labor migration: an overview', *Asian and Pacific Migration Journal*, 4: 211–32.

——R. Ball, C. Inglis, and P. Gutman (1993), *Global Population Movements and their Implications for Australia*, Australian Government Publishing Service, Canberra.

——and Ansanul Habib (1991), 'Emigration and development in South and Southeast Asia', in Demetrios G. Papademetriou and Philip L. Martin (eds.), *The Unsettled Relationship: Labor Migration and Economic Development*, Greenwood Press, New York: 163–80.

Stalker, Peter (1994), *The Work of Strangers: A Survey of International Labour Migration*, International Labour Office, Geneva.

Stark, Oded (1978), *Economic-Demographic Interactions in Agricultural Development: The Case of Rural-to-Urban Migration*, UN Food and Agricultural Organization, Rome.

——(1980), 'On the role of urban-to-rural remittances in rural development', *Journal of Development Studies*, 16: 369–74.

——(1982), 'Research on rural-to-urban migration in less developed countries: the confusion frontier and why we should pause to rethink afresh', *World Development*, 10: 63–70.

——(1984a), 'Migration decision making: a review article', *Journal of Development Economics*, 14: 251–59.

——(1984b), 'Bargaining, altruism, and demographic phenomena', *Population and Development Review*, 10: 679–92.

——(1991), *The Migration of Labour*, Basil Blackwell, Cambridge.

——and David E. Bloom (1985), 'The new economics of labor migration', *American Economic Review*, 75: 173–8.

——and E. Katz (1986), 'Labor migration and risk aversion in less developed countries', *Journal of Labor Economics*, 4: 134–49.

——and David Levhari (1982), 'On migration and risk in LDCs', *Economic Development and Cultural Change*, 31: 191–6.

——and Robert E. B. Lucas (1988), 'Migration, remittances and the family', *Economic Development and Cultural Change*, 36: 465–81.

——and Mark R. Rosenzweig (1989), 'Consumption smoothing, migration and marriage: evidence from rural India', *Journal of Political Economy*, 97: 905–26.

——and J. Edward Taylor (1989), 'Relative deprivation and international migration', *Demography*, 26: 1–14.

——— (1991*a*), 'Migration incentives, migration types: the role of relative deprivation', *Economic Journal*, 101: 1163–78.

——— (1991*b*), 'Relative deprivation and migration: theory, evidence, and policy implications', in Sergio Díaz-Briquets and Sidney Weintraub (eds.), *Determinants of Emigration from Mexico, Central America, and the Caribbean*, Westview Press, Boulder, Colo.: 121–44.

——and Shlomo Yitzhaki (1986), 'Remittances and inequality', *Economic Journal*, 96: 722–40.

——— (1988), 'Migration, remittances, and inequality: a sensitivity analysis using the extended Gini Index', *Journal of Development Economics*, 28: 309–22.

——and Shlomo Yitzhaki (1988), 'Labor migration as a response to relative deprivation', *Journal of Population Economics*, 1: 57–70.

Statistics Bureau of Japan (1995), *Japan Statistical Yearbook 1995*, Statistics Bureau of Japan, Management and Coordination Agency, Tokyo.

Statistics Canada (1992), *Immigration Canada: Immigration Statistics 1990*, Statistics Canada, Ottawa.

——(1995), *Canada Year Book 1990*, Statistics Canada, Ottawa.

Stern, Claudio (1988), 'Some methodological notes on the study of human migration', in Charles W. Stahl (ed.), *International Migration Today, 2: Emerging Issues*, University of Western Australia for the United Nations Economic, Social, and Cultural Organization, Perth: 28–33.

Straubhaar, Thomas (1986), 'The causes of international labor migrations: a demand-determined approach', *International Migration Review*, 20: 835–56.

——(1992), 'The impact of international labor migration for Turkey', in Klaus F. Zimmerman (ed.), *Migration and Economic Development*, Springer-Verlag, Berlin: 79–134.

——(1993), 'Migration pressure', *International Migration*, 31: 5–42.

Stuart, James, and Michael Kearney (1981), *Causes and Effects of Agricultural Labor Migration from the Mixteca of Oaxaca to California*. Center for US-Mexican Studies, University of California at San Diego, La Jolla.

Sullivan, G., and S. Gunasekaran. (1992), 'Is there an Asian-Australian brain drain?' in C. Inglis, S. Gunaskeran, G. Sullivan, and C. T. Wu (eds.), *Asians in Australia: The Dynamics of Migration and Settlement*, Institute of Southeast Asian Studies, Singapore: 157–92.

Sumalee, Pitayanon (1986), 'Thailand', in *Middle East Interlude: Asian Workers Abroad: A Comparative Study of Four Countries*, UN Economic, Social, and Cultural Organization, Bangkok: 61–84.

Sussangkarn, C. (1995), 'Labour market adjustments and migration in Thailand', *ASEAN Economic Bulletin*, 12: 237–56.

Swamy, G. (1983), *International Migrant Worker's Remittances: Issues and Prospects*, World Bank, Washington, DC.

Swanson, Jon C. (1979*a*), *Emigration and Economic Development: The Case of the Yemen Arab Republic*, Westview, Press, Boulder, Colo.

——(1979*b*), 'The conseqeunces of emigration for economic development: a review of the literature', *Papers in Anthropology*, 20: 39–56.

Sword, Keith (1995), 'The repatriation of Soviet citizens at the end of the Second

World War', in Robin Cohen (ed.), *The Cambridge Survey of World Migration*, Cambridge University Press, Cambridge: 323–6.

Szoke, László (1992), 'Hungarian perspectives on emigration and immigration in the new European architecture', *International Migration Review*, 26: 305–23.

Takenaka, Ayumi (1996), 'Limits of ethnicity and culture: ethnicity-based transnational migration and networks of Japanese-Peruvian sojourners', Paper presented at the Annual Meeting of the American Sociological Association, New York, 16–20 Aug.

Tan, Edita A., and Dante B. Canlas (1989), 'Migrant's saving remittance and labour supply behaviour: the Philippines case', in Rashid Amjad (ed.), *To the Gulf and Back: Studies on the Economic Impact of Asian Labour Migration*, International Labour Office, Geneva: 223–54.

Tapinos, Georges (1975), *L'immigration etrangère en France*, Presses Universitaires de France, Paris.

Tarrius, Alain (1987), 'L'entrée dans la ville: migrations Maghrébines et recompositions des tissus urbains à Tunis et à Marseille', *Revue Européenne des Migrations Internationales*, 3: 131–48.

Taylor, Alan M. (1994), 'Mass migration to distant southern shores: Argentina and Australia, 1870–1939', in Timothy J. Hatton and Jeffrey G. Williamson (eds.), *Migration and the International Labor Market, 1850–1939*, Routledge, London: 91–118.

Taylor, J. Edward (1986), 'Differential migration, networks, information and risk', in Oded Stark (ed.), *Migration Theory, Human Capital and Development*, JAI Press, Greenwich, Conn.: 147–71.

——(1987), 'Undocumented Mexico-US migration and the returns to households in rural Mexico', *American Journal of Agricultural Economics*, 69: 626–38.

——(1992a), 'Remittances and inequality reconsidered: direct, indirect, and intertemporal effects', *Journal of Policy Modeling*, 14: 187–208.

——(1992b), 'Earnings and mobility of legal and illegal immigrant workers in agriculture', *American Journal of Agricultural Economics*, 74: 889–96.

——(1995), *Micro Economy-wide Models for Migration and Policy Analysis: An Application to Rural Mexico*, OECD, Paris.

——(1996), 'International migration and economic development: a micro economy-wide analysis', in J. Edward Taylor (ed.), *Development Strategy, Employment and Migration: Insights from Models*, OECD, Paris: 1–31.

——and Irma Adelman (1996), *Village Economies: The Design, Estimation and Application of Village-Wide Economic Models*, Cambridge University Press, Cambridge.

——and Dawn Thilmany (1993), 'Worker turnover, farm labor contractors, and the California farm labor market', *American Journal of Agricultural Economics*, 75: 350–60.

——and T. J. Wyatt (1996), 'The shadow value of migrant remittances, income, and inequality in a household-farm economy', *Journal of Development Studies*, 32: 819–912.

Teitelbaum, Michael S. (1989), 'Skeptical noises about the immigration multiplier', *International Migration Review*, 23: 893–9.

Thahane, Timothy T. (1991), 'International labor migration in Southern Africa', in Demetrios G. Papademetriou and Philip L. Martin (eds.), *The Unsettled Relationship: Labor Migration and Economic Development*, Greenwood Press, New York: 65–88.

Thomas, Brinley (1973), *Migration and Economic Growth: A Study of Great Britain and the Atlantic Economy*, Cambridge University Press, Cambridge.

Thomas, Dorothy S. (1941), *Social and Economic Aspects of Swedish Population Movements: 1750–1933*, Macmillan, New York.

Thomas, William I., and Florian Znaniecki (1918–20), *The Polish Peasant in Europe and America*, William Badger, Boston.

Thomas-Hope, Elizabeth M. (1985), 'Return migration and its implications for Caribbean development', in Robert Pastor (ed.), *Migration and Development in the Caribbean: The Unexplored Connection*, Westview Press, Boulder, Colo.: 157–77.

——(1986), 'Transients and settlers: varieties of Caribbean migrants and the socio-economic implications of their return', *International Migration* 24: 559–72.

Thompson, Gary, Ricardo Amón, and Philip L. Martin (1986), 'Agricultural development and emigration: rhetoric and reality', *International Migration Review*, 20: 575–98.

Thuno, M. (1996), 'Origins and causes of emigration from Qingtian and Wenzhou in Europe', Paper presented to the Conference on European Chinese and Chinese Domestic Migrants, Oxford University, 3–7 July.

Tiglao, R. (1996), 'Welcome exchange', *Far Eastern Economic Review*, 29 Feb.

Tilly, Charles, and C. H. Brown (1967), 'On uprooting, kinship, and the auspices of migration', *International Journal of Comparative Sociology*, 8: 139–64.

Tingsabadh, Charit (1989), 'Maximizing development benefits from labour migration: Thailand', in Rashid Amjad (ed.), *To the Gulf and Back: Studies on the Economic Impact of Asian Labour Migration*, International Labour Office, Geneva: 304–43.

Tinker, Hugh (1977), *The Banyan Tree: Overseas Emigrants from India, Pakistan, and Bangladesh*, Oxford University Press, Oxford.

——(1995), 'The British colonies of settlement', in Robin Cohen (ed.), *The Cambridge Survey of World Migration*, Cambridge University Press: 14–20.

Todaro, Michael P. (1969), 'A model of labor migration and urban unemployment in less-developed countries', *American Economic Review*, 59: 138–48.

——(1976), *Internal Migration in Developing Countries*, International Labor Office, Geneva.

——(1980), 'Internal migration in developing countries: a survey', in Richard A. Easterlin (ed.), *Population and Economic Change in Developing Countries*, University of Chicago Press, Chicago: 361–401.

——(1989), *Economic Development in the Third World*, Longman, New York.

——and L. Maruszko (1987), 'Illegal migration and US immigration reform: a conceptual framework', *Population and Development Review*, 13: 101–14.

Toepfer, Helmuth (1985), 'The economic impact of returned migrants in Trabazon, Turkey', in Ray Hudson and Jim Lewis (eds.), *Uneven Development in Southern Europe: Studies of Accumulation, Class, Migration and the State*, Methuen, London: 76–100.

Tolbert, Charles M. II, Patrick M. Horan, and E. M. Beck (1980), 'The structure of economic segmentation: a dual economy approach', *American Journal of Sociology*, 85: 1095–116.

Tomasi, Silvano M. (1984), *Irregular Migration: An International Perspective*, Special issue of *International Migration Review*, 18: 406–813.

Torrado, S. (1982), 'El exodo intelectual Latinoamericano hacia los Estados Unidos durante el período 1961–1975', in Mary M. Kritz (ed.), *Migraciones Internacionales en las Américas*, Centro de Estudios de Pastoral y Asistencia Migratoria, Caracas: 19–33.

Torrealba, Ricardo (1987), 'International migration data: the problems and usefulness in Venezuela', *International Migration Review*, 21: 1270–8.

——(1988), 'Tendencias recientes de la migración internacional hacia Venezuela: resultados de una encuesta nacional de migración', *Estudios Migratorios Latinoamericanos*, 3(10): 127–47.

Torres, A. T. (1992), 'Features of the migration of men and women in the Philippines', Paper presented to the International Colloquium: Migration, Development and Gender in the ASEAN Region, University of Malaya, Pahang, 5–6 Oct.

Trigueros, Paz, and Javier Rodríguez (1988), 'Migración y vida familiar en Michoacán', in Gustavo López (ed.), *Migración en el Occidente de México*, Editorial el Colegio de Michoacán, Zamora: 201–21.

Truong, T. D. (1996), 'Gender, international migration and social reproduction: implications for theory, policy, research and networking', *Asian and Pacific Migration Journal*, 5: 27–52.

Tsay, C. L. (1995), 'Labour importers: Taiwan', *ASEAN Economic Bulletin*, 12: 175–90.

Twaddle, Michael (1995), 'The settlement of South Asians in East Africa', in Robin Cohen (ed.), *The Cambridge Survey of World Migration*, Cambridge University Press: 74–7.

Ugalde, Antonio, Frank D. Bean, and Gilbert Cárdenas (1979), 'International migration from the Dominican Republic: findings from a national survey', *International Migration Review*, 13: 235–54.

United Nations (1975), *La Transferencia de Tecnología: Dimensiones, Efectos Económicos, y Cuestions de Política*, United Nations, New York.

——(1980), *Patterns of Urban and Rural Population Growth*, United Nations, New York.

——(1991*a*), *1989 Demographic Yearbook*, United Nations, New York.

——(1991*b*), *Remesas y Economía Familiar en El Salvador, Guatemala, y Nicaragua*, Comisión Económico para América Latina y el Caribe, Naciones Unidas, Mexico.

——(1992), 'International migration trends and policies', in *World Population Monitoring 1991*, United Nations, New York: 170–212.

——(1993), 'Hijratu El-Amala El Arabia' (Arab Labor Migration), Paper presented at the Arab Population Conference in Amman, UN Economic and Social Commission for Western Asia, Jordan, 4–8 April.

——(1994), *The Migration of Women: Methodological Issues in the Measurement and Analysis of Internal and International Migration*, UN International Research and Training Institute for the Advancement of Women, Santo Domingo.

——(1995), 'International migration policies and the status of female migrants', in the *Proceedings of the UN Expert Group Meeting on International Migration Policies and the Status of Female Migrants*, UN Population Division, New York: 1–300.

Urrea Giraldo, Fernando (1989), 'Evolución y caracterización sociodemográfica y socioeconómica de la migración Colombiana en un contexto comparativo', in Gerónimo Bidegain (ed.), *Las Migraciones Laborales Colombo-Venezolanas*, Nueva Sociedad, Caracas: 41–64.

US Immigration and Naturalization Service (1991), *1990 Statistical Yearbook of the Immigration and Naturalization Service*, US Government Printing Office, Washington, DC.

——(1992), *1991 Statistical Yearbook of the Immigration and Naturalization Service*, US Government Printing Office, Washington, DC.

——(1993), *1992 Statistical Yearbook of the Immigration and Naturalization Service*, US Government Printing Office, Washington, DC.

——(1994), *1993 Statistical Yearbook of the Immigration and Naturalization Service*, US Government Printing Office, Washington, DC.

——(1996), *1995 Statistical Yearbook of the Immigration and Naturalization Service*, US Government Printing Office, Washington, DC.

Van Amersfoort, Hans (1995), 'From workers to immigrants: Turks and Moroccans in the Netherlands, 1965–1992', in Robin Cohen (ed.), *The Cambridge Survey of World Migration*, Cambridge University Press, Cambridge: 308–12.

Vandemann, A., E. Sadoulet, and A. de Janvry (1991), 'Labor contracting and a theory of contract choice in California agriculture', *American Journal of Agricultural Economics*, 73: 681–92.

Van Dijk, Pieter J. C. (1978), 'Foreword', in Rinus Penninx and Herman Van Renselaar, *A Fortune in Small Change*, REMPLOD, The Hague: 7–12.

Van Roy, Ralph (1984), 'Undocumented migration to Venezuela', *International Migration Review*, 18: 541–57.

Vasquez, Noel (1992), 'Economic and social impact of labor migration', in G. Battistella and A. Paganoni (eds.), *Philippine Labor Migration: Impact and Policy*, Scalabrini Migration Center, Quezon City, Philippines: 41–67.

Vatikiotis, M. (1995), 'On the margins: organized crime profits from the flesh trade', *Far Eastern Economic Review*, 14 Dec.: 26–7.

Vázquez, Josefina Zoraida, and Lorenzo Meyer (1985), *The United States and Mexico*, University of Chicago Press, Chicago.

Vega, William A., Bohdan Kolody, Ramon Valle, and Judy Weir (1991), 'Social networks, social support, and their relationship to depression among immigrant Mexican women', *Human Organization*, 50: 154–62.

Velosa, María (1979), *Mercados de Trabajo y Salarios Diferenciales en la Zona Fronteriza*, Ministerio de Trabajo y Seguridad Social de Colombia, Bogotá.

Vertovec, Steven (1995), 'Indian indentured migration to the Caribbean', in Robin Cohen (ed.), *The Cambridge Survey of World Migration*, Cambridge University Press, Cambridge: 57–62.

Vivolo, Robert L. (1984), 'Emigration and agriculture in a Sicilian village', in Daniel Kubat (ed.), *The Politics of Return: International Return Migration in Europe*, Center for Migration Studies, Staten Island, NY: 73–7.

Walker, Robert, Mark Ellis, and Richard Barff (1992), 'Linked migration systems: immigration and internal labor flows in the United States', *Economic Geography*, 68: 234–48.

——and Michael Hannan (1989), 'Dynamic settlement processes: the case of US immigration', *Professional Geographer*, 41: 172–83.

Wallerstein, Immanuel (1974), *The Modern World System I: Capitalist Agriculture and the Origins of the European World Economy in the Sixteenth Century*, Academic Press, New York.

——(1980), *The Modern World System II: Mercantilism and the Consolidation of the European World-Economy, 1600–1750*, Academic Press, New York.

Walsh, Brendan M. (1974), 'Expectations, information, and human migration: specifying an econometric model of Irish migration to Britain', *Journal of Regional Science*, 14: 107–18.

Warmsingh, S. (1997), 'International Contract Migration in Rural Udonthani', Unpublished Ph.D. dissertation, Dept. of Geography, University of Adelaide, Adelaide.

Warren, Robert. (1995), 'Estimates of the undocumented immigrant population residing in the United States, by country of origin and state of residence: October 1992', Paper presented at the Annual Meeting of the Population Association of America, San Francisco, 6–8 April.

——and Ellen Percy Kraly (1985), *The Elusive Exodus: Emigration from the United States*, Population Reference Bureau, Washington, DC.

Watanabe, Susumo (1969), 'The brain drain from developing to developed countries', *International Labour Review*, 99: 401–33.

Watters, R. (1987), 'MIRAB societies and bureaucratic elites', in A. Hooper (ed.), *Class and Culture in the South Pacific*, Centre for Pacific Studies, Auckland: 32–55.

Weiner, Myron (1982), 'International migration and development: Indians in the Persian Gulf', *Population and Development Review*, 8: 1–36.

White, Michael J., Frank D. Bean, and Thomas Espenshade (1990), 'The US 1986 Immigration Reform and Control Act and undocumented migration to the United States', *Population Research and Policy Review*, 9: 93–116.

Whiteford, Scott (1981), *Workers from the North: Plantations, Bolivian Labor, and the City in Northwest Argentina*, University of Texas Press, Austin.

Wiest, Raymond E. (1973), 'Wage-labor migration and the household in a Mexican town', *Journal of Anthropological Research*, 29: 108–209.

——(1979), 'Implications of international labor migration for Mexican rural development', in Fernando Camara and Robert Van Kemper (eds.), *Migration across Frontiers: Mexico and the United States*, Institute of Mesoamerican Studies, State University of New York, Albany: 85–97.

——(1984), 'External dependency and the perpetuation of temporary migration to the United States', in Richard C. Jones (ed.), *Patterns of Undocumented Migration: Mexico and the United States*, Rowman and Allanheld, Totowa, NJ: 110–35.

Wilpert, Czarina (1984), 'Returning and remaining: return among Turkish migrants in Germany', in Daniel Kubat (ed.), *The Politics of Return: International Return Migration in Europe*, Center for Migration Studies, Staten Island, NY: 101–12.

——(1988), 'Migrant women and their daughters: two generations of Turkish women in the Federal Republic of Germany', in Charles Stahl (ed.), *International Migration Today, 2*, University of Western Australia for the United Nations Educational, Social, and Cultural Organization, Perth: 168–86.

——(1992), 'The use of social networks in Turkish migration to Germany', in Mary M. Kritz, Lin Lean Lim, and Hania Zlotnik (eds.), *International Migration Systems: A Global Approach*, Clarendon, Oxford: 170–89.

Wilson, Kenneth, and W. Allen Martin (1982), 'Ethnic enclaves: a comparison of the Cuban and black economies in Miami', *American Journal of Sociology*, 88: 135–60.

Wilson, Patricia A. (1992), *Exports and Local Development: Mexico's New Maquiladoras*, University of Texas Press, Austin.

Winsberg, Morton D. (1993), 'America's foreign born', *Population Today*, 21: 4.

Wiznitzer, F. (1993), 'Western Europe's invisible iron wall keeps immigrants out', *Le Monde*, 31 May.

Wong, K. Y. (1983), 'On choosing among trade in goods and international capital and labor mobility (a theoretical analysis)', *Journal of International Economics*, 14: 223–50.

Wong, Morrison G. (1986), 'Post-1965 Asian immigrants: where do they come from, where are they now, and where are they going?', *Annals of the American Academy of Political and Social Science*, 487: 150–69.

Wonsewer, J., and A. M. Teja (1982), *Informe Final del Proyecto 'Condicionantes Económicos de la Emigración Internacional en el Uruguay en el Período 1963–1975'*, Centro de Investigaciones Económicas, Montevideo.

Wood, Charles H. (1982), 'Migration remittances and development: preliminary results of a study of Caribbean cane cutters in Florida', in William F. Stinner, Klaus de Albuquerque, and Roy S. Bryce-Laporte (eds.), *Return Migration and Remittances: Developing a Caribbean Perspective*, Smithsonian Institution, Washington, DC: 291–308.

——and Terry L. McCoy (1985), 'Migration, remittances, and development: a study of Caribbean cane cutters in Florida', *International Migration Review*, 19: 251–77.

Wooden, Mark, Robert Holton, Graeme Hugo, and Judith Sloan (1994), *Australian Immigration: A Survey of the Issues*, Australian Government Publishing Service, Canberra.

Woodrow, Karen A. (1988), 'Measuring net immigration to the United States: the emigrant population and recent emigration flows', Paper presented at the Annual Meeting of the Population Association of America, New Orleans, 7–11 April.

World Bank (1994), *World Development Report 1994*, Oxford University Press, New York.

Wright, Eric O. (1979), *Class Structure and Income Determination*, Academic Press, New York.

Wright, Richard A., Mark Ellis, and Michael Reibel (1997), 'Large metropolitan areas and the linkage between immigration and internal migration in the United States', *Economic Geography*, 73, forthcoming.

Wu, C., and C. Inglis (1992), 'Illegal immigration to Hong Kong', *Asia and Pacific Migration Journal*, 1: 601–22.

Yap, L. (1977), 'The attraction of cities: a review of the migration literature', *Journal of Development Economics*, 4: 239–64.

Yoon, InJin (1991), 'A Comparative Historical Study of Asian Immigrant Entrepreneurship', Unpublished Ph.D. dissertation, Dept. of Sociology, University of Chicago, Chicago.

Young, W. C. (1987), 'The effect of labor migration on relations of exchange and subordination among the Rashaayda Bedouin of Sudan', *Research in Economic Anthropology*, 9: 191–220.

Zabin, Carol, and Sallie Hughes (1995), 'Economic integration and migration: a case study of indigenous Oaxacan farm workers in Baja California and the United States', *International Migration Review*, 29: 397–422.

Zelinsky, Wilbur (1971), 'The hypothesis of the mobility transition', *Geographical Review*, 61: 219–49.

Zhou, Min, and John R. Logan (1989), 'Returns on human capital in ethnic enclaves: New York City's Chinatown,' *American Sociological Review*, 54: 809–20.

Zlotnik, Hania (1987), 'The concept of international migration as reflected in data collection systems', *International Migration Review*, 21: 925–46.

——(1992), 'Empirical identification of international migration systems', in Mary M. Kritz, Lin Lean Lim, and Hania Zlotnik (eds.), *International Migration: A Global Approach*, Clarendon Press, Oxford: 19–40.

——(1993), 'South-to-north migration since 1960: the view from the south', in *International Population Conference, Montreal 1993*, International Union for the Scientific Study of Population, Liège: 3–14.

——and B. Hovy (1990), 'Trends in European migration: what the data reveal', Paper presented at the Symposium on the Demographic Consequences of International Migration, Netherlands Institute of Social Analysis, Amsterdam, 27–9 Sept.

Zolberg, Aristide R. (1989), 'The next waves: migration theory for a changing world', *International Migration Review*, 23: 403–30.

——Astri Suhrke, and Sergio Aguayo (1989), *Escape from Violence: Conflict and the Refugee Crisis in the Developing World*, Oxford University Press, New York.

Zubrzycki, Jerzy (1981), 'International migration in Australasia and the South Pacific', in Mary M. Kritz, Charles B. Keely, and Silvano M. Tomasi (eds.), *Global Trends in Migration: Theory and Research on International Population Movements*, Center for Migration Studies, Staten Island, NY: 158–80.

Zucker, Lynne G., and Carolyn Rosenstein (1981), 'Taxonomies of institutional structure: dual economy reconsidered', *American Sociological Review*, 46: 869–83.

Index

LaVergne, TN USA
19 December 2009
167599LV00001B/2/P